T0365671

CHURCHES FOR SALE
WHERE HAVE
THE CHRISTIANS GONE?
A Choir Boy's Perspective

S.N.DURU

ARCHWAY
PUBLISHING

Archway Publishing books may be ordered through booksellers or by contacting:

Archway Publishing
1663 Liberty Drive
Bloomington, IN 47403
www.archwaypublishing.com
844-669-3957

Scriptures are taken from the NEW KING JAMES VERSION (NKJV):
Scripture taken from the NEW KING JAMES VERSION ®. Copyright©
1982 by Thomas Nelson, Inc. Used by permission. All rights reserved.

ISBN: 978-1-6657-6877-1 (sc)
ISBN: 978-1-6657-6876-4 (e)

Library of Congress Control Number: 2025906686

Print information available on the last page.

Archway Publishing rev. date: 04/08/2025

CONTENTS

DEDICATION

Dedicated to the memory of my brother, Herbert Nnadi Nwobodo Duru, who served in the Second World War under the Royal West African Frontier Force; to the children starved to death in the Biafra War; and to the foreigners and humanitarians who donated, served or died for their conscience.

Motto: Speak the truth, but not so truthful as to offend anyone.

PREFACE

Unlike many books on library shelves, this book requires a prerequisite that should be read and digested. The prerequisite is the allegory of the Six Blind Men and the Elephant by John Godfrey Saxe, available on the Internet. Depending on where the six men groped, the Elephant was like a wall, a spear, a snake, a tree, a fan or a rope. None of them could see the whole Elephant because they were blind.

People are born into a culture, a religion or denomination and can follow it generation after generation without a reality check. Many nations are divided between North and South or East and West. They see issues from their cultural or geographic perspectives. Even conservatives are divided between the spiritual conservatives who conserve spiritual values, the cultural conservatives who conserve cultural values and those on both sides. American Democrats and Republicans know the human tendency to see truth from a partisan perspective. Those who have lived in one and only one culture, are prone to a monocular vision of the world.

"Life's Little Instruction Book" volume Two (by H. Jackson Brown)[1] offers this advice: "Don't dismiss a good idea simply because you don't like the source." In American politics, hard - core Republicans and hard-core Democrats do dismiss facts from a source they don't like. The same is true in religion. Jesus Christ was not born to a priest or king, but to a carpenter. St. Peter, the leader of the Church was not a theologian. He was a fisherman with no academic credentials. John Godfrey Saxe's allegory prepares the reader to see the global vision, not the ethnic vision; the global perspective, and not the cultural or geographic perspective; the global Truth, and not the cultural truth; and ultimately, embrace one fundamental Truth called the Golden Rule - Treat others the same way you want them to treat you. It makes sense to anyone who is human regardless of culture, ethnicity, gender, religion or political ideology.

An astronaut in space belongs to no nation in his body but in his mind. If he belongs to no nation in his body and mind, he is enlightened and civilized. That's the mindset required to read this book. Nobody in modern Europe frets over what the pagan Roman empire did to them but over what Christians, including Adolf Hitler, have done to them in the past 2,000 years of Christianity. That mistake by past generations should not be continued by any human being today. Yet, nations led by Moscow and nations led by Washington, D.C., are relying on technology for more efficient instruments for mutual destruction; not on God's way for mutual coexistence.

There is often a motive that drives an action. My previous book "When Culture Overrules God and Reason" was driven by two epiphanies. First, where would the Lamb of God be born if not in a manger for sheep? The birth of Jesus Christ in a manger was not fortuitous. Second, the experience of St. Peter who walked on water by faith and began to sink out of fear, demonstrates the inverse relation between Faith and Fear. These two epiphanies have remained unnoticed. Now, "Churches for Sale" is not a treatise on Church sales. It is an expose' of how corrupted, theoretical and intellectualized Christianity has affected every facet of life leading up to declining trust, declining faith, declining Church attendance, empty pews and Churches for Sale.

Apart from Church decline that should concern every Christian, this book is also driven by other realities. First, nobody should give advice that will lead the recipient to regret. Second, in matters of faith, it is more important to listen to God than to men. It is said that war is too important to be left to the generals. The same can be said about Economics and Religion because they affect everybody. In the Old Testament, the Almighty God chose the Prophets. In the New Testament, Jesus told His disciples:" You did not choose Me, but I chose you." The spiritual leaders of all religions were not chosen by God Almighty. They are volunteers.

It is an embarrassment that in all the struggles to solve the social maladies of the past century, the moral leadership has not come from the Church but from the street. Without critics - and activists - nothing will change. Surely, Christians need scholars in ethics, Church history, and Gospel doctrine. They need to know the culture and environment of the first century, and the problems Christians faced in order to contextualize the Scriptures. But no scholar has been to heaven and back, to become an expert beyond what is in the Gospel of Jesus Christ.

Now, after 2,000 years of Christianity, why are Christians selling churches? Why are some churches - sacred places of worship - on life support? Based on the Golden Rule, the Great Commandment and the New Commandment, if Christianity is about good relations between peoples and between them and the God of Creation – and it is - why is the world the way it is after 2,000 years? And why is the United States of America the way it is today after 2,000 long years of the Gospel? "We live in an evil world," some preachers say. For over a millennium after the Apostles passed away, the church controlled the world through the Kings and Emperors of Europe. Who was the ruler of the evil world?

CHAPTER 1

Churches for Sale

It takes a Rip Van Winkle not to notice that some neighbors with Christian names no longer go to church. Or to notice that some churches have been turned into commercial-use buildings. It takes a Christian Rip Van Winkle not to care. "The first step to solving a problem," said Will McAvoy, "is recognizing there is one." A parishioner who draws attention to empty pews and how to fill them will be considered disloyal. They either leave to become "backsliders" or keep quiet and watch the decline go from bad to "Church for Sale." Here are the problems.

In late October 2017, the Associated Press published an article titled "Churches Find Second Life as Breweries: Holy Spirits Given New Meaning in Youngstown." A 1923 Presbyterian church in Youngstown, Ohio, that was turned into a brewery prompted the article.

"With stained glass, brick walls and large sanctuaries ideal for holding vats and lots of people," according to the reporter, "churches renovated into breweries attract beer lovers but can grate on the spiritual sensibilities of clergy and worshippers.

"At least 10 new breweries have opened in the old churches across America since 2011 and at least four more are slated to open in the next year. The trend started after the 2007 recession as churches merged or closed because of dwindling membership. Sex abuse settlements by the Roman catholic church starting in the mid-2000s were not a factor because those payments were largely covered by insurers." The reporter further noted, "Cincinnati's Taft's Ale House kicked off its grand opening in the 167-year-old St. Paul's Evangelical Protestant church with a 'blessing of the beers.'"

The Atlantic of November 25, 2018, published an article titled "America's Epidemic of Empty Churches." The writer observed that three blocks from his Brooklyn apartment,

> a large brick structure stretches toward heaven. Tourists recognize it as a Church—the building's bell tower and stained-glass windows give it away— but worshippers haven't gathered here in years.
>
> The 19th-century building was once known as St. Vincent De Paul church and house a vibrant congregation for more than a century. But attendance dwindled and coffers ran dry by the early 2000s. Rain leaked through holes left by missing shingles, a tree sprouted in the bell tower, and the Brooklyn diocese decided to sell the building to developers. Today, the Spire Lofts boasts 40 luxury apartments, with one-bedroom units renting for as much as $4,812 per month. It takes serious cash to make God's house your own, apparently.
>
> Many of the nation's churches can no longer afford to maintain their structures—6,000 to 10,000 churches die each year in America— and that number will likely grow. Though more than 70 percent of our citizens still claim to be Christians, congregational participation is less central to many Americans' faith than it once was. Most

denominations are declining as a share of the overall population, and donations to congregations have been falling for decades. Meanwhile, religiously unaffiliated Americans, nicknamed the "nones," are growing as a share of the U.S. Population.

In "Leaving Christianity: Changing Allegiances in Canada since 1945" (McGill-Queen's University Press 2017),[2] Brian Clarke and Stuart Macdonald laid out detailed statistics of the decline in church attendance. After the Second World War, according to the authors, the baby boom flooded Sunday schools with children to replace their grandparents. Then church attendance peaked in the 1960s and began to decline. The writers show that the nondenominational and interdenominational groups grew in the 1980s while the mainstream denominations declined. They all experience sporadic growth at one time or another only to decline. They report that the Canadian cultural ethos of consumerism favors no religion, and so it is no surprise that no religion remains a growing, robust trend. The citizen has been turned into a customer by corporations and a taxpayer by the government. Many youths have never been part of a church. Baby boomers' children have little or no exposure to Christian beliefs and practices apart from Easter and Christmas.

How Have the Mighty Fallen?

The Roman Catholics used to make up almost half the population. The decline of Roman Catholicism is very depressing because nobody doubts the sincerity of the men and women who took a vow of poverty to serve God and humanity. According to the authors, there used to be a church within walking distance. Seminaries provided priests for the churches. Convents provided nuns for schools, hospitals, and nursing homes. The church bell rang at noon to say the Angelus. On Sunday, it summoned the faithful to mass in their Sunday best. With secularization, declining church attendance, profession of no religion, and children raised with no religion, convents have become condos, and some churches have been desanctified and turned into restaurants.

The authors end with a dire conclusion that borders on capitulation. "Let us be clear," they state, "we are not calling for a religious revival. As our findings have shown, such a mass change in sentiment is not very likely. Nor would we advocate a re-Christianization of Canadian Society. When Canada's churches held social power, often they did not use it wisely, and the social pressure that existed before the 1960s for religious conformity should not be underestimated. Religious diversity, and the attendant freedom to choose one's religion or not to have any religion at all, is something to be valued by all Canadians, Christians included" (244–245).

It is a fact that some disaffected Christians have gone from one denomination to another. Some have left the church completely. A city magazine columnist wrote an article about the church his parents attended in the city of Calgary in the 1960s. Abandoned churches are often listed as commercial real estate, he observed. "I haven't thought about St. Andrew's in decades," he wrote. "Thirty years have passed since I last walked through the carved wooden doors. Earlier this year, though, I learned that the church was for sale." He recounted his childhood experiences at the church and added, "I feel no spiritual affiliation with the church anymore. I've long since stopped believing in the God I prayed to and knelt before in St. Andrew's wooden pews. Nothing that happened in that church feels important or transformative to me now. The church, instead, stands as a temple of more everyday recollections. The building houses my memories of last lasagnas and polkas and bingo cards. Of bespeckled priests and the sudden splash of holy water. Of first suits and first neckties."

The Hutterites have read the same Gospel as other Christians. They live in a trust-and-obey community that cares for the body, mind, and soul. It is inconceivable that a Hutterite will cease to believe in God. Unlike other religions, anyone forced to be a

Christian is not a Christian. Anyone born into a Christian family is a nominal Christian until he or she is born again. Being a born-again Christian is based on faith that is based on conviction. A born-again Christian lives by the Golden Rule, the Great Commandment and the New Commandment and can never become an atheist or an agnostic regardless of what other people do in the secular society. But the church establishment has to teach how to be born again.

The priests deserve some empathy. Nobody can be a minister of state or the president of the United States, for example, without joining a political party institution. Similarly, some men and women who want to serve God and humanity have gone to the extent of taking a vow of poverty and celibacy to conform to an institution doing the same old dogma over and over, expecting to save the world. If the theology is flawed, it will not save the world. Offering forgiveness of sins (absolutions) will not save but corrupt the world. The clergy and laity must be born again and live by the Golden Rule, the Great Commandment and the New Commandment and be equally accountable to God Almighty. Some of those priests and nuns retire in poverty from a thankless job.

One of the numerous sects in America publishes *The Philadelphia Trumpet*.[3] In the November-December 2017 edition, page 16, an article was titled "A Religious Revival in Europe?" It stated Capernaum Church in downtown Hamburg, Germany,

> is much busier than it used to be. The main hall accommodates 500 worshipers. Under the building's previous owner, the Evangelical Church, only about 20 people showed up each week. But for its new owners, the hall is not big enough.
>
> Why the dramatic change? Because it is now the Al- Nour Islamic Center. The change is symbolic of the trend sweeping Europe. In London, since

2001, 500 Churches have become private homes, and more than 400 mosques have opened. In 2016, seven French Churches were demolished, 26 put up for sale, and many more converted into offices, apartments, gymnasiums, etc. Meanwhile, since 2003 nearly 1,000 French Mosques have been built.

So, it seems odd to talk about a Christian revival in Europe. Churches are dying. Religion is playing a smaller role than ever in people's everyday lives.

But in politics, religion is making a major comeback. Politicians are talking about their nation's religious heritage more than ever. They are using it to differentiate themselves from Muslims. They talk about its importance to their culture. Although Europeans aren't going to church or letting religion tell them how to live their lives, they are looking to religion to tell them who they are.

Culture wishes hatred, death, and destruction on enemies. That is the cultural truth. Here is the global or eternal truth: "But I say to you, love your enemies, bless those who cause you, do good to those who hate you, and pray for those who spitefully use you and persecute you" (Matthew 5:44). Advertently or inadvertently, the Christians in Europe might have done that. But hundreds of their churches have disappeared. How about Eastern Europe? The article notes,

> As early as 2014, the Catholic magazine *First Things* noticed this trend emerging in Central and Eastern Europe: "In Hungary, Croatia, and elsewhere in Eastern Europe, a pro-family, pro-life revolution and a rediscovery of Christian roots is occurring.

"Unnoticed in the shadow of a secularized West, religion's public role has been growing in the East since the collapse of communism (January 17, 2014.)

"This process has sped up dramatically as Europe's migrant crisis has worsened. Since 2013, around 2.5 million migrants have applied for asylum in the European Union. The EU does not track the religion of asylum seekers, but the vast majority are from Muslim-dominated countries. According to Pew Forum in 2010, about 19 million Muslims lived in the EU. So, the EU has had roughly a 10 percent jump in its Muslim population due to the refugee crisis alone.

"As thousands of Muslims have arrived every year, bringing their religion with them and setting up numerous mosques, European leaders have shifted their rhetoric away from strict secularism and have begun to emphasize how Christian the nations are." In other words, some politicians are holding the Gospel, not because they want to live by the Golden Rule, the Great Commandment and the New commandment, but because the Gospel separates "us from them."

Tacit Atheism

In an address to a congregation at St. German's Cathedral on the isle of Man, in October 2000, the Archbishop of Canterbury, Dr. George Carey drew attention to prevailing tacit atheism in Britain. He noted that most people no longer believe in eternal life but desperately seek to postpone death by medical means. He had to speak out at a time when attendance at Church of England Sunday Services had dropped below one million. He did not want to be remembered as the archbishop who nursed a dying church.

The situation, the archbishop said, was so serious that it demanded both lay people and the clergy of the whole Church of God to be mobilized to fight to restore "authentic Christianity." It has not happened. The situation may be worse today. There is no doubt that the corruption of the Gospel that began since slave trade and slavery has led to the "tacit atheism." Some Bishops have seen their Christians in public office, do to others what they don't want others to do to them. That disobedience of God's Golden Rule is the proximate cause of nearly all of man's woes on earth. It is tempting to give up or retire and let the dead bury their dead. Yet, the seeds for the morass in the world today were sown by Church leaders several centuries ago.

If those who control religion, politics and the News media are habituated to the status quo, change in society will be snail slow. Religion and politics are too important to be left in the hands of a few. The problem of empty pews cannot be solved without the views of those who sit on the pews. Albert Einstein cautioned against doing the same thing over and over expecting a different outcome. For his part, the archbishop cited the words of a German theologian, Prof. Jurgen Moltmann: "A Church that cannot change becomes a fossil church. It becomes an unimportant sect on the edge of a rapidly changing and progressive society. Men and women run away from such a church. Only the old, the tired and the resigned retained their membership."

The Backlash

In the Star Metro (Nov.1-3,2019), The Canadian Press had this caption: "Quebec Mosque founder urges talking through backlash." When residents north of Montreal learned of a plan to transform a local church into a Mosque and Islamic cultural Centre, according to the report, the reaction was so strong that parish leaders invoked the 2017 mass shooting of Muslims in Quebec City to justify putting the project on hold.

"Members of the diocese of Trois-Rivieres, Que., located along the St. Lawrence River between Montreal and Quebec City, sent a litany of angry and threatening emails to the parish. Others spoke out during public consultations held earlier in October.

"Rene Beaudoin, a parish member leading a committee on the future of the region's churches, said the outcry made diocesan Luc Bouchard think of the six Muslim men shot dead in a Quebec City Mosque in 2017. The bishop decided to stop the sale." Apparently, the children of baby boomers do not want to go to church to keep it open. Neither do they want to see it sold to become a Mosque. On July18,2022 the Canadian Press reported "42 Catholic properties sold to pay abuse survivors at former Newfoundland orphanage." The sale included 167-year-old Basilica of St. John the Baptist, located in the provincial capital. According to the report,"70 more church-owned properties across the island of Newfoundland will also be put up for sale."

Let us be wise enough to admit that the church of St. Peter and the Apostles was not Roman Catholic or Protestant. They received the Holy Spirit, became born again, and lived by the Golden Rule, the Great Commandment and the New Commandment. That mother church would not do what the post- apostolic church had done in the past 2,000 years. The number of Christian denominations in a nation cannot be ignored because it is part of the problem plaguing the church of Jesus Christ.

There are Adventists; Apostolic Christian; Associated Gospel; Baptist ;Brethren in Christ ; Charismatic Renewal ; Christadelphian; Christian and Missionary Alliance ; Christian Assembly; Christian Congregation; Christian Science; Churches of Christ, Disciples ;Church of God ;Church of the Nazarene; Doukhobors – Orthodox Doukhobors; Reformed Doukhobors; Evangelical Free Church; Jehovah's Witnesses ;Latter Day Saints (LDS) Mormons – Church of Latter Day saints; Reorganized Church of LDS ; Lutherans; Mennonite: Hutterite; Methodist Bodies - Evangelical ; Free Methodist; Methodist Episcopal; Missionary Church; Mission Covenant; Mission de l'Esprit – Saint; Moravian; New Apostolic; Pentecostal ;People's Church; Plymouth Brethren ; presbyterian; Quakers; Reformed Bodies – Christian Reformed; Canadian Reformed Church; Dutch Reformed Church; Reformed Church of America ; Salvation Army ;Spiritualist; Standard Church ;Unitarian; United Church; Wesleyan; Worldwide church of God ;Nondenominational ; Interdenominational; Eastern Orthodox - Greek Orthodox ; Armenian Orthodox; Ukrainian Orthodox; Serbian Orthodox; Russian Orthodox; Romanian Orthodox; Antiochian Orthodox Christian. They demonstrate the lack of a clear understanding of the Gospel of Jesus Christ. For examples, should the Armenians, Greeks, Romanians, Russians, Serbians and Ukrainians go to war, their Orthodox church would go along with them to offer prayer support. It is incumbent on all denominations to return to the Gospel and restore the Church of Jesus Christ.

Ask any leader of a denomination why there are so many denominations, the answer would be: "the rest are not like us." What would the Apostles think of all the denominations? They may not be able to recognize some of these Churches as Christians. A house divided against itself cannot stand. The same can be said of the Church but the real Church will stand because "the gates of Hades will not prevail against it," Jesus said. None of these denominations want to see their sunset. The theological differences between some denominations, such as the mode of baptism, are irrelevant to salvation. But there are denominations that are still preaching the same doctrine preached to the master class - Christian slave traders, slave masters, auctioneers and politicians - for over 200 years. They were to ignore the Golden Rule, the Great Commandment and the New Commandment and claim the righteousness of Jesus Christ as a free gift. They did not have to be born again. Everyone will be saved by

God's amazing grace except Adolf Hitler. When any thinking man or woman considers the thousands of religions, sects and denominations in the world, it is obvious that some sheep and shepherds are lost or gone astray. Some professions require malpractice insurance just in case something goes wrong. In religion, there is no malpractice insurance. Therefore, "buyer beware" applies to religion.

Christian denominations are the products of the sale of indulgences that sparked the Reformation led by a Roman Catholic priest named Martin Luther. Today, even conservative Christians are divided between Christians who conserve spiritual values, Christians who conserve cultural values, and Christians who are on both sides, neither hot nor cold. Other issues of contention are liturgy, Church governance, music instruments, Bible edition, the ordination of women, abortion, same - sex marriage and more. What the denominations have in common is the overarching and pervasive alienation of their members from both Church and State that have turned Christianity into a philosophy that is neither relevant to the living nor to the dead.

The Empty Pews: A Witness to the Decline of Faith

It is disheartening to see empty pews in churches whose predecessors built schools, churches, some hospitals in distant lands, and great Cathedrals at home, all to the Glory of God. They were faithful believers of what they understood. The Cathedrals were built when the world population was a fraction of what it is today. They should be overflowing but are half empty. So, why are some Churches dying? Why did Christians begin to sell churches after 2000 years? Why were the 1960s the turning point? As research shows, the decline in church attendance began in the 1960s. After the end of the Second World War the rest of the world looked up to the United States of America. If one can capture the mood of the time and as a witness, it was apparent that life did not make sense to many and probably does not make sense to many today.

The Vietnam war was an unjustifiable and very divisive war against the spread of communism an ocean away. President Kennedy who came to office to represent a new generation of Americans, joined Abraham Lincoln, James Garfield, William McKinley in the list of assassinated presidents. Rev. Dr. Martin Luther king, the Civil Rights leader, was assassinated. Senator Robert F. Kennedy, an advocate for social justice and moral leadership in politics, would also be assassinated. The moral sense of right and wrong that is called conscience, was activated in young adults. But the church as an institution was as irrelevant as it was during the struggle to end slavery. That's some of the plausible reasons why youth rebellion and the decline in church attendance began in the 1960s.

In parts of Eastern Europe, some Churches were filled to capacity in opposition to communism. When communism ended, Church attendance declined. The absentees joined the disaffected Christians of capitalism. The Gospel changes individuals who seek change; it has not changed the institutions that serve society where change is most needed. Since hypocrisy is a global currency, those who saw it in the church lost trust and the exodus from the church grew. As world problems increased annually, mature Christians also lost interest in Bible stories embellished and retold.

The state of the church or religion is a hot topic on social media. If Wikipedia is a reliable source, "Decline of Christianity – Wikipedia" paints a sad portrait of the church. It shows that the percentage of Christians in America has been declining steadily. Since the year 2000, some denominations have lost over 40% of their congregation and closed over 12% of their churches. In Minnesota, for example, the Evangelical Lutheran church has lost 200,000 members and closed 150 churches. The Catholic Church closed 81 Churches. The Archdioceses of Minneapolis closed 21 churches. The Archdiocese of Boston closed more than 70 churches between

2004 and 2019. Still, despite the contraction, there is a shortage of priests. Infant baptism decreased nationwide between 34 to 40 percent.

During the colonial and apartheid era, Mahatma Gandhi had conflicts with Christians in South Africa and India. The Christians did not understand the Christianity they professed. If any Christian were asked why they were saved and Gandhi was not, the answer would be:" I believe in Jesus Christ as my Lord and savior, Gandhi does not." That theology is a factor in closing churches in Minneapolis, Minnesota and several places around the world. More will be closed and sold post COVID -19 pandemic.

In Quebec, Canada, since the Quiet Revolution, according to Wikipedia, over 500 churches (20% of the total) have been closed or converted for non-worship-based uses. In Chile, atheism has grown from 21% in 2018 to 32% in 2019. They lost trust in the Church and then faith in God. In the Netherlands, atheists and agnostics are the majority. In 2015, according to the report, 63% of the population thought that religion does more harm than good. That must be the effect of terrorism. The number of people who never pray has grown from a minority to a majority of the people. Further research will determine if those who prayed are better off than those who didn't pray. One thing is certain and beyond dispute - the funereal state of the church and human relations will get worse unless church and state discovered what Christianity (following Christ), is all about. The mindset of Church gatekeepers has to change.

In the distant past, many Christians were led to believe in predestination. A Christian was saved because unlike pagans and atheists, he believes in Jesus Christ. Therefore, past, present and future wrongs are forgiven. That mindset that sustained slavery for over 200 years in protestant America and over 350 years in Roman Catholic Brazil, still exists today. The complainers then were the slaves and later, the Civil Rights activists. By the 1970s, right and wrong became a choice open to everybody. Since then, everyone has become a complainer about something.

Abortion was a serious issue. Babies were aborted even for economic reasons. Women bore the abuse and the consequences of abortion but the men involved in the pregnancy went Scot- free. What was concerting to rational minds was that the same men and women who saw life as sacred and professed to be pro-life were the same men and women who allowed children who were born, to languish in poverty. And those who grieved over the lack of prayer in school also opposed the social programs that pre-empt prayer. That superficial spirituality accentuated man's hypocrisy and eroded church attendance.

In the 1970s also, the evangelical pulpit complained a great deal about Satan. A running joke was "Satan made me do it." Today many are coming to realize that Satan does not live in the ethereal domain but next door. When the consequences of intellectualism, theoretical Christianity and abuse of trust contribute to the exodus from the church, the empty pews left by "backsliders "were seen by prophecy preachers as a fulfillment of Bible prophecy. That state of denial fueled more discontent. All church leaders read the same Bible and choose what they want. Some cite the Old Testament for their purpose. That purpose is not practical Christianity. A few of the captive audience frustrated by years of theoretical Christianity chose to leave.

When the law is slow to acts, some people take the law into their own hands. Some frustrated protestants become freelance pastors to take evangelism into their own hands. The solution, they believe, is to lease a hall or renovate an abandoned church, re-tool a website, preach inspiring and biblically based sermons and invite people to join a new and improved church. When they do not satisfy the needs of congregants, and run out of gimmicks, they joined the thousands of churches that close down each year in America, and let the dead bury their dead.

The world is the way it is today because the post-apostolic church has misrepresented Jesus Christ. It did not practice the Gospel. The culture was resistant to Christian civilization – the Golden Rule, the Great Commandment and the New Commandment. One commandment the church has been led to observe is the Eucharist, in remembrance of Christ offering Himself as the sacrificial Lamb of God. If the solution to empty pews is for the church to go Online in response to changing culture, how do you observe even the Eucharist Online?

How many listeners remember what their pastor preached two or three Sundays ago? What some of the "backsliders" care about is not what happens to the soul on Sunday but what happens to the mind and body the other six days of the week. The church should care if it represents Jesus Christ who came to do more than "preach good tidings to the poor." The Salvation Army was founded for that reason but the church cannot be government. The Gospel of Jesus Christ has been derailed since America's slave economy. And once again, "all we like sheep have gone astray." Now, extreme liberalism will drag the Church into paganism; and cultural conservatism will drag it into Mammonish Christianity. Christianity can only be saved by spiritual conservatives or born-again Christians (Pentecostals) who live by those commandments. It does not come naturally. Being governed like the Hutterites is the only bait that fishers of men need, particularly in the United States, to fill empty Church pews again. Trust and obey is the only way.

Nothing is sacred anymore. Still, Church for sale is a shock. What else is not up for sale? How does a place of worship end up for sale? Long after the Apostles of Jesus Christ passed away, all hell broke loose. The successors opened the Pandora's box and everything that can go wrong began to go wrong. Who opened the Pandora's box?

CHAPTER 2

Who Opened
the Pandora's Box?

Who opened the pandora's box? African men, women and children were enslaved, exploited and dehumanized. Men, women and children have been murdered and babies aborted. Some women have been denied suffrage because of their gender. Some men and women have been denied suffrage because of the color of their skin. Hatred, avarice, pride and prejudice have led to wars, destruction, death and misery. Some men and women have been robbed, oppressed and slandered. Some bullied schoolchildren have committed suicide because death was better than life. Infidelity, verbal, physical and sexual abuse have broken up many families. Some men and women are homeless or lonely. At this very moment, there are adults and young adults behind a computer or telephone somewhere on earth, trying to scam trusting people. And there are governments trying to control or sow seeds of discord in some other nations.

Now, when human beings have seen the devastation of wars and the mass starvation to death of babies and children ; when they have seen the world go from crisis to crisis without learning from the past ; when they have seen men use their office to do to others what they would not like others to do to them; when they have seen the Internet open new channels of immorality and scams; when they have seen broken relationships, declining trust and declining faith lead to Churches for sale, is it not a sin to remain silent when the solution is obvious? All these have happened and continue to happen for one reason – the disobedience of God's Golden Rule. There is no social problem or war, ancient or modern, that is not attributable to non-compliance to the Golden Rule.

Jesus Christ ended up on the cross because bearing the Truth has consequences. And so, the weak, even the educated, hesitate to disclaim malfeasance and misfeasance, past or present, for fear of losing the support of their friends or members. The fate of billions of souls may be too important for the silent majority to leave to a few volunteers. If your father is doing something you know to be wrong, it will be difficult to tell him because he is your father. If a husband is bringing home ill-gotten wealth, it will be difficult for the wife to report him to the police. It must have been difficult for sexually abused Roman Catholics to bring charges against men who occupy the office of God. So it is with reopening Church history.

How did we get to where we are today? Who opened the Pandora's box? This theme calls for a caveat to ease tension for the pastorate. The present generation is neither responsible nor accountable for the wrongs of history but to fix their consequences. Those wrongs are discussed in chapter three. One cannot criticize politicians without criticizing the church that raise them. There is the God of creation. Did He know that someone will do to others what he does not want others to do to him? God's Golden Rule – "And as ye would that men should do to you, do ye also to them likewise." Or Treat others the same way you want them to treat you. It makes sense to any human being. That has been the solution to man's social malady. Analytical minds cannot be fooled into complacency when economic advancement and moral values are heading in opposite directions. Who opened the pandora's box? In "Why You Can Disagree and Remain a Faithful Catholic" (by Philip S. Kaufman)[4], the author states: "One of the clearest of erroneous moral teaching is the Roman magisterium's authoritative approval of slavery. It is true that the New Testament never explicitly condemns slavery, but neither does it attempt to justify the institution. Indeed, St. Paul's pastoral approach in Philemon and his statement in Galatians that in Christ there is neither slave nor free (Galatians 3:28) helped create the atmosphere in the west that led to the gradual elimination of slavery."

He notes that St. Paul seemed to tolerate slavery (1 Corinthians 7: 20 – 21). But he was a missionary preacher and writer whose goal was to get people to believe in Christ. He notes that St. Paul was convinced that Jesus Christ will return in his own lifetime. Therefore, it was not important to dwell on social evils that will end with the Second Advent. And so, the magisterium, he notes, "would eventually use Paul's failure to condemn slavery as reason for supporting slavery, long considered an essential element in the structure of society." It is noteworthy that the Golden Rule – Treat others the same way you want them to treat you – is an implicit condemnation of all forms of malfeasance. Surely, Satan can cite the Scriptures for his purpose.

Roman catholic theologians note that celibacy began in the fourth century under Pope Damasus (366-384). But it was not enforced. In his account, Philip S. Kaufman notes that "Beginning with the local Council of Gangra in 362, affirmed by Pope Martin 1 in 650, the record is long and detailed. For example, in an attempt to enforce celibacy, the Ninth Council of Toledo in 655 decreed that the offspring of offending clerics should become permanent slaves of the Church. Pope Urban 11 in 1089 gave princes power to enslave the wives of clerics. During the Crusades, Pope Alexander 111 at the Third Lateran Council and Pope Innocent 111 at the fourth Lateran Council authorized enslavement of captured Christians who had aided the Saracens. As the fifteenth-and sixteenth-century explorations began, Pope Nicholas V in 1454 granted to King Alfonso v of Portugal and his son Prince Henry the navigator, 'full and free permission --- to capture, conquer and subjugate all Saracens and pagans whatsoever and other enemies of Christ ---and to bring their persons into perpetual slavery. " Yes, perpetual slavery.

Here it is important to revisit John Godfrey Saxes allegory of the blind men and the elephant as a reminder to see from a global perspective, like the Almighty, rather than from a parochial or cultural perspective. And understand why after 2,000 consecutive years of the disobedience of the Golden Rule, some Churches are being sold. The Church also resisted the abolition of slavery.

"In fact, American bishops considered slavery a political, not a moral issue," Kaufman continued. "Even after the civil war had begun, bishops at the Third Provincial Council of Cincinnati in 1861 wrote: The spirit of the Catholic Church is eminently conservative. They do not think it their province to enter into the political arena. "He notes that as late as 1866, after slavery had been abolished in the USA and several Latin American countries, the Holy Office (the Vatican predecessor of the present Congregation for the Doctrine of the Faith) issued an instruction reaffirming the moral justification of slavery. Eventually, in 1891, Pope Leo 111 spoke indirectly about slavery. According to Kaufman, "He wrote that human labor is personal, since the active force inherent in the person cannot be the property of anyone other than the person who exerts it, and it was given to him in the first place by nature for his own benefit." He notes that "the erroneous doctrine so firmly held and promulgated by the Roman magisterium for so many centuries was implicitly corrected by the Roman magisterium in 1891. However, the correction by Pope Leo was so mute that some of the biggest men in moral theology – Lehmkuhl, Prummer, Merkelbach, Genicot, and Zalba – didn't catch on. They still taught the morality of slavery down to the middle of the present century. Zalba wrote justifying slavery as late as 1958. He was one of the four theologians on the 'birth control commission' who voted to keep the church's prohibition of all use of artificial contraception.'

It was not until Vatican 11 in 1965 was Catholic teaching on slavery corrected. Even then, Kaufman wrote, "there was no hint that the council was correcting centuries of false teaching and practice in the Church. Rather, the bishops condemned the practices of others, especially the forced labor and slavery of the totalitarian states. Finally, in stark contradiction to centuries of explicit church teaching, Pope John Paul 11, in his encyclical, The splendor of Truth, included slavery in a list of intrinsic evils." The Polish pope must have read the Golden Rule at last. Many Roman Catholics still do not know why Pope Benedict from Germany resigned.

Kaufman wonders that" if the magisterium could be wrong in its approval of morality of slavery, could it not also be wrong in its absolute prohibition of artificial contraception, sterilization, and marriage after divorce? If such a doubt exists, then probabilism could be used in these and other cases of conscience." Let it be said that one of those other cases of conscience is the issue of continued celibacy despite the consequences of sexual misconduct and a shortage of priests.

To any high school student who has read the Gospel of Jesus Christ, it is shocking that the biggest Roman Catholic men in moral theology taught the morality of slavery down to the middle of the 20th century. For those past centuries, Roman Catholics were not allowed to read the Bible. Anyone who has read the Acts of the Apostles would know that the first century Church of Jews and Gentiles was Pentecostal. They received the Holy Spirit that replaced the resident evil spirit in man (Luke 11:13). It made them born again Christians who lived the Gospel - the Golden Rule, the Great Commandment and the New Commandment. With the Holy Spirit, they could never wage a war of conquest. They could never be slave traders and slave masters. Never.

The Romans drove that Pentecostal church underground. It is partially underground today. Living the Gospel was not amenable to the ego of superiority and the economic benefit of slave trade, slavery and colonialism that would follow. History was written by the victors. The narrative of religion had to be controlled by the victors too. They operated like the mafia and designed sacraments from birth to the last rites, with confession and forgiveness(absolutions) between birth and death. So, most Roman Catholics never knew that a Christian must be born again. To go from slavery to a faith tradition that dismantled the Pentecostal church of Christ based on the Golden Rule, the Great Commandment and the New Commandment is to go from slavery to purgatory, if there is one. They would need the grace of God.

In the mandate of the Great Commission, what did Jesus Christ ask his followers to teach in Matthew 28:20? It is incomprehensible, therefore, that the Jesuits - the Society of Jesus - owned and sold 272 of their slaves, with the permission of Rome in 1838, to save Georgetown University from bankruptcy. It makes their resistance to the abolition of slavery understandable. The enemies of an organization are usually on the outside. Christianity can never be Christianity if it has members resisting the Gospel from the inside.

Slavery pre-existed Christianity. But the church that used slavery to enforce celibacy; facilitated racialized commercial slavery in which it was also a participant, betrayed a sacred trust. It opened that Pandora's box and since then, everything that can go wrong has gone wrong. "And as ye would that men should do to you, do ye also to them likewise" or treat others the same way you want to be treated, makes sense to any human being regardless of culture, ethnicity, gender, religion or political ideology. That disobedience of God's Golden Rule is at the root of our problems. It began with distant generations and has been propagated. Wars, Colonialism, Slave trade, Slavery, Apartheid, Spiritual imperialism, Crimes, Terrorism,

Family dysfunction, Anti- Semitism, Islamophobia, Cyber-attacks and scams have followed as a consequence.

History was written by the victors. The Gospel of Jesus Christ was also schemed, translated, interpreted, managed and explained through the bias of patronizing victors. It was victor theology. They offered absolutions in lieu of being born again. They explained that salvation was based on faith alone. Jesus died for our sins or paid our sin debt. So, sin or malfeasance is no longer a barrier between man and God. And for nearly 250 years for Protestants and 300 years for Roman Catholics, clergy and laity lived off the avails of unpaid servitude. It shows how the Gospel of Jesus Christ and even the Old Testament were corrupted by the Gentile gatekeepers of Christianity. The Gospel aside, one would expect that the Church fathers, theologians and scholars, read Jeremiah 22:13 to wit: "Woe to him who builds his house by unrighteousness. And his chambers by injustice; who uses his neighbor's service without wages, and gives him nothing for his work "(NKJV).

In either the Old Testament or the Gospel, no bishop or pope saw a contradiction between faith and slavery. They erased the interface between right and wrong, and between Truth and deceit. They ignored the Golden Rule, the Great Commandment and the New Commandment- the very core of the Gospel that spells good relations between people and between them and God Almighty. There seemed to be no character difference between those who believed in God and those who didn't. From segregated Churches and graveyards, clergy and laity in Dixie went "home to be with the Lord "without reconciliation and without restitution for centuries of slavery. It was all based on the victor's theology. Presidents who owned slaves and abused "the least of these My brethren" were given State funerals and sent "home to be with the Lord." To go home to be with the Lord without doing the will of the Lord is not amazing grace, it is amazing self-deceit. God's commandments were treated as suggestions. The African slaves were physically ruined but the slave masters, politicians and clergy were spiritually ruined. They gained the whole world but lost their souls. Even the world they gained was left behind because none took a penny to the grave.

Ignorant people are easily led astray. Politics and religion thrive on ignorance. If skin tone is the subject of prejudice in Christendom after 2,000 years of Christianity, do we know what the Gospel is about? If we don't know what the Gospel is about, how do we know what it means to be born again and obtain the visa to the kingdom of God? According to a Gallup survey, the percentage of Americans who believe that they are born again is higher among those with no college education. And they are concentrated in Dixie where Christians who fought and died to sustained slavery were honored with statues and monuments. Sadly, Africans and African Americans are the greatest consumers of religion as well as the greatest victims. Just as history was written by the victors, the Church that created a master class in Dixie defined being born again to be synonymous with evangelicalism. Nicodemus was not asked to be evangelical or evangelistic. He was asked to be born again. When Jesus Christ was condemned to death, the Roman soldiers twisted a crown of thorns on His head, mocked Him, spat on Him (being a Jew), and led Him away to be crucified on a cross. And in all that, all that we have to do is accept the free gifts and carry on with malfeasance, if you can believe the evangelicals. And once saved always saved.

So, Christians ignored the Golden Rule, the Great Commandment and the New Commandment to suffer slave trade, slavery, wars of conquest and colonialism. That is how Christians subjected Africans to over 200 years of slavery in Protestant Dixie, over 300 years of slavery in Roman Catholic Brazil, and include segregation, apartheid and colonial rule. That's victor theology, not the Gospel of Jesus Christ. Now, when evangelicalism based on me-dieval imperial victor theology and medieval prejudice are melded with a lifestyle still opposed to the Golden Rule, it turns educated people away from the church and away from Christianity.

"Except a man be born again, "Jesus said, "he cannot see the kingdom of God" (John 3:3). Any Christian can presume to be born again but a Christian who would do to others what he would not want others to do to him is not a born-again Christian. The life of the Christian slave traders, slave owners and master class is instructive. Christianity is about good relations between people and between them and God Almighty. It can only be attained by being born again. There is one born-again doctrine that changes lives and limits malfeasance. There is another that pretends to change lives but reliant on Amazing Grace. A Christian must choose one or the other. A Christian who is comfortable in a segregated church that does not reflect the kingdom of God has not been changed. A Christian who cares about babies in the womb but turns a blind eye to children languishing in poverty has not been changed. A Christian who is not born again cannot fake it. We must keep that in mind. By the criterion described in chapter 13 (Christianity for Dummies), many should reconsider if they are truly born again. Nobody can deceive God.

Weekly confessions and absolutions do not change lives or the world. Belief in Jesus Christ per se does not change any life or the world. Sacraments and rituals did not change the lives of those clergy and laity who lived off the avails of slavery for centuries, and became habituated to inhumanity. Without reconciliation and without restitution, many generations went home to be with the Lord from segregated churches. It took thinking human beings to give their lives in a war to end slavery and relentless inhumanity. Unless a man is born again, he cannot live by the Golden Rule, the Great Commandment and the New Commandment, and be the human being the Almighty expects him to be. That is the Gospel.

Abraham Lincoln understood the Gospel better than many theologians of his day. The slave masters who occupied the White

House figuratively, held the Bible as a symbol of oppression. The church fathers and victors perverted what Christianity is about. One does not have to go to a seminary to read and understand the Bible and God's will. There is the Golden Rule (Luke 6:31). In fact, there is no greater tool for conflict management or resolution than God's Golden Rule. Treat others the same way you want to be treated makes sense to anyone who is a human being. Also, there is the Great Commandment (Luke 10:27). There is the New Commandment (John 13:34). There is the Parable of the Good Samaritan that defines a neighbor (Luke 10:25 – 37). There is "Bear ye one another's burdens---"(Galatians 6:2). There is the Beatitudes (Matthew 5:1 – 16). There is the expectation to love your enemies (Matthew 5:44). "There is neither Jew nor Greek, there is neither slave nor free, there is neither male nor female; for you are all one in Christ Jesus "(Galatians3:28 NKJV), to underscores a common humanity. There is woe to those who do to others what they don't want others to do to them (Jeremiah 22:13). Nobody has to go to a Seminary to understand the will of God, and how to be a good person for the good of society.

So, how could the Theologians and Scholars in Universities misunderstand the Gospel? How would the clergy and laity live off the avails of slavery for centuries and saw no contradiction between their lifestyle and the faith they professed? Instead, they adapted the Bible to serve the master class. But there is no mass admission into heaven. Rather, each man must be born again; not through sacraments, confessions and absolutions but by asking for the Holy Spirit (Luke 11:13) to enable him to keep those commandments. That is the summary of the Gospel. The rest of the scriptures are commentary. A man is born again when the Holy Spirit burns the Golden Rule, the Great Commandment and the New Commandment into his character. However, there will always be men and women who don't believe in the living God. There will always be men and women who don't believe in Jesus Christ. For atheists and agnostics, the Great Commandment and the New Commandment may be optional. But the Golden Rule is not. Treat others the same way you want to be treated or don't do to others what you don't want others to do to you transcends culture, ethnicity, gender, religion or political ideology. For anyone who is a human being, the Golden Rule is not optional. From the family level to the national level, and from the national to the international level, there is hardly a relationship problem that does not hinge on the disobedience of God's Golden Rule.

The Grace of God is not an amnesty for all. The first Gentile gatekeepers of the Church used the faith to exercise power. And so, slave trade, slavery, colonialism and evangelism all worked in tandem to serve the master class. For nearly 2,000 years Roman Catholic parishioners were not allowed to read the Bible or associates with Protestants who read the Bible. Was it to avoid misunderstanding the Bible or to keep them in the dark? Does the complicity of the imperial Church fathers in centuries of slave trade and slavery, suggest that the failure to teach converts to observe the Golden Rule, the Great Commandment and the New Commandment was an honest mistake? In that slave economy, the church owned slaves. It is patently obvious that the church fathers created a master- class culture that ruined the lives of African Americans for centuries. It may also have ruined the souls of those who for centuries "go home to be with the Lord" without doing the will of the Lord.

The ancient world was controlled by the gods. In Greek mythology, when Atlas carried the world on his shoulders, there were many gods and goddess in control of different realms. The god mother was more revered than the god or son. Could that account for why the liturgy designed by the medieval Church fathers revered the Virgin Mary more than Jesus Christ who is more than a human being? It is wise to reexamine religion through the eyes of the 21st century, not the eyes of the first century. When imperial Rome established Roman Catholicism, over 90 percent of the world's population was illiterate. In this 21st century it is the reverse. It is not easy to mislead intelligent people. Therefore, every individual can compare the mandates of the Great Commission and the outcome and determine if the blueprint has been followed. Regardless of their academic credentials, Christians who have not read the Gospel and the mandate (Matthew 28 :19 – 20), are not different from the illiterate people of the third century. The disposition to blame Satan for everything that is wrong on earth has not changed even after 2,000 years of experience.

The Acts of the non-Apostles

Before the Reformation by disgruntled priests led by Martin Luther, there was Jan Hus (1369 – 1415), a Czech theologian and philosopher. Like many, Hus became a priest in order to escape poverty but opposed many aspects of the Imperial Church, including the sale of indulgences. Since the church was run by humans, he argued, it was inherently flawed. He was right. A few centuries later, the church would own African slaves. In 1838, the Jesuits - the Society of Jesus - sold 272 of their tobacco plantation slaves to save Georgetown University from bankruptcy.

Hus was arrested and burned at the stake for heresy against the doctrines of the Roman Catholic Church. While being burned, he predicted that God would raise others whose call for reform would not be suppressed. That was before the Protestant Reformation. The genuine reform that will restore the original Church of Jews and Gentiles is yet to happen.

John Wycliffe (1330 – 1384) was an English philosopher, theologian, Roman Catholic priest and Bible translator. He criticized the beliefs and practices of the imperial church. In 1415, 31 years after his death, Wycliffe was condemned as a heretic, exhumed and burned.

William Tyndale (1490 – 1536) was an English priest, linguist and Bible scholar. He translated the New Testament into English so that ordinary people could read and see for themselves. He was condemned for heresy and burned at the stake.

Joan of Arc (1412 – 1431) led the French army to repel the English in the Hundred Years' war. She believed in divine law only and not in man's church law. She was condemned as a heretic and a witch and burned at the stake. The same Imperial Church would later make her the patron saint of France. Similarly, the Romans crucified St Peter and later named him the first pope.

Galileo Galilei (1564 – 1642) was an Italian astronomer, physicist and engineer. As an Astronomer, he suggested that the Earth revolves around the Sun. That was different from what the infallible church wanted people to believe. He was charged for heresy and incarcerated until his death.

Pope Leo X (1475 – 1521) was known to be wasteful and hedonistic. According to him," Since God has given us the papacy, let us enjoy it." Did God give the Romans the papacy? With the dispersion of the Jews, the Almighty did not need Levites anymore. If He placed any nation in control of the Church, that Church would not own slaves and live off the avails of slavery. For Pope Leo X, the sale of indulgence was a payment to absolve sins. After the Protestant Reformation, absolutions (forgiveness of sins) became free of charge.

Pope Pius X11 (1876 - 1958) was the wartime Pope. He was said to have maintained good relations with Adolf Hitler and did not speak up against the Holocaust.

The Imperial Church did not hesitate to burn at the stakes, those who did not believe everything the church wanted them to believe. The last heretic to be burned at the stake was Edward Wightman (1566 – 1612). He was an English Anabaptist minister who believed that human souls did not go to heaven or hell but remained in the grave until Judgment Day. Whether he was right or wrong, he had the right to believe it. That belief did not disqualify him from the Kingdom of God if he was born again and lived by the Gospel - the Golden Rule, the Great Commandment and the New Commandment - which the imperial church did not do. Instead, they built cathedrals, now half empty, to serve both God and Mammon. Some are tourist attractions in remembrance of the past. The poor were neglected. In 1739, John Wesley founded the Methodist Church, to minister to the poor and address social issues. In 1865, William and Catherine Booth founded the Salvation Army to rescue the poor from neglect. The original church of Jesus Christ can neither be restored by the rich nor by the poor but by the middle class, if they can be found.

Where are witches today? Women suspected of being witches were routinely burnt at the stakes by the medieval mind. Notice that the church Establishment was the Judge, Jury and Executioner. It controlled Europe which controlled the rest of the world. Now, the church that opened the Pandora's box blames culture for everything that is going wrong in the world.

The theologians of the Reformation did not see anything wrong with the enslavement of people who looked different. They worried about the sale of indulgence but being born again is more important than the sale of indulgence. Jesus Christ identified the Broadway that leads to destruction and the narrow and difficult way that leads to life. Even after the Reformation, if a spiritual Pied Piper led the masses down the Broadway, will there not be numerous wars? Will there not be colonial wars, World Wars, the Holocaust, slave trade, slavery, segregation, apartheid, hatred, family conflicts and breakups and more. The Pandora's box is still not empty. The nuclear bombs are not out yet. Furthermore, the Reformers created denominational differences that are totally irrelevant to salvation. Like the mother Church, they missed what is important - a Christian must be born again and live by the commandments, including the Golden Rule. One generation does not have to follow the footsteps of the preceding generation. They do, if they are born into a denomination or religion that is dogmatic. In many poor countries, the difference between pagans and Christians is that the latter go to church on Sundays and claim to be sinners saved by grace; or have their weekly transgressions erased by absolutions, to clean up for the next week.

Billions of Christians cannot watch societal change and decay and remain silent. I have lost a son to religion because he has to receive weekly absolutions and venerate the Virgin Mary as the mother of God. In some parts of Africa, some Roman Catholic parents who never read the Bible were denied communion because a son or daughter married a Bible – reading Protestant. The African church is not fully independent. Evidently, the polarization in many nations in a struggle between right and wrong has been evolving for 2,000 years. Evangelism, as will be shown later, was a superficial mission. To err is human. Does that include the Church? The assumption of papal infallibility has made it difficult to admit to past mistakes including celibacy and the sale of indulgences.

The Nazis were a prominent cultural militia. Every culture has a cultural militia. They do to others what they don't want others to do to them. Or lead the people astray. Actions have intended and unintended consequences. The problems of today are the consequences of the legacy from past generations. When the Jewish Church leaders abandoned Christianity to the Gentiles, it has consequences. When the Roman magisterium used slavery to enforce celibacy, it has consequences. When the church became an accomplice in over 200 years of slave trade and slavery, it has consequences. When the Arabian Cultural militia used their cultural religion to invade parts of the world and occupy Egypt and parts of Africa, in the pursuit of spiritual imperialism, it has consequences. When the church, post Reformation, still did not teach converts to observe all that Jesus Christ commanded, particularly the Golden Rule, it has consequences. When the Christian cultural militia led their nations to invade, colonize and merge discordant tribes into one nation, it has consequences. Some of those consequences are ethnic hatred, anti-Semitism, Islamophobia, mass migration, populism, family violence and divorce, scams, wars and the killing of some survivors of slavery by men in uniform.

After the death of Prophet Muhammad, Arabians got into the business of conquest and slavery using their new religion. Some people do to others what they don't want others to do to them. The Gospel of Jesus Christ came to tame the animal instinct in man. No people group in the world has been more adversely impacted than Africans by the corruption of the Gospel of Jesus Christ. That is why Africans and African Americans must be at the forefront to change the Church that stood for might is right, to the Church of Jesus Christ that stands for the Golden Rule. It makes sense to any human being. In the year 2020, the asphyxiation to death in nine minutes, of an African American named George Floyd, by a policeman on a street in Minneapolis, Minnesota, was caught on camera. There was a global revulsion and social convulsion over that 21st century barbarism. The statues of prominent imperialists were defaced. The statues of some slave traders and confederate soldiers were pulled down. In all the turmoil, the fountainhead of that original racism remained out of sight. It is the Church that used slavery to enforce celibacy. And in collaboration with slave traders, slave masters, auctioneers, church clergy and laity lived off the avails of the enslavement of Africans for about 300 years.

The participation of the clergy in the enslavement of one group of people by another erased the interface between right and wrong. That is what Americans are still struggling with to this day. The Democrats and the Republicans can blame each other for all that is wrong in America. But to any rational mind, there is no doubt that the Church bears a great responsibility for the social problems in the nation. The Church is said to be "eminently conservative." Cultural conservatives do to others what they don't want others to do to them. In the absence of the Apostles, who speaks for Christ? The Jesuits (the society of Jesus) sold 272 of their inventories of slaves to save Georgetown University from bankruptcy. To this day, the Church has expressed no repentance and no reconciliation with God or man before sending their members "home to be with the Lord." According to the Bible, "If My people who are called by My name will humble themselves, and pray, and seek My face, and turn from their wicked ways, then I will hear from heaven, and will forgive their sin, and heal their land" (2 Chronicles 7:14). There has been no response. If that is the mind of the Almighty and immutable God, it stands to reason and common sense, that He does not care about the cultural center that is called Church but about individual Christians who are born again and live by the Golden Rule, the Great Commandment and the New Commandment.

Early in 2020, conscience-driven activists expressed their moral indignation on the streets of America and much of the world. The Golden Rule is the interface between the right side and the wrong side of history. Apart from the name "Christian, "there is nothing in common between the spiritual conservative Christians and the cultural conservative Christians who control the world order and have been at war with God and the Gospel that is counterculture. Evidently, the war to emancipate the slaves in Dixie did not change the Church that raised the slave traders, auctioneers, slave masters, and politicians. It did not change the Church and clergy, high and low, who lived off the avails of unpaid servitude for centuries.

The cultural conservative Christians who would do to others what they don't want others to do to them still dominate the spiritual conservative Christians who treat others the way they would like to be treated. The nominal Christians still dominate the born-again Christians. Prayers and absolutions cannot and have not changed the Church. Can an incumbent be the leader of change? Every inhuman event will fade in memory, to be followed by another inhumanity. If the wrongs of the past do not reflect who we are, we must expedite action to redress them. Reliance on prayers to solve the problems of unrepentant world has no effect and cannot erase history. How can the church be forced to undergo repentance and change? Is it by joining the exodus from the church? Out of the decadence of the church that stood for might is right, will emerge the church of Jesus Christ that stands for the Golden Rule. Otherwise, there is nothing to prevent a nuclear conflict between the East and the West.

It has become a regular cliché that things will get worse before they get better. Things will surely get worse as more concerned and rational minds boycott the church. Then, the church fathers will be forced to review the role of the church Establishment in history, and begin to fulfill all the terms of the Great Commission or be replaced by a new generation of volunteers who would preach the Gospel and teach converts to observe all things whatsoever that Jesus Christ commanded.

Human beings are supposed to have differences of opinion. But God's Golden Rule – "Treat others the same way you want them to treat you" has veto over differences of opinion. The empty pews and churches for sale speak to over a thousand years of doing the wrong things over and over, expecting a different outcome. It speaks to the long list of wrongs done to man by man and to groups by groups. If denominational headquarters are following the footsteps of the church fathers that opened the Pandora's box some 2,000 years ago; if the pastorate continues to do the same wrong things over and over, expecting a different result," church for sale" will be as normal and regular as "house for sale." Opening the Pandora's box has been the beginning of our sorrows. As individuals and as an institution, the role of the church in over 200 years of slavery is sickening. When the Jewish and Gentile church abandoned the faith to the Roman Empire, the lion and the bear were allowed to evangelize the jungle. Until there is repentance and return to the theology of the first century church, going to church is a perpetuation of hypocrisy and self-deceit.

"We live in an evil world," some preachers say. For over a

millennium, after the Apostles passed away, the church controlled the world through the Kings and Emperors of Europe. Who was the ruler of the evil world? Americans have fought for the emancipation of slaves, for suffrage for women, civil rights and social justice. When a priest or pastor is aware that the church, they inherited also used slavery to enforce celibacy; and for centuries clergy and laity lived off the avails of unpaid servitude, does it make sense to berate the evil world, culture, humanists, liberals, universities and godless communists for the evils in the world when the church fostered that world? For centuries, the world was controlled by the church and slave holders. If that was not an evil world, when did the evil world begin? We still live in a world where evil seems to prevail, and it is even aided by Christians. In all of the above, who was the adversary of the commoners by resisting God's Golden Rule? Was it Satan? Was the church not part of the problem? Were women not denied suffrage by their sons? Yes, "we have met the enemy, and they are us."

Suppose the Almighty sends every man, woman and child into exile in Mars or another planet. Will this still be an evil world? The evil spirit or Satan or the spirit of disobedience will follow them into exile because the evil spirit dwells in a man or woman who has not been born again, a man or woman who has not genuinely asked for the Holy spirit (Luke 11:13) to replace the evil spirit or the spirit of disobedience. Babies are born into a religion, denomination and culture. Those who become hate monger and racists are good people who inherited ignorance through victor theology. Still every December we are reminded about peace and goodwill to all on earth. In 2,000 years, it has not happened because the institution designed to mold character and facilitate it was hijacked and bastardized. If current evangelists continued to follow the footsteps of the imperial church fathers; if they care about the soul of the dead but not about social justice and the wellbeing of the living, they will turn away more of the educated people from their church. And more churches will be closed and sold because they do not believe that anyone would die and "go home to be with the Lord" without doing the will of the Lord.

The Truth of the Matter

The Roman Empire was the greatest empire in human history. The imperial power that fed Christians to Lions at the coliseum for entertainment, drove underground the Pentecostal church of Christ composed of Jews and Gentiles. In that early church history, to be the bishop of Rome or Pope, was a bloody contest. The Pope exercised authority over the Kings and Emperors of Europe. When the imperial power lived by the antipode of the Golden Rule, and crucified people, how can the Golden Rule be practiced in the Empire and beyond?

Evil is always initiated by men, not women. The first and second generations of men in the Trans-Atlantic slave trade and slavery must have struggled with their conscience. For subsequent generations born into the business, slavery became a normal way of life. It was blessed by the church Establishment. Even the men in robes, who were performing wonderful liturgy became habituated to the inhumanity. Activists and environmentalists will notice that the world has never been threatened physically or environmentally by the half-naked "primitive people" in the jungle who live simple lives. The sad events of history show that those who were right in centuries past, are seen today to be wrong in the light of Christian civilization. Being right then was based on a cultural truth, not the Gospel Truth. The church Establishment was based on the cultural truth; it ignored the Gospel Truth, and was part of the world in which might was right.

And so, slavery lasted for nearly 250 years in the U.S. and over 350 years in Roman Catholic Brazil, despite the Golden Rule, the Great Commandment and the New Commandment - the very core of the Christian faith they professed. The great tragedy is that since those centuries of slavery to this day, most Christians have been going "home to be with the Lord "without doing the will of the Lord. The church has not changed. Where those men and women end up only God knows. The slaves were ruined physically but the slave masters and their clergy were ruined spiritually. A genuine Christian who is born again lives by the Golden Rule and will never be involved in hatred, slave trade, slavery, colonialism, segregation, and apartheid or go to war except in self-defense. That is obvious. And if common sense is common, it is equally obvious that if the church fathers were faithful to the spirit of the Gospel, and mandate of the Great Commission, there would have been no protestant denomination.

Arabians whose ancestors were Christians in the first century will also admits that if the church fathers did not abuse power but observed God's Golden Rule from the first century to this day, there would have been no need for Islam; and all the turmoil of the Middle East would have been averted. Treat others the same way you want them to treat you makes sense to any human being. Yet, for centuries, clergy and laity lived off the avails of the unpaid servitude of African men women and children. In 1838 the Jesuits- the society of Jesus - sold 272 of their slaves to save Georgetown University from bankruptcy. That is a shameful fact that shows how different the Church is from the Church of Jesus Christ. Now, in a more civilized world, there are men - and women in particular - who lament what "we" have done to other people. Social problems will never be solved without separating the ambiguous 'We" from the dogmatic cultural militia or cultural conservatives who still do to others what they don't want others to do to them. In the U.S., for example, no party is responsible for what the other political party does. No nation, even now, can find the route to civilization without going back 2,000 years to the Golden Rule.

The church that owned and sold slaves, and lived off the avails of slavery for centuries was a sick church. After 2,000 years of Christianity the church, with a growing population of divorcees has become resigned to morbidity. The number of divorced Christians in the world shows that something is wrong in Christianity. After 2,00 years, the war between Russian and Ukrainian Christians shows that the Gospel is not part of the cultural fabric of any nation. After 2,000 years, a church whose member in uniform would handcuff a man whose ancestors survived centuries of slavery by Christians, kneel on his neck on the pavement for nine minutes to kill him; that church has an ingrained chronic disease. Why does the church have a chronic disease? Is the diseased church incurable? As enlightened youths of tomorrow condemn slave traders and slave masters during man's savage past, they must also see the imperial church as a disservice to the soul of their nation. That church needs a second Reformation because it has not changed.

If there is a Conference of Bishops that is in silent denial of the events of the past 400 years; and neither condemns nor condones the egregious wrongs Christians still do to one another; and withholds a national act of regret, remorse, Truth and Reconciliation with God and man, "church for sale" is long overdue. If the men and women who wear the cross, hug the Bible and peddle hatred are Christians, "church for sale" is also long overdue. The cultural conservative Christians and dogmatists have turned the U.S. into a poster child of man's defiance of God Almighty.

From the beginning to the end of human history, nothing has gone wrong or will go wrong in human relations that is not connected to the failure of the church Establishment to observe and also teach converts to observe God's Golden Rule – Treat others the same way that you want them to treat you. That disobedient spirit that began with slavery is the same spirit that is destroying Christian families. Karma calls the chickens home to roost. And so, students, particularly African students whose people bear the brunt of history - from colonialism to slave trade, slavery, segregation, apartheid and more - cannot but be ashamed of their own church that has not changed course. They have continued to hate and kill each other through a corrupted religion that has yet to teach them to observe all things whatsoever that Jesus Christ commanded. If the students didn't learn, the teacher didn't teach.

Nevertheless, Christianity will survive with fewer denominations. The church that is Pentecostal and understands how to be born again and live by the Gospel will survive. That is the whole purpose of man. For 2,000 years, the church has been a masquerade of the Pentecostal church that was led by St. Peter. Peter was crucified and so was the Pentecostal church. Human beings make mistakes. Consider this: If the world is propagating a faulty theology and doctrine generation after generation, will it get better or worse? If the world is propagating the Gospel – the Golden Rule, the Great Commandment and the New Commandment – generation after generation, will it get better or worse?

CHAPTER 3

The Church Establishment: Regent or Executor?

Those who worship any deity are expected to know from their Scripture, his will for humankind and if it makes sense on a global context. If adult children have conflicting views of their father, do they have the same father? If humanity has conflicting views of the God of Creation, are they accountable to the same God and what directives keep them accountable to that God? Christianity is about good relations between peoples and between them and the God of Creation. That's what makes it authentic. Anyone who professes to be a Christian or a non-Christian should read the will of the God of Creation expressed in the Gospel of Jesus Christ and determine if it makes sense. And based on that will, ask why the world is the way it is today after 2,000 years; not 20, not 200, but 2,000 years of Christianity.

There is the Golden Rule (Luke 6:31). It is golden because it makes sense to anyone who is a human being. There is the Great Commandment (Luke 10:27). It is great because it is comprehensive. It covers relations with God as well as relations with people. Jesus used the Parable of the Good Samaritan (Luke 10:30 – 37) to show that a neighbor is anyone who behaves like a human being. Finally, there is the New Commandment (John 13 :34). That is the will of God for humankind. It is the core of the Gospel and the foundation of Christianity. It makes sense to any rational mind and they are the very words of Jesus. To make these precepts actionable, you are to ask for the Holy Spirit, to replace the resident and endemic evil spirit - the spirit of disobedience in man. "If ye then, being evil, know how to give good gifts unto your children:" Jesus said, "how much more shall your heavenly Father give the Holy Spirit to them that ask Him? (Luke 11:13). The rest of the Scriptures are commentary.

Hidebound by tradition, the Pharisees whose ancestors related to the God of Israel through Moses, Joshua, Prophets and Kings, demanded to know where Christ's authority came from. Centuries of prophecy showed that He, the Messiah, would be born in Bethlehem. It was common knowledge. He was born in a manger for sheep in Bethlehem. Where would the sacrificial Lamb of God be born if not in a manger for sheep? It is detailed in my previous book "When Culture Overrules God and Reason. "To further prove Himself, Jesus performed miracles; healed the sick by command; raised the dead by command; walked on water; died on the cross as the sacrifice to end all animal sacrifices; rose from the dead on the third day as predicted; and returned to heaven. It was finished. His disciples and followers were willing to die for the Gospel in an empire that crucified deviants. He had issued a mandate to them in the Great Commission: "Go ye therefore, and teach all nations, baptizing them in the name of the Father, and of the Son, and of the Holy Ghost: Teaching them to observe all things whatsoever I have commanded you" (Matthew 28 :19 - 20.) Notice the last clause of that mandate - "Teaching them to observe all things whatsoever I have commanded you." Has it happened? That is the problem. With all of the above in mind, why is the world the way it is today after 2,000 years of Christianity? Where was the Golden Rule? There were numerous wars in Europe between Christians, up to the 20th century. The War of the Roses, according to historians, was a family feud. Where was the Golden Rule? Africa became the new forbidden fruit post anno domini. Christians began commercial slave trade from West Africa, and colonized the entire continent but spared Ethiopia. For over 300 years in Brazil and over 200 years in the United States, African men women and children were enslaved by Christians until they were stopped through a civil war. Even the Roman Catholic Jesuits owned and sold slaves. The emancipated Africans were to endure lynching, segregation and over 400 years of repression without restitution. The Pandora's box was wide open.

World War 1 took about 38million lives. World War II took about 50 million lives, including about six million Holocaust deaths. The Christians in Moscow and Washington, D.C. have been in perpetual conflict. What is holding them back from war is not the fear of God, but the fear of a nuclear war and death among politicians. For generations, women struggled for suffrage from the patriarchal Establishment. African Americans still struggle for civil and human rights from the patriarchal Establishment. Around the world, thousands of people, particularly women, are killed every year. Specifically, over 45,000 are killed each year just for being female. The divorce rate among Christians is not much different from the rate among the Pagans. Germans, Italians and Japanese citizens in North America were once treated as enemy aliens. Muslims in North America complain about Islamophobia and discrimination while some of the relatives they left behind are killing Africans and Christians. There are robberies, terrorism, scams, Cybercrimes and human trafficking every single day. In the light of the Gospel of Jesus Christ reviewed at the beginning, why have all these malevolent events happened in 2,000 years of Christianity despite the Golden Rule, the Great Commandment and the New Commandment? Are they the consequences of the church that went astray?

The Regent Church Establishment

A king who is a minor, incapacitated or cannot speak for himself is represented by a Regent. While an Executor follows the instructions of a will, a Regent is independent. He has his own agenda. Since God's will is in the Bible, He does not need a Regent but an Executor of His will. The Romans took over the Jewish-Gentile Church with the spirit of imperial superiority complex, not the spirit of service. The pastorate took advantage of the silence of God Almighty, who does not supervise the world like a referee. The post- Apostolic pastorate became a Regent for God Almighty, wielding imperial power beginning with the authorization of slavery.

The leaders of ancient Israel did not serve as Regents but as Executors of God's will, expressed in the Ten Commandments under the Old Covenant. Some Christians have used the Bible as a storybook or a book of quotations. Some even see it as a self-help book. But the Bible is about the will of God. Since the church Establishment assumed the role of Regent rather than an Executor of God's will in compliance to the Great Commission, imperial power demanded a paradigm shift - the victor theology. The clergy was, and should be the most important office in the land. That was the case in ancient Israel. But the strongmen of an empire cannot condescend to obey the Golden Rule, and stoop to wash the feet of commoners. It is said that history was written by the victors. They controlled the narrative of history. Similarly, the imperial Rome that controlled Europe, also shaped the narrative of the Gospel of Jesus Christ. Later, the Protestant victor in America will shape a different narrative.

Before King Henry V111 formed the Church of England, and before the Reformation, the church was controlled by the greatest and most sophisticated empire in human history. It is human nature to exploit ignorance. Under the British empire in Africa, for example, there were court messengers who interpreted English for the British

Magistrates. Many got rich by demanding from the illiterate people, more money than the Magistrate imposed. Under the Roman empire, Jewish tax collectors demanded more than was imposed. And so, the Roman church fathers exploited the ignorance of an illiterate world and fed them victor theology. Christian converts were not allowed to read the Bible to see what it says. What were they hiding? The Epistles, particularly the Pauline Epistles were preached more than the Gospel of Jesus Christ. Why? The Apostles were guarded in what they said. They could be crucified. St. Paul even seemed to support slavery and for keeping women in their place. They did not want to "ruffle feathers." So, the Apostles were in a situation like Uncle Tom in the antebellum South where some slaves fought in the Civil War for the Confederate States of Alabama, Arkansas, Florida, Georgia, Louisiana, Mississippi, North Carolina, South Carolina, Tennessee, Texas and Virginia – ostensibly, to stay enslaved.

The Roman Catholic Victor Theology

As the greatest and most sophisticated empire, the influence of Caesar's Romans in science, Law, and Senators who resist change, persists to this day. By the fourth century, the Bishop of Rome was in control of the church, not as an Executor of God's will - the Golden Rule, the Great Commandment and the New Commandment - but a Regent, doing the will of culture in the name of God. While the Pharisees introduced hundreds of Laws that made Judaism a burden, the church Establishment introduced church laws. The Roman Rota is the highest courts of the church. There is the Magisterium in control of doctrine. And the Bishop of Rome, the pope was the head Regent of God's Kingdome on this side of heaven. He was more than a King. Frankly, if Rome was a continuation of the Pentecostal Church that St. Peter led, the Pope should be more than a King.

As the church evolved from pope to pope, there were seven sacraments, from cradle baptism to the last rites or extreme unction. It offers a dying person, prayers for forgiveness, mercy, the intercession of the Saints and a clean slate to enter heaven because they have denounced their sinful nature - at last. The "sinful nature" places responsibility on God the Creator. But man is given the freewill to do what is right or wrong. Abraham Lincoln, John Brown, William Wilberforce, Mother Teresa and many others, for example, did not denounce their sinful ways at the hour of their deaths. They did so while in good health. And so can any man or woman. And surely, many Christians live by the Golden Rule as evidence of being born again.

Over the centuries, church doctrine held that Mary was always a virgin. But Matthew 13:55 - 56 proves otherwise. Was the doctrine an excuse for celibacy? Clerics used to be married. The last married pope was Pope Adrian 11 (867 – 872). New traditions were added. The rosary was issued for the battle against evil. There was holy water because the devil hates holy water. There was purgatory for final purification. The Priests were called "Father," contrary to Matthew 23:9. To miss mass on Sunday was sin. Around the world, church service was conducted in Latin, the language of the Roman empire. They upheld belief in transubstantiation. The wine and the bread baked in the oven for communion were real blood and body of Jesus Christ, not symbols. You have to believe it. My illiterate married niece whose father was a titled man was baptized and given the name Mary. Such adults, take a couple of days to memorize their new Christian name. Being illiterate, they believed whatever they were told and did not understand a word of Latin.

Confession must be made to be in a state of grace to receive communion. The power of the church was absolute. There was a power struggle between the Roman contenders for the papacy, like the potential kings who fought for the throne. Between 1378 and 1417, there were three rival popes. There was also a power struggle between European Kings and the pope. The claim of "The Divine Right of Kings" was not based on sacred scripture. But if governance was based on the Golden Rule, the Great Commandment and the New Commandment, the claim would have been credible. And as the Executor of God's will, the executive monarchy would have lasted to this day. Sadly, the Kings were not Executors of God's will. They faced the ecclesiastical gatekeepers of the church who claimed to be the vicar of Christ on earth. Jesus Christ promised to send the Holy Spirit to His followers. Some will argue that the Holy Spirit is the real vicar or representative of Christ.

The Jesuits, the society of Jesus, owned slaves. In 1838, with the permission of Rome, they sold 272 slaves to save Georgetown university from bankruptcy. So, the church bought and sold slaves; the clergy and laity lived off the avails of slavery for centuries; they erased the interface between right and wrong; and offered absolutions to wrongdoers. That was a Regency, a secular church that served the interest of culture, in the name of God. It was not the vicar of Christ. Neither church nor State were the Executors of God's will.

The monarchy also claimed "Rex non potest peccare" – the king cannot do wrong. The Pope had to come up with a response. Pope Pius 1X whose papacy begun in 1846 and ended in 1878 came up with the Doctrine of Papal Infallibility. Yet, throughout his reign, the clergy and laity lived off the avails of the servitude of African men, women and their children. About 750,000 Americans would die on both sides in a civil war that could have been prevented if the infallible Pope condemned slavery. The sale of indulgences or tickets to heaven was too much for Martin Luther, a Roman Catholic theologian. He rebelled against the abuse of power. The movement he started led to the protestant denomination. In Africa, Asia and Latin America, the illiterate Christians with no sense of history believe that Martin Luther was born a Protestant and Protestants are destined for hell and no longer part of the church of St. Peter," the first

Pope." But the Pentecostal Church of St. Peter went underground. Without the disobedience of the Golden Rule there might be no Protestant denomination, and no new religions after Christianity. Cradle Christians did not read the Bible to see what they professed. Over the centuries, the grandchildren developed an aversion to Bible reading. With sacraments all laid out, why bother to read the Bible? So, they never knew that a Christian must be born again to see the kingdom of God (John 3:3). They never knew that a Christian must ask for the Holy Spirit to be born again (Luke 11:13) and observe the Golden Rule (Luke 6:31), the Great Commandment (Luke 10:27) and the New Commandment (John 13:34). These are the precepts that should have prevented the long list of sad events in human history. A Regent Establishment can rationalize what they do.

The imperial church also sowed the seed of self-destruction. Compulsory celibacy has led to sex abuse lawsuits and church closures. And since parishioners began to read the Gospel and ask questions, the Catholicism based on victor theology designed by imperial Rome is bound to unravel after 2000 years. Why did the Jesuits, the society of Jesus own slaves? Why did the church use Christianity to practice racism to serve culture? Nobody who understands the Gospel of Jesus Christ will believe that the church - clergy and laity - that lived off the avails of slavery for over 200 years in the U.S. and over 300 years in Roman Catholic Brazil, served any useful purpose either to the living or to the dead who left all their wealth behind. Were they inspired by the Holy Spirit or a different Spirit? If the church of slave trade and slavery was not inspired by the Holy Spirit, without remorse, repentance, restitution and reconciliation with God and man, has the Holy Spirit returned to the church?

To anyone born on the other side of the Atlantic Ocean, the African American history is like a fairy tale. Did Christians really do all that is recorded? If the Golden Rule, the Great Commandment and the New commandment are in the Bible, has the pastorate ever taught the Gospel of Jesus Christ? If it has, how many slave masters and their politicians lived by the Golden Rule? The Church has yet to express repentance for modern man's original sin. Africans cannot hold back the Truth because no people group has suffered more than Africans since the Church went astray. They have suffered both from flawed Christianity and the engendered Islam.

The Protestant Victor Theology

Before the Reformation, the one and only theology was the victor theology of Rome, the seat of the Roman empire. Some religions need reformation to modernize them. The Reformation in Christianity was not to modernize the Gospel of Jesus Christ. It cannot be modernized. A message from God Almighty cannot be modernized. The Reformation was to free the counter -culture Christianity from culture. The 16th century reformers left the Roman Catholic Church because of the sins of Rome. Slavery was not one of them. When people are made to believe that every word in the Bible is the word of God, it lays the foundation to spin and cite the Scriptures to create the false and convenient theology for their purpose - sustain cultural and economic interests. They told lay people who did not attend a seminary what they wanted to hear: "Christianity is about believe in Jesus Christ. He died on the cross to pay for our sins. You are saved by grace alone, and not by what you do." Romans 10 :9 and Ephesians 2: 8 – 9, not the Gospel, were cited as proof. Those who say the sinner's prayer, confessing Jesus Christ as Lord and Savior; that He died on the cross for their sins, become baptized, are born again and bound for eternity. Their sins are mailed on the cross and once saved always saved. God has decided who would be saved. Therefore, occasional malfeasance is covered by God's Amazing Grace. That is seen to be "The good news "; no sweat.

Evangelicalism became synonymous with being born again. The Holy Spirit is not needed. In essence, the difference between a Christian and a non -Christian is belief in Jesus Christ; that the blood of Jesus Christ on the cross canceled our sins. It did not. That is the victor theology or the Dixie gospel for protestants. If our sins are nailed on the cross, there is no need to go to church anymore. We are then licensed to do to others what we don't want others to do to us. That is not Christianity. It is the Dixie or Southern gospel or the Protestant victor theology that fostered slave trade and slavery without any guilt of conscience. It now emboldens and animates "Christians" who carry "Faith and Blue" placards to oppose "Black Lives Matter" demonstrators in support of people who survived slavery and still have no respite in Christendom. The "Faith" is the Southern Gospel. In religion and politics, the Gospel of Jesus Christ was unsuitable for the powerful men of an empire, particularly an empire that crucified deviants who transgressed cultural norms. To abide by the Golden Rule, and wash the feet of the lower class and commoners would be condescending towards the lesser mortals. The strongmen of an empire in control of the highest office in the land cannot do that. The Gospel had to be schemed and tailored for continued subjection; not for equality but for hierarchy. They nullified the intent of the Gospel of Jesus Christ and erased the interface between right and wrong. It opened the door to wars of subjugation and conquest, colonialism, slave trade, slavery, segregation, apartheid and more. One colony would go from one colonial power to a superior colonial power.

As the Lamb of God, the blood of Jesus Christ canceled offering periodic animal sacrifices for people of the Christian faith and for no other religion. Asking for and receiving the Holy Spirit to enable a Christian to obey God and live by those Commandments is what cancels sins. The Apostles of Jesus Christ received the Holy Spirit on the day of Pentecost. That was the birthday of the Church. The followers of Jesus Christ became born-again. A repentant person who accepts Jesus Christ as Lord and Savior is a Christian. The new Christian or nominal Christian or churchman or woman must ask to receive the Holy Spirit (Luke 11:13). The Holy Spirit replaces the resident and endemic Evil Spirit in a man. When the Christian lives by the Golden Rule, it is the visible evidence of a born-again Christian who will likely live by the Great Commandment and the New Commandment. They didn't in Dixie where opposition to plantation capitalism (slavery) was opposition to their Christian faith and way of life. They were willing to fight and die for the Southern Gospel, and they did. Since the powerful or victors control the narrative of history and religion, polls show that about one -third of Americans Christians believe that they are born again. And that the greatest concentration of "born-again Christians" is in Dixie where clergy and laity fought and died to sustain slavery. If a Christian is a follower of Jesus Christ, the church of the slave economy were not even Christians. It was self-deceit.

Only an individual knows what is stored in their soul. When asked if the churchman or woman is born again, the proximate answer is always yes. It is better to ask: "In the past one year, have you done to anyone what you don't want them to do to you?" That is the litmus test of a born-again Christian. Posters can start from politicians. Compassion, fairness and honesty cannot be acquired through the ears and eyes but by inviting the Holy Spirit to replace the resident spirit of disobedience. To tell Johnny to be a good boy will not make him a good boy. To slap him on the wrist for bad behavior will not change his character. That has been the flaw of the victor theology dispensing Absolution or Amazing Grace, as Regents rather than the Executors of God's will already in the Bible.

A visit to the Caribbean revealed to me that the clergy, slave traders and slave masters were not godless communists. They were very religious Christians. Many islands were carved up into Parishes of St. Peter, St. James, St. Mary, St. Thomas, St. Andrew, St. George, St. Joseph, St. Michael, St. Philip, Christ Church, etc. For one who has read the Gospel of Jesus Christ, the corruption is surreal. How did pastors and priests who read the Gospel of Jesus Christ and saw the Golden Rule, the Great Commandment and the New Commandment minister to men who were buying and selling human beings – men, women and children - to be enslaved for life? And together, clergy and laity lived off the avails of slavery for over 250 years. What can it be but a victor theology that turned the Gospel of Jesus Christ upside down and created a secular Church? And they were buried in church yards as a steppingstone to heaven, if you can believe it. Skin-tone prejudice is a social construct based on medieval ignorance. The thought of a man from a noble family being enslaved just because of the tone of my skin was overwhelming. They believed that the lifestyle they were born into was God ordained because "As it was in the beginning, is now, and ever shall be, world without end. Amen."

The world then and now is not as it was in the beginning. Based on the scriptures, if Christianity is about good relations between people and between them and the God of Creation, why is the world the way it is today after 2,000 years of Christianity? Why is the East and West in perpetual state of war? What does it mean to be an Executor of God's will? The answer is in the mandate of the Great Commission: "Go ye therefore, and teach all nations, baptizing them in the name of the Father, and of the Son, and of the Holy Ghost: Teaching them to observe all things whatsoever I have commanded you: and lo, I am with you always, even unto the end of the world" (Matthew 28:19 – 20). Notice that a key clause of the mandate has not been fulfilled after 2,000 years, namely, "Teaching them to observe all things whatsoever I have commanded you." How many Christians and politicians have been taught to observe the Golden Rule, the Great Commandment and the New Commandment? That is the role of an Executor of God's will. The secular Church has been the Executor of the will of culture. It is not the people that have to change. It is the clergy that has to change and start teaching the Gospel, not victor theology. The clergy and laity that colonized defenseless people and lived off the avails of slavery for some 300 years did not observe all that Jesus Christ commanded. If the students didn't learn, the teacher didn't teach. The teacher is still not teaching. That is the legacy of victor theology.

Notice also the support the evangelists should expect - "and lo, I am with you alway, even unto the end of the world." Some sincere and committed Christians have gone to the backwaters of the world and faced persecution. The Holy Spirit or Jesus Christ was not with them because the Gospel and the victor theology are not the same. The persecutors do not resent the Gospel but the victor theology that spurred colonialism, slave trade and slavery for centuries. The persecutors might even use a cultural religion to persecute unbelievers. An Executor Church would do the will of God for the salvation of humankind. But the Regent church Establishment did the will of man for culture. Some tried to serve both God and culture. People do things the way it has always been done. The clergy and laity of the slave economy had a theological relationship with God. They were not born again. Can the blind lead the blind?

John Newton, the slave trader whose song, <u>Amazing Grace</u> has become an anthem, was one of the few who recognized that they were blind and lost. They were able to regain their spiritual sight, not because of the clergy but despite the clergy and their victor theology. Still, many are following the footsteps of Christians who were blind and lost. Christians and hate-mongers who resist social justice or the Golden Rule are not different from the church of the slave traders. Before blaming culture, Liberals and delinquent youths; and what the cultural conservative Christians called "the hoodlums and criminal class," those who have rational minds would recognize that the clergy and laity," the blooded stock "that lived off the avails of slavery for centuries, laid the foundation for modern-day moral delinquency. Take a look at the baby pictures of the men and women in prison. Everybody in the world was once an adorable innocent baby. What happened from the cradle to the prison is an indictment of the imperial secular church that owned slaves and did not teach converts to "observe all things whatsoever I have commanded you" as Jesus said. Unofficial research and common-sense show that the number of babies in a Hutterite colony who grew up to be criminals is insignificant compared to the general population. Yet, the church Establishment sees humankind, especially young adults, as the problem it is working to change. The Truth is that the church is the problem that has to change because it is a caricature, not a carbon copy of the Pentecostal church that St. Peter led.

If Christianity were a cultural religion, the founding culture would be practicing what is in their scripture as cultural religionists do. Christianity is a counter-culture religion that was hijacked by imperial Rome. Consequently, there is no religion in the world with a greater disparity between what is in the scripture and what is practiced. The mother Church of the First Century received the Holy Spirit and became born again Christians who lived by the Golden Rule, the Great Commandment and the New Commandment. That First Century church was not Roman Catholic or Protestant. By their very nature, the successors of that church led by St. Peter should never issue the Doctrine of Discovery and unleash colonialism, slave trade, slavery, colonial wars, world wars, the Holocaust, segregation, apartheid and racism. Never. The imperial Church of the past 2,000 years did not ask for the Holy Spirit (Luke 11:13) as Jesus Christ proposed, to replace man's evil spirit. Obviously, if the Gospel Truth be told, the post Apostolic Church had nothing in common with the First Century Church of Jesus Christ, except in name only. That is not a new dogma but common sense.

Apart from church participation in centuries of slave trade and slavery, the Doctrine of Discovery and the Scramble for Africa brutalized Africans in their homeland. In the Belgian Congo, for example, as many as 10 million Africans were killed in their homeland. An activist leader, Patrice Lumumba, was murdered, butchered and dissolved in acid. Anyone who has read the Gospel of Jesus Christ (Matthew, Mark, Luke and John) and the Acts of the Apostles, should notice that the imperial Church of the past 2,000 years has nothing in common with the First Century Church of Jesus Christ. Once the spiritual Pandora's Box was opened, there is no limit to depravity.

Records do not show that President Abraham Lincoln belonged to any Church. He was self-educated. How could he read the Gospel and understand it better than religious seminarians and institutions that bought, sold and enslaved men, women and children simply because they were powerless and their skin tone was different? His compatriots did not go to Church to worship God, but to worship culture through their victor theology. That may still be the case as the macho man piles on transgression after transmission without redress. Nobody has been to heaven and back. Anyone who can read Matthew, Mark, Luke and John like Lincoln, has all the information needed as Pilgrims on a barren land. Since he was assassinated, cultural conservative Christians who conserve culture, have continued to sabotage the Christian faith. Humans are evil by nature. And so, Jesus came to teach the Golden Rule and more, and offer the choice between the Holy Spirit and the resident Evil Spirit of disobedience. It is a choice that separates the human jungle from the animal jungle.

From The Acts of The Apostles to The Acts of Their Successors

Can anyone imagine St. Peter and other Apostles running a Church that bought, sold and enslaved men, women and children for 300 years? What followed after their death was a secular Church. Being born again can never leads to the sad events of history, including slavery. But the victor theology of imperial Rome and the Southern gospel of the evangelicals conditioned succeeding generations to circumvent the gospel of Jesus Christ. They turned Africans into chattels for plantation capitalism. In the centuries of church- endorsed slave trade and slavery, sharks trailed slave ships, according to historians. How many Africans were thrown into the Atlantic Ocean, only God knows. For those who survived the trans- Atlantic voyage, parents raised children to be sold and separated from them. Wives or husbands were sold and separated from each other. The churchmen and clergy could do all that because victor theology does not change lives; only the Holy Spirit can change lives.

School children cannot read the Gospel of Jesus Christ and believe that Priests and Pastors ministered to Christians who bought and sold human beings -men, women and children like their classmates, to be enslaved for life without pay. And for centuries the clergy who collected offerings, lived off the avails of the enslavement of brothers and sisters who looked more like the Adam and Eve they preached on in the Genesis account of creation. Even the Jesuits, the society of Jesus, owned slaves and with the permission of Rome, sold 272 of their inventories of slaves in 1838 to save Georgetown university from bankruptcy. How do you explain the association of Jesuits with slavery? Can any Christian who has read the Golden Rule, the Great Commandment and the New Commandment explain why the Jesuits would own slaves? The Dixie theology or Southern gospel would convert people and call Jesus "Lord, Lord "and do not what He says.

Americans in the North, did not want an expansion of slavery and the Southern brand of Christianity. When Abraham Lincoln and Stephen Douglas held seven debates focused on slavery, they were covered by newspapers across the nation. At the end of one of those debates, according to historians, Lincoln was carried on the shoulders of some of his supporters because of his performance. His pro- slavery opponents reported in their media that Lincoln was so exhausted that he was carried away. Fake news is not new. The truth has often been distorted since Satan appeared in the garden of Eden. That is still the case. Without the church, Abraham Lincoln read and understood the Gospel, as schoolchildren today would read and understand it. Mahatma Gandhi, who confronted Christians in apartheid South Africa and the colonial masters in India also read and understood the same Gospel. He opined that the greatest asset of Christianity is Jesus Christ; and the greatest liability are the Christians.

Any human being who understands the Gospel and what it means to be a follower of Jesus Christ will be ashamed of the Acts of the successors of the Apostles. And may even be ashamed to be a human being in the light of slave trade and slavery. There is hardly anyone today who has not been impacted by slavery, wars, colonialism, imperialism, racism, sexism, Islamophobia, anti-Semitism, divorce, scams, cybercrimes and more because of the Regency of the church. There is hardly a social problem in the world that is not linked to the disobedience of the Golden Rule. If the students didn't learn, the teacher didn't teach. The protestant apostles of prophecy will never be apostles of the Golden Rule. Africans endured about 300 years of slave trade and slavery because of the tone of their skin. Yet, they saw rabbits change their skin color every year. In the light of the Gospel today, whose humanity is in question - the slaves or the slave masters? If Adam and Eve were created or evolved, and were naked from year to year, they must have lived on a hot continent and were dark skinned. They were Africans. Everybody is an African.

It took men and women who had a living conscience to wage a civil war to end slave trade and slavery. Based on conditioned misbelief, the Dixie church went to war to kill or be killed in order to sustain slavery forever. Presidents Abraham Lincoln who led the civil war was assassinated. He was succeeded by a Southerner, vice President Andrew Johnson. He rescinded the proposed 40 acres of land and a mule to resettle emancipated families. He was known to be an owner of about 150 slaves and a racist to the core. He was a Democrat. But as the Democrats changed with time, Abraham Lincoln's spiritual conservative Republican party became a cultural conservative party preaching personal responsibility, not societal responsibility. Some became politician to prevent the use of government to serve the common good. So, government must be small, even when they claimed to care so much about creating jobs. The Republican party became the voice of the master class defending plantation capitalism while the Democrats became the voice of those begging for women's suffrage and African Americans pleading for civil rights and inclusion. Who created this lifestyle?

St. James, who is rarely quoted wrote:" For as the body without the spirit is dead, so faith without works is dead also" (James 2:26). Anyone who has been to church for 10 years, must have heard enough of what Jesus said and what St. Paul in particular said. Doing what they said is the problem. Some of what they said is considered to be a radical socialist agenda. The church of the slave masters had a macho man's interpretation of the Gospel of Jesus Christ. After 400 years, no attempt has been made to established Truth and Reconciliation Commission to reconcile with God and man over America's original sin. Instead, to keep the underclass down, the cultural conservatives have relied on gerrymandering, voter suppression, and intimidation to keep those who inherited poverty from slavery, away from the ballot box in the world's greatest democracy.

Spiritual conservatives conserve spiritual values while cultural conservatives conserve cultural values. How does a cultural-conservative Christian live with his conscience? That has not been a concern since the corruption of the Christian faith. The underlying problem in America is not politics. Government is not the problem. The mainstream media is not the problem. Communists are not the problem. The police are not the problem. The church is the problem. The corruption of the Gospel of Jesus Christ is the problem. Americans are still fighting a war on Truth. The descendants of Africans who were enslaved for centuries are still resisting repression while their government is focused on human rights abuses elsewhere.

The mandate of the great commission is to convert all nations,

"Teaching them to observe all things whatsoever I have commanded you." It includes observing or obeying the Golden Rule. It did not happen. The Establishment became the Regent of God Almighty, not the Executor of God's will. Even after slavery, compliance to the Golden Rule would have prevented the lost lives and treasures in several wars, including wars in Korea, Vietnam, Iraq and Afghanistan, and over 60 million refugees fleeing from ungodly governments by 2020. Abba Eban, an Israeli politician reportedly noted that" History teaches us that men and nations behave wisely once they have exhausted all other alternatives. "Is the church the exceptions? It has been said that some people never change. The Klan will never change until their church changes. The church itself is not expected to change if it serves as the Regent for God Almighty.

The leaders of ancient Israel did not serve as Regents but as Executors of God's will expressed in the Ten Commandments, under the Old Covenant. The imperial Church Establishment was not an Executor of God's Commandments in compliance to the Great Commission. It assumed the role of Regent and offered absolution or forgiveness of sins. For centuries, the successors have not seen the need for an "infallible "Establishment to seek repentance and reconciliation with God and the victims of history, even when it owned and sold slaves, and lived off the avails of unpaid servitude for centuries.

The Golden Rule, the Great Commandment and the New Commandment have social obligations. "Bear ye one another's burdens, and so fulfill the law of Christ" is a social obligation. God gives every nation their daily bread. The gap between the billionaire and the homeless or pauper, shows that the daily bread is not well shared under plantation capitalism. If the post- apostolic pastorate were the Executors of God's will, after 2,000 years of Christianity, every nation on earth would have universal education, universal healthcare, and universal employment for all families in their original habitat, just like a Canadian Hutterite colony. Sadly, there is not a single nation on earth that has such a national plan between now and doomsday. The good and the evil are growing together like crops and weeds.

In Dickensian England, the society was homogeneous. And the prisons also because the poor commit crimes everywhere. No baby is born to be a criminal, but neglect will turn them into criminals and street people. The neglect of the underclass was so appalling that William and Catherine Booth founded the Salvation Army in London in 1865, to care for the spiritual and temporal needs of the poor and destitute people fictionalized as Oliver Twist. If the church were the Executor of the will of God rather than a Regent, between then and now, the UK would have been like a Canadian Hutterite colony with education, healthcare and employment for every family. But the Pentecostal Holy Catholic Church had disappeared.

Armenia - A Regency

Armenia has some of the oldest churches in Christendom. About 97percent are Christians. As far back as 301 AD, the Armenian Apostolic church founded in the first century became the state religion. Based on those commandments; and based on 'Bear one another's burdens and so fulfill the law of Christ," after 2,000 years of Christianity, there is no reason why homogeneous Armenia should not be like a Canadian Hutterite colony. That is the will of God for every nation. But the secular church based on victor theology reversed the will of God. And so, in 2020, Armenians would pray to God who is no longer listening, get a blessing from the secular church and go to kill or be killed in a war with predominantly Shiite Azerbaijan that should also have been like a Canadian Hutterite colony in compliance to the commandments and their social implications.

Some European nations with a similar experience as Armenia

have turned their back on the church and became even more secular in order to live in religion-free conflict in their native land. Nobody in Africa, Asia, America, Europe, or anywhere else should feel insecure in their own native land in this 21st century. It is all because the imperial church opened the pandora's box and became a Regent and not the Executor of the Golden Rule, the Great Commandment and the New Commandment after they crucified St. Peter. Many Christians and non -Christians have become disillusioned with the democracy that protects plantation capitalism and demonizes socialism. Until there is a Second Reformation, the world will continue to drift from crisis to crisis leading to more empty pews and churches for sale. It is easy to notice an institution that is growing. "Church for sale" is not the sign of an institution that is growing. The Second Reformation needs a new breed of Christians, perhaps an Alpha generation, who will trust and obey; and stop acting as God's Regents converting people to a life of hypocrisy and conflicts.

Rev. Dr. Billy Graham of North Carolina was the most famous evangelists of all time. He converted millions of people around the world to Christianity. How many became born again Christians and politicians who lived or governed by the Golden Rule, the Great commandment and the New Commandment, only God knows. It was no surprise that President John F. Kennedy and Rev. Dr. Martin Luther king would be assassinated in the Southern States - Kennedy in Texas and King in Tennessee. In the homeland of the Ku Klux Klan, St. Paul's call to "Bear one another's burdens and so fulfill the law of Christ" (Galatians 6:2) is a radical left agenda. Universal healthcare ensures that fellow Christians do not die because the family cannot afford Medical Care. A major illness has led many families to bankruptcy. Yet, socialized medicine is anathema in the land of the evangelicals and great evangelists. If universal healthcare is anathema in the richest and most gospelized nation on earth, universal employment will be one of those "over -my- dead -body" proposals. A wise Southern Baptist remarked that Jesus Christ will not be welcome in some of their churches today. That's a genuine Christian who has read the Gospel encapsulated by the Golden Rule the Great Commandment and the New Commandment. The victor theology will send more people to hell than to heaven or paradise because most people do not go to worship God but culture. That was the case with the clergy and laity of the slave economy.

Spiritual conservative Christian conserve spiritual values. They are Christians in the inside. The cultural conservative Christians conserve cultural values. They are Christians on the outside. The two groups give the church a moral split personality. If the Golden Rule - Treat others the same way you want them to treat you - has been in the Bible for 2,000 years; and the world is the way it is after 2,000 years, it is obvious which group controls the church. There are preachers who describe the world as Satan's world. If religious identity is worn as a plaque on the outside, and the evil spirit is still inside, is it not humans that run the Satan's world? The slave economy that lasted for about 300 years, was not run by Mr. Satan but by humans. The greatest victims of the Satan's world are Africans. "Study the past if you would define the future," said Confucius of China. They have studied the past. An August 28, 2018 article in The Atlantic by Signal Samuel, was titled: China Is Treating Islam Like a Mental Illness." Was that because they have studied the past?

In every crisis, the U.N. Security council has been paralyzed. Some nations seem to react to the past. The ethnocentric and dogmatic cultural conservatives who control and lead the majority will do well to practice the Golden Rule before confrontation. African Americans, Asians Americans, Pacific Islanders and aboriginal Americans are not sure if they belong to the East or West. They want a world that lives by the Golden Rule and free from discrimination and confrontation because in God, there is no East or West. The arms manufacturers may have to do something else. This may be the point to revisit "The Six Blind Men and The Elephant" to be re-conditioned to see life from a global rather than a cultural perspective. In any habitat, if the Gospel is disabled; if the Golden Rule is null and void, some animals will be adversely affected. There is no Bishop or Pope today who will condone slave trade and slavery. There is no rational mind today who will justify slavery based on the Gospel of Jesus Christ. That generation of clergy and laity that lived off the avails of slavery have long gone to give an account of their lives. Yet, it is so difficult to denounce those who led the church down the garden path. And begin the process of reconciliation with God and man, so that the Gospel of Jesus Christ can breathe.

Dogmatism requires doing things the way they have always been done. Even so, in the past 2,000 years, there must have been Popes and Kings who were undogmatic at heart. But such good Popes and Kings can be hostages to their own handlers. "And why call ye me, Lord, Lord," Jesus said," and do not the things which I say?" With that in mind, what is the purpose of going to church with a pile on of transgression over transgression in defiance of God? Let us be honest. Slavery was physical harm and abuse to Africans. If the commandments of God are to be obeyed; if it is true (Ezekiel 18:20) that "the soul that sinneth, it shall die, "can anyone go home to be with the Lord without doing the will of the Lord? If slavery is a crime against humanity today, it was a crime against humanity then. If it was done out of ignorance, what about the wrongs Christians do today?

The truth is that Christians who are not born again will continue to do wrong to others because the resident evil spirit has not been replaced by the Holy Spirit. The Golden Rule has been in the Scriptures long before slave trade and slavery. It was given as a behavior modifier to the primordial instinct in man to do wrong to others. Did the God of Creation know that people will do to others what they don't want others to do to them? Did He know? Obviously, the church Establishment that raised those Christians were not executing God's will but the will of culture through victor theology. That is still the case. The Apostles performed miracles. They healed the sick. They did not forgive sins. The Acts of their Successors were a rebellion against God.

The Command of Loyalty

Those who described World War 1 as the great war, did not see World War 11 coming. Students around the world have wondered how Adolf Hitler was able to control millions of people for a few years, and lead them to a war that took millions of lives. What lesson was learned from that experience? It was frustration that offered him loyalty. In November 18, 1978, Jim Jones, an American cult leader led over 900 members of the People's Temple, to a mass murder suicide in Jonestown Guyana. His followers, who were mostly African Americans were frustrated by the evils of endemic racism and poverty that persist to this day. What lesson was learned from that experience? Frustration with the Democratic party that was content with half measures; that could not offer the universal healthcare developed nations take for granted; and Republican Senate leaders who acted like Senators in the Roman empire resisting change, led to the election of an outsider as president of the United States in 2016.

While he ruled like a president accountable to nobody, women described President Donald Trump as misogynist. In the 2020 election, more women voted for him than in 2016. African Americans saw him as a racist who stoked hatred and disdained African countries. In the 2020 election more African Americans voted for him that in 2016. To abuse people and still demand their loyalty is preternatural; to offer the loyalty is even more preternatural. While over 81million people voted for vice President Joe Biden which was a record, over 74 million Americans voted for President Donald Trump, also a record. The news media was described as "fake news" and in fund- raising messages for the 2020 election, and in "Election defense Fund," Trump's followers were told that "by coming after me, they are coming after you." It is a command for loyalty.

Students may wonder how Adolf Hitler and Jim Jones commanded the loyalty of people to their death. What they will not do is wonder how the Church Establishment that used slavery to enforce celibacy; and for centuries, clergy and laity lived off the avails of slavery; and without repentance or reconciliation, still commands the loyalty of billions of people. The men, from Priests to Cardinals, accused of sexual misconduct, are themselves victims of an imperial Church Establishment that is difficult to change because of a long-standing claim of Papal infallibility. Yet, every cleric is a volunteer, not an appointee of God Almighty. Imagine what the world would look like in 2,000 years if the Regent Church were an Executor that followed the full mandates of the Great Commission: to convert all nations," Teaching them to observe all things whatsoever I have commanded you." Imagine how the world would have been in 2,000 years if Christian converts were taught to observe the Golden Rule - Treat others the same way you want them to treat you. Would there have been numerous wars in Europe, colonial wars, colonialism, slave trade, slavery, World Wars, the Holocaust, scams, Ponzi schemes, segregation, terrorism, apartheid, cybercrimes, racism and more?

With victor theology, the Church came to Latin America since the 15th century. Six hundred years later, Latin America is mired in corruption, violence, mass poverty and untold wealth at the top. Clearly, victor theology is not a life changer. Again, If the students didn't learn, the teacher didn't teach. The teacher is still not teaching. Since the teacher didn't teach, by the seventh century, Arabians got their own religion. It was weaponized to invade and colonize parts of Africans including Pharaoh's Egypt and as far as Spain and Portugal, in the name of a brand-new religion, Islam. Africans were dispossessed, some were killed or enslaved. The Pharaohs were exhumed for tourism and native Egyptians could do nothing against terror. Centuries later, in the name of national glory (not Christianity), European powers colonized all Africans including the colonizers. They began slave trade and slavery that lasted for nearly 250 years in the U.S. and 350 years in Roman Catholic Brazil, the first to start and the last to stop slavery.

Africans are not the ones complaining about an evil world.

Nobody speaks for them. But why did spiritual imperialism from the East coast and slavery from the West Coast befall defenseless people? One sin leads to another. Now, Christians have been killed in churches, Muslims have been killed in Mosques and Jews have been killed in Synagogues. Were all these preventable?

About a thousand years before Jesus Christ came, the Israelites got this message from God Almighty, the God of Israel:" If my people, which are called by my name, shall humble themselves, and pray, and seek my face, and turn from their wicked ways; then will I hear from heaven, and will forgive their sin, and will heal their land. "(2 Chronicles 7:14.) It didn't happen. Under the Roman empire, Jesus Christ came to a God-forsaken world, with a New Covenant for all humanity. Among them, "Treat others the same way you want them to treat you" will ensure that the human jungle is different from the animal jungle where the weak are the prey. It is a key to human civilization. It was ignored. The victor theology became the narrative of the Gospel of Jesus Christ. The secular Church replaced the Pentecostal Church of Jesus Christ. Africans have been the greatest victims of the disobedience of God. If religious people can do so much to Africans and still go to heaven or paradise, the atheists and "godless communists" watching, will be glad to go somewhere else. The clerics of monotheism led believers to the sin of slave trade and slavery for centuries, colonial wars, World Wars, colonialism, segregation, lynching, apartheid repression and all that can emerge from the Pandora's box. That is worse than what the Pharisees who led the Israelites did and were forsaken for 400 years before the Messiah came. Today, in many nations, even Church and State, clergy and laity, indirectly live off the avails of prostitution and strip clubs through taxation.

"God is a Spirit:" Jesus said," and they that worship him must worship him in Spirit and in truth." With a long list of malfeasance since slave trade and slavery, can those who believe in God, go to worship in Spirit and in truth and not feel that we also live in a

God-forsaken world? The cultural - conservative Christians who enjoyed the assets of slavery but resist restitution because they are not responsible for the sins of the past, do not show that they are any different in spirit from the wrongdoers of the past. With a pile on of transgression over transgression, there is no remorse, no repentance, no restitution, and no reconciliation with God or man. Yet, there are men of the cloth who act as if all those sad events of history never happened. "Jesus loves you," they proclaim, and suggest that God Almighty is still waiting to attend to your needs. Grandparents know that it is not true. But the show must go on. The Almighty God does not need anybody. To heaven, one soul may be as important as one dollar is to a billionaire.

Why The World Is, And Should Be God-Forsaken

Prayers cannot be answered in a God-Forsaken world. The Almighty God punished the Israelites for disobedience. They endured captivity in Assyria and Babylon. The message of 2 Chronicles 7:14 fell on deaf ears. In the inter-testament period of about 400 years, they were completely forsaken for disobedience. Then the Almighty sent Jesus Christ, the Messiah, to open the door of faith to all humanity beyond Israel. With an inclusive New Covenant, He taught the way to eternal life. As the Lamb of God, He died on a cross to end animal sacrifices for believers and returned to heaven.

As an imperial power, after the apostles passed away the Romans took control of the church composed of Jews and Gentiles. They drove the Holy Catholic Pentecostal Church underground and introduced victor theology that ignored the Gospel summarized by the Golden Rule, the Great commandment and the New Commandment. The imperial church did not live by the Golden Rule – "Treat others the same way you want them to treat you." The Jewish Christians abandoned Christianity and returned to Judaism.

The Arabians founded their own religion, Islam, and also ignored the Golden Rule. They used their religion to invade parts of Africa and Europe and the Middle East (vide: Stephenblanton.org/growth). The Crusaders drove them back except from Africa, where they forced their religion on Africans and enslaved some Africans because their doctrine allowed slavery.

On the other side of the Continent, Christians traded African men, women and children like cattle and enslave them in the New World. For over 200 years, Protestant clergy and laity; and for over 300 years, Roman Catholic clergy and laity lived off the avails of slavery. With the permission of Rome, the Jesuits – The Society of Jesus - sold 272 of their slaves to save Georgetown university from bankruptcy.

With the blessing of their own Bishops, Christians fought numerous wars, including two World Wars. There was the Scramble for Africa and Colonialism. Long after the Civil War that freed Africans from slavery, there was a prosperous African American community known as the Black Wall Street in Tulsa Oklahoma. On May 31, 1921 it was attacked by land and air, and wiped out of existence because of hatred and jealousy. Their success challenged the frontier spirit of exceptionalism, rugged individualism and structural racism. About 300 were killed and buried in unmarked graves, and 10,000 were left homeless. Nobody was held to account to this day. History was not only written by the victors; some were not written. Tulsa is the base of a pre-eminent televangelist and founder of Oral Roberts University. If what happened to African Americans happened elsewhere in the world, the villains would be described as Godless savages. But these were Christians raised on victor theology.

Between 1925 and 1961, unmarried pregnant women gave birth at Roman Catholic care home at Taum, Ireland. About 800 died and were buried in unmarked graves. Some of the children were sent for adoption as far away as Australia. And in May 2021, the remains of

215 children were discovered in unmarked mass grave at Kamloops, British Columbia. It was one of over 400 Indian residential schools run by the government and church authorities in the 19th and 20th centuries. The goal was the forcible assimilation of the aboriginal peoples of Canada. An estimated 6,000 children some as young as five years old, never came home. Their parents were never notified. A few weeks after the discovery, six Roman Catholic Churches on Indian reservations were burnt down. Several churches in cities were vandalized. Then, in remorse, some Junior High Schools were festooned with posters proclaiming "Every child matters." It took 2,000 years of Christianity to learn that every child matters. Will it take another 2,000 years to learn that no corpse has left this planet with one penny and underscore the need to run a just society?

History is about what people who have power did to those who were powerless. The victor theology of the Church normalized injustice and racism fueled by the theory of evolution. A world created by evolution will be unlivable because there is no accountability to a higher power. A world that believes in Jesus Christ as Lord and Savior without compliance to the Golden Rule, the Great Commandment and the New Commandment, will also be unlivable. That was the sin of the victor theologian and church in the slave economy. They lived by bread alone and did to others what they did not want others to do to them. Those who were different were savages. In the New World, indigenous peoples were a menace more than human beings to be evangelize. Even as Christians, the emancipated African slaves also became a menace to the cultural conservative Christians. Since they were no longer available to be enslaved, some were sent back to Liberia, West Africa. When God's work is not done in God's way, it is no longer God's work. Yet to apologize or not to apologize, even for centuries of slavery, centuries ago, is a catch -22 for the doctrine of papal infallibility.

To be civilized is to have a conscience. The world is being changed by men and women with a conscience. Christianity is no longer among the religions that nurture children to hate. In May 2021, Germany officially admitted that the 1904 mass killings of the Herero people who rebelled against their colonial rule in Namibia were a genocide. Without waiting to be sued at the International Court, it promised $16 billion in development aid. Will it be kept and over what period? About 75 percent of the Herero people and 50percent of the Nama people, 100,000 people in total, were killed. Some were used for medical experiments. The skulls from other Colonies - Cameroon, Rwanda, Tanzania and Togo- were also used. The brutality and inhumanity in the Belgian Congo were such that King Leopold 11 was condemned by fellow imperialists. Some apologists argued that the King never went to the Congo. However, they do not exonerate Adolf Hitler because he never fired a shot. The cultural conservatives only care about what other people do to them but not what they themselves do to others. They believe that those outside their group, exists for their convenience. It is clear from history that based on the Golden Rule, the Great Commandment and the New Commandment, the post-apostolic church has not been the Church of Jesus Christ.

King Henry V111 left the Church of Rome for private reasons and founded the Church of England. Germany's Martin Luther rebelled and led the Reformation that created the Protestant de-nomination. Slavery was not among their concerns. Germany's Pope Benedict XV1 served from 2005 to 2013 and resigned. In June 2021, Germany's Cardinal Reinhard Marx published in multiple languages online, his letter to the Pope offering to resign as arch-bishop. The catholic church's mishandling of clergy sexual abuse cases led him to declare that the church had arrived at "a dead end." In 2018, a church -commissioned report concluded that in Germany alone, at least 3,677 people were abused by clergy between 1946 and 2014. More than half of the victims were 13 years old or younger at the time of the abuse. Church insiders are beginning to see the defects of the medieval victor theology of imperial Rome that led the world down the garden path.

A Voice of America news report of August 14, 2018 showed that over 300 Roman Catholic priests in Pennsylvania had sexually abused more than 1,000 children in a period of 70 years. And a BBC News reports of September 18, 2014 showed that some Bishops sometimes have doubts about God. These are manifestations of a church that went astray and is coming to a dead end. Man's victor theology replaced the Gospel of Jesus Christ and demanded celibacy from those who want to serve God. The Vatican has also faced some financial embarrassments that could have been prevented if women took care of the money.

The French Revolution (1787 – 1799) was a rebellion to change the relationship between those who ruled and those who were ruled. It ended up with Emperor Napoleon Bonaparte and the reign of terror. It also diminished the importance of the Church. In Russia over a century later, the Bolshevik revolution of 1917 overthrew the Church and States that luxuriated at the expense of Serfs and peasants. They introduced Christianity without Christ and called it communism. They were opposed by the U.S. where African men, women and children were bought, sold and enslaved for centuries under plantation capitalism with faith in Christ. Both sides have been in conflict ever since. So, in the West there was plantation capitalism with faith in Christ. In the East, there was Christianity without Christ.

However, while the ideological cold war has ended, both sides are still in an internal struggle between excessive wealth and excessive poverty to this day. The world tends to demonize those who want to change the status quo established by victor theologians. They are given derogatory names. In the East, they were called "Bolshie" and in the West, they were called "lefty "or "Crackpot." Notice that the highest concentration of churchmen and women described as "born again Christians" is in Dixie where people owned slaves and fought and died to sustain slavery. In those thirteen Southern States, St. Paul's charge to bear one another's burdens and so fulfill the law of Christ is described by the political class as a" radical socialist agenda "or a" radical left-wing agenda. "Good is evil and evil is good.

The world prefers change through evolution rather than revolution. In that slow process, the victims of injustice are ruined physically while the villains are ruined spiritually. It is an ill wind that does nobody any good. Man is mortal. Since Adam and Eve walked on this planet, nobody has ever left with one penny. From the French Revolution to the American Civil war against slavery and plantation capitalism, to the Bolshevik Revolution, it is obvious that the underlying problem is the corruption of the Gospel by victor theology. The Golden Rule, the Great Commandment and the New commandment disappeared in that theology. Was the church that was supportive of slavery and serfdom inspired by the Holy Spirit? The answer is no. Has the church changed and shown remorse, repentance and reconciliation with God and man? You be the judge.

In the past 2,000 years, both Roman Catholic and Protestant Christians have lived and died professing belief in "the Holy Catholic Church." What they attended and spread overseas was not the Holy Catholic Church but a secular Church base on victor theology. The secular church engaged in slave trade and slavery; and in wars of conquest, colonialism, segregation, apartheid and for 200 to 300 years, clergy and laity lived off the avails of slavery until stopped through a Civil War. The Holy Catholic Church led by St. Peter was a Pentecostal church filled with the Holy Spirit. They can never do what the secular church has gone. Never. The secular church has not changed. There has been no repentance, restitution and reconciliation with God and man. There is nothing meek in a defiant macho church based on victor theology.

There are men and women who wonder why they are suffering and their prayers are not answered. Some children have died because in some denominations, their parents depended on divine healing in a God-forsaken world. Research will show that problems solved in the West through prayers are also solved in the East without prayers. Meteorogists can forecast rain for two or three days before it falls. Several generations ago, farmers prayed for rain. When it fell, they gave credit to their prayers. We probably live in a God-forsaken world.

Let us recall that the Israelites were forsaken for disobedience. In Africa in this 21st century, Coptic Egyptians have become sec-ond -class citizens in their own fatherland. East Africa is still being terrorized through another victor theology. A United Nation's report released in June 2021 showed that since the Islamist group, Boko Haram launched its first attacks in 2009 to 2020, about 350,000 people have been killed. Nearly 90 percent were children. Modern history has been a pile on of transgression upon transgression. Since the Apostles passed away, monotheists have done worse than the Israelites who were forsaken. Those who are preaching that God Almighty is answering prayers and blessing people have either not read the Old Testament or they are deliberately deceiving their con-gregation to keep them coming. Has the Almighty turned a blind eye to the wrongs people do? Do all lives matter to God? If the God of the Old Testament is the God of the New Testament; if cultural conservative Christians and Muslims did all that is recorded and unrecorded in history; and if there is no remorse, repentance, resti-tution, and reconciliation with God and man, common sense, if it is common, suggests that the world has been forsaken yet again until the Second Advent. If the world is not forsaken, obviously Black Lives do not matter to the God or god of the slave traders, slave masters, terrorists and Boko Haram. The god of pagans is on the side of the big battalions. But the Almighty God has the last word.

Before Jesus Christ came, the Pharisees and spiritual leaders of Israel believed that they were still in the good graces of Jehovah. They did not know that they were worshiping culture, not God Almighty. Through victor theology, monotheists may also be worshiping culture rather than God Almighty. That's evident because there is not a nation on earth where the Golden Rule, the Great Commandment, and the New Commandment are part of their cultural fabric. Not one. Sir Winston Churchill reportedly said: "History will be kind to me, for I intend to write it." Like history, the narrative of religion has also been controlled by the victors. Who is on the Lord's side? The clergy and laity that lived off the avails of slavery for centuries were clearly not on the Lord's side. Without living by those commandments, a Christian cannot claim to be on the Lord's side. Nevertheless, as in the first inter-testament period, some people are still able to find peace with God and the narrow way to salvation.

If China is restraining religion, it may be because the leaders have studied the past. They don't want to be like Africa, ravaged from left and right by religious cultural conservatives. History allows people to see ancestral malfeasance and repent. Without repentance there can be no change. The cultural conservatives want to cover up African history, American history and the insurrection of January 6,2021 in Washington, D.C., even when they were not directly involved. It is like birds of the same feathers protecting one another generation after generation. Before they are led into more conflicts, the men and women of genuine faith must begin to practice the Golden Rule and demand the same from others. It is the only way to avoid conflicts and evangelize those who practice Christianity without Christ. Whether we believe in it or not, based on what men have done without repentance or reconciliation, we live in a God-forsaken world. No nation can fix their politics without fixing their religion.

CHAPTER 4

A Moratorium on the Epistles

The Pioneer Days

Under the Homestead Act in the U.S.A. and the Dominion Lands Act in Canada, new immigrants could receive free land to encourage settlement. New residents to a community received a "Welcome wagon" loaded with provisions. That was the horse- and- buggy pioneer days. Those pioneer settlers can relate to the pioneer Christians of the first century. Free land made life easier for settlers. Such beneficence does not apply today. Historians cannot extrapolate the colonial pioneer days into the 21st century. Neither should theologians extrapolate the church pioneer days of the first century into the 21st century. The bar was set low just to get them to believe that Jesus Christ was the prophesied Messiah.

The Roman Empire was a time of fear and insecurity. It was a time of Pax Romana or the Peace of Rome; a time when deviants were promptly crucified. It was a time when the God of Israel was seen as a tribal god, like the pagan gods. It was a time of spiritual

Stone Age. Like the pioneer days in America, the bar was set low to encourage people to believe in the Living God of Creation and the Messiah. In the Dark Ages, when nobody knew the Living God, Abraham believed in God and it was counted for him as righteousness. Will anyone today be counted as righteous just for believing in God? Being born again is more than believing in God. It goes beyond Judaism. Apparently, as in the pioneer days in America, the Apostles lowered the bar to encourage transition to the new faith.

Paul and Silas were imprisoned for preaching the Gospel. There was an earthquake, the doors flew open and their chains fell off. If a missionary were in a similar situation today, will there be an earthquake? They told the prison keeper:" Believe on the Lord Jesus Christ, and you will be saved, you and your household." (Acts 16:31 NKJV). Does that apply today? That would apply to the first century pioneer days, not today. Dogmatic evangelism teaches that every statement in the Bible is the word of God. How many Christians are sure that if a man believes on the Lord Jesus Christ, his entire family would be saved?

In the days of the Pharisees, to confess Jesus as Lord and Savior was dangerous. Context matters. St. Paul wrote to the church in Rome: "That if you confess with your mouth the Lord Jesus and believe in your heart that God has raised Him from the dead, you will be saved." (Romans 10:9 NKJV). And "Everyone who calls on the name of the Lord will be saved "(Romans 10 :13 NKJV). Do those verses apply today? If anyone, anywhere on earth calls and the name of the Lord while on a death bed, will he or she be saved? There is no short -cut to heaven. Did St. Paul forget the words of Prophet Ezekiel: "The soul that sinneth it shall die. The son shall not bear the iniquity of the father, neither shall the father bear the iniquity of the son: the righteousness of the righteous shall be upon him and the wickedness of the wicked shall be upon him "(Ezekiel 18:20.)

St. Paul also wrote to the Church in Ephesus:" For by grace you had been saved through faith, and that not of yourselves; it is the gift of God, not of works, lest anyone should boast." (Ephesians 2: 8-9 NKJV). St. Paul is our favorite Apostle. He made salvation look very cheap. That verse was the basis of Martin Luther's Protestantism. But that was the first century pioneer days. St. James, whose Epistle or letter is rarely preached, wrote:" Show me your faith without your works, and I will show you my faith by my works. You believe that there is one God. You do well. Even the demons believe - and tremble!" (James 2:18- 19 NKJV).

In the 1950s, students wrote with fountain pen and ink. Bleach was a novelty. A brilliant itinerant British evangelist came to our school to conduct morning prayers. He dabbed some ink on a white handkerchief. Each dab of ink represented sin. With a few dabs, the white handkerchief was soiled with ink. He dipped the hand-kerchief in a basin of undiluted bleach, squeezed it, and it came out white again. It was magic. That's how the blood of Jesus Christ washes away our sins, he said. Nobody will see that illustration and not believe in Jesus Christ. The theology comes from 1 John 1:7, not from the Gospel. To believe in Jesus Christ is one thing. To be born again is another. A Pagan who believes in Jesus Christ without being born again, will become more ungodly because his sins are always cleansed. He is immune from condemnation. And so, with-out repentance and change of behavior, Christians still go to war to kill one another after 2,000 years of the Gospel. They have been redeemed. Their sins have been washed away. Once saved, always saved. The Golden Rule, the Great Commandment and the New Commandment are irrelevant. Are they?

The slave traders, slave masters and auctioneers went on with their business for centuries because their Priests and Pastors led them to believe that faith in God was all that was required for admission into heaven. Evidently, a lot of misunderstanding among the numer-ous Christian denominations is based on the Epistles, not the Gospel of Jesus Christ. The apologists for slave trade, slavery and apartheid cited the Epistles. Church goers have heard more from the Epistles than from the Gospel of Jesus Christ. Nothing, according to St. Paul, "shall be able to separate us from the love of God which is in Christ Jesus our Lord "(Romans 8:39 NKJV). Is it not a license to ignore God's commandments? Does it not make the Golden Rule, the Great Commandment and the New Commandment null and void? For 250 to 300 years the Church of the slave traders believed that the Commandments no longer apply because Jesus Christ died for our past, present and future sins. No, He died to bring an end to periodic animal sacrifices for Christians, not for cultural religions. Any institution premised on a doctrinal deviation from the Gospel is a cult. Selected verses of the Epistles shaped the victor theology that discarded the Gospel of Jesus Christ. Hence, slavery lasted for centuries until human conscience rebelled and prevailed. Besides, it was in their economic interest to trust but not obey God.

Some female theologians will also argue that the suppression of women was based on the Epistles, not the Gospel of Jesus Christ. It is clear that since the post-Apostolic era, millions of Christians have died and are still dying without being born again. The Epistles have been studied and preached as if man's salvation depends on them. Salvation depends on the Gospel that expects a man to be born again and live by the Golden Rule, the Great Commandment and the New Commandment. The New Testament is about the words of Jesus Christ, not the words of St. Paul. Yet, church goers have heard more of the Epistles than the Gospel and wonder why the world is not better after 2,000 years of distraction from the Gospel. In fact, it is possible to justify American history based on the Epistles. It is impossible to justifying the history based on the Gospel of Jesus Christ. It may be heretical but these considerations call for a moratorium on the Epistles - letters or sermons addressed to the first century Christians, not to us. The Epistles are ready-made sermons. Without them, there will be more worship and less sermons because the focus would be on the Gospel of Jesus Christ. A few centuries ago, an advocate of a moratorium would face an

Inquisition. But every generation is more enlightened than the previous generation.

There is a lesson to learn from the horse -and-buggy pioneer days in North America. The historical circumstances made it possible to offer free land and a Welcome Wagon to new settlers. New immigrants today do not qualify, if they can be admitted in the first place. The Epistles or letters were Sermons to pioneer Christians at a time when it was difficult and dangerous to abandon traditional beliefs and customs for something new. It was a period of transition from the Old to the New Covenant. The messages of the Epistles are not a substitute to the Gospel of Jesus Christ. They are not complementary to the Gospel and should not supplant the Gospel and keep the Church disconnected from the Gospel. The victor theology does not prevent man's inhumanity to man. It is a misrepresentation of God Almighty and Jesus Christ.

Few clerics preach the Epistle of St. James, an Epistle that stands the test of time. It does not serve victor theology. The Pauline Epistles and victor theology overshadowed the Gospel of Jesus Christ for centuries. Millions of Christians have been to church for decades and never heard that a Christian must be born again. And that a born-again Christian lives by the Golden Rule, the Great Commandment and the New Commandment. They show a life that has been changed. That is what prevents wars, slave trade, slavery, family dissociation and social problems. Those transgressions cannot be prevented by weekly absolutions or forgiveness of sins on behalf of God Almighty.

"Ask, and you will receive---" How many Christian grandparents asked and received? Extrapolating apostolic authority and promises to the modern Church has made Christianity frustrating to grandparents, but not to grandchildren who are still naïve. Mixing the Old Covenant and the New Covenant Scriptures has made Christianity irrelevant in the lives of common people. New Testament Christians live by the Golden Rule, the Great Commandment, the New

Commandment and their social implications because they are born again. That's what Christianity is all about. As creatures of culture, some Christian neophytes in the first century, had one foot in the Old Testament and one foot in the New Testament. They were neither hot nor cold. That Old Testament Christianity persists to this day through prosperity preachers.

The Gospel is like a cookbook. Reading a recipe does not fill an empty stomach. The recipe requires action. Reading the Bible did not prevent the numerous wars in Europe. Bible study did not prevent slave trade, slavery, colonial wars, World Wars, the Holocaust, segregation, apartheid and the forever social injustice. The Pauline Epistles were written to pioneer Churches in transition, not to churches in this century. Suppose the Epistles were not discovered. If they were not discovered, more attention would have been focused on the Gospel. The world would have been better because there is not a statement in the Gospel that encourages or leads to hatred, slave trade or slavery.

A Christian must be born again, as Jesus said. Human beings have a resident evil spirit with the propensity to do wrong. If the men of the cloth can do wrong, the parishioners can also do wrong. The church is fallible. For generations, those who received weekly absolutions have not been encouraged to ask their heavenly Father for the Holy Spirit to replace the endemic Evil Spirit (Luke 11:13). The Apostles believed in Jesus Christ. It was not enough. They received the Holy Spirit on the day of Pentecost. It is how to be born-again and observe all that Jesus Christ commanded. Those who ask with sincerity, can receive the Holy Spirit within weeks or months. It would have prevented all of those sad events of human history.

The Regent and secular Church Establishment that owned and sold slaves, did not understand or want to comply to the Gospel of Jesus Christ. Based on the Gospel, we can conclude that the Church of the slave traders offered no abundant life to the living or eternal life to the dead. Now, given the divorce rate among Christians; the forever social injustice in a nation where the church owned and sold slaves; and where a policeman can handcuff an African American and kneel on his neck to kill him, that conclusion may still be true to this day. Access to God is through Jesus Christ (John 14:6). Instead of attending, African Americans and those who understand the Gospel, can demonstrate in front of the Church of culture until it becomes the Church of Jesus Christ that complies fully to the mandate of the Great Commission. Ignorance is killing us. Terrorism is killing us. Religion is killing us physicality and spiritually. It is not the religion from God but the religion from man.

In the past 2,000 years, religion has been about exercising power as Regent, not about serving God as the Executor of God's will. That power dynamic is a legacy of imperial Rome. It's a shame. It is difficult for a pagan to be a Christian after reading African American history that is shaped by Christians. If evangelism is about serving God, it should be preaching how to be born again and live by the commandments, and not about how to avoid them. The slave traders slave masters and their clergy read in the Scriptures that "The just shall live by faith." What faith? For nearly 300 years they lived by faith. But it was a false faith rooted in victor theology and superficial spirituality.

The victor theology restructured the Gospel, a counter -culture religion, to serve culture. The Golden Rule was made null and void. Salvation by grace alone and weekly absolutions became the gateway for slave traders, masters and clergy to "go home to be with the Lord. "That was a monumental tragedy. Before the saints go marching in, they start marching here on earth. To go home to be with the Lord without doing the will of the Lord is not Amazing Grace; it is amazing self -deceit. The clerics forgot that doing the work of the Lord and doing the will of the Lord can be completely different. Many clerics of the slave economy were sincerely doing the work of the Lord. But they were not doing the will of the Lord. It is true of many clerics today.

"Not everyone who says to Me, 'Lord, Lord,' shall enter the kingdom of heaven," Jesus said, "but he who does the will of My Father in heaven." (Matthew 7:21 NKJV). It is all in the Gospel. Is it not risky to count on salvation that is based on victor theology that doesn't require a Christian to obey the commandments? The empty pews and "church for sale" presage the beginning of the needed Second Reformation to transform both the Roman Catholic and the Protestant denominations from institutions that stood for might is right to the Church of Jesus Christ that stands for the Golden Rule, the Great Commandment, the New Commandment and their social implications ---the "will of My Father in heaven".

There are times when a medical report or a legal document has to be translated or interpreted. It is common knowledge that history was written by the victors. The Gospel of Jesus Christ was also interpreted and repackaged by the victors. If the Christians of the slave economy were asked: "How do you know that you are saved?" The answer would be: "It is because the Bible tells me so." If those who fought to sustained slavery during the American civil war were asked the same question, the answer would be the same – "the Bible tells me so." That convenient and preferred scripture did not prevent the numerous wars of the past and present. And the sad events of history that have not ceased after 2,000 years of Christianity.

For about 250 years in Protestant America and about 300 years in Roman Catholic Brazil, Christian clergy and laity lived off the avails of unpaid servitude. They passed away and "went home to be with the Lord, "if you can believe it. There has been no apology, restitution or reconciliation with God and man because the victor theology has not changed. Our spiritual leaders, whatever religion it is, were not appointed by the God of Creation. They are volunteers. To wait for God to hold them accountable will be too late for the millions of Christians who do not trust and obey but will also go home to be with the Lord without doing the will of the Lord. All the malfeasance of today are still happening because of the ineptitude of the church that went astray. And until that church changes, the USA will never be the city on a hill.

Today, slave trade or slavery is considered to be a crime against humanity. Was it not a crime against humanity during the slave economy? The victor theology did not prevent the crime, rather, it sustained it. The victor theology did not prevent Christians from going to war to kill fellow Christians. It did not prevent Christian governments – the products of victor theology - from selling weapons to kill fellow Christians while sending humanitarian food to the other side to feed starving children, as in the Biafra War. The Epistles, particularly St. Paul's letters to the first century Christians are more likely to be heard in churches than the Gospel of Jesus Christ that changes lives.

"My food," Jesus said, "is to do the will of Him who sent Me, and to finish His work "(John 4:34 NKJV). When on the cross He said: "It is finished!" (John 19:30), it was finished. Nothing could be added to the message of salvation. The Epistles are not complementary to the Gospel. They can become a distraction. They certainly did not change the lives of slave traders, slave masters, their clergy and politicians for over 300 years. It is the Gospel of Jesus Christ that changes lives. It is by being born again to keep the Golden Rule, the Great Commandment and the New Commandment that produces a new creation worthy of eternal life. The sad events of history and the disenfranchisement of women do not reflect the born-again experience. The Epistles per se could not prevent or end slavery in America. The slave traders, slave masters, and clergy were not liberals, socialist or spiritual conservatives like Abraham Lincoln and William Wilberforce. They were cultural conservatives who believed that other people exist for their convenience. That mindset persists to this day. So, slavery was ended by war through the righteous indignation of genuine, conscience- stricken Christians against unrepentant and hardened hearts. Clearly, Acts 16:31; Romans 10:9 and Ephesians 2:8-9 do not lead anyone to be born again. They may be shortcuts to heaven for pioneer Christians but not for an enlightened world.

Similarly, the reward and punishment regime used to train the people of the Old Covenant are not transferable to the people of the New Covenant. To believe that it is transferable can only lead to frustration and disappointment with God. "I have been young, and now am old," King David wrote, "yet I have not seen the righteous forsaken, nor his descendants begging bread." (Psalm 37:25). That does not resonate with the grandparents who went through the Great Depression or the panhandlers on the streets of New York, Los Angeles, London and other major cities of the world. Since Christianity is about good relations between man and man, and between them and the God of Creation, the theme of the New Covenant church is" Trust and obey." That is important to remember before we can study the Bible to death without obeying God. What is the Church to obey? It is the Golden Rule, the Great Commandment and the New Commandment. That is the good relations between people, and between them and God Almighty. That is the summary or synopsis of the Gospel and the solution to a host of problems because they have social implications.

On Justification

The Doctrine of Justification came from St. Paul. "Therefore, as through one man's offense judgment came to all men, resulting in condemnation," he wrote, "even so through one Man's righteous act the free gift came to all men, resulting in justification of life." (Romans 5:18 NKJV). "When God sees you," said a cleric "He sees Jesus." Welcome to heaven. That was how the church lived off the avails of slave trade and slavery for centuries. They were justified. Amazing Grace for the slave trader was injustice for the slaves. Those who believed in the Fatherhood of God did not believe in the brotherhood of man. Some fought and died to sustain slavery and their way of life. How many were born again? How many would see the Kingdom of God? They did not know and were not taught that a follower of Christ must be born again and live by the Golden Rule, the Great Commandment and the New Commandment.

A teenager said to his Bible study peers: "In 2 Thessalonians 3;10 Jesus said: "If any would not work, neither should he eat." Was he wrong? Every Scripture read on the pulpit is said to be "The word of the Lord." Who can blame him? If the Epistles were not discovered, the church would have focused attention on the Gospel and realized that Christianity or following Christ, is about good relations between peoples and between them and God Almighty.

On tribulation

Two thousand years ago, anyone who did not speak your language was a potential enemy. The influence of the Gospel, and the Gospel alone, has changed that. But imagine the introduction of a new religion that is counterculture. The Apostles were bound to face hostility. So, Jesus Christ cautioned His disciples, not you or me, that they will face tribulations. They did. Now, some Christians believe that a life without adversity, tensions and problems is unbiblical. Nobody should go looking for tribulations. When do we separate what is applicable to the pioneer Christians from what is applicable today? In the pioneer days in Canada, for example, it was illegal to carry bow and arrow on the street. There must be a reason for that. The aboriginal people carried bow and arrow. That law may still be in the books, but it is out of date. Yes, we have done the things we ought not to do and not done the things we ought to do. If it is a tradition to be won as a badge of honor with no desire to change; if prayers were said only to give instructions to God Almighty; if prayers are said for the wrong reason and for people in authority who are not born-again Christians and who do not intend to live by the Golden Rule, more Churches will be sold.

There is no doubt that Bishops believe in Jesus Christ. Jesus said: "And these signs shall follow them that believe; In my name shall they cast out devils; they shall speak with new tongues; they shall take up serpents; and if they drink any deadly thing, it shall not hurt them; they shall lay hands on the sick, and they shall recover." (Mark 16: 17-18). Such verses are hardly read in church. If all that was said to the people in the first century, applies to the people of the 21st century, how many Bishops will be willing to pick up snakes? Life is a test of faith. If the Bishops could do all that is stated above, there is hardly a human being in the world who will not become a Christian. Life will no longer be a test of faith.

Divine Inspiration and Divine Dictation

In the primordial world, before serpents were cursed to crawl on their belly, we would assume that they had many legs. Did they? There would be vestiges of those legs. In Joshua 10:13 it appears that it is the sun, not the earth that moves. Astronomers who argued against that Scripture became heretics. The condemnation of Galileo Galilei (1564 – 1642) has come to symbolize the dogmatism of Christians who see every word in the Bible as the word of God. The Scriptures were written by divine inspiration. There is also divine dictation. The Ten Commandments fall under divine dictation because they came directly from God Almighty. The words of Jesus Christ in red letters are also divine dictation because the Father and Son are one. The statements in divine dictation are immutable. But some in divine inspiration and not. They do not stand the test of time. That makes the Scriptures less confusing.

Those whose relatives have died from snake bites, mosquito-borne malaria parasites or tobacco – induced lung cancer, will question the notion that everything God made is very good, according to Moses in Genesis. Perhaps some exist to keep man mortal. The Old Testament, Israel's encounter with the Almighty God can be used as a reference guide. The Epistles, the letters or sermons to Christian Pioneers 2,000 years ago, should also be used as a reference guide, not the Gospel. Much of the contents are still relevant because human nature is a carbon copy of past generations. A moratorium on the Epistles will allow the Church to refocus on the Gospel that changes lives.

Life on earth has been difficult for some individuals and for some people groups. When you think about the millions of people killed in two World Wars; the millions of Jews gassed to death; the numerous colonial wars in Africa, Asia and the New World; the slave trade and slavery that lasted for over 300 years ; the countless Africans thrown into the Atlantic Ocean by slave traders; the America's Civil War in which Christians fought and died to sustain slavery; the designation of the survivors of slavery as three-fifths of a person; and the endless conflicts and wars, you have to ponder what limit men can go by listening to the Epistles.

The Gospel of Jesus Christ is very clear. To tell Johnny to be a good boy will not make him a good boy. He must ask for the Holy Spirit to change him. If the students didn't learn, the teacher didn't teach. Some teachers have a cultural vision of the world while embracing a religion that is counterculture. They saw every statement in the Bible as the word of God but selected the ones to live by and ignored the most important precepts, namely, the Golden Rule, the Great Commandment and the New Commandment. Disobedience of the Golden Rule accounts for the inhumanity perpetrated by the cultural conservatives of Christianity, Islam and Judaism.

Even now, there is no harmony between the Christians in Moscow and the Christians in Washington, D.C. It speaks to the need to shelf the Epistles and preach the Gospel of Jesus Christ. For Christians who are tired of platitudes and theoretical Christianity;

and for Scriptures that apply to the Hebrews and pioneer Christians, calls to prayer can be annoying when so many are alienated from the Truth. It was difficult to be godly in the slave economy where speaking the Truth brought the condemnation of the Establishment and beneficiaries of slavery. William Wilberforce, a spiritual and compassionate conservative spent decades in verbal combat with cultural conservative Christians in the British parliament. For them, to end slave trade and slavery was a mortal threat to free market capitalism.

Abraham Lincoln, a spiritual and compassionate human being had to go to war to end slavery because the Church itself owned slaves and could not renounce slavery. John Brown and thousands of others gave their lives to end commercial slavery. The wrongdoers found Scripture in the Epistles (not the Gospel) to justify their actions. The Bible was even used to justify apartheid in South Africa. Consequently, those deeds degraded the Christian faith, perhaps irreparably. Those Epistles or letters are still being heard in Churches more than the Gospel of Jesus Christ. Still, after 2,000 years, the battle against social injustice is far from over. Social evolution is a very slow process. There is an enduring resistance to Christian civilization. How many Christians remember what their pastors preached two or three Sundays ago? Many pastors don't remember either. Sermons tend to go into one ear and out through the other. Sermons can lead people to God but do not change lives. It is the Holy Spirit that changes people, when invited, and makes them a new creation.

The Apostles' Creed

Did the persecuted and dispersed Apostles get together to formulate the Apostles' creed? Critical minds believe that both the Apostles' and the Nicene Creeds were formulated by the church under the Romans from the fourth century, long after the Apostles had passed away. According to Wikipedia, "The expression 'Apostles' Creed' is first mentioned in a letter from the Synod of Milan dated AD 390, referring to the belief that each of the Twelve Apostles contributed to an article to the twelve articles of the Creed. This belief was explicitly challenged by the orthodox delegates at the Council of Florence (1431 – 1449), and was shown to be historically untenable in the 15th century by Lorenzo Valla. "

Lorenzo Valla was a moral Italian Catholic priest and scholar known to expose forgery. The Creed is an indoctrination on what to believe and nothing about responsibility and the outcome based on the belief. The Apostles, according to the Creed, also believed in "The Holy Catholic Church." The church that most Christians have been raised in is not the Holy Catholic Church. That church was the Church of the Apostles led by St. Peter who was crucified. It was a Pentecostal Church based on the Gospel. They were filled with the Holy Spirit and lived by the Golden Rule, the Great Commandment and the New Commandment. That Pentecostal Church filled with the Holy Spirit could never be involved in slave trade, slavery, wars, colonialism, segregation, apartheid and all that the secular church continued to do to this day. Open – minded scholars of Church history note that the Council of Nicea held in 325 AD was presided over by Emperor Constantine, the new convert. He likely introduced pagan practices into what will become official Roman Catholic doctrine with liturgy in the language of Rome – Latin. Even December 25, a pagan feast day was too cold for shepherds to be in the field.

To any novice who has read the Gospel of Jesus Christ and the Acts of the Apostles, it is obvious that the Pentecostal Church led by St Peter could never support the Doctrine of Discovery, colonial wars, colonialism, slave trade, slavery and more. The Romans changed the Church.

Now, imagine this scenario, which may not be farfetched. A powerful politician used his secret service to assassinate a foreign leader whose desire was freedom from foreign control. When his

own death was near, he summoned his pastor to assure him that
when the roll is called up yonder, he will be there. His pastor pulled
out a Bible and read Romans 10 :9: "That if you confess with your
mouth the Lord Jesus and believe in your heart that God has raised
Him from the dead, you will be saved." (NKJV) The politician
confessed and said that he believed. The pastor turned to Acts 16:31
where the jailer asked Paul and Silas what he must do to be saved.
"Believe on the Lord Jesus Christ," they said "and you will be saved,
you and your household." (NKJV) The politician said he believed.
That may be valid in the first century. Will the politician and his
family be saved just for believing in Jesus Christ? Finally, the pastor turned to Ephesians 2: 8-9:" For by grace you had been saved
through faith, and that not of yourselves; it is the gift of God, not of
works, lest anyone should boast" (NKJV). The politician accepted
the free gift, yes, free gift, and felt relieved that he is saved. They
sang Amazing Grace and end with a prayer. This is victor theology,
not Christianity.

The Gospel of Jesus Christ summarized by the Golden Rule,
the Great Commandment and the New Commandment has been
made null and void. Jesus came to fulfill the law, not to abolish it.
We are not under the law of Moses. But the law of grace does not
abrogate the Golden Rule, the Great Commandment, and the New
Commandment. The Grace of God does not excuse slave trade,
slavery, war, murder and all the ungodly acts of the secular Church.
It is obvious that the Epistles or Sermons to the first century pioneer Christians were misapplied and corrupted to serve economic
and social Darwinism. The cultural conservative Christian and
social Darwinists believed that some people, including women, exist
for their convenience. Hence, Roman Catholic Jesuits saw nothing
wrong with owning slaves.

If motivational speakers can change everyone, poverty will be
eradicated. Similarly, if the Epistles can change the church, all the
sad events of history would have been avoided. There would have

been social justice for all by now. It takes the Gospel and the Holy Spirit to change lives. The record of sermons preached in any church will show that St. Paul was more quoted than Jesus Christ Himself. That's how it was in the centuries of slavery. Does anyone need to read more ancient writings such as Baruch, Judith, Maccabees and Tobias – excluded from the Protestant Bible. They are distractions. Christianity can be turned into a complicated academic exercise. Yet, St. Peter, the leader of the Church was not a theologian. He was a fisherman with no academic title. Jesus Christ was not born in the home of the high priest or the king of Israel as one might expect, but in the home of a carpenter. "God moves in a mysterious way," wrote William Cowper, "His wonders to perform.". So, "Don't dismiss a good idea simply because you don't like the source." It happens in politics and religion, and frustrates the critics of the elites.

Mahatma Gandhi was raised in a cultural religion. While in Law School, he also studied the Gospel. It is an embarrassment that he showed practical Christianity to the Christians of his day who would use the Epistles to justify slave trade, slavery, colonialism, segregation and apartheid. Gandhi came to the conclusion that Jesus Christ is the greatest asset to Christianity and Christians the greatest liability. For his exemplary life, Mahatma Gandhi emerged from the pages of history as the man who practiced Christianity.

It is easier to live with a mistake made by you than a mistake made for you. The victor theology is a mistake made for you. Christianity is counterculture. Jesus Christ came to establish Christianity and change the thousands of cultures on earth into one common spiritual culture accountable to the only God of Creation. Instead, it is the cultures that are changing Christianity; the more powerful the culture, the greater is the resistance to Christian civilization. In no religion but Christianity is there a greater divergence between what is in the Scripture and what is practiced. Now, a more educated and civilized world is up against centuries of victor theology that relies on rituals and does not change lives. It does not

require a person to be born again, and become a new creation who
lives by the commandments. Rather, it requires a person to be the
recipient of weekly absolutions for endless malfeasance. The victims
of that endless malfeasance are leaving the Church.

The Truth of the Matter

A vehicle is built to move people and goods from one location to
another. It can also be used to kill people. The Pauline Epistles is
like a spiritual vehicle the devil can use to serve his purpose. Some
people will argue that after darkness comes daylight. Others will
argue that after daylight comes darkness. We must listen to both
sides of an argument with the context in mind. According to dogmatic evangelicals, to believe that Jesus Christ died for our sins is
all that is required for salvation and citizenship in heaven. It is not
good works, baptism or church attendance, they say. That dogma
has not changed despite slave trade, slavery, segregation, apartheid,
colonialism and endless wars. If good works cannot save you, does
it mean that you should not do good works? If Baptism cannot
save you because the thief on the cross was not baptized, does it
mean that you should not be baptized as a sign of membership?
If belief in all that is required, then believers can stay home once
they believe.

The Epistles must be contextualized like the pioneer days in
America. What was the condition when the Epistles were written?
The Romans did not hesitate to crucify deviants. Imagine writing
a critical editorial in a nation under a brutal dictator. Also, the
Pharisees did not tolerate any change to centuries of doctrine. While
the Gospel of Jesus Christ has proved to be immutable and stands
the test of time, for the Pharisees and the Romans, a global religion
was an affront to entrenched cultural religions. Contexts matters in
Scripture.

The Apostles raised the expectation of pain and suffering for the Pioneer Church. Pain and suffering were inevitable because their rulers were not believers. Should Christians expect pain and suffering today when their rulers are believers? The fathers of the Reformation used selected verses of the Epistles to predetermine the narrative of the Gospel of Jesus Christ. For example, Africans and women are the greatest victims of the Epistles. What is described as a "Bible- believing church" is one that abuses the Pauline Epistles as terrorists use Scripture to abuse people.

The Church in Corinth had a lot of problems. St Paul wrote: "Were you called while a slave? Do not be concerned about it; but if you can be made free, rather use it" (1 Corinthians 7:20 – 21 NKJV). He also wrote: "Let your women keep silent in the Churches, for they are not permitted to speak; but they are to be submissive, as the law also says. And if they want to learn something, let them ask their own husbands at home; for it is shameful for women to speak in church" (1 Corinthians 14:34 NKJV). Who can blame the Taliban? The law cited was the law of Moses, not the Gospel of Jesus Christ. The "Bible- believing church" believes that a woman should not be on any pulpit.

Jesus Christ came that humankind may have abundant life. Is slavery abundant life? The church owned slaves. If the Epistles were not discovered, the world might have been better than it is today because more people, including those African slaves, would have had an abundant life. Those who want to live in hypocrisy can live in hypocrisy but not at the expense of someone else. If every pastor is preaching the same message, there will be only one denomination and the text will be the Gospel of Jesus Christ.

Unfortunately, William Shakespeare was right: "The Devil can cite the Scripture for his purpose." That is because the Epistles offer a buffet of Scriptures to cite. If the Epistles were not discovered, the church fathers would not have capitalized on salvation by faith alone (Ephesians 2:8). It is nowhere in the Gospel. It became the Amazing

Grace and a license to continue a lifestyle that included wars, conquests, slave trade and slavery. Did God Almighty abrogate the commandments because He so loved the world? Rather than amnesty, did He prefer to send Jesus Christ so that mortal men would stick a crown of thorns on His head, spit on Him for His Jewish descent and nail Him on the cross just to offer salvation with no strings attached? Real salvation has strings attached. It is compliance to the Golden Rule, the Great Commandment and the New Commandment with the help of the Holy Spirit.

Nevertheless, the Pauline Epistles have some Gospel Truth that should be cited. To the Galatians, St. Paul wrote: "For, brethren, ye have been called unto Liberty; only use not liberty for an occasion to the flesh, but by love serve one another. For all the law is fulfilled in one word, even in this: Thou shalt love thy neighbor as thyself (Galatians 5:13 – 14). How do you love your neighbor without being Pentecostal? If Christ or the Holy Spirit lives in you, would you colonize and enslave people or go to war to kill, except in self-defense? Many Africans who have no knowledge of the role of the church in slavery have been led to believe that the church Establishment is the gatekeeper of Heaven. Therefore, they dare not leave, even when Jesus Christ is being misrepresented.

The Apostles of Jesus Christ had apostolic authority. (Mark 16: 17- 18). Any Christian who believes that every promise in the Bible applies to both pre and post - apostolic Christians should pick up snakes to prove it. The church fathers and the church Establishment once controlled the world. The world cannot be the way it is today if they lived by God's Golden Rule, and not by corrupting the Epistles of St. Paul.

History tends to repeat itself. "In those days," according to Scripture, "there was no king in Israel, but every man did that which was right in his own eyes" (Judges 17: 6). Now, there are hundreds of Christian denominations, sects and Conferences. Without the Holy Spirit; without being born again, everyone is doing what is right in their own eyes. Any cleric can find a verse in the Epistles (not the Gospel), to support an irrational view. During the COVID - 19 pandemic, some churches did not encourage their members to be vaccinated. They were to rely on prayers because it is in the Bible. One denomination reportedly lost 17,000 members. We hope that they were all born again. Nobody should follow a spiritual Pied Piper to hell.

Are all the hundreds of Christian denominations on the right track? Is it possible or even probable that some are converting and leading people into the Broadway to destruction? In ancient times, there were philosophers, men and women who did what is right because it is right, and not because of a reward after death. They lived a life based on the Golden Rule. Then the Imperial Church introduced the Doctrine of Discovery that led to colonialism, slave trade and slavery. The Epistles became a spiritual buffet where some theologians went to select what they want to believe. That God Almighty sent Jesus Christ to die for our past, present and future sins opened the floodgates to malfeasance. The Golden Rule was no longer Treat others the same way you want them to treat you but "He who has the gold makes the rules." That is still Christianity today despite the fact that in 10,000 years nobody has gone to his grave with his gold.

For the sake of goodwill, all religions including Voodoo, are said to be equal. That may be comforting to cultural religionists. Christianity is not the religion of any culture. It is counterculture. The foundation members were Jews and Gentiles. Since no institution can guarantee salvation or issue a visa to heaven or paradise, buyer beware applies to religion.

Finally, 2,000 years ago, the world population was less than one billion. Some restless believers expected Jesus Christ to return in their lifetime. St Peter said to them: "The Lord is not slack concerning his promise, as some count slackness, but is long suffering toward us, not willing that any should perish but that all should come to repentance "(2 Peter 3:9 NKJV). Was it the word of God or St. Peter's opinion? Will all ever come to repentance? If Jesus returned when the world population was one billion, millions of souls would have perished. If Jesus returns when the world population is 10 billion, billions of souls will perish. The longer the delay, the more souls will perish. It is hard to believe that Judgment Day may be 2,000 years away. One thing is certain: The Almighty will not offer amnesty, and then apologize to the people of Sodom and Gomorrah. Not even a billion souls are indispensable to God. Therefore, it is wise to heed the advice of King Solomon: "Fear God, and keep his commandments: for this is the whole duty of man" (Ecclesiastes 12:13).

CHAPTER 5

The Deer in the Jungle

An evangelist recognized that a deer stays alert, to stay alive from the day they are born. "In a sense," he noted," you and I are a lot like those deer. From the day we are born Satan schemes to claim our souls." A student cannot learn if the stomach is empty. Before gaining access to his soul, a man's wellbeing cannot be ignored. The homeless men and women on the major streets of the world don't care about Satan or his claim on their souls. The deer have their own way of communication. Suppose the preachers among them told them to run faster and jump higher to stay alive from the lions and the bears, generation after generation. They are promised that those who believe in a doctrine and die, going through the hoops of life will have eternal life. If stories from their Scripture are told and retold and nothing changes; if all they hear are recycled theoretical religion, anecdotes and platitudes; and if after 2,000 years nobody has heard from those enjoying eternal life, the deer will be tired of more Sermons. Will it take those animals over 2,000 years to recognize the need to change the dynamics of their environment? Human beings do.

Preaching to the deer does not change the jungle. Does the deer need to read a book titled "Confronting your fear"? Do they want to read "How to weather the storms of life?" Do they want to read about the jungle life fictionalized? Is "A strong faith in tough times" the solution to their problems? One would expect some deer to suffer from mental illness based on their experiences. Will books on Romance be helpful? Yet their bookshops are filled with such books and books on motivation and fiction that do not redress the reality of jungle life. Every week there are anecdotes about the deer that jumped higher to escape death; the deer that ran faster to escape; the deer that prayed and the lions ran in a different direction; and the young deer that squeezed into a small hole to wait out a bear. Their priority is not peace with God but peace with other animals. And Sermons about love do not change the status of the deer. Unlike humans, they cannot change the dynamics of their environment.

The preachers of prophecy in the 1960s have passed away, like their predecessors. Their alarm bells of prophecy rang hollow in their own lifetime. The men and women they chastised for their interest in Rock and Roll are grandparents today. Their nation has no universal healthcare or job security to this day. If the Gospel of Jesus

Christ is about good relations between people and between them and God Almighty, did their fixation on prophecy or Rock and Roll serve any useful purpose? Was it not better to focus on improving the human condition? A young deer can run faster and jump higher to escape death. But with age, it will be unable to run faster and jump higher to escape death. Is it not better to change the dynamics of the jungle so that the deer can live in peace and grow old?

The Church that laid the foundation stone for America's social problems has not changed. A Christian must show evidence of being born again. Nobody can be born again just by saying a prayer. But just as it was in the slave economy, Christians are told that they are born again just by saying a prescribed prayer. The sermons are focused on motivating the individual, not on changing the urban jungle for education, healthcare and employment for every family. Those who have no control over their lives are always praying to God but nothing changes. If the deer are muzzled, the jungle will never change. So, activists need a loud voice.

Why did the Almighty give us the Golden Rule? Did God know that someone would do to others what he does not want others to do to him? When you are the deer in the urban jungle, your survival depends on demanding that those who claim to be Christians, observe God's Golden Rule. That's what changes the dynamics of the urban jungle. In Sermons and speeches, all the attention has been on the individual but no attention has been paid on the structure of the human jungle. Is it not better to change the human jungle and nourish both body and soul? That's what the Gospel of Jesus Christ demands. The environment does not change until the mind changes. The Church leaders can change the urban jungle because Christianity makes the impossible possible. With God, all things are possible. If the Church, the salt of the earth cannot practice the Golden Rule - "Treat others the same way you want them to treat you" - what religion on earth will practice it? A lot of people complain about the government. Some complain about society, culture or the wrongs done by friends and relatives. Whatever happens to you, the advice has been to pull yourself up by your bootstraps. Now, the Internet has added a new dimension to the trepidations of life. The truth is that the God of Creation provided protection for all social problems. It is called the Golden Rule.

The Apostles of Jesus Christ told their followers: "It is not desirable that we should leave the word of God and serve tables. Therefore, brethren, seek out from among you seven men of good reputation, full of the Holy Spirit and wisdom, whom we may appoint over this business." (Acts 6: 2-3). The men had to be filled with the Holy Spirit in that Holy Catholic Pentecostal Church of the Apostles. If denominational headquarters summon the courage to tell Christians to elect politicians of such caliber, the world will change for the better in a year or two. That birds of the same feathers flock together is a useful tool to identify doves and hawks. The sad events of history cannot be attributed to Liberals, Socialists or Spiritual Conservatives but to Cultural Conservatives who conserve the cultural values of human nature to obstruct Christian civilization.

In Canada, Hutterite leaders have changed their jungle, and reduced the use of economics as a tool for predation. Can it happen in the rest of Christendom? Humans were created to be different from wildlife. It is not enough to care only for family and stash away money for retirement. The lions and bears care only for family and in so doing have destroyed other lives. "Jesus loves you "means nothing to homeless people and their colleagues using drugs to drown their problems. They don't care about Satan's claim on their souls. They don't care about free copies of the Bible. The Gospel or Good News is good news not only for the soul but also for the body. The emphasis has been on the soul. But when the body does not come to Church, the soul does not come to Church.

People who have been through a difficult life or seen the sad events of life are more likely to question the existence of God. They need a functioning society that reflects the love of Jesus Christ they hear about. Babies and children have died from starvation because a mother's love does not fill an empty stomach. Neither does the love of Jesus Christ. If the greatest force in the world is love, according to the preachers, why are some Christians resistant to universal health-care and universal employment that would get so many veterans off the streets? Some fought overseas to keep communism at bay. The Gospel is embraced by billions of people in the world. One of the key precepts is the Golden Rule. So, why is the world the way it is today after 2,000 years of Christianity? When the wrongs that humans, even Christians, do to others are seen as the work of Satan, it allows the church to do nothing but wait for the return of Jesus Christ to bind Satan.

A few centuries ago, women who were suspected of being witches were routinely burned at the stakes in Europe. If witches are no longer in Europe, they must be in Africa. Since Satan no longer walks the streets in Europe, new missionaries see him in every nook and cranny in Africa. Where is Satan, the scapegoat we blame for every wrong on earth?

Where is Satan?

It is convenient to blame Satan or the Devil for all the evil on earth. What does Satan or the Devil look like and where is he? If Satan will be bound for a thousand years, between now and then, where is he? If we don't know where Satan lives, we can never solve our social problems. When Satan was "cast down," where did he go? If Satan were an entity challenging God Almighty for thousands of years, why should he not have been destroyed? The God who created the world by the word of His mouth can destroy it or Satan by the word of His mouth. The Almighty destroyed Sodom and Gomorrah for less than what Satan is said to be doing since Adam and Eve walked on this planet. God Almighty cannot be getting along with Satan. In the Garden of Eden, the Devil was represented by the talking snake as the agent of temptation to arouse the spirit of disobedience. Is the snake in the bush, crawling on its belly still the Devil? When Jesus Christ was tempted, the Devil was not the snake. Also, when Peter who later became the head of the Church rebuked Jesus, He said to Peter: "Get behind me Satan! You are an offence to Me, for you are not mindful of the things of God, but the things of men." (Matthew 16:23 NKJV). Was Peter, the Satan? Satan has also been shown as a dragon. The people in ancient cultures spoke in metaphors and allegory. The Devil or Satan is neither in heaven nor in the ether. The Devil is the spirit of disobedience, or the embodiment of the disobedience of God. Satan or the Devil is synonymous with the disobedience of God just as Quisling is synonymous with a traitor. Being the first to do what they did became a symbol. The Devil, Satan, the spirit of disobedience or the Evil Spirit is the default mode in man.

Adam and Eve sinned. They did not steal, commit adultery or murder. They ate the forbidden fruit and disobeyed God. That is sin. That propensity to disobey God is in every human being created with a free will rather than a robotic mind. The free will has two sides - obedience and disobedience. The Holy Spirit is a prompter of what is right or wrong. The evil spirit or human nature is a prompter of a perversion of what is right or wrong. To fail to accept the Holy Spirit and obey the commandments but blame Satan for every wrong in society is disingenuous. Can anybody name a wrong done to him or her by Satan, rather than a human being?

Since there is good and evil in everyone, there is good and evil in the world. Submission to divine authority mitigates that propensity to do wrong. In the distant past, the Church attempted to exorcise the evil spirit from man. It was not successful. Satan cannot cast out Satan. The Holy Spirit and the Holy Spirit alone can replace the evil spirit. Replacing the evil spirit must be the desire of a willing host (Luke 11:13). Are human beings intrinsically good or evil? In many parts of the world, the willful nature demands the freedom to express human nature, apart from the common good. A nation with education, healthcare and employment for every family would be called "a Communist or Socialist utopia trampling on our freedoms and rights." That means trampling on human nature. Human nature has no concern about an economic structure that creates multibillionaires while some families and children in need are dependent on prayer. Apparently, in every generation, those men who do what is in human nature seem to be dominant.

Nations have a government and the opposition to the government. Satan has been overrated as the head of the opposition to God's sovereignty. The Almighty God has no opposition but disobedient people. Jesus said:" But why do you call Me 'Lord, Lord,' and not do the things which I say?" (Luke 6:46 NKJV). For humans, any policy that is not based on God's Golden Rule is not inspired by the Holy Spirit. Imagine a world where everybody lives by the Golden Rule – Treat others the same way you want them to treat you. Imagine a world where all Americans live by the Golden Rule. Would there be wars, slave trade, slavery, racism, cybercrimes, family violence and misogyny? What is preventing that world? It is man's spirit of disobedience otherwise known as Satan. The world will get better the sooner we stopped blaming Satan and took responsibility for what we do or fail to do under the influence of the Holy Spirit or the evil spirit. Being born again allows the Holy Spirit to replace the evil spirit or the spirit of disobedience. Satan lives in us, not in the sky. When God Almighty revokes man's free will, that is the end of Satan.

A Tale of Two Faith Traditions

In the 1950s a group of American missionaries came to Africa to proselytize. They told people in bare-foot poverty not to worry because Armageddon was imminent and non- members of their group will perish. They pointed to all the bloody wars and suffering in the world and opined that when the kingdom of God comes, every problem on earth will be fixed. Paradise will be restored here on earth. They had pictures of the Lion in a lush pasture playing with children in the new kingdom. Their literature also suggested that man is trying to do the impossible by going into space because the heat of reentry will incinerate the satellite and crew. Russia's Sputnik in 1957 was a shock.

It is easy to convince people who are suffering that the end is near; that the kingdom of God is at hand. It is not. It's one of the ways to keep hope alive and do nothing to change the human condition, generation after generation, and century after century. The African converts did not participate in civic affairs to make life better. They have passed away. Now their grandchildren are peddling the same doctrine and are still waiting for the kingdom of God to come.

Jesus Christ was here on earth some 2,000 years ago and will be back. But for the God of eternity, 2,000 years is like a nanosecond or a drop in the ocean of time. Believe it or not, in the next one or two millennia, astronomers are unlikely to see the signs that will precede the return of Jesus Christ (Mark 13:24-26). That truth will not deter those who peddle hope and do nothing more than offer band -aid solutions in Africa and elsewhere. It will be a long wait for the coming kingdom of God. Sadly, those who leave groups considered to be cults will discover that the "cults" are more friendly, more respectful and inclusive than the mainstream religions. It can be a very difficult transition for deserters. A Christian can be an expert in theology without being born again. How long will some religious groups continue to keep hope alive?

Now, consider another faith tradition. In a Canadian Hutterite colony, parents wake up in the morning and go to work. Their children go to school. And being Canadians, they have universal healthcare. That is a holistic lifestyle and a different faith tradition. That is how people who believe and obey God live. They have not separated the body, mind and soul. Notice that they do not wait for the coming kingdom of God to end suffering. What else does a person need? A community that caters to the body, mind and soul is not for everybody. There are men for whom a conflict -free life, even heaven or paradise will be boring.

The Hutterites do not have a food bank for needy people. They do not have homeless, lonely or jobless people or gangs. They do not have to pray to God because they cannot pay their medical bills. They do not pray for rain, they dig wells. There are no unemployed people in the chapel unhappily singing" Great is Thy faithfulness--- All I have needed, Thy hand hath provided." They are not in perpetual need for help because they live the Gospel. They do not exploit human suffering and don't need motivational speakers and their books.

Those who are poor but rich in faith can be exploited. They do not need the prayer of Jabez to solve everyone's problems. It doesn't. There is no conflict between business and labor. They do not need an army, a police force or security guards to keep them safe. Safe from who?

And they are not going around the world in search of enemies. Is it not better to live by faith and also do the will of God on earth as it is in heaven rather than dwell on prophecy, the Great Tribulation and the Second Advent that may not happen in another 2,000 years? The Hutterites can "taste and see that the LORD is good "and show that the trials and tribulations of life are manmade. When we obey God, social problems disappear. For example, the Hutterites and the Mennonites are brethren in Christ. The former live in a colony, the latter live in the city. The Hutterites in the colony live a holistic life. They have education, healthcare and employment for all families. On Sunday, their chapel is full. That is not the case among the mainline churches in the city. It can be. They can live in a multi-faith and multi- cultural diversity with the same universal education, healthcare and employment without being communal, and see their churches full again. It can only happen when the cultural conservative Christians who control humankind are converted to genuine Christianity and be compassionate conservatives who care for both body and soul for all.

Imagine 58-year-old Anne, a Canadian Hutterite who lives with her husband in an economy based on education, healthcare and employment for all families. On Sunday, they worship in their chapel and are happy to sing "Great is Thy faithfulness ---All I have needed Thy hand hath provided." Imagine also 58-year-old Rita in the neighboring city church. She has been encouraged to keep praying; keep her eyes on the cross; Jesus is the answer; God is our source. Rita is one of the millions who are enchanted by fellow Christians who do nothing but raise the hope that prayer will solve the next problem, even when it didn't solve the last. They are "prisoners of hope" who need to be rescued from prayer fatigue.

As a member of the growing number of single- person house-holds, Rita has been unemployed for a year. At that age, the men and women whose trust has been betrayed find it difficult to establish a trusting relationship again. Rita is in financial distress. Financial advisers expect people to save for retirement and have an emergency fund. But she has gone from unemployment to unemployment and lived from paycheck to paycheck for years. She has a telephone land line and can't afford a cell phone. She still remembers that two doors from their apartment, an elderly man for whom death was better than life, took his life. It came to light when notes began to accumulate at his door for a couple of weeks. It took a week to fumigate his apartment. When you see endless conflicts, starving children, suicide, family violence and divorce as feigned love turns into hate; and see joblessness and homelessness without abatements, a sermon is like flogging a dead horse. It can be annoying to those like Rita who have been going to church for decades. Inhumanity is when the future of one life is controlled by another.

When Rita hears that Jesus said: "Give and it shall be given unto you;" it is like rubbing salt into her wound because she can't afford to give. She hates when they sing "Great is Thy faithfulness --- All I have needed Thy hand hath provided." She lost hope when she heard a Radio pastor say that "Help is a prayer away." Now, Rita does not go to church anymore to worship hypocrisy and self-deceit. She is also disappointed with God. But to Anne, Christianity offers abundant life here on earth and eternal life hereafter. She does not have to wait on the Lord. Many grandparents waited and nothing happened. Her church experience is relevant to the living and the dead. Sadly, to Rita, her church experience has no relevance to the living. And may not be for the dead if they are not taught to be born again and live by the Gospel. So, what is her church there for? That's a question for victor theologians. Does theoretical Christianity offer her eternal life through hardship? Some religious groups are led while others are controlled. The groups described as cults don't want to hear anything other than what they believe. The same is true of their critics whose own members are suffering from theoretical Christianity and prayer fatigue.

The proletarian poor on main street are more numerous than the men of Wall Street. Yet, it is the few that controls the many. Ask the unemployed people if the government should be used to help people. The result will be different from a survey of a segment of the general population who do not feel the pain of others. Under ballot- box democracy, the poor majority should control the government because, many centuries ago, Democracy was conceived to serve the common good. If it has not, it is pseudo- Democracy. For genuine Democracy to endure, the world must know by whose authority a politician rules over his or her parents, grandparents, teachers, professors, classmates and pastors, if any. Unfortunately, the poor will go to the polls to vote against their interest by figuratively electing a Trojan horse. The government will be hijacked by the lobbyist lurking in the Trojan horse. They serve the rich on Wall Street which offers the greatest temptation to live by bread alone.

And so, when the government of the people, by the people and for the people is a hoax; when a boycott of the polls changes nothing; when a boycott of amoral companies has no effect on their stock price; when prayer is of no avail; and in 2,000 years the Almighty God of the Old Testament has not sanctioned politicians or controlled Satan, a few people like Rita can profess to be atheists. In surveys, they are listed as "no religion." But the seed of faith is still inside. She is not the atheists associated with evolution - that would be insanity - but a creationist contemptuous of the church that would see her as a" backslider." She did not turn her back on Jesus Christ, but on the church of man. In the Canadian Hutterite colony, spiritual enlightenment has spared Anne from suffering but not Rita who hears sermons that suggest that unabated suffering and tribulation are part of prophecy. Nevertheless, she is lucky to be a Canadian where healthcare is guaranteed to all.

Let us be clear. The church was born on the day of Pentecost. it was a Pentecostal church. Then or now, the Pentecostal church (without the ostentatious glossolalia) that raises born again Christians who live by the Gospel, appeals to uncorrupted teenagers with primordial innocence. It also appeals to their grandparents based on their lived experience. Living by the Golden Rule is the only way to know a Christian who is born again. It is the criterion for salvation. There is no other way. The church of culture that raises Christians who do to others what they don't want others to do to them should not appeal to men and women who reason with rational minds. That is the church that has to be closed down through boycotts for the good of humankind.

Mainline churches have been losing men and women like Rita who are "disappointed with God." The churches that make people like Rita prayer dependent, discouraged and drift away, described them as "backsliders." It is the work of Satan the enemy, they say. The clergy and laity do not walk in each other's shoes. Whereas the Annes of the world have leaders who obey God's commandments and their social implications, the Ritas of the world have leaders who take cover under secularism, even as Christians. Hence, Christians are led by victor- theology Christians in a way that undermines faith in God. The victims should be disappointed, not with God but with politicians and the pastorate that raised them. How can anyone watch human life look like wildlife and be disappointed with God, but not with the denominations that do not understand and live by the Gospel as the Hutterites do?

Those denominations raised the State actors. Is belief in God or in Jesus Christ, the beginning or the end of faith? For some it is the beginning. But for others it is the end of faith. A king does not run the kingdom. It is the functionaries on his majesty's service that run the kingdom according to his will. A dictator does not run the State. It is the bureaucrats that run the State according to his whim. The Almighty God does not solve problems on earth. The fateful allow God to use them to do his will on earth as it is in heaven. The Hutterite clergy is a faithful servant bearing fruit. When Christians do wrong to others, they are practicing paganized Christianity. Those who raised them are not faithful servants. That is the concern of Rita and those of us like her who have left the church for several reasons. Consider the 2022 brutal war in Ukraine. What Christians do to others after 2,000 years of the Gospel suggests, paradoxically, that the church can only be saved by a boycott of the church that resists Christian civilization.

Some Activists who care more about human life than money demand universal basic income. That is not a concern in a Hutterite colony with universal employment. The clergy and laity in mainline churches need to work in each other's shoes. Being told to keep your eyes on Jesus will not fill and empty stomach. The Hutterites doing the will of God on earth as it is in heaven know that. Their church or chapel is a place to worship God; not a Sunday school, teaching students who never graduate. The city church parishioners will hear about what God is doing in faraway places; how He has led someone to do one thing or another and how they are digging wells in Africa. Can God also lead the Church to run a society or a nation like the Hutterite economy that serves every family? There is no ebb and flow of life in a Hutterite economy. They have designed a steady- state economic homeostasis that overrides the ebb and flow of life. Evidently, there is a correlation between the way people are governed, church attendance and empty pews. When you have been looking for work for months or years; when the government of the people run by Christians lays you off in order to balance a budget deficit that is recurrent, you don't go to church and joyfully sing: "Great is Thy faithfulness --- All I have needed, Thy hand hath provided. "

Politics and religion thrive on ignorance. In Canada, a Baptist preacher got into politics and introduced universal healthcare. In the United States with the applause of his congregation an evangelical preacher proclaims that Washington, D.C is their problem, Christ is the solution. Yet he is resistant to universal healthcare and believes that an economy based on education, healthcare and employment for all families is godless socialism. They have created God in man's image. God is no longer on the side of righteousness but on the side of sinner since slave trade. He no longer requires repentance but like a waiter, He is waiting to answer prayers and bless everybody. In the 2008 Great Recession, thousands of their congregants lost their homes. Their prayers in a Godforsaken world were not answered. Some clerics count on the short memory of grandparents. Their grandchildren are unaware of the past. They are in church listening to Bible stories and motivational sermons of smoke and mirrors. They cannot see the forest for the trees until they, too, become parents and disillusioned grandparents. It is an endless rotation of children, parents and disillusioned grandparents. That has been Christianity for 2,000 years. Some Christians can lose hope from what they read.

In the 2019 edition of The Shepherd's Guide, a Christian Business and Ministry Directory in Alberta, some clerics had a list of Scriptures for every problem. There is Scripture to read when you are worried, depressed, have sinned, when losing hope, seeking peace or when people have failed you. And when your bank account is empty, you read Psalm 37. You can read Psalm 37 and nothing will happen. This Protestantism that ignores the Gospel, leads to frustration, empty pews and Church for Sale signs. A practical Christian like Pastor Dietrich Bonhoeffer noted that "one act of obedience is worth a hundred sermons." The faithfulness of God will not make sense to the grandchildren listening to 100 more sermons until they visit a Canadian Hutterite colony. Bonhoeffer omitted what many pastors don't want to hear – To obey is better than prayer. When an economy is based on education, healthcare and employment for all families, to "bear one another's burdens and so fulfill the law of Christ" is no longer a burden. It also reduces needless prayers. But in Dixie, that is godless socialism. So, the smoke and mirrors of spiritual hypocrisy continues generation after generation in a world that blames Satan for what men do.

St. Paul offers three options for those who want to cite the Scriptures to serve their purpose. There is "Bear ye one another's burdens and so fulfill the law of Christ." (Galatians 6:2). There is "For every man shall bear his own burden." (Galatians 6:5.) And there is" But my God shall supply all your need according to his riches in glory by Christ Jesus." (Philippians 4: 19). The context is different but they offer community living, rugged individualism and dependence on God respectively. The Hutterites choose to bear one another's burdens and in so doing, nobody bears a burden. No Hutterite is dependent on charity. The youths are neither jobless nor suicidal. They are not part of Satan's world. Every family can stand on their own feet and support church and missions. They exemplify the will of God being done on earth as it is in heaven. It is the practical Christianity that the city dwellers are missing. If the Apostles of Jesus Christ ran a government, what kind of government will it be? Any born-again Christian knows that it would be a SOCIALIST government free from hatred, prejudices and discrimination. Nobody would be homeless or jobless. That's easy to visualize in a homogeneous culture.

Scandinavian countries were less imperial and less encumbered by the consequences of colonialism. They could be the first to have education, healthcare and employment for all families like the Canadian Hutterites, without being communal. That is Christianity. What is tugging at the soul of the biggest and most diverse nation on earth, is the clash between culture and a counterculture religion. Outside a Hutterite colony, is there a church that bears one another's burdens, if their government does not? The correct answer is no. Is there a church that the Apostles of Jesus Christ would recommend? You be the judge. There are prosperity preachers who ask their audience to wait for the right time like Abraham. Decade after decade, recession after recession, the captive audience are entertained with anecdotes of men and women who overcame the enemy. They encourage rugged individualism, which means that you are on your own.

The Gospel of Jesus Christ shows that rugged individualism is a fraud. And who is the enemy? Satan. If Satan is the enemy, guilty of all he or she is accused of doing, generation after generation, how can it be that the Almighty God cannot control or get rid of Satan. Why is the enemy opposed to education, healthcare and employment for all families? And why is that enemy not in a Canadian Hutterite colony? When an economy is based on education, healthcare and employment for every family, Satan seems to disappear. There is no Satan to blame. When people do the will of God, the spirit of disobedience or the enemy disappears. The enemy is within us. If Christians looked carefully, the enemy is the spirit of disobedience in the neighborhood, including the neighborhood church. From teenage years to now, I can name a dozen wrongs people have done to me. I cannot name of a single wrong that Satan has come to me. Nobody can.

The enemies of an organization are usually on the outside. It bears repeating that Christianity can never reach its potential if it has members resisting the Gospel from the inside. That resistance was evident in the American civil war. The victor theology has helped the antichrist. In many communities, band- aid solutions have been institutionalized even when they are known to cost more than permanent solutions. That's the will of cultural conservatives. The food bank is a cultural solution. With employment for all families, a Hutterite colony does not need a food bank. There is little or no social problems or crimes induced by poverty. An unjust society is expensive to police and contributes to a budget deficits and debt. The unrestrained and undisciplined freedom to own guns lead to gun deaths every day. The same unrestrained and undisciplined freedom to resist vaccination prolonged the covid-19 pandemic and increased the casualties. By contrast, aside from their holistic economy, the Hutterites have restrained and disciplined freedom to do what is right, not the freedom to do what is wrong. Consequently, they do not need policing. Their moral and ethical living lead to what Jesus Christ described as abundant life. What New York City or Chicago spends on policing, is enough to make everyone in Haiti rich.

There were moments when prophets like Habakkuk and Kings like David wondered if God is still there in heaven. The Almighty is not supervising the World. When cities are like a Hutterite colony, they share their daily bread. No family has too many loaves while some have none. And nobody wonders if God is still there to respond to every need or punish every transgression. The public may wonder how some professionals fare in their jobs. How do medical personnel cope with what they see and still have a normal life? How do teachers cope with abused and abusive children who come to school with their family problems? How do the police cope with the family violence they see and the people they shoot dead, and still have a normal life? How do pastors cope with all the family problems they deal with and still have a normal life? The people who get into these professions develop a psychological immunity as a coping mechanism. Without a doubt, future generations will find those jobs easier when their policymakers are either born-again Christians or atheists who run an economy based on education, employment and healthcare for every family.

Protestant Christians have written books on God's promises in the Old and New Testaments. Are the promises not contingent on obedience? Believers cannot call Him "Lord, Lord," and not do what He says (Luke 6:46). Jesus is said to be the answer. How is He the answer for starving children and the beggars on the streets? How can He be the answer without obeying the commandments and their social implications? Theoretical Christianity based on victor theology is a show. When a church is sold, it is the end of the show. The show operator is not the pastor. No pastor can change society. Not even Rev. Billy Graham. The show operator is the Establishment. The

Church Establishment has not determined the summary or the core of the Gospel of Jesus Christ. If in 2,000 years, the Establishment is in denial of past malfeasance and does not expect from policy-makers a caring economy like a Hutterite economy, has the theology changed? Will the church survive this indifference by 3,000 AD? The church must be more than a prayer house or an entertainment center. As automation reduces employment in the next 1,000 years, will Christians be coming to pray to God who does not build facto-ries to employ people? The church will be deserted. Those who will inhabit this planet a thousand years from now will reap the seeds we sow today just as we reap the seeds that were sown a thousand years ago. Actions have consequences.

Children born and raised in a city can be forgiven for believ-ing that eggs come from a grocery store. They need an excursion to a farm to see the chickens that lay the eggs. On their way to church, children have seen their parents drive past beggars and homeless people and look the other way. Where do they go to see practical Christianity? Where do they go to see the abundant life they heard about in Sunday schools? Where do they go to see the Great Commission fully implemented? They also go to a Canadian Hutterite farm where "teaching them to observe all things whatso-ever I have commanded you "is on display. There are no absolutions here. They observe the Holy Eucharist and also observe the Golden Rule, the Great Commandment, New Commandment and their so-cial implications. The Hutterite children study the gospel is Sunday school as God's guidebook or instruction Manual. Their parents put the instructions into practice. They don't care about what happened 1,000 years ago or what will happen 1,000 years from now in the name of prophecy. What they care about is now. The first law of na-ture is self-preservation. An economy based on education, healthcare and employment for every family is the definition of security. In a colony there is no informal economy. But outside the colony those who are excluded by" hardworking people "find ways and means to survive. One of those ways is prostitution, now called sex workers. No child will regret being born in in a nation that has the abundant life that Jesus Christ came to offer 2,000 years ago.

Can anyone read the Gospel of Jesus Christ and not know that self-help or rugged individualism is a fraud? However, communal life is not for everybody. With its cultural diversity, the city life cannot be a communal life with a common ownership of resources and a dress code. The Hutterite work ethic – "Arbeit macht das Leben suss" - or work makes life sweet, leaves no room for indolence.

The lesson from a Canadian Hutterite colony is that an economy based on education, healthcare and employment for all families is possible to those who believe. If there are practicing Christians in the city, can they do the same for every family? Practical Christianity would have been spread with evangelism, from the defunct Roman empire to the rest of the world before colonialism brought diverse cultures together to make it seem impossible now. Do we need to resurrect Mahatma Gandhi to teach us how to practice Christianity?

Roman Catholics and Protestant Anglicans believe in the Holy Catholic church. Does it exist. If the moral principles of a religion are not practiced, the religion serves no useful Purpose to the living. It becomes entertainment or a ritual. Christianity is serving no useful purpose to the homeless and beggars on the streets. Many politicians have run their government in a way that destroys faith. Now, many mainline churches are half empty after peddling theoretical Christianity based on victor theology for too long. And have continued to do the same things over and over, expecting a different outcome. It is not different from those waiting for the coming kingdom of God. The discontent of disaffected Christians applies to both Church and States. Declining church attendance and low voter turnout in elections are expressions of that discontent.

Antisocial elements demanded rugged individualism and for centuries, Christians focused attention on lifting yourself up by your bootstraps. But the future of Christianity depends on community, not on individualism. It depends on bearing one another's burdens, not on lip service. It depends on changing the dynamics of the human jungle, not on the motivation of the individual. The church service that some people see as entertainment or the pastoral show can continue as long as the pastorate teaches being born again and compliance to the Gospel. They lead the church to education, healthcare and employment for all. It frees the Gospel that is stuck on the pages of the Bible to come alive. That is the will of God. That is practical Christianity. It is the yoke of Jesus Christ that makes for easy and abundant life. There is no doubt that it creates less stress for everyone including teachers, the clergy, medical and legal professions. The alternative is the yoke of culture - the yoke of greed and hatred.

In these two faith traditions, who is practicing Christianity? Christianity is following Christ; it is a way of life, not a sermon. How can the will of God be done on earth as it is in heaven when the masses are led to be prayer dependent? The poor do not want charity or an economic policy that keeps them prayer dependent. They want to be like the Canadian Hutterites with education, healthcare and employment for every family. That's the will of God. One of those faith traditions can produce men and women who can "taste and see that the Lord is good." Their practical Christianity makes the impossible inevitable because with God all things are possible. The other tradition can only produce men and women who are disappointed with God in their prayer and expectation fatigue.

If a sheep can be lost, can a shepherd also be lost? The Almighty God, I believe, would prefer His commandments to be obeyed than to see the beggars and homeless people watch life's lottery winners praise God for what he has done for them. Surely, the church does not and should not run the economy. But its members do, even in a secular society. When history was young, the rulers of the world were pagans. For pioneer Christians to endure pain and suffering was understandable. Why should Christians endure pain, suffering and tribulations when their leaders at Christian? One of the pillars of the Gospel is the Golden Rule - Treat others the same way you want them to treat you. It makes sense to any human being regardless of culture, ethnicity, gender, religion or political ideology. It is only possible through the Holy Spirit. Many atheists are more compassionate than some religious people. So, which group is in control of the nations of the world? Is it those who believed in God or those who don't believe in God? If it is those who believed in God, like the Hutterites, education, healthcare and employment for all families should have been government policy over a thousand years ago. When governance or political discuss is not based on the Golden Rule, the officials are not inspired by the Holy Spirit but by a different spirit.

About 2,000 years ago, some Christians believed that they were living in the last days. Today some Christians are still living in the last days and will not lift a finger to help people in need and advance civilization. The Hutterites could care less about the last days. They leave the faith. A person who is thirsty needs water to drink, not a lecture about the chemistry of water. if you want something to happen, stop praying and make it happen. While personal transgressions were condemned in the Bible, collective transgression was also punished. It is important to focus more attention on the collective transgression of society that allows personal transgressions to breed. It will reduce the inclination to do wrong. The decisions church leaders made or did not make a thousand years ago still has consequences today. A child who puts his finger in a fire suffers the consequences, not his mother. Nobody should suffer the consequences for someone else's actions. Nobody suffers from the actions or policies inspired by the Holy Spirit. A Christian politician who lays off government employees to balance a recurrent budget deficit is not inspired by the Holy Spirit. It does not happen in a Hutterite colony because they have been raised to live by the Golden Rule. To avoid the call for clinical psychologists and psychiatrists for the youths who will need antidepressants a decade hence, now is the time to follow the lead of the Hutterites and structure society to serve the common good.

How many Christians in Africa live by the Gospel - the Golden Rule, the Great Commandment and the New Commandment? How many Americans do the same? Each year, thousands of people die from suicide in America and thousands die from despair in Africa. Keeping hope alive did not keep them alive. If Christians do not follow the Hutterites to practice Christianity, it makes no sense to convert more Africans and Asians to hypocrisy, and lead them to believe that God will answer their next prayer. It will not happen. Haiti was an exception. But left to African slaves alone, slavery would not have ended. Left to South Africans alone, apartheid would not have ended. And left to colonized people alone, colonialism would not have ended. Change comes when among those who exercise power and control, a critical mass has a revived conscience.

The verdict of history on moral power vs. carnal power is clear. So, there will be healthcare, education and employment for families in America when evangelical Christians have a conscience revived by the Gospel of Jesus Christ beyond Amazing Grace. Politicians should have a goal beyond winning the next election. There is no reason why a nation run by genuine Christians cannot plan for education, healthcare and employment for all families by the year 2030. If it is more likely to happen in China than in the United States where most of the leaders are Christians, what does it say about their Christian faith and democracy? If Christianity does not return to its base - the Golden Rule, the Great Commandment and the New Commandment, it will be permanently deformed by the victor theology that sustained slavery and pseudo- democracy for over three centuries.

'It takes fire," the preacher says, "to refine gold and heat to get tea from a tea bag". Those platitudes only promote the endurance of social injustice and support the antisocial victor theology resisting collective actionable responsibility. They do not apply in a Hutterite colony where genuine Christians live by the Gospel. Preaching without practicing the Gospel is destroying Christianity. The message Christians hear today in church is the same message Christians heard in over 300 years of slavery. What is different are the preachers. Church Sermons make sense when politicians run an economy based on education, employment and healthcare for all families. If Jesus is the answer, that is the answer and nowhere is the answer more evident than in a Canadian Hutterite colony. They have abundant life here on earth, and eternal life hereafter. The pastors serve as the Executors of God's will, not as Regents of God who cannot speak for Himself. The Hutterite's holistic life is also "the will of God in Christ Jesus concerning you". After 2,000 years, if Christians have not figured out how a nation should be managed, realtors will be like vultures looking for dead churches to convert to commercial use.

How important was prophecy to the Christians who passed away in the past 2,000 years? Prophecy is one of the distractions from the Gospel. Within the past century, many prophecy preachers in North America have passed away. They did not live long enough to see the end time they preached about. The same will apply to the zealots of prophecy today. It is used as a distraction from teaching Christians to observe the commandments and their social implications. Those who mislead are the first to warn you about men who are deceitful. But any institution that is based on deception or abuse will eventually collapse. It cannot withstand God's moral law. People can listen to endless anecdotes of men and women who won a lottery and be reminded that they could be the next. Similarly, Old Testament Christians feed their members stories of what God did in the Old Testament and is waiting to do the same today despite a pile of transgressions. That is the nature of sermons that keep false hope alive generation after generation without practicing the Gospel. Some congregants are told to be patient for God to remove the obstacles on their way. Who placed the obstacles? The Old Testament

Christians do not know that in a Canadian Hutterite colony, New Testament Christians have no obstacles.

Looking back in history, the church that owned and sold slaves did not practice Christianity. The members who lived off the avails of the enslavement of African men, women and children did not learn the Gospel - the Golden Rule, the Great Commandment and the New Commandment. If the church lived the Gospel, after 2,000 years the church would have been like a branch plant producing the engines that run the State. That States would have been like a Canadian Hutterite economy where all parents go to work, children go to school, and all are covered by universal healthcare. In that" abundant life" here on earth, and eternal life hereafter, their members can" taste and see that the LORD is good." They go to church as a place of thanksgiving and worship, not as a club for entertainment.

When Christians flock to a church that is entertaining, within a few generations most churches become entertainment Centers. That is not Christianity. Church membership is declining because the doctrine is not sound and Sermons do not fill and empty stomach. Some members have unfulfilled expectations. Those who are grown up physicality and spiritually no longer believe that God shall supply all their needs according to His riches in glory by Christ Jesus. It did not happen to their grandparents and will not happen to them in the foreseeable future. The Christians of the slave economy were led to believe that they can go home to be with the Lord without doing the will of the Lord. The Establishment has the capacity to fool the people of every generation to believe that they can also go home to be with the Lord without compliance to the Golden Rule, the Great Commandment and the New Commandment.

Being civilized is a measure of how distant the cave man has walked away from his wildlife habitat. Since the Great Commission, the Hutterites have walked the farthest from the cave man. They have become, not the most developed but the most civilized community on earth. The Christian civilization is the ultimate civilization. To lay treasures on earth, die and leave everything behind should make no sense under predatory capitalism. And no useful purpose is served in a life lived in hypocrisy. No nation can be changed by a leader, no matter how good he or she may be. A nation is transformed by asking for the Holy Spirit to replace the endemic evil spirit and live by the commandments; not by spiritually lawless Amazing Grace.

The Bottom Line

Why is the world the way it is today after 2,000 years of the Golden Rule? Did the church go astray and ignored to practice it? Until the third century, the old -time religion was Pentecostal. They received the Holy Spirit. It was good enough for the Apostles and should be good enough for you. Christianity is about good relations between people, and between them and God Almighty. That is the Truth not yet preached. We know that from the Golden Rule, the Great Commandment and the New Commandment. Jesus said that a man must be born again to see the kingdom of God (John 3:3.) A man is born again by asking for the Holy Spirit (Luke 11: 13), to replace the evil spirit, the default mode in man. That is the Truth. The church did not ask. Jesus used a practicum (Matthew 10:5-15), to demonstrate the conduct of evangelism. The Doctrine of Discovery did the opposite of the will of God. That is the Truth. If the imperial victor theology that sustained slave trade and slavery for 300 years has not changed, is the new- time religion good enough for you? That is the question. Victor theology does not change lives. It is a theology without ethics. It did not change the slave - trading church and clergy for centuries. Reliance on Amazing Grace and weekly absolutions will not change the world. Conversely, the Gospel of Jesus Christ replaces the evil spirit and changes lives. It minimizes malfeasance generation after generation to the point of minimal policing.

Now, while some churches are declining, and closing for preaching to the choir for too long, there are also mega-churches. Are they mega because they are spiritual or mega because they are entertaining? A church whose members are doing to others what they don't want others to do to them is not the Church of Jesus Christ but the Church of culture. It is obvious that based on the Golden Rule, the Great Commandment, and the New Commandment; and based on "Bear one another's burdens and so fulfill the law of Christ," if the Church lived the Gospel, after 2,000 years of Christianity, every nation should have been like a Canadian Hutterite economy. If not, Satan must have derailed God's program through surrogates. Some preachers complain about the evil world. Who was in control of the evil world in the centuries of slave trade, slavery and colonization? The Hutterites are not all saints. But they live in an environment that makes it easier to be saint than a criminal.

When did the United States become a developed nation? When did New York City become a developed city? A long-developed nation or city is still developing because development has no end. What it needs is to be civilized. Consider New York City and a Canadian Hutterite colony. The colony has employment for every family, education for their children, universal health care for all and life beyond the grave. That's abundant life (John 10:10). The city is more developed but the colony is more civilized. Similarly, America's cities are more developed but rural America is more civilized and has no homeless people. Global warming may be a warning to be more civilized and less developed. So, copy the Hutterites. Furthermore, Prophet Jeremiah proclaimed God's plan for the faithful: "For I know the plans I have for you," said the Lord, "plans to prosper you and not harm you, plans to give you hope and a future" (NKJV). The Canadian Hutterites live that plan. What is holding back God's plan for your life?

Two hundred years ago, parents here on earth gave birth to the people in the world today. They fought, killed and struggled to make a living. Some starved babies and children to death in order to get rich from the parent's natural resources. Now, more than 90 percent of them have been forgotten or even despised by their own descendants because of their deeds. Suppose they knew that they would be forgotten by their descendants after two or three centuries. They would have been more humane, more sober, and more rational in their relationship with one another. "Treat others the same way you want them to treat you "made sense then, and still makes sense to anyone who is a human being because it is a basic principle.

In North America, there are families referred to as "church hoppers". What are church hoppers looking for? They are looking for a Hutterite church outside a Hutterite colony. There is no such church. But a government whose policies line up with the provision of abundant life is long overdue.

CHAPTER 7

Evangelism

There are hundreds or thousands of Christian denominations around the world. Does it suggest that Christians do not agree on what Christianity is all about? Does it show that there are hundreds of ways to follow Christ? In North America, a Bible belt can also be a racist belt. A tourist can drive through a town of less than 8,000 people and find over ten denominations. There might be a Baptist church, Alliance church, United church, Roman Catholic church, Anglican church, Presbyterian church, Church of the Nazarene, Lutheran church, Main Street Pentecostal church, Church of Jesus Christ of Latter -day Saints, The Salvation Army and Kingdom Hall of Jehovah's Witnesses. For salvation, some rely on weekly absolutions. Some rely on adult baptism. Some rely on belief in Jesus Christ and nothing more. Some rely on the structure of Church administration. Ask any pastor if their group is going to heaven while all other Christians go to hell, there is no clear answer. Buyer beware!

First, let us be clear what the Gospel is all about. It is more than a doctrine. It is a way of life. It is about good relations between people and between them and the God of Creation. Like car manufacturers, the Almighty issued operating instructions that must be followed. Every literature, document or manual can be summarized.

So, the Gospel of Jesus Christ is summarized by: (1) The Golden Rule – "And as ye would that men should do to you, do ye also to them likewise (Luke 6:31). That means, treat others the same way you want them to treat you.; (2) The Great Commandment – "Thou shalt love the Lord thy God with all thy heart, and with all thy soul, and with all thy strength, and with all thy mind; and thy neighbor as thyself."(Luke 10:27); (3) The New Commandment - "A New Commandment I give unto you, that ye love one another; as I have loved you, that ye also love one another. "(John 13:34). These precepts, are herein referred to as the Gospel. They come with the offer of the Helper, the Holy Spirit (John 14:26; Luke 11:13) who replaces the evil spirit and helps a convert become born again and keep those commandments. That is what Christianity is all about.

So, why is the world not better than it is today after 2,000 years of Christianity? Most people on earth have been affected directly or indirectly by wars, murder, divorce or family dissociation, robbery, scams, violence or neglect. Therefore, Christians need to re-examine the mandate of the Great Commission because it is the key to understanding why the world is not better than it is today after 2,000 years of Christianity. It is the key to understanding why some Churches have been sold and more will be sold. It is the key to understanding the disillusion and disaffection that led some to feel disappointed with God. If the Truth be told, they should be disappointed with man or the Church and State Establishments, not with God.

Life is only fair when it is lived according to the will of God. It is unfair to about 30,000 people who take their lives through suicide each year in America. Evangelism was executed in man's way, not in God's way. Jesus Christ gave His disciples a practicum on evangelism (Matthew 10:5 – 14). "And whosoever shall not receive you, nor hear your words, when you depart out of that house or city, shake off the dust of your feet," He said. At the end of his mission on earth, He gave a clear mandate to His followers in the Great Commission:" Go ye therefore, and teach all nations, baptizing them in the name of the Father, and of the Son, and of the Holy Ghost; teaching them to observe all things whatsoever I have commanded you: and, lo, I am with you alway, even unto the end of the world." (Matthew 28:19-20). Who changed God's plan? Do human beings make mistakes? Do they abuse their office? A chaotic world looks like the product of evolution because God's guidelines were ignored. In 1493, Pope Alexander V1 proclaimed the Doctrine of Discovery. It was the antithesis of the practicum on evangelism. He granted some European nations that have been evangelized, the legal and moral justification to seize, colonize, and subjugate the pagans outside Europe, and reduce them to perpetual slavery. It was the opposite, even a defiance of the practicum that Jesus Christ demonstrated. Another Papal bull declared Australia as terra nullius or no man's land. It could justify extermination of the Aboriginals. Some decapitated heads were preserved as trophy.

There is an Evil Spirit in man. Jesus said: "If ye then, being evil, know how to give good gifts unto your children: how much more shall your heavenly Father give the Holy Spirit to them that ask Him? (Luke 11 :13). The Regent Church fathers didn't ask for the Holy Spirit but offered sacraments, confession and forgiveness of sins (absolutions), designed for mass admission to heaven or paradise. All that a Christian had to do is accept Jesus as Lord and Saviors and carry on. So, a Christian is a pagan who believes in Jesus Christ and nothing more. There is no mass admission or Broadway to Holy heaven. Jesus said: "Enter by the narrow gate; for wide is the gate and broad is the way that leads to destruction, and there are many who go in by it. Because narrow is the gate and difficult is the way which leads to life, and there are few who find it. "(Matthew 7:13 -14). Are there churches and people on the Broadway today? Clearly, the default position is hell, not heaven. How do you enter by the narrow gate if the "substitutionary death of Jesus Christ," as theologians call the crucifixion, has "paid for our sins or nailed our sins to the cross"? That theology that accommodated slave trade and slavery for over

250 years in protestant Dixie and over 300 years in Roman Catholic Brazil is not the Gospel of Jesus Christ. It is victor theology.

How many times do preachers remind listeners that this is an evil world? The slave- trading church controlled that world when the Spirit-filled Holy Catholic mother Church ended. By not asking for the Holy Spirit to replace the evil spirit in man, the church allowed the ugly side of man to thrive. Nothing has changed. "Compassion: A Global History of Social Policy" by Professor Alvin Finkel is a depressing account of imperial power. If a private institution did what the church Establishment allowed, that institution will be charged for crimes against humanity. History makes people uncomfortable because it was brutal. Today is a day in history. What men and terrorists still do can make future generations ashamed. What religious people did centuries ago would make a normal teenager ashamed to be a human being.

Nobody should be too critical of those who are not the Establishment but the successors of the Roman Empire Establishment. To be a Pastor, Priest, Nun or an Evangelist is an extraordinary sacrifice. In a materialistic world, the men and women who took a vow of poverty and celibacy in order to serve the Almighty are worthy of beatification and a place in heaven. But following the theology and liturgy designed by medieval minds make no sense in the 21st century. Children cannot be rebuked for the sins of their parents but for following their parent's footsteps. To err is human. But when we are criticized, the first reaction is to be defensive. And even crucify the messenger. The first reaction should be to assess if the criticism has some validity that merits changes, particularly when the mistakes were made by men who passed away over a thousand years ago. It requires an open mind. Do the new gatekeepers of religion and laity have an open mind to see the mistakes of the old gatekeepers of centuries past? And then feel the pain of those who were enslaved and colonized through power theology? If not, the reader may revisit "The Blind Men and the Elephant" by John Godfrey Saxe. The allegory helps to see the world from God's perspective and not from a cultural perspective.

If gold is tarnished, bronze looks better. When Christians auctioned off men, women and children for slavery; to the Atheist, Voodoo, the religion of the slaves looked better than Christianity, the religion of the slave masters. When slave traders, slave masters, auctioneers and their priests, lived off the avails of unpaid servitude in the New World, including New France, Voodoo looked more moral. One can imagine how the slaves in America and the Caribbean were treated when Haiti fought off Napoleon's troops. It was all because the church fathers conveniently excluded teaching the slave masters and themselves, to "Observe all things whatsoever I have commanded you "as Jesus said. That is still the case to this day. It takes a born-again Christian to see the world from God's perspective.

"Go ye therefore, and teach all nations." That was done. "Baptizing them in the name of the Father and of the Son and of the Holy Ghost." That was done. "Teaching them to observe all things whatsoever I have commanded you:" That's where the problem lies. Was that segment lost in translation or ignored for convenience? The victor theology smothered that clause because it is a disservice to imperialism. The Holy Communion is a sacrament. As the body of Christ, the church cannot fail to observe it. But in 2,000 years how many Christians were taught to be born again and live by the Gospel? It did not happen. Imperialism smothered that mandate. Still, it was easy to believe that relatives who were not born again went home to be with the Lord, particularly, when buried in the church graveyard.

In the exercise of worldly power, the church fathers used slavery to enforce celibacy and opened the pandora's box. They were the first Christians to disobey God's Golden Rule – Treat others the same way you want them to treat you. Slavery lasted for about 250 years in America and was ended, not by the church Establishment that owned slaves and defended slavery, but by men and women of goodwill. It took Abraham Lincoln to tell the church that "If slavery is not wrong, nothing is wrong." He was not a member of any church. In fact, in Dixie, nothing was wrong if you believed in Jesus Christ because He died for your past, present and future sins. That was the doctrine. This spurious Broadway doctrine for endless malfeasance has endured. The Broadway must be overcrowded as a consequence of the half-truth. Sacrificial lambs died for past sins, not for the present or future sins.

Everything that can go wrong was yet to go wrong. The greatest and deadliest of the things out of the Pandora's box was flawed evangelism that perverted the Gospel. For example, the Jesuits, the society of Jesus, of all people, owned about 300 African slaves. They sold 272 slaves to save Georgetown university from bankruptcy. How could they teach the Golden Rule with moral authority? It is abundantly obvious that church leaders perverted the Gospel of Jesus Christ. They misrepresented Jesus Christ. Additionally, even if they understood the will of God, theocracies knew that religion is a powerful tool to control people. Having lost the moral authority to teach the Golden Rule, the church fathers offered weekly absolutions or forgiveness of sins to every confessor including themselves, in lieu of being born again. For centuries, the laity never read the Bible to know that a Christian must be born again, as Jesus said. Students graduate from college and begin to practice their profession. Christians should graduate from Bible study, become born again and live by the Gospel. It has not happened. Nobody graduates from Bible study. If they do, it would be reflected in governance. They were not taught. If the students didn't learn, the teacher didn't teach.

How do you teach the Golden Rule to people under colonial rule? African slaves were not allowed to learn to read and write. If they read the Gospel, it would be obvious that the slave master's faith was based on hypocrisy. So, they were not allowed to read and write. The Moravians tried to teach them. Clearly, evangelism did not fulfill all the mandate of the Great Commission. The partial compliance explains why the world is not better than it is today after 2,000 years of the Gospel. Latin America, for example, has enough Saints to be venerated every single day of the year. Yet, after over 400 years of Christianity, Latin America is plagued by social turbulence. Were they really following Christ? The leaders and followers were never taught to be born again Christians who live by the Gospel. Instead, they received weekly absolutions or forgiveness of sins. How can any man change, if his sins are forgiven every week? That was the same theology that sustained slave trade and slavery for centuries.

If there is no law, lawlessness will be understandable. But there is. If there is no God, wars, terrorism, and inhumanity will be understandable. But there is the God of Creation who knows man inside and out. Since human beings will do to others what they don't want others to do to them, He issued the Golden Rule. "Treat others the same way you want them to treat you" makes sense to anyone who is a human being. And it comes with the offer of the Helper, the Holy Spirit, if only one would ask. The Christmas week, for example, is a week of mass decorum. It is not genuine because, without the Holy Spirit, it is a superficial change. The hypocrisy fizzles out in January. A Latin American woman interviewed on BBC's Hardtalk said: "I have been married three times. If I live long enough, I might be married four times." The epidemic of divorce is the product of the victor theology that nullified the Golden Rule and enslaved Africans for over 300 years in Roman Catholic Brazil. Now, the vast majority of the world's population see through the eyes of the Gospel, not through the eyes of the victor theology that led to slave trade, slavery, colonialism and endless conflicts.

Consider this: Adolf Hitler's mother was known to be a devout Catholic. If Adolf Hitler, Benito Mussolini, Napoleon Bonaparte, Joseph Stalin and Francisco Franco were taught that a Christian must be born again; that a born-again Christian lives by the Gospel, world history would have been very different. Living by the Golden Rule is one visible proof or evidence of a born-again Christian. The corruption of every facet of life goes back to the failure to teach converts "to observe all things whatsoever I have commanded you." The victor theologians led Christians to believe that they don't have to live by the Gospel. The empty pews and "Church for Sale "signs result from declining trust and declining faith. The evangelical pulpit can blame the "backsliders," but according to an old adage, if the students didn't learn, the teacher didn't teach. "And why call ye Me' Lord, Lord,' Jesus said, "and do not the things which I say?" (Luke 6:46). That is a good question for the evangelicals who do not teach members how to live by the Golden Rule but by Amazing Grace.

Jesus also said: "By this shall all men know that ye are my disciples, if ye have love one to another." (John 13:35). If a Christian would go to kill fellow Christians, except in self-defense; sell weapons to kill fellow Christians or invest in instruments of bloodshed; and do to others what he does not want others to do to him, obviously, the faith is a sham. It is self-deceit, perverted religion and flawed evangelism. To follow Jesus Christ is to do the things that He said to do – the Golden Rule, the Great Commandment and the New Commandment. It is counter culture. The victor theology blends culture and Christianity. It is no longer Christianity because culture directs the way people behave. One leads to peace and goodwill to all. The other leads to wars, colonialism, slave trade, slavery and more. In Haiti, for example, the Masters blended Christianity and Culture while the slaves blended Christianity and Voodoo. It leads to chaos.

Sudan is illustrative of the flaw in evangelism. After 20 years of bloody conflict between the Christian South and the Janjaweed Arab militia, the U.N. helped the South to secede from the Muslim North in 2011 to avoid another Biafra. Based on the Gospel of Jesus Christ which they professed, one would expect the Christians to live in harmony, regardless of ethnicity. But by 2013, the "Christian"

South was at each other's throat. Why? Just as Christians slaughtered each other in two World Wars, Southern Sudan descended into the hell of ethnic cleansing. Like everywhere else, Christian converts were not taught that a Christian must be born again; that a born-again Christian lives by the Gospel. Otherwise, he or she is not born again. Treat others the same way you want them to treat you makes sense to any human being regardless of culture, religion, ethnicity, gender or political ideology.

Why would anyone kill his wife and child? Born again Christians do not kill each other. Those who are not do. Why are the Christians in Moscow and Washington, DC in perpetual conflict? It is the same reason. When "teaching them to observe all things whatsoever I have commanded you" is made null and void, spirituality based on quantity replaces spirituality that is based on quality. The old church fathers strongly believed and taught, not evolution, but Creation and the descent of humankind from one couple named Adam and Eve. But while the enslavement of one of those descendants was normal in America, in South Africa the tone of the skin determined the value of a human being. Now under # MeToo, the women whose predecessors saw nothing wrong in slavery and apartheid want men to know that gender should not determine the value of a human being.

With few exceptions, the Third World nations were once under Christian colonial powers. It was an opportunity to highlight the difference between a global religion and cultural religions. Why is Christianity now on the defensive? Why is it in decline? Since the imperial medieval church fathers opened that pandora's box - with the use of slavery to enforce celibacy - every facet of life and subsequent events have been leading up to" church for sale." Christianity is on the defensive because evangelism lost the moral authority to preach and teach the full Gospel of Jesus Christ that includes the Golden Rule. The church that should separate itself from the world used imperial power to create and become the world it now complains about. It is obvious that many of the hundreds or thousands of denominations are going the wrong way. Yet, with a sense of moral superiority, and mindless of history, anyone with a microphone can call on listeners to donate money to evangelize "the darkest corners of the world" with a doctrine that does not change lives. Anyone who does not understand the Gospel should not teach the Bible. The gap between the Gospel of Jesus Christ and what is practiced must be closed.

If the church were a corporation with shareholders, there would have been a change of management over 1,000 years ago or after two World wars. The church Establishment does not issue a visa to heaven or guarantee eternal life. It is composed of volunteers. In a sense, through the collection plate, the parishioners or laity are shareholders. Jesus Christ rescued His followers from the Pharisees who held the Jews as spiritual hostages in the name of God. Can the same happen to Christians? When we are led to believe that our sins -past, present and future - are forgiven; that once saved always saved; and then resist social justice, and do nothing to make amends for past wrongs, it is not Christianity but self -deceit. That was the mindset that kept slavery alive for over 300 years. Buyer beware applies to religion.

Without a doubt, if the Great Commission proceeded as expected, there would have been no new religions in both the Old and the New Worlds. After 2,000 years, every nation would have been like a Canadian Hutterite colony with education, healthcare and employment for every family, and life beyond the grave. That is the abundant life that Jesus Christ came to offer (John 10:10). It is an economy based on the social implications of the Gospel. The imperial church derailed it. The Hutterites do not have to choose between their stomach and their conscience. They do not have to choose between support for employers or support for employees. They live life holistically in a steady- state economy that is a model of God's world, not Satan's world. Other Christians hear about the end-time without experiencing the abundant life that Jesus Christ came to offer. It cannot be emphasized enough that "teaching them to observe all things whatsoever I have commanded you" is more than the Eucharist. When we think of the failure of church leaders to fulfill the mandate of the Great Commission and the resultant European wars, World Wars, colonial wars, colonialism, slave trade, slavery, apartheid, pornography, scams, unemployment, homelessness, terrorism, family violence and divorce, what is the solution other than to boycott the church and begin anew?

After 2,000 years of Christianity every nation on earth should have been like a Canadian Hutterite colony through the influence of the Gospel, even if the people do not believe in God. The world cannot get there in the next 2,000 years by doing the same things over and over expecting a different outcome. Many evangelists have used John 3:16 like the message of a town crier. So, converts would believe in Jesus Christ and still live the ungodly cultural values of human nature. That was the case with the slave traders, auctioneers and slave masters for about 250 years in America and 300 years in Roman Catholic Brazil when they had segregated graveyards. That is still the case to this day in segregated churches and neighborhoods. The Church of the slave masters has left an indelible mark.

The Will of God

The Israelites believed in God. The Arabians believed in God. The Christian Gentiles believed in God. They all knew that Satan can believe in God without doing the will of God. Everyone is a catalyst for change. If there are numerous Christian denominations, is it because they don't know the will of God? Now, after 2,000 years, if monotheists don't know the will of God, they may never know. So, what is the will of God? Under the Old Covenant, the Hebrews had learned and were guided by the Ten Commandments. Then Prophet Micah summarized God's will for each one: "He has shown you, O man, what is good; and what does the LORD require of you but to do justly, to love mercy, and to walk humbly with your God?" (Micah 6:8). In the New Covenant for all of humankind, the will of God is still good relations between man and man, and between them and the God of Creation. That is self-evident from the Gospel.

The Parable of the Good Samaritan broadened the concept of neighbor. That is Christianity. Everything we need to know is in the Bible and what we know is more important than what we don't know. His will is for personal and collective wellbeing and accountability. So, life is a test in the exercise of free will. Adam and Eve did not kill anyone. They did not rob anyone. They did not commit adultery. They ate the forbidden fruit. Disobedience of God is sin. Abraham was shown to obey. He passed the test. So, we are here on earth to participate both individually and collectively in the struggle between obedience and disobedience of God. In that struggle, some are inclined to obedience, some are inclined to disobedience, and the rest are on both sides or neutral. Those inclined to obedience are the few on the narrow and difficult way.

In some denominations, the prophecy preachers see wars, starvation and empty pews as a fulfillment of prophecy. Therefore, they are justified to do nothing. In some other denominations, they receive weekly absolutions and spiritual palliative care until they depart to heaven. Is there any hope when leaders do not learn from history? In the first World War about 20 million people were killed without divine intervention. In the second World War about 50 million people were killed including six million Jews. Israel's expected Messiah did not come to intervene. In the Biafra War, people watched hundreds of thousands of babies and children starve to death. There was no divine intervention. In the Middle East, Arabians still kill themselves, spreading refugees whose impact will not be known for generations. There is no divine intervention. And in Israel it takes a miracle to form a government. In 2020, thousands of Italians died in the Covid- 19 pandemic. Prayers from the Vatican did not help. In the past 2,000 years, what does God's silence teach us? It is: "obey My commandments. See you at the end of your history." The question now is: will the commandments be obeyed even by Christians?

The Volunteer Clergy

As far as we know, in Judaism, Christianity and Islam, nobody was appointed like Prophet Moses, King David or Saint Peter. What we have are volunteer spiritual gatekeepers. Now, what language and words can show that our problems are the result of the failure or refusal of the volunteers to implement "teaching them to observe all things whatsoever I have commanded you," as Jesus said. The Golden Rule – "Treat others the same way you want them to treat you" makes all the difference in human relations. And it makes sense to anybody who is a human being regardless of culture, ethnicity, gender, religion or political ideology. About 2,000 years ago, strongmen of the cloth had to choose one of two pathways. While wearing that cloth, they chose the way of culture, not the way that is counterculture.

The world is still on that Broadway of culture, not the narrow and difficult Gospel way. Nobody today, not even the Pope can be blamed for the mistakes made and institutionalized over a thousand years ago. But the failure or refusal to teach billions of Christians to observe all things that Jesus Christ commanded, including the Golden Rule, is a crisis of leadership that has been building up for centuries. It is frustrating to see volunteers do the same things over and over expecting a different result while holding the rest of humankind as spiritual hostages. In the Acts of the Apostles, for example, converts were led to receive the Holy Spirit to enable them live the Gospel. Power corrupts. Their successors offered absolutions or assurances that once saved always saved. And so, "all we liked sheep have gone astray," yet again.

The Habakkuks of the world would think that a mass boycott of the church or more empty pews will alert the church fathers who control the spiritual compass. It will not. Some church fathers see declining church attendance, wars, starving children and crime as the signs of the last days or a fulfillment of Bible prophecy, not the consequences of a flawed theology. They cite St. Paul's private letter to Pastor Timothy: "Now the Spirit expressly says," he wrote, "that in latter times some will depart from the faith, giving heed to deceiving spirits and doctrines of demons, speaking lies in hypocrisy, and having their own conscience seared with a hot iron "(1 Timothy 4:1-2 NKJV). Suppose these Epistles were not discovered! If many Christians have lost faith in the church leaving empty pews; if evangelism has stalled for lack of funds; and if some churches are being sold and converted to commercial use for the growing culture of materialism, all these are seen as a fulfillment of that prophecy. Therefore, there is no need to change. Does "church for sale "presage evangelism that has reached the point of diminishing returns?

The end is not near. Dooms Day is not at hand. Most Christians who leave the pews empty did not depart from the faith, but from victor theology, theoretical Christianity and the abuse of office. St. Paul's private letter to Timothy cannot be a self-fulfilling prophecy that allows good Christians to do nothing and let the church collapse. After 2,000 years, the laity has yet to see the Gospel translated into a caring society like a Canadian Hutterite colony because they subscribe to victor theology. What they see on television are politics and law "speaking lies in hypocrisy." Parents who were misled by their own parents will likely mislead their children. Professors who were misled by their own professors will likely mislead their students. And theologians who were misled by their predecessors will likely mislead their congregation. That has been the history of the church before and after the Reformation. The Reformers worried about the sale of Indulgence. But not being born again is more serious than the sale of Indulgence. How many Christians today believe that denominational differences are relevant to salvation; that celibacy is essential to a call to serve; that the Pope including those who ignored slavery for over 300 years can be infallible; and that a priest can offer absolution or forgiveness of sin to his parents? Theologians who were misled by their predecessors will likely mislead their successors and parishioners. When and how will it end?

The year 2020 may be the year that exposed how man's self-interests trumped the eternal verities of the Gospel. It all began when slave trade, slavery, colonialism and evangelism all worked in tandem because the old Establishment structured Christianity in their own image - the image of an imperial power. Today the new gatekeepers who control religion are in their denominational head-quarters, following the footsteps of the old gatekeepers and doing the same things over and over expecting a different result. They and they alone, not you and me, not even the local pastor, can change the trajectory of the church by completing all the terms of the Great Commission. Millions of relatives have been converted or were born into Christianity. Millions have been offered weekly absolutions. Millions have been assured that once saved, always saved. And millions have died without being taught that a Christian must be born again and live by the Gospel. How do you teach the Golden Rule to people in slavery or under colonial rule? To teach them to observe the Golden Rule would be an admission of guilt. That quagmire can deter a U-turn.

So, we keep going with the theology that Jesus has died to pay our sin debt – past, present and future. That is self-deceit. The God of Creation knew, didn't He, that not only in Israel but everywhere, cultural conservatives like the Pharisees will do to others what they don't want others to do to them. That is the reason for the Golden Rule. The victims and villains of slavery, Nazism and colonialism belong to a past generation. What prevents a U-turn from victor

theology? Conversion produces quantity; obedience to what is commanded produces quality. That's what is missing in evangelism to
this day. It has to be said again and again before the Apostles say it
at the end of history: If the students didn't learn, the teacher didn't
teach. People volunteer to do what is right not what is wrong. Now,
imagine a tourist who went to a faraway country. He came home
with a very cheap Rolex watch. It looked very real but it was an
imitation. A Christian, even a born-again Christian cannot be Jesus
Christ, but can be an imitation of Jesus Christ. It has not happened
because "teaching them to observe all things whatsoever I have
commanded you" has been ignored and there is nothing ordinary
Christians can do.

Televangelism

Does televangelism contribute to empty pews? Every televangelist
must have a catalogue of entertaining anecdotes. Some are about
overcoming adversity, rarely on preventing adversity. Sports heroes
have been used to promote Christianity. Someone believes that they
will lead people to become Christians just like marketing sports
shoes. The publicity may well be distractions from compliance to
the Gospel and its social implications. As seen on television, the
church has been changing. The church is not a show, a bookshop, a
place for entertainment or a school that teaches students who never
graduate. It is a place of worship. From what they see on television,
pagans and atheist must wonder if Christians go to church to worship God or to be entertained. Does anyone there feel the presence
of the Holy Spirit or feel entertained when they leave? Even before
the mandate expressed in the Great Commission is fully understood
and practiced, Christianity has morphed into an entertainment and
marketing industry.

Some preachers have published over a dozen books that their

followers buy and read to understand the mysterious Bible. Yet chapter 13 of this book (Christianity for Dummies), shows that the Gospel of Jesus Christ is not difficult for a teenager to understand. If God wants people to be saved, why would He make it difficult to understand? How do you become a born again Christian if you have been distracted from being born again? How do you observe the Golden Rule if born into a culture that does not treat others the same way they want to be treated? "When Culture Overrules God and Reason" shows that the church is part of the culture that overruled God and reason when it used slavery to enforce celibacy and became a slave holder. Since culture directs human behavior, the church was resistant to Christian civilization. There is a difference between "telling" and "teaching." In a Canadian Hutterite colony, for example, the worship and telling experience is in the chapel. The teaching or practical experience is in the activities of daily living. Day after day, every negative events in the news should be weighed against God's Golden Rule. In every event, the question should be -would it have happened if those involved learned to observe the Golden Rule?

Since clergy and laity lived off the avails of unpaid servitude that only ended through a civil war, there is nothing that suggests that in liturgy, routine or habit, the church Establishment has changed. There has not even been repentance, contrition or reconciliation with God or man. The world will not change course until the policy makers are converted from the Dixie brand of Christianity to the Hutterites brand of Christianity. If the church does not acknowledge and redress the wrongs of the past and teach new converts to observe all that Jesus Christ commanded, including the Golden Rule, obviously, the church has lost its mission and relevance. The rise of Adolf Hitler was a presentiment of the coming antichrist. The church did not teach the Gospel and still does not teach the Gospel. That negligence paved the way for Adolf Hitler and may be paving the way for the antichrist. Instead, victor theology taught that the crucifixion of Jesus on the Roman cross was the Gospel. That it was a substitutionary death that paid our sin debt to allow us to continue life as usual. But He was on the cross as the Lamb of God to end all animal sacrifices.

The U.S.A is the world's largest social laboratory. The journey from the distant past to the present shows the snail-slow progression of social evolution, even in a Bible belt. How does the rest of the world explain America's gun culture? It may be based on fear. That fear is more intense in Dixie than in Washington State or Alaska, for example. Unofficial research based on common sense indicates that it may be the fear of retaliation on the slave masters by the survivors of slavery. But that generation has passed away. A PBS television program "Finding Your Roots" shows that there are African Americans who bear the genes of the slave masters. Some were slave masters themselves. Yet, every year Americans kill relatives more than they kill enemies abroad. And spend more on military hardware than on social justice.

Every generation has a duty to repair the damage done by their predecessors. There is no such interest where churches are segregated. This again shows the failure of evangelism to fulfill the mandate of the Great Commission – "teaching them to observe all things whatsoever I have commanded you." In the past one thousand years or more, how many Christians were taught to observe the Gospel? That is the problem. A Christian must be born again. If African and African American Priests and Pastors are not teaching parishioners to be born again and observe all that Jesus Christ commanded, including the Golden Rule, they are perpetuating the victor theology that ruined their lives. That is the lesson to learn after all the sad events of 2,000 years of Christianity.

The world is in a mess and there is no end in sight because if Christians do not practice the Gospel, who will practice it? It is more important to practice the Gospel than to practice Christianity that means different things to different people. Jesus did not tell the woman condemned for being a sinner to continue and come back for absolution; but to "go and sin no more." The Puritans, the Quakers and Moravians waned because they could not compete with the denominations that offered an easy Broadway to salvation through weekly absolutions or Amazing Grace. Now the next are the few Pentecostals who know that a Christian must ask for the Holy Spirit (Luke 11 :13) to be born again and stop doing to others what they don't want others to do to them. Unfortunately, some Pentecostal zealots have turned away potential good Christians by insisting on speaking in tongues.

Since slave trade and slavery, and since the Reformation, some denominations have sent their dead "home to be with the Lord" through weekly absolutions while others have done so through His Amazing Grace; all without doing the will of the Lord. Unfortunately, no relative can phone or send an email to confirm that those who have been sent home to be with the Lord are really there. Why did the God of Creation command the observance of the Golden Rule? The slave economy shows that in every culture, there are men and women who do to others what they don't want others to do to them even as they carry or wear the cross. The slave trade, slavery, colonialism, segregation and apartheid cannot be erased from history. At the end of World War 11, it became clear that a cultural-conservative minority can mislead the majority. Good people must no longer allow bad people to define them through a theology that does not change lives. That is the hope that will make the future better than the ungodly past.

The fact that Christian denominations are numerous suggests that Christianity means different things to different denominations. The obfuscatory dogma from the Medieval Age of Ignorance has been iteratively embellished, leaving many converts unsure of what Christianity is about. Is Christianity about good relations between people and between them and God Almighty or is it that Jesus died for our sins and made the commandments null and void? The former is the Gospel, the latter is victor theology. Even after the

Reformation both the Roman Catholics and Protestants did not see buying and selling men, women and children to be enslaved for life, as evil capitalism. They continued business as usual because Jesus died for man's past, present and future sins. Our sins have been nailed on the cross, thanks to the Romans. The narrative was that if you believe in Jesus Christ, you can do as you please. The commandments are irrelevant. If the dogma did not change the lives of the slave traders, slave masters and clergy, why will it change anyone today? Since victor theology does not change lives, the people who will be in church next Sunday are not the people who can change society. It is like preaching to the deer in the jungle. Some Christians struggling with the contradictions of Christianity have left the pews empty.

The Gospel has failed to bring peace to the world because it has not been practiced. The victor theology is not the Gospel. It no longer appeals to any rational mind today. It turned the Gospel of Jesus Christ upside down and fostered numerous wars, slave trade, slavery and colonialism. It enabled the clergy and laity to live off the avails of slavery for centuries. There is yet no remorse, no repentance, no contrition, no restitution and no reconciliation with God who is obligated to answer prayers. The Almighty God punished disobedient Israel, and allowed them to endure captivity in Assyria and Babylon. It is not in God's divine nature to ignore sin and answer prayers.

In two World Wars, millions of people prayed before they died. There was no divine intervention. Some of the six million Holocaust victims probably prayed. There was no divine intervention. In the Biafra war (1967 - 70) hundreds of thousands of babies and children were starved to death despite the prayers of their mothers. Is there a greater need for God's response than for dying children? In the Covid- 19 pandemic over five million people died despite many prayers. In the next pandemic, nothing will change. There will be prayers and no response. Life makes sense to those who believe that we live in a God-forsaken world just as it was for 400 years before

Jesus Christ came. There was a precondition for God to answer prayers: "If my people, which are called by my name, shall humble themselves, and pray, seek my face, and turn from their wicked ways; then will I hear from heaven, and will forgive their sin, and will heal their land." (2 Chronicles 7:14). It was ignored. Man has to act before God will respond. It didn't happen in ancient Israel. Perhaps they didn't know who and where to initiate the call to action. Today we know who and where to start. It is Europe not America. The victor theology, slave trade, slavery, colonialism, and the bloodiest wars all began from Europe. The Truth can be uncomfortable but it sets people free.

Revival

Evangelical Christians are forever praying for revival. Those who call for prayers for revival and for living the Christian life (whatever it means to them) always look elsewhere not within. They expect repentance and revival to begin with the man and woman on the streets not with the Church Establishment that supported and lived off the avails of slavery for centuries without repentance. How does God answer prayers without repentance, without restitution, and without reconciliation? How does a Christian live the Gospel without being directed to ask for the Holy Spirit who makes it possible to be born again and live by the Gospel? To trust Jesus as Lord and Savior is not enough to change lives or the world. To called Jesus "Lord, Lord" and do not what he says does not change lives or the world. The slave traders, slave masters and clergy trusted Jesus as Lord and Savior. They had "In God We Trust" stamped on their currency. They did not live by the Gospel. They did not trust and obey. When the slaves were creating prosperity at their own expense, it was easy for the master's family to count their blessings, trust but not obey.

The United States has a long list of global evangelists. There was Reverend D. L Moody, Reverend Billy Sunday, Reverend Rex Humbard, Reverend Oral Robert, Reverend Evelyn Wyatt, Reverend Billy Graham, Reverend Robert Schuller and Reverend Pat Robertson to name a few. Evangelist Billy Graham traveled around the world to convert millions of people to Christianity. How many became born again Christians only God knows. Still, America is in social chaos. In September 2023, Wallace Smith, an American magazine editor asked: Why is our civilization becoming so uncivilized – dominated by a culture of hate and contempt for one another"? Christian civilization requires a man to be born again and live by the Golden Rule, the Great Commandment and the New Commandment. Paradoxically, even Christians are resistant to Christian civilization. The Church of Jesus Christ came to fix the world. Now, both the church and the world are dying a slow death because Jesus Christ was misrepresented when the Apostles passed away. Every generation has been following their footsteps without the vision to change course.

After 2000 years do we know who is on the Broadway and who is on the difficult and narrow way? Do we know the sheep and the goats? Every culture has resisted Christian civilization because culture directs human behavior. The Gospel is counterculture. The Golden Rule, the Great Commandments and the New Commandment are all counterculture. The much-cited St Paul charged: "Bear one another's burdens and so fulfill the law of Christ "(Galatians 6:2 NKJV). To those who are dyed in culture, this is godless communism. Yet, as Christians, they look forward to the return of Jesus Christ or to be in heaven. What kind of government are they looking forward to? The Kingdom of God is not a democracy. The Gospel will not become part of the cultural fabric of any nation until the vast majority are born again. If the above evangelists could not change even their home State to continually live by the Gospel, none of the numerous televangelists we see today can change their hometown. If this is true, televangelism must be nothing but a profitable show. If Evangelical Christians understand the Gospel and believe in God, they must demand a government that runs the economy like the Canadian Hutterites. They have employment for every family, education for their children, universal health care for all, and life beyond the grave. That is the abundant life that Jesus came to offer 2,000 years ago. That economy is long overdue.

The Old Covenant teaches what God has done in the past. A Christian must choose between what people who have not been to heaven and back say about God and what God Almighty says in the Bible about Himself. It is presumptuous if not arrogant, to appear to know more about God than what is revealed in the Bible. Exodus 34:6-7 shows that He is the God of mercy as well as the God of justice. A murderer and his victim cannot end up in heaven. He punished the Israelites for disobedience and allowed them to fall into captivity in Assyria and Babylon for disobedience. The people were forsaken for 400 years before Jesus Christ came.

During slavery, the Church had revival camp meetings. When hundreds of people came forward to accept Jesus Christ as Lord and Savior, it was said to be a revival. Those men and women described as "Sinners saved by grace" returned home to continue slave trade and slavery. Since those camp meetings, a Christian is still understood to be a sinner saved by grace and not liable to the Golden Rule, the Great Commandment and the New Commandment. Such pockets of Christians have been revived again and again because the Holy Spirit was not there. Victor theology is not a life changer.

When the church is resistant to Christian civilization, it does not need a revival but a second reformation to a free church that conforms to the will of God; a church that for once, teaches converts to ask for the Holy Spirit and live by God's commandments that Victor theology made null and void. An evangelistic crusade to revive Christians and convert new ones has never changed a nation.

Sinners saved by grace will always do to others what they don't want others to do to them.

In the 1970s there was "Jesus' people" in America. It fizzled out because the Protestant victor theology is not the Gospel. Theoretical Christianity is theoretical Christianity. "My God shall supply all your needs" was not part of the experience of those youths. Anyone born into what is known as a Christian family can easily be disillusioned. Believing in Jesus Christ as Lord and Savior did not solve their problems. They needed practical Christianity like the Hutterites. But to get along people go along even in Dixie. So, nothing changes. There is no cleric who was appointed by God Almighty. They are all volunteers. In tragedy after tragedy those who have volunteered to serve are asked why God allows pain and suffering. And why bad things happen to good people. They do not have a good answer. Given man's history of malfeasance without repentance and reconciliation, can one answer be that we live in a Godforsaken world? God's work must be done in God's way, not in man's way. The prerequisite to answer prayers, 2 Chronicles 7:14, applies to Jews and Gentiles because God has not changed.

Bertrand Russell was born into a Christian family. He published Why I am not a Christian, a critique of the religion he was born into. Similarly, Ibn Warraq published a critique of Islam titled Why I am not a Muslim. No rational mind can be converted based on what Christians and Muslims have done in history. The Acts of the Apostles show that the first century Church of Jews and Gentiles was inspired and directed by the Holy Spirit. The Roman strongmen of the cloth who took over the Church were faced with two pathways. One pathway was the Gospel way that involves the Golden Rule, the Great Commandment and the New Commandment. The other pathway was the imperial culture way. While wearing the garb of Christianity, they chose the culture way in a religion that is counter culture. They designed sacraments from cradle to grave, with confession and absolution along the way. That victor theology was the paganized Christianity that discarded the Gospel. A Christian convert no longer has to ask for the Holy Spirit and be born again or regenerated. That is how victor theology, the culture way, led to numerous wars in Europe, and two bloody World Wars. That is how the culture way led to colonial wars, colonialism, slave trade, and slavery. That was how clergy and laity lived off the avails of slavery for centuries. That was how the Jesuits, the society of Jesus, owned and sold 272 of their tobacco plantation slaves to save Georgetown university from bankruptcy.

For God to heal the land, it requires more than a personal response. It requires a national response. It requires repentance, restitution and reconciliation with God and man. It has not happened because the Establishment is either defiant or believes in infallibility. The preachers on radio, television and on the pulpits in North America blame modern culture for everything that is wrong in the world. And their perceived anti-Christian sentiments by the liberal elite. Have they considered Truth and reconciliation with God and man after centuries of slave trade and slavery endorsed by the Church? And the fact that for centuries, clergy and laity lived off the avails of slavery in the evil world? We cannot know God or do what is right without suspending ethnocentricity. If parishioners assemble because they have shared values, an African will be foolish to embrace a religion that enslaved their people for centuries.

The same applies to aboriginal peoples and colonial peoples. But the problem is not religion, but the victor theology that replaced the Gospel. The culprits of the imperial past have all passed away. Today, the culprits and not the Liberals, Socialists or the spiritual conservatives who treat others the same way they want others to treat them. The culprits are the cultural conservatives and agnostics resistant to change and amends to the wrongs committed in the past by men of similar mindset. Hence, nobody can preach the Gospel – the Golden Rule, the Great Commandment and the New Commandment – without being attacked by the men who conserve the cultural values

of human nature. "That's not who we are" has become the mantra
for progressives still resisting those who conserve culture. Slave trade,
slavery and colonialism are milestones in human history. Terrorism
will also be in the historical past. Those who have been tortured will
agree that it is the spirit of God that separates the human being from
the human animal. The Gospel is the future. The victor theology is a
theology against the will of God Almighty. It is futile. The tragedy is
the millions of lives still being lost fighting against the will of God.

Christian governments are known to sell arms to one side in a
conflict and give "humanitarian aid" to the children on the opposite
side dying from starvation. It is antichrist. In spite of the past and in
spite of the resistance to Christian civilization, genuine Christians
can still change the world by practicing the Golden Rule and demanding the same from their neighbors. There is no other choice. It
is easy to blame slave traders, slave masters and empire builders for
historical malfeasance. It is easy to blame one President for fanning
the flames of endemic racism in America. China has not forced
any nation to buy its products. But it is easy to blame China for
trade deficits and mistreatment of its minorities. It is easy to blame
Arabians for Islamic terrorism; and Iran, Russia, and North Korea
for a multitude of transgressions as if we are perfect. What is not easy
to do is recognize the role of the Church Establishment in the state
of the world today. The Church was an accomplice in slave trade
and slavery; it erased the interface between right and wrong, truth
and fallacy; sold slaves to save Georgetown university from bankruptcy; and for centuries, clergy and laity lived off the avails of slavery without contrition, regret, remorse, restitution or reconciliation
with God and man. No nation can fix their politics without fixing
their religion. The Klan cannot change until their church changes.
Those who have suffered historical or present injustices; those who
are victims of crime or neglect; and the children of broken homes
all have a major role to play in civilization.

The Gospel is the blueprint for Christian civilization. It is counterculture. Every culture has been resistant to Christian civilization. Even the Church that participated in slave trade and slavery for centuries was and is resistant to Christian civilization. The slave masters invested in the misery of others. They went to church to thank God for his blessing and Amazing Grace. They died and left the treasures they laid on earth at the expense of their souls. They were misled by victor theologians who ignored the Gospel and used other scriptures as a distraction. Today, their successors who seek the same lifestyle see Galatians 6:2: "Bear one another's burdens and so fulfill the law of Christ" as a radical left agenda. They will also leave their treasures behind in less than fifty years. History repeats itself when similar minds regain power. If no corpse has left this planet with treasures, it makes sense to use government to care for every family like socialist Scandinavia.

Africans, African Americans and native Americans who preach the victor theology they learned in Bible colleges and Seminaries are participants in their own degradation. They should have been preaching the Gospel of Jesus Christ that requires a Christian to be born again and live by the Gospel, not by Amazing Grace. That is what prevents man's inhumanity to man. The slave traders and slave masters were conservative Christians. But there are two kinds of conservative Christians. Spiritually conservative Christians are Christians in the inside. They are born again. They live by the Golden Rule. They treat others the same way they want others to treat them. But like the slave traders, slave masters, and clergy, culturally conservative Christians are Christians on the outside. They are not born again. Therefore, they do to others what they don't want others to do to them. Every conservative party has the two groups struggling for control.

In the selection of David as king of Israel, the Bible states: For the LORD does not see as man sees, for man looks at the outward appearance, but the LORD looks at the heart." (1 Samuel 16:7). The spiritually conservative Christians do not want to be the Lion's family in the human jungle. But the likes of Adolf Hitler and his henchmen who performed experiments on Africans and Jews, are Christians on the outside. They want to be seen as the Lion's family of the human jungle. The church did not teach them to be born again. Is it doing so today? The men who were spiritual on the outside have done more harm to humanity than all the atheists and pagans combined. Nobody was born into the world to be abused by those men (usually men) who have no fear of God or regard for the Golden Rule. If compliance to the Gospel - the Golden Rule, the Great Commandment and the New Commandment - is the test for salvation, how many clergy and laity have passed the test in the past 2,000 years?

The victor theology was designed for imperial interest, not for salvation. The church today is an anachronism if it is not based on the mandate of "teaching them to observe all things whatsoever, I have commanded you." Has it changed? In Lebanon there are Christians whose ancestors were among the first century Christians. The wise men from the East could also be their ancestors, Arabian astronomers. Lebanese Christians understand that if evangelism taught converts to be born again and observe those commandments, all the sad events in history including terrorism, could have been averted. To treat others the same way you want them to treat you, reflects a global religion. But Surah 4:89; 5:18; 6:101; 8:12; 9:30; 9:35 – 36; 47:4; and 98:6 reflect a cultural religion that should be left to culture. An open Pandora's box can produce alarming results, including what has been documented in Stephenblanton.com/growth. If the Gospel is about good relations between people and between them and God Almighty, monotheists must choose either the saving Truth or the victor theology that allowed slave traders, slave masters and clergy to live off the avails of slavery for centuries because – "Jesus died for our sins; Jesus paid our sin debt; our sins were nailed on the cross."

History will show that men who professed to believe in God have killed more people than atheists and pagans combined. Nevertheless, some Christians have done a lot of good and their influence has tamed the world. But because some are born again and others are not; some are spiritually conservative and others are culturally conservative; some are Christians in the inside and others are Christians on the outside; some are doing good and others are not; some live by the Golden Rule and treat others the same way they want to be treated while others do the opposite; the two groups give the church a split personality. As dance partners, they do two steps forward and one step back. The Old Covenant has many interesting events. The Psalms and Proverbs have many good advice. But the Old Covenant is not the New Covenant. Compliance to the Gospel and their social implications is what is required in the New Covenant. It is the essence of the Christian faith.

Spreading the victor theology that sustained slave trade and slavery for centuries is not doing Africans or the world any good. Jesus Christ told His disciples: "If the world hates you, you know that it hated Me before it hated you" (John 15:18). The first century Christians were persecuted for doing the will of God. Christians can also be persecuted for not doing the will of God but the will of culture through victor theology. Some African and Asian leaders who struggled to end colonial rule by Christians were imprisoned for demanding freedom. After colonial rule, some African and Asian Christians were persecuted as surrogates of colonial powers, even when the new persecutors were crass in the abuse of human rights. In all the centuries of wars, treaties and more wars, the Church had no moral influence on society including the society of slave traders. The victor theology and culture were integrated. Similarly, in developing countries the church does not have a moral influence on society. The political culture and victor theology have been partners resisting Christian civilization.

The Bottom Line

Jesus said:" If ye then, being evil, know how to give good gifts unto
your children: how much more shall your heavenly Father give the
Holy Spirit to them that ask him? "(Luke11:13). In 2,000 years, if
this Scripture means anything, how many Christians have asked
for the Holy Spirit? That is the mode of regeneration or being born
again. The second issue here is the Great Commission. It includes
"teaching them to observe all things whatsoever I have commanded
you." In 2,000 years, how many Christians have been taught to
observe the Gospel? It comes through the Holy Spirit. It is the core
of the Christian faith - good relations between people and between
them and the God of Creation. That's the essence of the Christian
faith and means the same in every language and every Bible translation. Clearly if the students didn't learn, the teacher didn't teach.
In fact, the teacher deliberately didn't teach and didn't want to
know the characteristics of a born-again Christian because it did
not serve imperial interest. With those two considerations in mind,
it is obvious why the world is the way it is today after 2,000 years of
Christianity. It will get worse without a Second Reformation that
leads to compliance to the Gospel of Jesus Christ. Christianity based
on Amazing Grace, confession and absolution is not changing the
world and will never change the world. The Church that has become an entertainment center cannot ask people to repent because
it makes them feel guilty or uncomfortable.

Those who peddle unconditional salvation and blessings through
Amazing Grace are not doing themselves and their congregation any
good. The fact that the Almighty is not responding to prayers of petition for basic needs should ring a bell. The only prayer the Church
needs is the Lord's prayer. That's the prayer they need in a Hutterite
colony. Is it not time to try something different? The Romans formulated the victor theology based on sacraments from birth to
death, as an alternative that does not require Christian converts to

ask their heavenly Father for the Holy Spirit, become born again, and live by the Gospel. It leads to equity. Compliance would have prevented all the sad events of history. The great institutions of learning, like Harvard Divinity School, existed for about half a century before the end of slavery. Did they teach the Gospel - the Golden Rule, the Great Commandment and the New Commandment? Or did they watch slave trade, slavery, wars and the epidemic of divorce today and not questioned the incongruity between the Gospel and reality?

If Christianity did not bring peace and goodwill even among Christians who fought so many wars, including two bloody World Wars; if the world is the way it is after 2,000 years of Christianity; the great institutions of learning and the Doctors of Divinity must wonder why! Is the Gospel flawed or not followed? It is either one or the other. Those who live inside a box cannot see the horizon. Several centuries ago, when a king was converted to Christianity, his subjects became Christians. Then "democratically elected" politician replaced the monarch. Perhaps nothing will bring people to God more than converting politician, the new monarchs, to a genuine faith. Those who are born again and live by the Gospel have no fear of what happens after death. But like the slave traders and clergy, those who rely on absolutions and Amazing Grace have reason to be afraid of death.

Presidents and prime ministers send soldiers to kill or be killed in war. When the end is near, they have good reason to worry about life beyond the grave. President Dwight Eisenhower asked Reverend Billy Graham how people can really know if they are going to heaven. President Lyndon Johnson knew that the world listens when a president dies. So, he told Reverend Billy Graham:" Don't use any notes and no fancy eulogizing either. I want you to look into those cameras and just tell 'em what Christianity is all about. Tell 'em how they can be sure they can go to heaven. I want you to preach the Gospel. "Amen to that.

In the past, parents wanted a priest in the family. What they want today is a lawyer in the family. Still, it does not prevent siblings from fighting over their inheritance. As designed by Victor Theology, the priesthood can be a thankless job. Unlike the Protestant denominations, the Roman Catholic denomination has faced decreasing number of priests. Between 1965 and 2012 according to records the number of parishes in the USA without a priest rose from 530 to 3215. Africa is one continent with no shortage of priests. In spite of sexual abuse scandals, celibacy is still a requirement for ordination. Voluntary celibacy and the ordination of women can solve the problem. It will take a second Reformation to change the imperious institution.

An inquiry commissioned by the French Catholic Church in 2018, released their report in October 2021. It showed that since 1950, the clergy have sexually abused some 216, 000 children in France alone. Some were as young as 10 years. The abusers were as many as 3,200. According to a BBC report of 6 February 2019, "Pope Francis has admitted that clerics have sexually abused nuns, and in one case they were kept as sex slaves. He said in that case his predecessor, Pope Benedict, was forced to shut down an entire congregation of nuns who were being abused by priests. "The Vatican's women's magazine, Women Church World, has revealed that in some cases, nuns were forced to abort priest's babies. A female theologian in New Zealand who suffered abuse at the hands of a priest in Lima Peru told the BBC:" The people I trusted, the ones representing God, were fake." Can a sinner forgive sins? Some Christians go to church to receive absolutions or forgiveness of sins week after week. Is it valid? To be fair, the vast majority of priest are devout Christians and the "fake" ones were also the victims of forced celibacy.

Human institutions are prone to corruption. The women sex slaves were abused. Africans were enslaved. The Jesuits, the Society of Jesus, were the biggest slaveholders in America. In 1838, they sold 272 of their slaves to save Georgetown University from bankruptcy.

In an article titled "The Future Of The Catholic Church "(www.firstthings.com on 8.28.23), Russel Shaw wrote: 'In a radio address back in 1969, a young German theologian named Joseph Ratzinger, the future Pope Benedict XV1, saw hard times ahead for the Catholic Church. It will "become small and will have to start afresh more or less from the beginning," he predicted, and the process would be painful. But though smaller, the Church of the future will have been "re-shaped by saints" to become a beacon for people seeking answers to questions of meaning, for which the arrogant secularism of those dark times will have no reply.' That day cannot come soon enough for the millions who will pass away without being born again. Clearly, it is a transition from quantity to quality, from nominal Christians to born again Christians. Pope Benedict XV1 resigned as head of the Roman Catholic church in 2013. If he could not restore the Roman Catholic church to what he envisaged, Roman Catholics may want to know who controls their spiritual destiny.

A Second Reformation

The emancipation of slaves was achieved through war not from the pulpit of a corrupted faith and counterfeit Christianity. The American Civil War did not change the tenor of the church, Roman Catholic or Protestant. It did not restore the moral standard of the Gospel. Christians who believe that the Church of that era went home to be with the Lord can continue doing church as usual. Everyone can be a nominal Christian but few will be born again Christians who live by the Gospel. Those who wear the cross and do to others what they don't want others to do to them show that "the heart is deceitful "but nobody can deceive God. Salvation by either weekly absolutions or by Grace alone is self-delusion because "Not everyone who says to Me "Lord, Lord, "shall enter the Kingdom of heaven," Jesus said, "but he who does the will of My Father in heaven

(Matthew 7:21 NKJV). So, based on Scripture, did the clergy and laity who lived off the avails of slavery for 300 years do the will of God Almighty? Did they go home to be with the Lord? Their doctrine has not changed.

Like the slave traders and clergy, Adolf Hitler, Benito Mussolini, and Joseph Stalin were Christians. Mother Teresa and the rest of us are also Christians. How many variants of a Christian are there? To comply to the Gospel and treat others the same way you want them to treat you, defines a Christian. It is possible through the help of the Holy Spirit. The Apostle John wrote: "Whoever has been born of God does not sin, for His seed remains in him; and he cannot sin, because he has been born of God" (1John 3:9 NKJV). Many Christians have not heard that verse in church. And what is His seed? It is the Holy Spirit. The Holy spirit is the spiritual vaccine against the evil spirit in man. A spiritual rebirth is different from a life of confessions and absolutions. Or merely professing faith in Jesus Christ and wishfully believing that once saved, always saved through God's Amazing Grace. Do Amazing Grace and weekly absolutions nullify the Gospel - the Golden Rule, the Great Commandment and the New Commandment? Obviously, hoping to go home to be with the Lord without doing the will of the Lord is not Amazing Grace, it is amazing self-deceit. It is better to have the wisdom to prevent problems than the expertise to explain what happened after the event.

How will evil or Satan be defeated? Man was created with a free will to obey or disobey; to pursue virtue or vice; to be good or evil; to submit to the Holy Spirit or to the evil spirit called Satan. From slave trade and slavery to the Emancipation; from colonialism and apartheid to freedom; from segregation and disenfranchisement to Civil Rights; from World War 1 and 11 to the European Union, all show that good will overcome evil despite continued resistance to the will of God. That trend leads to optimism and strengthens faith in God because He has the last word. When man's free will is revoked, he can no longer do wrong. The end of Satan will not happen soon enough.

Governments and citizens pay their debt and begin to accumulate new debt. if Jesus paid our sin debt, then we can begin to accumulate new sins by not doing what He says. That is not consistent with "go and see no more." Yet, it was the mindset of the clergy and laity during the centuries of slavery. It is still the mindset of too many clergy and laity to this day. Some Christian denominations simply usher all their members into heaven through weekly absolutions whether the Almighty God likes it or not. They don't need to be born again and sin no more with the help of the Holy Spirit. It is a deadly victor theology. If the church of the slave economy has no hope in the theology that did not change their lives, what hope do we have in following the same victor theology?

Joshua told the Israelites: "And if it seems evil to you to serve the LORD, choose for yourselves this day whom you will serve, whether the gods which your father served that were on the other side of the river, or the gods of the Amorites, in whose land you dwell. But as for me and my house, we will serve the LORD (Joshua 24 :15 NKJV). Christians have a similar decision to make: to serve God or culture. Most politicians do not go to church. What do they know that their electors do not know? Those who believe that the clergy and laity of the slave economy did not "go home to be with the Lord "; and those who believe that the church has not changed, should join the politicians in the exodus from the church to force change. It will not change without a second Reformation. The church will never be what it is supposed to be until we let the imperious church that stood for might is right to collapse and be reborn as the Church of Jesus Christ that stands for the Golden Rule. It is the only way to end conflicts within families, the community, the nation and between nations, particularly the impending conflicts between the East and the West.

A mere 120 years ago, our predecessors were doing what we are doing today. They were inventing, fighting, killing, reproducing, stealing, laying treasures on earth, etcetera. Every single one has passed away. Some died very poor. Some died very rich. Where are they now? Both the rich and the poor passed away and left everything behind just like the rich man and Lazarus. About 120 years from now, everyone alive today will be dead and that history will repeat itself. The billionaires will leave everything behind. King Solomon had hundreds of wives and concubines and all the gold, silver and livestock he could accumulate. The Almighty gave him the wisdom to know the difference between vanity and eternal varieties. He wrote:" Let us hear the conclusion of the whole matter: Fear God, and keep his commandments: for this is the whole duty of man" (Ecclesiastes 12: 13). This history will continue to repeat itself as long as evangelism allows people to abide the evil spirit and claim that Jesus Christ came just to die to free believers from condemnation.

CHAPTER 8

The Symbiosis between Church and State

Let us be clear what Christianity is all about. It is to underscore the incongruity in a partnership of the political culture and a counter -culture religion that is supposed to be separate from the world but became part of the world. The Golden Rule, the Great Commandment and the New Commandment manifest good relations between people and between them and God Almighty. It is herein referred to as the Gospel, and it is. Being a Christian is not about believing in or adhering to the teachings of Christ. It is believing in AND adhering to the teachings of Christ. It is a way of life facilitated by asking for the Holy Spirit. So, Christianity is about good relations between people, and between them and God Almighty. It has to be.

In the distant past, anyone who did not speak your language was an enemy or a potential enemy. They were not "us" but "them." Those who did wrong to the people of other cultures eventually did wrong to the people of their own culture. Who would have believed in that distant past that even in the 21st century those who crossed their cultural militia can suffer the fate of a journalist named Jamal Khashoggi who was killed and dismembered like sheep by his own people? Evil deeds are erased by short memory to make room for the next one. Two thousand years ago, Christianity came to prevent all the sad events in human history and promote compassionate leadership. Still, all have happened because of the corruption of the Gospel of Jesus Christ. In the exercise of worldly power, even after the Reformation, the Gentiles who were the gatekeepers of Christianity became an accessory to the very disorders the Gospel was designed to prevent. Roman Catholicism and Protestantism fought over Latin liturgy, Latin Bible, celibacy of the clergy, the doctrine of transubstantiation, observance of sacraments, church governance by the presbytery or by the episcopacy (bishops), predestination or salvation by good works, papal infallibility and more.

While the monarchies struggled for power between themselves and their subjects, the Roman Catholic and Protestant Church leaders struggled for the hearts and souls of the monarchs. In that struggle for influence and power, they established self- serving partnerships. In all that cacophony, the Church ignored what Christianity is all about - good relations between man and man and between them and the God of Creation. Surely, Satan can cite the scriptures for his purpose. The Epistles aided in that purpose - the corruption of the Christian faith. St. Peter was appointed the head of the Church. Based on what Christians hear in the church, it is obvious that St. Paul was the de facto head of the Church. If the Epistles were not discovered, the world might have been better than it is today. The rulers of the world were pagans. Yet, St. Paul wrote: "Let every soul be subject to the governing authorities. For there is no authority except from God, and the authorities that exist are appointed by God. Therefore, whoever resists the authority resists the ordinance of God, and those who resist will bring judgment on themselves. (Romans 13:1-2 NKJV).

Was he blessing a feudal system? Both the Roman Catholic and

Protestant Establishments believed that on this side of heaven, the Almighty God created inequality and kingdoms were to enforce it. There were clerics vs. laymen; lords vs. serfs; masters vs slaves; and men vs. women. It should be no surprise that the church was opposed to the abolition of slavery to the very end. In that feudal structure, the burden of paying taxes fell on the commoners. To this day, nothing irritates cultural conservatives more than taxes. Church and State became mutually dependent. The enemies of the State were the enemies of the Church and vice versa. Since victor theology was self – sustaining, deviants were suppressed and labelled as heretics. The system was not designed to have compassion for the underclass that Jesus called "one of the least of these My brethren."

Kings and wars tend to go together. In 1327, after over 1,000 years of the Gospel, there was the hundred years' war between England and France. In 1493, Pope Alexander V1 divided the world from the North Pole to the South Pole. He gave Spain the western hemisphere and Portugal the eastern hemisphere. It was a recipe for conflicts between European Kings. By the 1500s there was the Trans-Atlantic commercial slave trade and slavery by men who professed the Christian faith. They needed to grow sugar for their drinks and tobacco to relieve stress. There would be plagues, epidemics and pandemics with mass casualties despite prayers. Some will survive. Some women could be hanged as witches. A massacre of French protestants (Huguenots) would lead to war. All these have happened after 1500 years of the Gospel - good relations between people and between them and God Almighty.

The Romans were the first to establish a standing army that enhanced empire building. By the 1600s mass killing with an army would become an industry. The Thirty Years War (1618 - 48) was probably the beginning of the military industrial complex. In this century, there would be the English Civil Wars (1640 – 1660). There would be the battles for Maritime Supremacy and empire building.

All have happened after 1600 years of the Gospel - good relations between man and man and between them and the God of Creation.

In 1700, there would be the Great Northern War for thrones. The year 1756 would begin the Seven Years' War. Napoleon Bonaparte would rise up and invade countries at will. Britain that came from behind to overtake other nations will begin to ban slave trade after years of opposition to William Wilberforce. There would be colonial wars to control the New World. In that Age of Imperialism, there would be wars to seize Africa in "The Scramble for Africa." This time, in Africa and Asia, it will be to acquired resources, not slaves. By the end of that century, there would be the Boer Wars (1880 – 81; 1899 – 1902) in South Africa. All have happened after 1900 years of the Gospel- good relations between man and man and between them and the God of Creation. In 1865, after nearly 2,000 years of the Gospel, William and Kathrine Booth founded the Salvation Army to care for both the body and soul of those neglected in the partnership or symbiosis between Church and State. London was by and large a homogeneous society.

The 20th century would be yet, the bloodiest in human history. There would be the first World War in which Christians slaughtered fellow Christians by the millions. There would be the Spanish Civil War to control power. And then, there would be the Second World War in which Christians again, slaughtered fellow Christians by the millions; and the Holocaust to settle a long-standing antisemitism. When Church and State are blended in a secular democracy, in war and peace, the national church and State became one and the same in a common purpose. The imperial church was part of the world, not a beacon of morality guiding the nation and the world to do what is right in the sight of God Almighty. And more so when the Golden Rule was made null and void through victor theology. Name a social problem in the world that has no bearing on the disobedience of God's Golden Rule – Treat others the same way you want them to treat you. Adolf Hitler was not one of those who committed atrocities in Africa. Adolf Hitler was Adolf Hitler because he pushed human nature to the limit. He was raised in the system that thanked God for the Sacraments or for Amazing Grace, and he could invoke the name of God. They were not required to be born again or even fake it.

Christian evangelism was always in tow with colonial enterprise, converting pagans to paganized Christianity that had lost the Gospel. it is obvious that at home and overseas, the Church fathers did not teach converts or themselves "to observe all things whatsoever that I have commanded you" as Jesus said, which includes the Golden Rule. Since they received absolutions, most Christians never learned that a Christian must be born again. And with the help of the Holy spirit, live by the Gospel. Offering absolutions is like playing God. In the Boer Wars, as in all wars, on both sides of a conflict, the local church or denomination was on the side of their people, right or wrong, just or unjust. Rome has never said: "Roman Catholics fighting this war are fighting an unjust war." In the UK, Canterbury has never said:" Anglicans fighting this war are fighting an unjust war." The Southern Baptist with headquarters in Nashville, Tennessee has never said:" Baptists fighting this war are fighting an unjust war." It would have made a difference in all wars including the civil war to sustained slavery. It would have made a difference in the Nigeria- Biafra war where thousands of babies and children were deliberately starved to death when big oil ruled the world economy.

In January 2022, Russia and Ukraine were on the verge of war. The Apostles of Jesus Christ would have asked Russia and NATO to justify their military expenditures. Sadly, as usual, the Church on both sides offered unspoken support for their side. Are church sermons changing the world? If after 2,000 years of the Gospel, Russia and NATO are mortal enemies, where is the Gospel of Jesus Christ? Where is the Golden Rule, the Great Commandment and the New Commandment? It is written: "Therefore every tree which does not bear good fruit is cut down and thrown into the fire." (Matthew 3:10 NKJV). Is that the fate of the Church? Is victor theology bearing good fruit? Let us be honest to God and to ourselves. The Church of Rome that introduced slavery, first, as a tool to enforce celibacy, and later as a commercial enterprise, made it difficult to teach the Golden Rule. The church of a colonial power could not teach the Golden Rule to colonized people. The Priests and Pastors of the slave economy could not teach them the Golden Rule. Even the Jesuits of Georgetown university owned hundreds of slaves. That corruption of the Gospel of Jesus Christ has undermined social evolution, embarrassed and alienated mindful Christians. They are labelled as "backsliders" for leaving the church; the church that is in a symbiotic relation with the State and is not known to condemn bad governance. If the church had no moral influence on the government, it no longer has influence on anyone. Moral values become subjective. The Church becomes a house divided against itself. Yet collectively, the Church can determine who forms the government in western democracies.

In 2020, the world faced a pandemic that claimed over five million lives. In some communities, African Americans were about 30 percent of the population but 70 percent of the dead. Their fellow Christians had opposed universal healthcare for decades, probably out of hatred. If modern church leaders cannot stand up for Jesus for fear of losing their tax-exempt status; and continue to do the same things over and over knowing that nothing will change, then it is incumbent on non-denominational Christian activists to stand up for Jesus. They may be up against Christian politicians who are themselves products of the church that failed to teach converts to live by the Gospel. If the students didn't learn, the teacher didn't teach.

The church Establishment has done well to join parishioners to observe the Eucharist or the Holy Communion. In 2,000 years, has it taught parishioners to be born again and observe the Gospel and the social implications? If silence is complicity, no institution has been more silent on social injustice than the Church. For the church to subvert the economic interest of the underclass and still lead them in prayer is hypocritical. Even some corporations have taken baby steps to advance social justice. The church withholds criticism of State functionaries to protect their tax exemption. That's "scratch my back and I will scratch your back." - a historical symbiotic relationship. In all the struggles in history for freedom, be it the emancipation of slaves, segregation, apartheid, civil rights, the enfranchisement of women and police brutality against African Americans, the Establishment church was silent. To refrain from demanding social justice and good governance in order to protect tax exemption, is to run with the hare and hunt with the hounds. The Gospel is counterculture. The church whose gatekeepers are volunteers have to choose between serving culture or serving God Almighty. If "Bear one another's burdens and so fulfill the law of Christ" is godless communism, the church will be empty.

An online post by a retired Episcopal priest (September 13, 2018) reads: "Christianity made a Faustian bargain with Empire in the fourth century. At that point, we ceased to be a viable movement embodying the principles of the Jesus of the New Testament, i.e., ranging ourselves on the side of the poor, marginalized, and powerless instead of cozying up to power at the expense of justice. American religion at the present moment is Exhibit A for Christianity being detached from the countercultural Jesus, who is now for great numbers of people identified with systems such as capitalism and phenomena such as nationalism that he never remotely espoused." In Africa, most Bishops are not known to demand good governance and social justice. Many are seen to cozy up to the men in power for self-aggrandizement. In the social evolution that Christianity envisaged, the Caesars and Senators would ultimately be humanized by the Gospel, become born again Christians who live by the Gospel and their social implications. The church Establishment

made a detour. The Caesars and Senators never became born again
Christians. What are the characteristics of a born-again Christian?
A born-again Christian lives by the Gospel. The most visible charac-
teristic of a born-again Christian is compliance to the Golden Rule.

Three people groups have suffered the most in Church history.
The first group is the Africans who were enslaved and dehumanized
for about 300 years. The second group is the Jewish people subjected
to antisemitism and the Holocaust that claimed about six million
lives. The third group is the Irish. Secrecy covered up Ireland's
Mother and Baby Scandal. Women said to be "Fallen Women" were
sent to several Roman Catholic run homes to deliver their babies.
Many of those women worked at Magdalene Laundries without pay
from 1922 to 1996 as penance. Thousands of their babies died from
malnutrition, neglect or trauma. Some children grew up and were
sent to industrial schools. Some were sent overseas for adoption but
not by protestants to be sure that they do not lose their soul. It was
an abuse of power by Church and State. An Irish survivor testified
that they were treated as low Caste. "You wouldn't do to an animal
what was done to me," he wrote. They were also under colonial rule.
"Train up a child in the way he should go:" wrote King Solomon,"
and when he is old, he will not depart from it." (Proverbs 22:6). With
that in mind, and the symbiotic relationship between Church and
State, the aboriginals in Canada faced the same abuse of children.
The government provided the funds while the church ran the schools
to "kill the Indian in the child." Several thousand children never
returned home. As a Regent, the church Establishment exercised
absolute power.

In 2021, a man and a woman who represent two of the three
groups most abused by the church became President and vice
President of the United States. They can begin the process of Church
Reformation by demanding an apology for the Church's abuse of
power; reconciliation with God and man for the centuries of slave
trade and slavery; and the transformation of the Church from a

Regent to an Executor of God's will," teaching them to observe all things whatsoever I have commanded you." as Jesus said. It may not happen. The dominant cultural conservatives who count on mortality and a short memory to close the chapter on historical wrongs, may never learn to be born again and open a new page. The silence of the Church in the emancipation of slaves, civil rights, social justice and suffrage for women presages a future when powerful nations are led by hardcore atheists and agnostics. There may be no Church to speak the Truth to power. The church of the clergy and laity that lived off the avails of unpaid servitude for centuries; the church Establishment that sold 272 slaves to save their institution from bankruptcy, had erased the interface between right and wrong, and between Truth and falsehood or fallacy. Nobody is responsible for the sins of past generations. It is incumbent on believers now, to transform the church of culture that stood for might is right, to the Church of Jesus Christ that stands for the Golden Rule. It calls for a Second Reformation.

The Bottom Line

All souls are equal. But life is designed for division of labor; for equity in life and equality in the afterlife. Israel was created to be a moral nation, a model to the rest of the world. Deuteronomy 15:11 records that "For the poor shall never cease out of the land: therefore, I command thee, saying, Thou shalt open thine hand wide unto thy brother, to thy poor, and to thy needy, in thy land. "With that in mind, Jesus said: "For ye have the poor always with you; but me ye have not always." (Matthew 26:11). Those who are privileged are judged by how they extended equity to those He called "the least of these my brethren." In every nation, people recognize that Adolf Hitler was a bad man but do not recognize that they have bad men too.

Since hypocrisy is a global currency, no group wants to hear anything negative about one of them even if it is true. Among the millions of Africans who were enslaved, some had a higher I.Q. than their slave masters who had power, guns and privilege. Similarly, in every nation there are men and women with a higher I.Q. than the rich but are poor or under employed; not because of natural selection but because of cultural selection. The slave trader, slave masters and clergy who saw one people group – fellow children of Adam and Eve- as hewers of wood and drawers of water, were close to Adolf Hitler on the inhumanity spectrum. On that inhumanity spectrum, every adult is somewhere between a baby and Hitler. Because of victor theology, in 2,000 years and counting, the Church has failed to inculcate the Golden Rule in the cultural fabric of any nation.

Towards the end of His ministry, Jesus prayed that "They," the Church, "are not of the world, even as I am not of the world." (John 17:16). The imperial church became the world. Has it changed? When it ruled the world through colonial powers, every nation learned about Christianity through the language of the colonial powers. It was an opportunity to teach the people that the Gospel of Jesus Christ makes Christianity a global religion that is more redemptive than cultural religions. It did not happen. The imperial church was not in a position to teach the slaves, colonized and aboriginal peoples to observe the Golden Rule it violated. That is still a problem for the modern church Establishment. In medieval times, the way out of the dilemma for Rome, was to institute Sacraments. It did not require a Christian to be born again and live by the Gospel. For Reformers, the way out was to claim Amazing Grace - Jesus died for our sins and paid our sin debt. For defending the Sacraments, Pope Leo X conferred on King Henry V111 a title - "The defender of the faith." Christians were not allowed to read the Bible. The church fathers kept the flock ignorant. Those Romans and Reformers have shaped the spiritual destiny of humankind. Jesus said to Nicodemus, the Pharisee:" Most assuredly, I say to you, unless one is born again, he cannot see the kingdom of God" (John 3:3).

Suppose a born-again Christian lives by the Golden Rule – Treat others the same way you want them to treat you. How many Christians were saved when clergy and laity lived off the avails of slavery for about 300 years? Nobody is indispensable to God Almighty. Still, there are biblical scholars and theologians who are quoted like experts who had been to heaven and back. None has seen the dissonance between the Gospel of Jesus Christ and the conduct of the clergy and laity who lived off the avails of slavery for centuries; and the Christians who still do to others what they don't want others to do to them. How did 2,000 years of the Gospel seem to pass unnoticed?

How did 2,000 years of Christianity seem to pass unnoticed? A second 2,000 years can equally pass like the first, if Christianity does not mean living the Gospel. There are magicians who say to their audience: "The more you look, the less you see." Christians have not notice that the Gospel is about good relations between people and between them and God Almighty. It is summarized by the Golden Rule, the Great Commandment and the New Commandment. That is the Gospel. The rest is commentary. Many have not been allowed to see the forest for the trees. And in this symbiosis between Church and State, the Church still cannot criticize the State. The reward is tax exempt status.

And so, while some parishioners are jobless or needy, some Pastors are preaching to them about prophecy or the ancient Kings of Israel that diverts attention from the Gospel and practical Christianity. The politicians raised in the system tell the poor and needy, about the ideology of limited government and low taxes; that they don't believe in the use of government to solve problems. It is like a world run by the Mob and magicians. The distractions made it possible for 2,000 years to pass and not notice the real Gospel. Nobody has yet left this planet with their wealth. Still, culture overrules God and reason guided by victor theology. The chaos in the world shows that victor theology is coming to an end. Nobody in Moscow, Beijing or Washington D.C. knows whether the theology that has controlled the world for 2,000 years will end in a nuclear war. Meanwhile, the Church that opened the Pandora's box remains silent. No nation can fix their politics without fixing their religion.

CHAPTER 9

Prayers For What?

The Golden Rule, the Great Commandment and the New Commandment show that the Gospel of Jesus Christ is about good relations between people and between them and God Almighty. If that is true, and it is, why is the world the way it is after 2,000 years of Christianity? Why are so much prayers needed every weekend? And when did humans begin to pray? The Scriptures do not show that Adam and Eve prayed. Moses began intercessory prayers for the Hebrews during the formation of Judaism. That was the Old Covenant. In the New Covenant, Jesus Christ prayed to commune with God the Father who sent Him on a Mission. People talk to their parents here on earth and use prayer as a wireless communication channel, to talk to their Father in heaven. Jesus had to be asked before He taught His disciples how to pray. Even so, He admonished His followers not to pray standing in public places like the hypocrites, but to pray in private.

There are church leaders today who pray for a global television audience to see. The Lord's prayer, and request for the Holy Spirit, the Helper (Luke 11: 13) may be the only prayers needed in the post - Apostolic era. Jesus Christ did not come to teach prayer. He came to teach good relations between people and between them and the God of Creation. Secondly, He came to die as the Lamb of God. Humans have a tendency to go overboard. Prayer was not meant to be a substitute for action. It has been abused and used as a substitute for action. For example, is it not easier to pray for persecuted Christians than to demand freedom of religion through the United Nations, at the risk of economic interest? Is it not easier to pray decade after decade for peace in Jerusalem than to demand the Golden Rule from both sides of the conflict in the Middle East? The church Establishment would have done so if it has a clean slate on observing the Golden Rule. Prayer is cheap.

In the exercise of worldly power, the Roman Magisterium treated the Golden Rule as a suggestion rather than a divinely ordained moral imperative. Accordingly, a Christian can receive weekly absolutions and does not have to be born again and observe or live by the Golden Rule, the Great Commandment and the New Commandment herein referred to as the Gospel. How can a son disobey his parents and turn round to ask for pocket money? A child must do the will of his father before asking for his blessing. How can we disobey God and use prayer to give Him orders on what to do? He can incinerate this planet and there will be no lawyers to file an appeal.

During his reign, wise King Solomon noted that the fear of God is the beginning of wisdom. With over 3,000 years of hindsight, Homo sapiens and astronomers should be much wiser than King Solomon. If an atheist was born blind, and received his sight in middle age, God's creation will be seen with a great deal of amazement. Atheists are born and raised to take God's creation for granted just as the teenagers take television and cell phones for granted. When he considers the hills and majestic mountains, the open prairies as far as the eye can see, the expanse of the oceans to infinity, and the whole weight of the earth suspended in space, the atheist should be inclined to sing "How Great Thou Art"; a song written by a man less informed about the complexity of life and outer space. Yet the world is swayed by agnostics. Those who believe in God obey His commandments. The agnostics who are not sure that there is God influence the masses to live in the middle ground between belief and unbelief, a state one Archbishop described as "tacit atheism." It has become the modus operandi of the secular culture. The fear of strongmen has long replaced the fear of God and wherever it does, the Truth recedes.

Ordinary citizens find it difficult to get an appointment to see a Mayor, Prime Minister, Governor, President, a Monarch or Pope. Yet, the Almighty God is like a waiter taking orders to serve man. If man's orders are not filled, it is because the Almighty is not a waiter. Humans take orders from God, not the reverse. Giving instructions to God through prayer has not been productive. In fact, most prayers are answered after death. What is productive is compliance to His commandments and their social implications. The Canadian Hutterites know that to be true. God or man, one has to listen to the other.

When adherents of Judaism, Christianity and Islam pray, it is to tell God what to do and who to bless. The Almighty God does not take instructions. If He answered the prayers of every one, many will be dead because of what they have done to each other. His Golden Rule solves all kinds of social problems if obeyed. It should have started since the Romans took over the Church. If a Christan is by definition a person who believes in some of the teachings of Jesus Christ, or a person who has been baptized, the slave traders, slave masters and clergy were Christian. Was the Church Establishment that lived off the avails of slavery for 300 years inspired by the Holy Spirit or a different spirit?

The Israelites were punished collectively, even for the sin of one man, Achan. They were led into captivity in Assyria and Babylon. Why? "Because they obeyed not the voice of the LORD their God, but transgressed His covenant, and all that Moses the servant of the LORD commanded, and would not hear them, nor do them."

(2 Kings 18:12 NKJV). They also got this prophetic message: "If My people who are called by My name will humble themselves, and pray and seek My face, and turn from their wicked ways, then I will hear from heaven, and will forgive their sin and heal their land "(2Chronicles 7:14 NKJV). This is God's precondition to answer prayers. Nothing changed. The people were controlled by men who didn't believe in cause and effects. They believed that they were His people whether they obeyed or not. They did not obey. That was over 3,000 years ago. In the 400 years of intertestamental period or the "400 Silent Years," the Israelites and the world were Godforsaken. Did they know? Is it possible to live in a Godforsaken world and not know?

Jesus Christ came to teach the Gospel; open the door of faith and eternal life to both the Jews and Gentiles; died on the cross as the Lamb of God, the sacrifice to end all sacrifices so that deformed animals will no longer be offered for sacrifices. He returned to heaven. Neither the Jews nor the Christians who are now also called by His name have complied to 2 Chr.7:14. Christian or Christ follower means different things to different people. Mother Teresa, for example was a Christian. So were the slave traders. If we call Jesus "Lord, Lord," and do what He says, Christianity and the Gospel would be synonymous. But if we pretend to believe in God, and pretend to obey His Commandments - the Golden Rule, the Great Commandment and the New Commandment, God will also pretend to answer our prayers. We have to stop pretending. It takes a thinker or a scientific mind to recognize that if God Almighty did not respond to prayers in numerous wars, the Holocaust, epidemics, pandemics and financial distress, something must be wrong. If a congregation is not worshiping and doing the will of God Almighty, they must be worshiping and doing the will of Culture or other gods. Can a man work for Coca Cola and expect Pepsi to pay him? Can he work for Satan and expect God Almighty to answer his prayers? Man was created to be free to obey God for his own good, not to be a slave to prayer.

When Jesus Christ was here on earth, the Egypt of the Pharaohs was an African country. It became a European country and in the Age of Jihad, North Africa became Arabian. The Coptic Egyptians became strangers in their own fatherland and their Pharaohs were later exhumed for revenues from tourism. From the west coast of Africa, other men who believed in the same God, bought and sold Africans for over 200 years of slavery. And also colonized the entire continent in their Scramble for Africa. In the colonial administration, aboriginal peoples were treated as savages. Some heads were decapitated and preserved as trophy. The men who professed to believe in God also fought many wars at home, colonial wars abroad, and in two World War, killed over 50 million people, including the Holocaust death of about six million Jews. All these show that the Gentiles have done far worse than the Israelites who were forsaken.

Haiti defeated Napoleon's troops and in 1804, became the first Black nation to be independent from Christian nations. The brutality of slave life made Haiti one of the richest colonies in the world. But for daring to be free, what the Christians did to Haiti, to keep it the poorest nation in the western hemisphere would make Satan blush with shame. Hurricanes and earthquakes periodically destroyed whatever is on their path, including Churches. They have left some survivors asking: "Does God really exist?" The sky has to fall on Haiti to prove that we live in a Godforsaken world. Life makes sense to those who believed that we do live in a Godforsaken world. Cuba has suffered similar isolation for using every means possible to serve the common good. The Christian men involved in historic atrocities passed away leaving their treasures behind. That nobody has ever left this planet with his wealth has not deterred the hoarding of wealth.

In all the atrocities since the Apostles of Jesus Christ passed away, there has been no repentance, no restitution, and no reconciliation with God and man. Still, you can be told that if you were the only sinner on earth, Jesus Christ would have died for you. That

Jesus Christ would have died for one person out of over eight billion people shows how important man is to God Almighty, if you can believe it. Where is the fear of God? If the Almighty and righteous God punished or abandoned the Israelites for disobedience; if the Gentiles have done worse than the Israelites, what reason is there to believe that this is not a Godforsaken world? For clerics to believe that the Almighty God is cheering and answering prayers is not only an insult to the intelligence of the survivors of historical wrongs, but a mockery of God Almighty. It is also disingenuous for the contemporary clergy and scholars to act as if the Almighty no longer cares about disobedience, and call it Amazing Grace. A bus driver deserves the respectful silence of his passengers but not when he is heading down and abyss.

Those who inherit assets also inherit liabilities. Both the slaves and masters worked for life and took nothing away. The assets are here on earth. The dehumanizing effect of three centuries of slavery cannot be reversed even in a century. Yet, Christians who were born into Christianity and have not read the Gospel fear that an apology for the wrongs of the past will lead to calls for compensation. Spiritually conservative Christians who conserve Christian values and culturally conservative Christians who conserve cultural values are both Christians and conservatives but do not have the same values. Those who are Christians in the inside and those who are Christians on the outside do not share the same values. That is the Achilles heel of the conservative party.

Some Christian literature have Bible answers for every human problem from A to Z. They include promises made to the ancient Israelites who were undergoing training that was based on reward and punishment. In the New Covenant, does "Ask, and ye shall be given" apply to the post-Apostolic Christians? "Ye have not chosen me, but I have chosen you, and ordained you, that ye should go and bring forth fruit, and that your fruit should remain: that whatsoever ye shall ask of the Father in my name, he may give it you" (John

15:16). That's who the promise is for. Grandparents know that they asked and did not receive. When do we separate what was applicable to His disciples and the first century Christian neophytes from what is applicable to us in the 21st century? When do we separate the past from the present; the first century from the 21st century; the Old Testament people from the New Testament people?

Misleading people discredits the Gospel. If prayer is the key that unlocks God's storehouse, based on lived experience those grandparents don't believe it. The sermons laced with platitudes and anecdotes did not solve their problems. Born again or not, older Christians are losing interest in Bible stories embellished and retold. That's what turns off those grandparents - 2,000 years of theoretical and intellectualized Christianity. The Almighty has not spoken in two millennia as He did through the prophets. The so-called backsliders may be baffled by the long silence since man is so important. But to the God of eternity, two thousand years is like a nanosecond or a drop in the ocean of time. Besides, why would He answer prayers and bestow blessings on an unrepentant world contemptuous of the Gospel since slave trade and slavery?

Now, after 2,000 years of hindsight, what lesson have we learned about God? If you have no food, you can pray until the cows come home, God will not send you food from heaven. If you are homeless, He will not send you a house from heaven. If you are jobless, He will not build a factory and employ you. In the U.S.A. Christians pray to be cured of different diseases including cancer. Is the success rate better through prayer than without prayer? The answer is no. Research will show that in the West, if a disease is in remission through prayer, in the East it can be in remission without prayer. The prayer of Jabez does not apply to anyone else but Jabez. Good things and bad things happen in all nations. The Almighty is not offering any reward or special blessing to anyone before the end of history.

When the unsinkable Titanic sank in April 1912, about 1,500

people drowned. Some others survived to tell the story. There was hardly anyone who did not pray. It is said that God answered some prayers by allowing some to live, and others by allowing them to die. Did He? The Almighty God does not play favorites. It is written:" For He makes His sun rise on the evil and on the good, and sends rain on the just and on the unjust," (Matthew 5:45). In fact, the favorites may be the born-again Christians who died and went home. No individual is more important to God than the millions who died in two world wars and the thousands of babies and children starved to death in Biafra and Yemen in spite of prayers.

The Old Covenant was about reward for obedience and punishment for disobedience. In the New Covenant, reward and punishment are deferred to the end of history or Judgment Day (Matthew 25: 31 – 46). There are television evangelists constantly asking for money but are indifferent or even opposed to universal healthcare and universal employment which are permanent solutions to the social problems of their audience. Christianity is not a show. Christianity is not a sermon. It is a way of life. Universal healthcare and universal employment make moral as well as economic sense. But Christianity is being undermined, not by Atheists but by insidious Christian insiders who don't want a change in the structure of the jungle but to cheer the deer to run faster and jump higher and be dependent on prayer for survival from day to day.

Many Americans listened to prosperity preachers who told them to expect the favor of God who will solve their problems. They lost their savings, their homes or both in the Great Recession of 2008 or for medical reasons. The question is always asked why bad things happen to good people or "Why do good people suffer?" Good people are those who do no evil but allow evil to thrive. However, God does not reward "good people" until Judgment Day. The Swift do not always win the race; the most intelligent do not always get the riches; the godly do not always win the war; the most deserving does not always win the lottery because this is a Godforsaken world.

It may be less obvious but bad things also happen to bad people. If Ponzi wants to double your money, he should first double his own money as proof. A prayer expert or prayer warrior needs to do the same for himself as proof. False prophets will be known by their fruits (Matthew 7:15 – 16). When Christians are made to pray for their needs; if the only one prospering is the prosperity preacher traveling in a private plane, some lose trust and even their faith in God.

There are jobless parishioners who have not heard a sermon from the Epistle of James for years. James 2: 15- 17 is instructive. Those who need help need help, not prayers. To use prayers to re-direct people's problems to God is an abuse of prayer. In the U.S.A countless prayers are said by men and women who face financial ruin because of health issues. Being diabetic is not a function of skin color. America's Appalachia and poor minority communities have a sugar rich, polluted and stressful life environment. The covid-19 pandemic killed the poverty class in large numbers if they have diabetes, asthma, high blood pressure and couldn't afford Health Insurance and a primary care doctor. In some communities, African Americans were about 70 percent of the dead where they constitute about 30 percent of the population.

Many culturally conservative Christians have resisted universal healthcare for generations. They see it as godless communism. To suggest universal employment will be condemned as pie in the sky or a pipe dream. Thousands of people, including war veterans are homeless. But in the 2020 COVID -19 pandemic, Congress approved an historic two trillion dollars in the first phase, to combat the disease. Many rich governments spared no expense to combat the pandemic because it is a disease that is no respecter of persons. Some problems need action others need prayers. Those who are homeless, jobless or unable to pay for healthcare or have no peace of mind, all need prayers. In neighboring Canada, Rev. Tommy Douglas, a Baptist preacher got into politics and introduced universal healthcare to his home province of Saskatchewan in 1962. It became a national program in 1966. He saw government, not prayer, as the instrument to improve lives. Universal healthcare ensured that Canadians do not die because of poverty or skin tone. One would have expected an American preacher to follow that example. It will not happen.

According to the Scriptures, to obey is better than sacrifice. By the same token, to obey is better than prayer. With universal healthcare Rev. Tommy Douglas has spared generations of Canadians from needless prayers. With universal employment Hutterite leaders have spared generations of their families from needless prayers and expectation fatigue. Hard work is more productive than prayer. What needless pain we bear because we are not led like the Hutterites. In fact, the answer to prayer is to pre-empt prayer by observing God's commandments. That is what the Canadian Hutterites have done. Prayer is not the first but the last resort. Their Church leaders are literally doing the will of God on earth as it is in heaven. Since Christianity is practiced rather than theorized and intellectualized, they do not pray for the homeless or jobless. They have none. What they prayer for can be different from what other Christian families pray for.

Prayer can become an evil tool to prevent action. Praying for what human beings can and are supposed to do, is a waste of time. The answer to prayer is to pre-empt needless prayer with education, healthcare and employment for all families. The Cultural conservatives will not allow it. Teachers and professors teach students until they graduate and begin to practice their profession. In Christianity, to graduate is to be born again and observe or live by the Gospel. Christians never graduate from Sunday school. It has not happened except in a Canadian Hutterite colony. There, the pastor appears to care for the spiritual and temporal needs of the flock. It is the structure that makes it possible so that he does not have to use prayer to evade solutions. The structure reduces the conflict between a worldly life and the spiritual life.

A wise professor noted that God is more interested in changing you than in changing your circumstances. It is the collective you. When your community changes, your circumstances will change. The Canadian Hutterite colony is an example.

But let us be honest. An economy based on education, employment and healthcare for all families should have started over a thousand years ago when every society was homogeneous. The mass migration of colonial subjects and cultural religions make the Christian ideal open to resistance. Prayers cannot end the persecution of Christians when some Christians and governments have economic relations with the persecutors. Yet, in prayer, the Almighty is asked to "help us to obey Your commandments." Or "make us willing to obey." Are we sincere? If we don't obey, it must be God's fault because He did not help us or make us willing to obey His commandments. That is why rational Pentecostalism is a superior theology. In rational Pentecostalism, a sincere Christian asks for the Holy Spirit (Luke 11 :13), and sooner or later begins to live by the Gospel. That's the evidence of the indwelling of the Holy Spirit in a born-again Christian.

Outside the abundant life of a Hutterite colony, most adult Christians have prayed and asked without receiving. How can God not answer a prayer asking to receive the Holy Spirit who changes lives? It is a selfless prayer that is bound to be answered. When they live by the Gospel - the Golden Rule, the Great Commandment and the New Commandment - they know that the prayer has been answered. It should have been church doctrine 2,000 years ago. It was not because the doctrine does not serve imperial interest. It would have prevented the Jesuits from owning slaves.

There is no Christian denomination that is flawless. The Pentecostals, unlike many other denominations, understand that a Christian must be born again through the Holy Spirit. But the faction that argues that speaking in tongues is for everyone discredits the denomination. The speaker in tongues and the concomitant interpreter are listed in 1 Corinthians 12:10 among spiritual gifts.

Born-again Christians do the will of God and have less need for prayers of need in what is said to be an evil world. A diagnosis is one thing; a cure is another. When people who profess faith in God are opposed to universal healthcare and universal employment for all families, this is not an evil world but a misguided world. The pastorate is the guide. Christians who pray and remind God to be God must first learn from the Canadian Hutterites that those who obey God can skip needless prayers. Sadly, from generation to generation, victor theology and liturgy allow us to disobey God respectfully.

Suppose all the people in the world are raptured, not to heaven but to Mars. Will this still be an evil world? The problem is the people. When "Thy will be done on earth as it is in heaven" is nothing but lip service, does an" evil or fallen world" let the pastorate off the hook? The guides are volunteers who inherited a flawed execution of the Great Commission that is yet to be rectified. A few centuries ago, the disobedience of God's Golden Rule affected only the slaves in America. Now, from divorce to scams, the consequences of the disobedience are catching up with everyone, everywhere and the solution seems to be prayers not compliance. Imagine for a moment, that the Virgin Mary has been praying for us sinners for the past 2,000 years and could be doing so for the next 2,000 years or the end of history. At what point does the Almighty say to Mary, "enough is enough"? Can parishioners be spiritual hostages to theology and liturgy designed by medieval minds at a time in mythology when the God mother was more revered and adored than the son?

King David could offer burnt offering and pray to God to end a plague (2 Samuel 24:25). Can spiritual leaders pray to God to end a pandemic? Why not? A thousand years before Jesus Christ came, the disobedient Israelites did not heed 2 Chronicles 7:14 and suffered the consequences. Then the promised Messiah came. He taught the way that leads to eternal life and opened the door of faith to both Jews and Gentiles. He died on a cross as the Lamb of God to end animal sacrifices that included deformed animals, before returning to heaven. For over 2,000 years, the people who claim to believe in the God of Abraham, Isaac, Jacob and Ishmael have also ignored the precondition for answered prayers. How can anyone rely on prayer when society has not paid heed to the pre-condition for prayers to be answered?

For over 200 years, Africans in slavery prayed for deliverance but there was no response. In numerous wars in Europe, millions of people died despite their prayers. There was no divine intervention. In the Holocaust, some prayed for the promised Messiah but the Messiah had already come. In the Nigeria-Biafra war that I witnessed, thousands of babies and children were starved to death despite the prayers of their mothers. In economic depression and recessions, families lost their homes despite their prayers. If prayer would have helped Mother Teresa to win a lottery jackpot to help the poorest of the poor, the church would have prayed. It didn't. There have been epidemics and pandemics in history. Millions or people died despite their prayers. Prophecy preachers will call them part of end -time events. They are not. Those who want to know end- time events can read Mark 13: 24 – 26.

The Covid -19 pandemic adversely affected Italy in March 2020. Within a 24-hour period, over 900 people died. Spain, another ancient Roman Catholic nation had over 800 deaths in one day in March 2020. About six million people died around the world. If the Church believed that prayer is efficacious, St. Peter's square would have been packed with people in supplication to God Almighty. It was deserted. The people will be back to pray and receive absolutions when the pandemic ends. Elsewhere protestant prayer warriors were in hiding. What does it say about their faith in prayer? When the pandemic is over and life returns to normal, the prayer warriors will reappear with ritual prayers as if this time, the Almighty will answer the prayers. If doing the same thing over and over expecting a different result is insanity, there is no greater insanity than praying for 2,000 years expecting a different result without fulfilling the precondition for prayers to be answered. Praying without lifting a finger is easier than doing the will of God. Should there be a Third World War, billions of people could die in a nuclear weapons exchange and there will be no divine intervention. Clearly, in a Godforsaken world, it is better to live with the Canadian Hutterites than to live with prayer warriors. Back in the 11th century, a Syrian poet Abu Maarri wrote: "The world is divided into two sects: Those with religion but no brains; And those with brains but no religion." Is he right?

Did the omniscient God know that David, as king, would commit a heinous sin? Yet, he was chosen as king. He was not a defiant sinner. Psalm 51 shows that God knew that he was a genuine godly man. If the imperial Church had the same spirit of remorse, contrition and repentance, it would have apologized for the sin that turned God Almighty away from humanity – the sale of men, women and children to be enslaved for life – an event that marked modern man's original sin. The victor theology is a defiant theology. King David wrote: "It is good for me that I have been afflicted, that I may learn Your statutes." (Psalm 119:71 NKJV). And "Oh, how I love Your law! It is my meditation all the day. You, through Your commandments, make me wiser than my enemies; for they are ever with me. I have more understanding than all my teachers, for Your testimonies are my meditation. (Psalm 119:97-99 NKJV). The world has been afflicted with colonial wars, slave trade, slavery, two World Wars, imperialism, the Biafra War with thousands of babies and children starved to death, family dissociation, terrorism, scams, epidemics and pandemics. What other solution can there be to social problems? Doing to others what you don't want them to do to you is the mother of inhumanity and suffering. The Almighty revealed Himself to Abraham and guided the Hebrews to be a light to the rest of humanity. Without the Old Covenant, most of us would not have believed that there is God because Christianity has been practiced in a way that promotes atheism.

Prayer and Lottery

What we have learned from 2,000 years of Christian experience is that it is unrealistic to tell people that God will solve their problems because it has not happened. Ancient peoples had oracles. There are some Christian denominations that use the Church as an oracle. Many go, not to worship God but to solve their health and economic problems particularly in poor countries. For Protestants it is prayers of need that bring them to Church. And for Roman Catholics it is absolution that brings them to Mass. Absolutions offer a false sense of security to those who continue to do to others what they don't want others to do to them. Truth be told, most prayers are not answered. If what we prayed and ordered God to do didn't happen is it our fault or God's fault? If we don't show kindness to others; if there is no peace in Jerusalem generation after generation; if wars continue to break out and Christians go to kill other Christians; if social problems persist despite all those prayers; and if we pray to God to help us keep His commandments but it doesn't happen, who is to blame? Is it man or God Almighty who does not take orders from His creation? Has prayer become a substitute for action?

Are there Christians whose cancer is in remission after prayers? Yes, there are. Are there non-Christians whose cancer is in remission without prayers? Yes, there are. Monotheists who are prayer dependent should compare the outcome with atheists. The probability of a positive or negative outcome is the same. Statistics shows that in the Netherlands, those who pray have become a minority. The next step is to determine whether those who pray are better off than those who don't. The Almighty is not rewarding anyone until the end of history or Judgment Day when the sheep will be separated from the goats. (Matthew 25: 32 - 46.)

Prayer is like lottery. In lottery and in prayer, the winner is placed on a pedestal as the norm rather than the exception. The millions who did not win know otherwise. Some lottery Corporations publish testimonies of their winners in every category. They are interesting to read but do not apply to the millions who lost. The vast majority who lost do not stop buying tickets. Neither does unanswered prayers deter anyone from praying for jobs or for peace in the Middle East. Every generation – children, parents, grandparents - will pass through the same revolving door without noticing that the Hutterites have a better way of life. The main purpose of prayer is not to give orders but to commune with our Father who is in heaven. The lottery corporations must have learned from religious institutions to place a winner on a pedestal.

The COVID-19 pandemic killed about six million people in the world. A religious organization told the story of one of their members. He landed in an ICU on a ventilator. For weeks he continued to deteriorate. His organs began to fail. He was placed on dialysis with a feeding tube. Those who loved him continued to pray. After months of persistent prayers, he recovered and returned to work. He told the people he knew that he is a living proof that God answers prayers. It is good to hear such testimonies of healing. But if a man wins a lottery, is it proof that everyone can win a lottery? Those whose prayers have been answered are lucky. They have won a lottery but not everyone wins a lottery. Some anti - vaccine preachers and their followers died in the pandemic because being vaccinated is an admission that prayer is ineffective and cannot be used as a bait to keep hope alive among the poor who have a list of needs.

The Christian Science Sentinel has "Testimonies of Healing "and prayers answered. In a June 4, 2018 edition, there was the healing of Asthma, a quick healing after a fall and the healing of cold symptoms, all by reasoning metaphysically and praying scientifically. In other editions, prayers healed migraines; a bad cold disappeared just before a musical performance; knee and ankle injuries were healed; recurring motion sickness disappeared; abdominal pain, gone; a dog's epilepsy healed; fever and sore throat gone; pet's parasitic condition overcome; a swift end to dental pain; no more prostate cancer symptoms; chest pain healed during Church; freed from flu symptoms; financial needs met. The list is long. Could the millions who died in Covid -19 pandemic have been saved if they went to the right place?

In the Biafra War (1967 – 70), hundreds of thousands of babies and children died from starvation despite the collective inter-denominational prayers of their mothers. How do we explain how God Almighty would answer the prayers of those individuals and even their pets, but allow the babies and children to die from starvation? Any human being, Christian or non-Christian willing to fast for a day can feel the agony of a child being starved to death for oil interest. And how can prayer warriors explain how the Almighty God would answer the prayer of a single individual but not the prayers for the millions of men, women and children who perished in two World Wars?

Surely, healing is possible through prayers. And like lottery, for everyone who is healed millions will not be healed. Such display of answered prayers is perhaps the most obvious and overt manifestation of theoretical Christianity. When those who win the lotteries of life give credit to God, it distracts attention from the unfulfilled Great Commission that makes everyone a winner. Still, we listen or read stories of spiritual and literal lottery winners. We know that it does not resonate with most people, but we like to listen year after year, and generation after generation. Never do we think of how to make everyone a winner. When everyone is a winner, it is no longer a lottery. It is taxation to serve the common good. Taxing people for the common good is not popular with anti-social cultural conservatives. So, we continue to pray for the less fortunate because prayer is cheap.

If prayer is needed, it is for things human beings cannot do, not for things they can do. That is an unpopular and uncomfortable truth. Religion can be a problem for African Americans when the Church is a place to be entertained rather than to worship God. And a place that some are told that Jesus has prescribed persecution and deprivation for them. Should anyone sit and court tribulation? They need a trip to a Canadian Hutterite colony to see where Christianity is not only preached but practiced through education, healthcare and employment for all families. Those born into a system do not know there is something better until they see it.

Trust and Obey

There are numerous religions, sects and denominations in the world. Obviously, some of the sheep and shepherds are lost. A few professions require malpractice insurance just in case something goes wrong. It is not required in religion. It is up to everyone to ensure that he or she is not being led astray. "Buyer beware "applies to religion. The Old Covenant shows that there is the God of Creation who revealed Himself several millennia ago, and wants His commandments to be obeyed. One of the greatest songs in the Church hymnal is "Trust and Obey." Some very liberal Churches have replaced Trust and Obey with "Amazing Grace." It is now an anthem for funerals.

God or man, one has to listen to the other. A pastor who does not demand compliance to God's commandments is leading the congregation astray. God's Amazing Grace derived from the Epistles does not nullify the Golden Rule, the Great Commandment and the New Commandment. Those commandments summarize the Gospel of Jesus Christ. "In God We Trust "is not enough. The Hutterite example to emulate is trust and obey. There are groups and nations that have been wronged in the past when doing wrong to others was a sport. Because they live counter to the Golden Rule, the conservative cultural militia bear responsibility for their nation's sins. It is incumbent on a new generation to reconcile with the past and open a new page rather than continue the wrongs of the past or venerates the icons of inhumanity. If Germany can open a new page, any nation can do that too, even if they are not Christians. "Treat others the same way you want them to treat you" makes sense to anybody who is a human being regardless of culture, ethnicity, gender, religion or political ideology.

John Greenleaf Whittier (1807 - 1892) wrote a hymn: "Dear God, compassionate and kind, forgive our foolish ways." Our foolish ways found expression in imperialism, slave trade, slavery, colonial wars, World Wars, apartheid, segregation, terrorism and more, despite the Golden Rule. When and how can our foolish ways end? The answer is as clear as day and night. It is not absolutions but the Golden Rule that will end our foolish ways when we allow the Holy Spirit to replace the resident evil spirit or human nature. We can go to Church and read the Ten Commandments one after another and ask God to "incline our hearts to keep this law." At the end of history or Judgment Day, our lawyers can argue that we did not keep the commands because God did not incline our hearts to obey. Are we playing games with God Almighty? Will the Almighty then apologize to the Canaanites; those killed in the Flood; to Sodom and Gomorrah; and other victims of our foolish ways and let bygone be bygone?

Any man or woman who does not live by the Golden Rule is not born again. The Almighty has William Wilberforce, John Brown, Mother Teresa and many others as examples of the men and women who saw the light and obeyed. Like Saints, the Canadian Hutterites will come marching in as a group that lived by the commandments and their social implications. The opponents of William Wilberforce and Abraham Lincoln were Christians. The role of those opponents in history was a discredit to their nations. Why do men who do to others what they don't want others to do to them profess to be Christians? Is it the creation of victor theology? When men like Adolf Hitler and others much less like him, do to others what they don't want others to do to them, some will argue that such men are not Christians. They are victor theology Christians. What was wrong for Hitler to do should be wrong for anybody else to do. For most nominal Christians, there is no desire to change.

Epidemics and pandemics show how the invisible can be more impactful than things that are seen. It is easier to obey the father you see on earth, not the Father in heaven you can neither see nor hear from. It separates faith from lack of faith. To approach God with the mind of a child is to trust and obey. There is no other way. The introduction of democracy - a government of the people, for the people, and by the people - did not bring an end to social problems. Everything is measured in the acquisition of wealth. There are leaders, Secretaries of State and their secret service whose citizens do not know about the covert operations done to other nations. What is made public in the media is what the other people do in reaction. If Christendom does not live by the Golden Rule, the emerging powers will not live by the Golden Rule. And so, the grandchildren would be left on a collision course with the future.

The proximate cause of all the social problems that call for prayers is the failure to obey the Golden Rule. It began with the church that used slavery as a tool to enforce celibacy and expanded to full- scale commercial slavery. Now, some of the children of the world regardless of religion, recognize that the role of government is to serve humanity not Marmon. They are taking a leadership role in environmental stewardship and social justice. It is a shame that children should lead adults to do the right thing. Children can be visionaries. A world going from crisis to crisis needs visionaries not the experts who show up, not before to prevent an incident but after the fact, to explain why things should have been done differently. The convergence of youths of different religions to solve social problems that shouldn't exist if Christians practiced Christianity now creates the fear of universalism.

Surely, there may be problems that are solved through prayer and fasting (Matthew 17:20 – 21). Those who wish to solve such problems by prayer should be prepared to fast to show the commitment and sincerity of their prayers. It should be the last resort to what cannot be done by man. Regardless of the discipline studied, the most important knowledge that students acquire in post-secondary education is how to think and reason. After 2,000 years of Christianity, if the Almighty God has not sent food from heaven to feed starving children; mobile homes to shelter the homeless; built factories to employ the jobless; imposed peace on Jerusalem and the Middle East; stopped an epidemic or a pandemic; destroyed those who persecute and kill the faithful in spite of their prayers, why do we continue to pray for the same issues generation after generation? Why do we return to St. Peter's square after a pandemic to continue doing the same things over and over expecting a different result? Is prayer and addiction? That would sound like blasphemy to cultural conservatives who have vested interest in the status quo. Outside a Hutterite colony, prayer is the lifeblood of the Church. So, speaking the truth is risky.

When the defenders of cultural values are more powerful than the defenders of global values, speaking the truth is always risky. Prayers did not end slave trade and slavery in America. Prayers did not end the Nazism and the Holocaust of the Second World War. Prayers did not end apartheid in South Africa. They all ended through the collective action of men and women of goodwill within and outside those nations. Prayers did not end the deliberate starvation to death of thousands of babies and children in the Biafra war. It ended with Pax Romana, aided by oil interests. Now, will prayers ever end the hatred, conscious and unconscious bias deep in the soul? Will prayers ever end the killing of innocent men, women and children in the name of religion?

Surely, every culture has an inalienable right to practice the religion of their culture but not the pursuit of such spiritual imperialism documented in www. Stephenblanton.com/ growth. Comfortable Christians have to stop praying for persecuted Christians and start practicing the Golden Rule to influence unbelievers. Everything else will fall into line. China treats the killing of people in the name of religion, as mental illness. Those who have the proclivity to do so are institutionalized for re-education. Every culture deserves to be governed by the values of their culture in their homeland. Women who go to Muslim nations cover their hair because when you go to Rome, you behave like the Romans. It is a two-way street.

Church history is not known for compliance to the Golden Rule. The church has been resistant to Christian civilization. Consequently, cultural religions including Voodoo, looked superior to Christianity. What is most exasperating is that there are enough intelligent people on earth who know that compliance to God's Golden Rule makes sense to any human being. And that if prayers did not stop the inhumanities of the past, it will not stop the inhumanities of the future. The Almighty God, in response to prayer will not kill the terrorists in order to save Christians or the people of any other faith. It will not happen.

So, why do those addicted to prayer continued to pray for the homeless, the jobless, the lonely, and for persecuted Christians without lifting a finger? Is it not addiction because prayer costs no money? The world needs the collective action of men and women of goodwill inside and outside the Middle East, to bring an end to the medieval practice of killing people who are different, particularly in Africa since the seventh century. And the repression of people because of their complexion. This is worth repeating: the answer to prayer is to pre-empt prayer by observing God's commandments. Trust and obey. There is no other way. We cannot tell God what to do and who to bless.

In the 1970s, there was "Jesus' people". It fizzled out because theoretical Christianity is theoretical Christianity. "But my God shall supply all your need --- "was not part of their experience. Those who were born into what is known as a "Christian family" can easily be disillusioned. Believing in Jesus Christ as Lord and savior with a superficial faith, did not fill the void in their lives. They needed practical Christianity like the Hutterites. But to get along, people go along, even in Dixie. So, nothing changes. A Church building packed with men and women who are Christians on the outside but not Christians on the inside, is not a church.

The most difficult thing for a pastor to do is to ask for money to run the church. The laity, including me, tend to put our spare change in the collection plates. Unless the denomination has one billion members, spare change is not enough. After 2,000 years of platitudes, those who still believe that with prayer the Almighty God will solve the financial problems of individuals and the church, are deceiving themselves. Without obeying God, like the Hutterites; without offering social security through education, healthcare and employment for all families, more churches will be up for sale post COVID- 19 pandemic. It does not take a prophet to see that coming. Televangelists will have to write and sell many more books to stay afloat. Prayers are not enough.

On Meditation

Meditation has not been part of the prayer life of most churches. It should be. As a preamble to prayer, meditation helps rid the mind of distractions. Invite the divine presence and focus on the metaphysical and ethereal space before praying reverentially, not for things human beings can do, but for things human beings cannot do. It is claimed that practicing meditation par se will reduce stress, insomnia, post-traumatic stress disorder, depression, feelings of hurt, anger, loneliness, anxiety, pain and high blood pressure. Metta or loving kindness meditation is said to help develop kind thoughts of yourself that then extends to other people; help in anger management and to acquire the self-control that breaks addiction dependencies. There is scientific evidence of communities in the world where food and exercise helped the people to live longer. Is there a community on earth where meditation changed lives and led to good relations between them and their neighbors? Unofficial research shows that the benefits of extended meditation are fleeting. Consequently, one must practice meditation a couple of times a day as a habit.

Jesus Christ told a Samaritan woman at a well: "But whosoever drinketh of this shall thirst again: but whosoever drinketh of the water that I shall give him shall never thirst; but the water that I shall give him shall be in him a well of water springing up into everlasting life." (John 4:13 – 14). By being born again, a Christian receives the benefits of meditation permanently, not daily. Disaffected Christians who were not led to be born again can over meditate and drift into a different faith tradition that has no redeeming value. When St. Paul went to Ephesus, he found 12 believers and asked them a crucial question: "Did you receive the Holy Spirit when you believed? "(Acts 19:2 NKJV). If it was not important, why would he ask? The mainline Churches never cared about receiving the Holy Spirit. Any man who is under the control of the Holy Spirit rather than the evil spirit, is a born-again Christian who lives by the Gospel and becomes a new creation. That is the baseline of a born-again Christian. The permanent benefits that it offers are more than the brief benefits of meditation. It leads to peace and joy. And most importantly, world history would have been different.

Several decades ago, some artists entered a competition to express the concept of peace on canvas. In the winning entry, the artists drew a hurricane destroying houses and trees. He also drew a very big rock. On the leeward side of the rock, there was a hole with a bird sleeping inside in the midst of the hurricane. That is like the peace that comes from being born again. You can go to church and gets a handshake wishing you" the peace of God." What St. Paul described as "the peace of God which surpasses understanding" does not come from a handshake but from being born again. The victor theologians are historically constrained to teach members to be born again and thereby expose the failures of the past. Some see religion and science to be mutually exclusive. But research will show that born again Christians, like the bird in the hollow of the rock, cope better than others in a pandemic or stress.

In war, thousands of babies and children have died from starvation despite the prayers of their mothers. Why would such a prayer not be answered? It was not a selfish prayer. Yet, God did not send manna from heaven. The medieval victor theology we inherited has no redeeming value in life or in death for the slave traders, slaves, slave masters, clergy and politicians. It is now leading to prayer fatigue. A man wrote to the American evangelist, Rev. Billy Graham and said: "How can I get close to God? Praying to Him is like praying to a brick wall; and although countless prayers of mine have been answered, it seems that my prayers just slide into the blackness of I- don't- know where. Do you think you could possibly help me? "{My Answer, My Answer, My Answer "by Billy Graham. Pocket Books, Simon and Schuster, New York, N.Y 1967 page 155}[5]. Such Christians should visit a Canadian Hutterite colony to see how people live in a Godforsaken world. No family prays to God for financial assistance. They don't pray for the homeless, the jobless, or the lonely. They have none. In the U.S.A, some women have prayed to God to let their husbands out of prison. In a Godforsaken world, they should not pray to God but to those who rule the world. Doing the work of God is one thing, doing the will of God is another. Praying to ask for the Holy spirit (Luke 11:13) to be born again and live by the Gospel and its social implications is a prayer that deserves to be answered.

The Middle East is the most prayerful region on earth. It is easier to see the sins of others than our own sins. With all the hatred and bloodshed that erupts from generation to generation, there are not many people in the world who believe that those prayer rituals go anywhere beyond the roof to be answered. The claim in every conflict by each side is that God was on their side. God cannot be on the side of culture. it is more important to be on the side of the God of all nations through compliance to the Golden Rule. That is the will of the true God. Jesus Christ revealed that the Pharisees and the religious Establishment were worshiping culture, not God Almighty. They didn't know. Similarly, the Christian clergy and laity who lived off the avails of slavery for over 300 years were worshiping culture, not God. They didn't know but nothing has changed. There is yet no contrition, no repentance, no restitution and no reconciliation with God and man. If we believe that the ritual prayers in the Middle East are not going anywhere to be answered should our ritual prayers be answered?

If the pre-Christian world was forsaken, is there any reason to believe that the post-Apostolic world of slave trade and slavery is not forsaken, yet again? We can assume that the prophetic message of 2 Chronicles 7:14 still stands because God is immutable. Among the Israelites who were taken into captivity for disobedience, there must have been a few godly men and women. The Jewish Teshuva or self-examination and repentance changes self but not society. Hence, some good people went into captivity. Good people suffer when society is misled. Did those Israelites in captivity believe that God's love is unconditional?

Suppose the Almighty sends every man, woman and child into exile in Mars or another planet. Will this still be an evil world? The evil or Satan or spirit of disobedience will follow them into exile because it dwells in the man or woman who has not received the Holy Spirit to be born again. In the centuries of slave trade and slavery, the church was in control of the world. Did the church preside over the evil world? It is difficult for those who became powerful to apologize to those who were powerless and abused. Hence, the church Establishment has yet to apologize and reconcile with the victims of history because they suffer no consequences. But the religious Establishments cannot pray to God in spirit and in truth and ignore 2 Chronicles 7:14. Nobody is above God Almighty.

For more than a thousand years, monotheists (not atheists) have piled on transgression on transgression without repentance, restitution, or reconciliation. The Almighty God is the same yesterday, today and forever. Hebrew history and common sense suggest that it is not in God's nature to ignore disobedience and bless people. Therefore, a church in denial doing damage control cannot expect prayers to be answered without repentance and reconciliation. The monotheists who are led to rely on weekly absolutions or Amazing Grace or the compassion and mercy of God, expecting disobedience to be ignored and prayers answered, may not be aware that "narrow is the gate and difficult is the way which leads to life, and there are few who find it." (Matthew 7:14). It is obvious that the default position is hell not heaven. Those who can set aside their ethnocentricity will recognize that if the Israelites can be forsaken for less malfeasance, there is no reason why the post -Apostolic world should not be forsaken. There is no reason why the Almighty will answer the prayers of men who believe that they are indispensable to Him; that Jesus Christ would again endure torture and die for even one sinner.

If you were a Holocaust survivor, would you expect God who didn't answer prayers then to answer prayers now? If you were a slavery survivor, would you expect God who didn't intervene for over 300 years to intervene now? If hundreds of thousands of babies and children died from starvation in the Biafra war despite the prayers of their mothers, do you expect God Almighty to be answering prayers for cats and dogs now? In all the tragedies of modern times, families lost lives, savings or homes. The prayer warriors and prosperity preachers did not help them. A thinker would recognize that we live in a Godforsaken world. A Godforsaken world may be a school of thought despicable to any expert who has a carrier staked on the status quo. But like it or not, in a Godforsaken world, prayers are not answered.

There is no person or institution that is more resilient than the church. All preachers in America can condemn universal education, healthcare and employment for all families, as godless communism. Christians will still go to pray to God for their healthcare and employment needs. They cannot miss the time for prayer request. That's resilience. In recession after recession, prosperity preachers have seen people lose their homes and still come back to hear about individuals who overcame adversity. They come because it is a show without admission fee. That's resilience. If that church were a corporation, it would have been sued out of existence for misleading advertisements.

In all the trepidations of the past 2,000 years, both Jews and Gentiles have not heeded or responded to God' precondition to answer prayers. Consequently, God Almighty has not responded to prayers. Yet the prayers keep coming. The Canadian Hutterites know how to live in a Godforsaken world. "Bear one another's burdens and so fulfill the law of Christ" should lead to divine economy, a just society that provides education, healthcare and employment for every family and pre-empts prayers of need. It gives credence to "Thy will be done on earth as it is in heaven." It will take another century or two to overcome the anti-social cultural conservatives. Meanwhile, their victor theology will continue to bring captives to religion and make them prayer dependent. That dependence on prayer will grow as technology reduces employment. If prayers have not produced jobs in the past, will it produce jobs in the future? Outside a Hutterite colony, prayer is the lifeblood of the church. Speaking the Truth is risky.

The Bottom Line

Confucius did not know God. In pre-colonial Eastern Nigeria, there were titled men who stood for moral values like Confucius. They did not know the living God or expect any reward after death. And like Adam and Eve, they did not pray to God. They lived by the

Golden Rule and did what is right because it is right. Suppose there
is no God, no heaven or hell. And given the fact that nobody in
history has left this planet with his wealth, treat others the same way
you want them to treat you, will still make sense to anyone who is
a human being. Those who are led to believe that a little talk with
Jesus will solve their problems, by and by, will be disappointed. Most
prayers and not answered. The Lord's prayer is all that is needed.
"Give us this day our daily bread," is not "give me this day my daily
bread." When a society has billionaires and beggars, it is obvious that
the daily bread is not being shared. Some of us have five loaves of
that daily bread while those who have none are on the streets. Did
God know that some people will do to others what they don't want
others to do to them? That is the reason for the Golden Rule. The
world does not need more Sermons and prayers; it needs practical
Christianity. Life in socialist Scandinavia will even be better with
universal employment. They don't need prayers except the Lord's
prayer.

A man who goes into the wilderness to do nothing but pray
for food will die from starvation. However, in the social life of a
Hutterite colony, he can pray. But for what? God answers prayers
but what kind of prayers does He answer? It is for things that are
beyond the ability of society to do. When all known wrongs are
righted, God may answer prayers but for things human beings cannot do. If a simple majority of the men and women in every chamber
in politics treated others the way they would like to be treated, the
world will be different. How does a society produce such politicians?
The gatekeepers of all religions are volunteers. Jesus Christ told his
disciples:" You did not choose Me, but I chose you and appointed
you---" (John 15:16 NKJV).

When Moses passed away the Almighty appointed Joshua as
a successor. When Peter passed away, did the Almighty appoint a
successor? If God appointed the Romans, there would have been no
slave trade and slavery. All spiritual leaders are volunteers. When all

hope is lost, and before a nuclear war, will the Almighty God end the paralysis of complacency and choose and appoint gatekeepers who will teach and raise born again Christians who live by the Golden Rule? That is something to pray for. It is like going back to the first century Pentecostal Church, uncorrupted by victor theology. Between now and then there will be tragic moments when good people pray but still die. In life or in death the faithful are not forsaken. Life is a test of faith until the end of history. There is enough to see to believe in God, trust and obey. There is also enough to see from tragedy and what humans do, and not believe in God. If the answers to a test are leaked to the students, will it still be a test? What happens if God answers all prayers. Will life still be a test of faith? And who is expected to do the will of the other - man or God?

Lived experience is passed from one generation to another. Grandparents have passed through the crucible of prayer and prayer fatigue. They have a duty to demand good governance that will pre -empt decades of the same prayer fatigue for the people they brought into the world. In the past 2,000 years, there has been numerous wars in Europe, including two bloody world wars. There has been slave trade, slavery for over 300 years in which clergy and laity lived off the avails of slavery. There has been colonialism, segregation, apartheid and the Biafra war in which hundreds of thousands of babies and children were starved to death for the control of Nigerian oil, when oil ruled the world. There has been epidemics and pandemics and in all these events, prayers did not stop the millions of deaths. The Israelites – clergy and laity - were punished collectively for disobedience, led into captivity and for 400 years completely forsaken until Jesus Christ came. They did not know that they were forsaken. If the God of the Old Testament is the God of the New Testament; if He is the same yesterday, today and forever; if the post- Apostolic world has done worse than the Israelites; without contrition, without repentance, without restitution and without reconciliation, what reason is there not to believe that the world is also forsaken? In the Covid-19 pandemic that could not be stopped by prayer, about six million people died. To return to normal, pretending that God is answering prayers will be an insult to the intellect of intellectuals. Are God's commandments null and void because someone discovered the Epistles? At the end of history, if God forgives those who were misled, will He forgive those who misled them? Matthew 18:6 may be a hint of things to come.

Finally, if the Romans were enslaved, would they attend the Church that enslaved them? Why should Africans? Africans and Jews are the victims of the two greatest atrocities of history – slavery and the Holocaust. If God didn't answer prayers, then but now, it would show that African and Jewish lives do not matter to God Almighty. Humans have a short memory. Through the annual Remembrance Day, politicians have not allowed the World Wars to be forgotten. But religionists are allowed to forget that in tragedy after tragedy, prayers were not answered. Consequently, prosperity preachers have the audacity to keep peddling hope and do nothing to cultivate the Canadian Hutterite economy that relieves prayer dependency.

In a pandemic, many evangelical Christians will refuse vaccination. For a pastor to be vaccinated is an admission that the prayers he peddles are ineffective. Still, without fulfilling the condition for prayers to be answered, the Church will until doomsday, be led to believe that God is answering prayers. To suggest that we live in a Godforsaken world where God does not answer prayers is seen as heresy. But I will be disappointed, and any African should be disappointed if God answers prayers in spite of centuries of slavery without contrition, repentance, restitution and reconciliation with God and man.

Since Christianity was born, there have been numerous wars for control and wars for liberation. If destruction is in his interest, the Devil's advocate will argue that prayers are being answered. For example, in World War 1, about 40 million people died. People prayed for the war to end. It did. In World War 11, about 45 million people died. People prayed for the war to end. It did. In the Spanish flu, about 50 million people died around the world. People prayed for the flu to stop. It did. In the American Civil War, about 620,000 men died. People prayed for the war to end. It did. In the Great Depression, praying Christians lost homes, jobs and savings. In the Nigeria – Biafra War, the world watched hundreds of thousands of babies and children being starved to death. They prayed for the war to end. It did. In the Covid-19 pandemic, over six million people around the world died. People prayed for an end. It did end. The Russia - Ukraine War will be like other wars. It will end. As long as God Almighty is answering these prayers, according to the advocate, there is no need for change because 2 Chr 7:14 is part of the Old Covenant. If it is not broken, don't fix it. The prayer line is always open for those who face home foreclosure, family violence, divorce, suicide, etc. It is wise to get out of the Broadway. Humanity has a choice to make: obey God and prevent problems or disobey God and continue to pray about problems.

Christianity is plagued with denominations. Does the world need a Christian dictator who would consolidate all churches in his nation into one; and bring the clergy into compliance to the mandate that begets born again Christians who live by the Gospel like the Church of the first century? That dictator can only come from Europe. Truth be told, Europe has shaped the course of human history. The victor theology, slave trade, slavery, colonialism, and the needed industrial revolution were conceived in Europe. It has a responsibility to God and humankind to lead a crusade of repentance and reconciliation that has not happened since the precondition to answer prayers was proclaimed some 3,000 years ago. The rest of the world, including the United States, would follow Europe's revived moral leadership. It may not happen when NATO and Russia are perpetual enemies. So, until Russia joins NATO, all you can do is brighten the corner where you are.

May the views expressed on these pages not diminish the need to talk to the Father in heaven through prayer. Nevertheless, God Almighty should not be expected to do what the faithful are supposed to do for themselves. The Canadian Hutterites understand that. Ask them. Everything humans need to know is recorded in the Gospel. Nobody has been to heaven and back to be an expert. There are no experts in religion or Christianity that has become a show. The only prayers the Church needs are the Lord's prayer and request for the Holy Spirit. Based on the non-compliance to 2 Chronicles 7:14, this is a Godforsaken world. Flogging a dead horse is one thing but flogging a decomposed horse is beyond belief.

CHAPTER 10

Capitalism, Culture and Empty Pews

This may be another juncture to revisit <u>The Blind Men and the Elephant.</u> That allegory is interjected as a reminder to see from a global or God's perspective. The Golden Rule – "Treat others the same way you want them to treat you" – does not apply to wildlife. The carnivores must eat fresh. But through economics, humans can eat fresh indirectly, by investing in the misery of others. The stock market, for example, may be the temple of capitalism. When a corporation lays off employees, believe it or not, the stock market price rises because we have become investors in the misery of others. So, when an economist wins the annual Nobel prize in Economics, and decade after decade the gap between the rich and the poor continues to grow, those who are left behind may be justified to nurse anti- intellectualism. Those who have expertise in chaos seem to be leading them from crisis to crisis. Albert Nobel must have expected his prize to go to those who find ways to eliminate poverty. Nevertheless, without the influence of a good religion that is practiced, human life can mimic wildlife.

Capitalism is not new in human history. What is new is industrial or plantation capitalism. Just as Nazism was the apex of imperialism, slave trade and slavery - buying men, women and children to work a lifetime unpaid; and breeding to sell men, women and their children at an auction as a business - were the apex of capitalism. They are indelible marks in human history. Some men must be stopped from playing God or Satan on earth. Plantation capitalism and racism have been profitable to the economic system that produces billionaires and paupers. It also unleashed an ungodly chain reaction and everything that can go wrong began to go wrong. That disobedience of God's Golden Rule created multiple pathways of disaffection and discontent that have led to vacant Church pews and the sale of Churches. It does not take a prophet to predict that after Covid - 19 pandemic is over; more Churches will be turned into commercial use.

For over 200 years, African slave labor laid the foundation for American greatness. In the civil war to end slavery; and the buying and selling of men, women and children by Christians and Muslims of Arabia; in the struggle for civil rights and suffrage for women, the church was not in the lead because it was part of the problem. As would be expected in a jungle, when God's commandments are not obeyed, it is the defenseless that suffers the most. We know from history which continent has suffered the most. It has come to light that the last slave ship, the Clotilda, arrived in Alabama in 1860 with 110 African captives from the kingdom of Dahomey (now Benin) for enslavement in America. It has also come to light that even the Jesuits, the society of Jesus, sold 272 of their slave inventories to save Georgetown university from bankruptcy. It was not the Church of Jesus Christ that owned slaves; erased the interface between right and wrong; and sowed the seed of the polarization that is crippling good governance. It was the church of man and culture. If the Church were any other business, it would have closed down centuries ago. But unlike Sodom and Gomorrah, a few good men and women are keeping the Church alive.

When President Abraham Lincoln was assassinated in 1865, he was succeeded by Vice President Andrew Johnson, a Democrat. According to historians, he lived and died as a racist. While he and others like him were responsible for their actions, the Church created the culture that raised them. President Andrew Johnson was also a slave holder. He rescinded the plan to resettle each family that survived about 250 years of slavery with 40 acres of land and a mule. It never happened and will never happen. The men, women and children who had no property, no money and no education inherited poverty. Collectively, their descendants including those languishing in ghettos would have been trillions of dollars richer today.

History is uncomfortable to read when it is about what people who had power did to those who were powerless. That is still the case when men who conserve human nature assume public office and repeat the history they find uncomfortable by doing to others what they don't want others to do to them. Some learn from history. Those who conserve culture and human nature repeat history. In the manner of the Romans, they exercise power like the gods of mythology. When a hen that used to flee from others has a brood, it turns into a hawk. Such is the case with cultural conservatives in office to conserve human nature. The Golden Rule is one of the precepts that make Christianity a counterculture religion. No genuine Christian will follow culture to do to others what they don't want others to do to them. When President Andrew Johnson passed away, he had a state funeral. Like all Christians of the time, they went home to be with the Lord based on God's Amazing Grace.

The Golden Rule, the Great Commandment and the New Commandment, referred here as the Gospel, were made null and void by the doctrine of victor theology. From Congress to the Judiciary, the iron hand of policing, the Court and Jury, cultural conservative Christians have controlled spiritual conservative Christians and the fate of African Americans. Whatever historians may write, a reformed Republican party and a revived Pentecostal

Church will thank recent events for exposing the undercurrent of endemic hypocrisy, racism, conscious and unconscious bias that kept people down in the service of capitalism and culture. Since president Abraham Lincoln was assassinated, his party would later be controlled, not by spiritual conservatives, but by cultural conservatives.

To conserve the past, they wrapped the Bible and the gun with the American flag at the altar of patriotism. Southern Democrats like Governor George Wallace, played the culture card but were marginalized. In nations involved in colonialism or chattel- slave economy, cultural icons who did to others what they did not want others to do to them had Streets, bridges, Parks, Airports and Schools named after them. In Dixie, the victims of history have for generations walked past the statues honoring confederate soldiers who did to others what they did not want others to do to them. The same applies to many cities in Europe. Ask a Christian in those centuries of slavery and imperialism: "How do you know that you are saved?" The answer would be "I know that I am saved because I believe in Jesus Christ." That mindset based on victor theology still persists to this day. Satan believes in Jesus Christ too. You are saved because you are a born-again Christian who lives by the Gospel. Compliance to the Golden Rule is the visible evidence of a born-again Christian. That's what changes the world, not belief in Jesus Christ as a license to do wrong.

The Scriptures show that the Pharisees were not born of the Spirit. Without being born again, people are in a relationship with a religion not with God. The disobedience of God is sin; and to wear the cross while doing so is a mockery of God Almighty. If the Gospel of Jesus Christ is a guide, the slave traders, slave masters, the auctioneers and clergy - the master class- were no closer to God than the Voodoo priests in an African hut. They were all sinners. In the United Kingdom people see the police to be on their side, protecting them from violence and criminals. In the U.S.A the disenfranchised youth, whose ancestors survived slavery and inherited poverty, see the police as agents of continued oppression to be resisted. What a difference 40 acres of land and a mule would have made if men did not do to others what they did not want others to do to them. To "study the past in order to divine the future," according to Confucius, is a natural response for self-preservation. But to study the past in other to fix the future is the godly response. The Church that owned slaves, and erased the interface between right and wrong is what has to be fixed. When God's commandments and not obeyed in the animal jungle some animals suffer. The Golden Rule separates human beings from animals. Without teaching religion, Schools can teach the Golden Rule in Social Studies. And why it makes sense to anyone who is a human being. In Dixie, where Black is the color of crime, neither reconciliation nor restitution has been made for centuries of slavery as mortals continue to die and go home to be with the Lord without doing the will of the Lord.

In June 1998, John William King and two colleagues tied up 49-year-old African American named James Byrd Jr. and dragged him from the back of a truck for nearly three miles on a Texas country road. His body was found in pieces. What did he do? He was born with a different skin color. That was his crime. His skin color was the skin color of Adam and Eve from whom all humankind descended. Adam and Eve lived in a hot climate without clothes. Cows born with different skin colors seem to be more humane than some "human beings." Atheists watch what religious people do to the defenseless. Texas is a great State in the Bible belt, with good people and many mega-churches. But it was also where President John F. Kennedy was assassinated in 1963.

Prosperity preachers have ignored social justice and led gullible people to believe that by repeating a prayer, a person is born again and be in front of the queue to lay treasures on earth. In Georgia, where hate crimes were not recognized, a video was released on social media in May 2020, for a murder in February 2020. It exposed one more vigilante justice that has gone on for centuries. An athletic

25-year-old Ahmand Arbery was jogging through a neighborhood on a Sunday afternoon. He was shot and killed by a retired police constable McMichael and his son, with the apathy of a hunter who had killed an animal. Was that the first for a retired police constable? He believed that Ahmand looked like a man who committed recent burglary in the neighborhood that was not reported. The justice department did nothing until the video was released. In their learned helplessness, the parents did nothing because "Uncle Tom's" people do not expect justice where might is right. That has been their way of life. Late in May 2020, an African American man named George Floyd was handcuffed on a street sidewalk in broad daylight. Derek Chauvin, one of four men in police uniform knelt on his neck for over 8 minutes while he pleaded: "Please, I can't breathe." By standers also pleaded for humanity. He died. It is easy to see the ease with which some kill their spouses. It takes an animal to kill a human being. Chauvin had two homes with his wife but went to squeeze life out of people who inherited the poverty of a church mouse, after over 200 years of slavery. The death resulted in violent demonstrations across the United States.

Mayor Jacob Frey of Minneapolis, Minnesota told the news media:" Being Black in America shouldn't be a death sentence. "All these events are the product of the victor theology that allowed clergy and laity to live off the avails of unpaid servitude for over 300 years. In many nations around the world, percipient young men and women who have no common faith with Christians but a common humanity, took to the streets to proclaim "Black Lives Matter." On June 7, 2020 protesters in Bristol England pulled down the bronze statue of Edward Colston, a prominent 17th century slave trader, and tossed it into the harbor. According to the BBC, Colston was "a member of the Royal African Company which transported about 80,000 men, women and children from Africa to the Americas."

A protester in Oxford wanted the statue of Cecil Rhodes gone because "he doesn't stand for my values," he said. In Belgium, colonial King Leopold 11 under whose reign millions of Africans were murdered in the Belgian Congo in order to possess their land and resources, was removed in the city of Antwerp. The statues of the icons of colonialism and slavery have become an embarrassment to the humanity of a modern generation with a better conscience. As an accomplice in over 200 years of slavery, the church that owned the slaves and should have taught converts to observe the Golden Rule, has been a disservice to God Almighty. God's commandments were not allowed to interfere with capitalism. Without a video in the murder of George Floyd, it would have been one of numerous unreported cases of police murder for the past centuries. What does it say about the value of a human being whose skin tone is different in a Bible belt and Christendom? What does it say about the men and women who have a good conscience but remained silent for generations? What does it say about the value of the Church after 2,000 years?

What is happening after 2,000 years of Christianity is evidence of a church that has lost its way and its relevance in spirituality but not in entertainment. So, why would Atheists and godless communists value the church? They would probably be happy to see all churches sold. There are institutions that cannot reform themselves. The church may be one and needs a new foundation. It will take a boycott of the church to rebuild, reconsecrate and reclaim the church of Jesus Christ tarnished by slavery. Out of the decadence and demise of the church that stood for might is right and lived off the avails of centuries of unpaid servitude, will emerge the Church of Jesus Christ that stands for the Golden Rule.

How do disenfranchised people do the right thing, the right way when the right way falls on deaf ears for centuries? The Civil Rights movement led by Dr. Martin Luther king did the right thing the right away. The peaceful demonstration he led has not eased the legacy of centuries of slavery. Neither has violent demonstrations. He was assassinated and memorialized - problem solved. In every tragedy and death, people sing John Newton's Amazing Grace and move on as if nothing happened until the next one. "I was blind," he wrote, "but now I see." A Christian who is not born again is still blind. A Christian who does not live by the Gospel is still blind. Light will not overcome darkness until the church of cultural conservative Christians is held accountable. To wait for God to hold the Establishment to account will be too late for billions of souls. Again, imagine that a thousand years ago, the pastorate taught Christian converts that a Christian must be born again; and that a born-again Christian, by definition, lives by the Gospel. All the sad events of history could have been averted. The chaos in the world today could have been averted. Even African American pastors have followed church tradition - doing the same thing over and over expecting a different result. What Christians do is part of church history. It has led to discontent, contempt and empty pews. Society changes when those who conserve the past change. Being born again would have prevented or ended slave trade and slavery but it took street wisdom, not religion, to know that it cannot continue forever. It will take wisdom, not religion to know that greed, hatred and terrorism cannot continue forever.

And those who emigrate to America should know that nobody goes to America to inherit the assets but not the liabilities of history. It includes new African and Asian immigrants. Some of us have lived in the new world, including Australia and New Zealand, because of Christopher Columbus and other explorers. But the end does not justify the means. The problem is the victor theology that allowed clergy and laity to live off the avails of slave trade and slavery, and ruined aboriginal peoples. There are men and women who have the good conscience to recognize that besides Adolf Hitler, their own cultural militia of centuries past did to others what they did not want others to do to them. Some families used scores of African slaves to lay treasures on earth, and died leaving everything behind. What did it profit them? There are also the modern day anti-social cultural militia jingoes who see nothing wrong with the past. Their watchword is "Do it to them before they do it to us." They are the reason why social justice has been slow. Their association with the church has tarnished the image of the church. If the wrongdoers of the past are not who we are, should we not expedite action to ameliorate the wrongs of the past? If they are who we are, then we don't have to expedite action or even ameliorate the wrongs of the past.

Let us be honest to God and to ourselves. The Roman Magisterium undertook the responsibility to faithfully interpret the word of God to humankind. If its members included Africans and the Asians, would they have supported slavery? If an African has been pope in the past one thousand years, would he have supported slavery? In over 250 years of slave trade and slavery in America, the church became habituated to malfeasance. The world, particularly the U.S. is reaping what the church fathers sowed through their participation in the enslavement of one group of people. Still, they went home to be with the Lord, if you can believe it. Clearly, as volunteers rather than appointees of God Almighty, a few church fathers should not determine the spiritual destiny of humankind. If war is too important to be left to the generals, more than war, the soul is too important to be left to volunteers who were not appointed by God Almighty. Their use of slavery to enforce celibacy was the beginning of modern man's original sin. It released a pandemic of social maladies that have plagued humankind to this day. Yet many men and women in politics and religion (even cults), don't want to hear anything but praise. The enlightened people who leave the pews empty don't want to go down the garden path. They recognize that it is not possible to go home to be with the Lord without doing the will of the Lord.

Students apprised of Harriett Beecher Stowe's "Uncle Tom's Cabin" about pre- civil war Dixie, can understand the righteous anger that drove men to fight and die to end the abuse and enslavement of people because they look different. Prayers could not end slavery. One might even spare the thought that the church whose members fought and died to sustain slavery; the church that like the modem Taliban, stood against the suffrage of their mothers; and never taught parishioners to observe the Golden Rule, that church deserves to be turned into commercial use. Even then, America's founding fathers who wrote the constitution understood human nature, and created checks and balances because some of them were unprincipled men who did wrong, and claimed to be Christians because it was part of the culture.

For centuries the slave traders, slave masters and auctioneers heard that" God loves you no matter what you do. "Is it the same God who sent the Israelites into captivity for disobedience? Even now, some Christians support and go to such churches that make them feel good. Some of their preachers have published over 10 or 20 books. Do you have to buy and read all the books to understand how to be born again and live by the Gospel? There is no denomination that would criticize the others for leading their flock astray. Or stand up for Jesus. In the parable of the talents (Matthew 25:14 – 30) Jesus Christ showed that making profit is not a wrong. Capitalism is not new. Before the industrial capitalism, there was private capitalism. Farming and selling to make money; buying and selling products to make profit are as old as the Old Testament. What is new is plantation capitalism that is predatory. It is capitalism without a conscience. To starve babies and children to death for oil, for example, is capitalism without a conscience.

The story of Ananias and Saphira shows that the first century Christians shared their resources. The community leaders did not control the means of production and distribution prescribed by communism. It was socialism or traditional capitalism with a social conscience. The self -righteous sociopaths have not only tried to confuse socialism and communism, but also suggest that socialism is linked to moral decay. Does the gospel - the Golden Rule, the Great Commandment and the New Commandment lead to capitalism or socialism? Does "Bear one another's burdens and so fulfill the law of Christ" lead to a capitalist or socialist manifesto? The most conservative administrations also have the greatest disparity between the rich and the poor. It is like an administration by slave masters. The mothers in developing nations don't understand or care about all the political and economic "isms," formulated after the end of slavery. They want education for their children, employment and healthcare for all families, just like the Canadian Hutterites. The Nordic nations understand that. They have a better understanding of the Gospel. Their model of socialism is taxing, but they also understand that no man has ever gone to his grave with his wealth. Where the economy is based on "cradle to grave "care, nobody needs to lay treasures on earth. But in North America, the financial advisers remind people how much they need for a "comfortable retirement." They do not only save for retirement after raising children, but also have money for grandchildren. It raises the bar on avarice and stress. As a holistic construct, faith-based socialism reduces family dissociation, prostitution, drug abuse and other social maladies that occur when culture overrules God and reason. The church that authorized slavery to enforce celibacy started the ungodly chain reaction that theologians complain about today.

In the 1960s, with the United States Agency for International development (USAID) that lived up to its name, and the Peace Corps volunteer program, President John F. Kennedy joined the missionaries and their spiritual conservative supporters to use goodwill to create a predictable future. They had a vision. Their foreign policy was not about building walls, but about building bridges and making friends through positive influence. Americans were honored everywhere on earth. Other advanced nations were tempted to have their own agency for international development. That spirit left after the Kennedy assassination in 1963. It was also a time when capitalism was made democratic through progressive taxation. Beyond an income limit, a tax payer would pay up to 80 percent on the excess income under progressive taxation. If there was a Golden Age of capitalism, it was when progressive taxation created a bottleneck to limit the number of millionaires. The revenue from the taxation helped fund social services to assist those at the bottom of society who did the most essential jobs. By the 1970s and 80s, greed took cover. Cultural conservative Christians drove out liberals from office in nation after nation. Foreign policy reverted back to making enemies to sell weapons. The liberals who did not want to be seen to be soft on communism succumbed to the culture of "us and them." The politicians who promoted selfish living knew that a nation becomes rich by buying raw materials and banana from the poor and selling bicycles and cars to them.

So, technology must be guarded from those outside the loop. East is East and West is West became the dogma of the cultural conservatives whose vision was to replace direct colonialism with indirect colonialism. Even Latin America was not part of the West. The policy was also creating a future that cultural conservatives cannot control; a future rife with mass migration of the people they do not like; a future that needs walls between nations. Selfish living means sitting in a speed boat and take pictures of men, women and children drowning in a leaky boat. Thousands of such men, women and children have drowned in the Mediterranean Sea.

In the COVID- 19 pandemic, former Colonies, even under the banner of Commonwealth, depended on surplus vaccines from the developed nations to save their own lives. Politics and self-preservation demanded vaccine nationalism. It can happen again. How many lives could have been saved if half the nations of the world got the technology to be self-reliant in a pandemic? This has been the trend since the end of the Kennedy administration. In every juncture in this book, it is important to remember that the Romans who took over the church did not teach Christian converts to observe all things that Jesus Christ commanded, including the Golden Rule. Neither did the architects of Protestantism. The gullible jingoes have been told that government was a hindrance to their progress; that a nation needs small government and less regulation; and that the government that governs the least, governs the best. It is jungle politics. They called for regressive taxation. Regressive taxation is predatory capitalism. It gives capitalism a bad image and has produced an explosion of billionaires.

How do corporations earn billions of dollars tax free? How do individuals who use public infrastructure, earn millions of dollars tax free while some families are struggling to survive? How does conscience allow one human being to take home millions of dollars a year, while driving past homeless and jobless people on the streets? When a Christian government transitions from humane capitalism to unfettered and predatory capitalism that allows a few to horde wealth they can't take to the grave; when it borrows to fight wars, terrorism and insecurity at home; when it allows tax averse corporations to keep revenues from mineral resources, and arms sales tax free; that government will be saddled with debt and budget deficits that call for reduced social services that dehumanizes the society. The government can be voted out of office only to return a few years later to repeat the cycle. If those in economic distress are made prayer dependent by the church, discontent with politics and capitalism would lead to discontent with the religion that raised the politicians. The result has been the exodus from the church. If the Bolshevik revolution was led by born again Christians, they would have changed the world. Even as we demonize "godless communism," we cannot be proud of godly capitalism that began at the slave auction of men, women and children.

From Inclusion to Predatory Capitalism

Capitalism stopped working for most people when it became predatory. Its regressive taxation replaced progressive taxation. And it privatized prisons in America, for the investors in the misery of others. In a capitalist economy, the many who are homeless, jobless or incarcerated in those prisons cannot see the benefit of religion, democracy, freedom and the rule of law. Most of the prisoners are better off in prison where they have food and shelter. Healthcare is tied to one's job in America. The underclass who are either jobless or easily laid off cannot afford Health Insurance. Those who are insensitive to the plight of others are in all walks of life and religions. It is the people who do harm physically, not those who do harm policy wise that end up in prison. Yet it is the policy makers that do more harm to society than those in prison.

Think about this: suppose a man bought a new car and followed the instructions of the manufacturer. If he continues to have problems with the car, he would be justified to question the competence of the manufacturer. Similarly, suppose the rulers of the world obeyed God's Golden Rule, the Great Commandment, New Commandment and their social implications. If life does not get better for all, mortal man will also be justified to question the competence of God Almighty his creator. It is manifestly obvious that if victor theologians obeyed God's Golden Rule, there would have been no slave trade and slavery. Instead of praying to God, it is more productive to pray to the rulers of the world, not God Almighty. They can choose to be Regents or the Executors of God's will. Regardless of their choice, the Almighty has the last word. In Egypt, the Pharaohs were buried with treasures for the afterlife. In Xian, China, an Emperor was buried with Terra Cotta chariots for war in the afterlife. Nobody leaves this planet with a penny. That has not stopped the hoarding of untold wealth even among Christians who have read the Parable of the rich man and Lazarus. And Scriptures that discourage laying treasures on earth. Human beings are said to be creatures of habit. When a billionaire passes away, it is in public interest to know how much he or she took to the grave.

During the slave economy, what mattered to the Christian slave traders, slave masters and their politicians was money. That is still the case today particularly, making money on weapons for blood-shed. Those men- they were men - passed away and left everything behind. The love of money is an addiction. That addiction has been aided by regressive taxation that encourages hoarding wealth. Is it not unconscionable if beggars and homeless veterans should live in the same city where a privileged few take home millions of dollars a year? Thanks be to the soldiers who fought and died overseas, to stop the spread of "godless communism." Some of those beggars go from car to car in mid- traffic, begging for spare change. One of them could be Jesus Christ in the flesh or a theophany. Is it possible that at the end of history, billionaire and millionaire-Christians and politicians opposed to social justice would say to Jesus: "When did we see you a beggar and did not help you?" It is true that billionaires become billionaires by chance and not by choice. Who would aspire to be a billionaire in a world with starving babies and children? But a Christian can choose to live by Romans 10:9 or by Galatians 6:2, both written by St. Paul. One is nominal Christianity; the other is practical Christianity. The two groups will not end up in the same Abraham's bosom.

In Psalm 14:1 and 53:1, the Psalmist notes that "The fool hath said in his heart,' there is no God. ' " Man's inhumanity to man may be one reason for unbelief. The Gentiles who face adversity and see inhumanity and unethical behavior question the existence of God they expect should intervene. Some Jewish people whose ancestors had a direct encounter with God Almighty question the existence of God who should have intervened in the Holocaust and sent the Messiah. He did send the Messiah to prevent the Holocaust by teaching the Gospel that was not obeyed. And he opened the door of faith to include the rest of the world. Before questioning the existence of God, why not question why we have not obeyed His commandments and ran an economy like the Hutterites, even in a homogeneous nation? A thousand years ago, for example, homoge-neous England, Scotland and Wales would have been governed like a Canadian Hutterite colony if evangelism fulfilled the full mandate of the Great Commission. By observing all things whatsoever that Jesus Christ commanded, with their social implications, education, healthcare and employment for all families will not be the "pie in the sky "or the "pipe dream" they are now. Cultural pluralism engendered by colonialism makes universal employment a pipe dream.

Pagans and atheists are asked to believe in God. But victor theology leads people to do to others what they don't want others to do to them or at best, are insensitive to the pain of others. That was the dilemma of the African slaves who miraculously, believed in God. Now, when believers cherish a lean and mean government, why believe? In communist nations, the citizens are not all happy with their governance. In capitalist nations, the citizens are not all happy with their governance. So how do you run an economy that makes it easier to obey God?

The Nordic countries prove that the closer a nation is to Christian civilization through compliance to God's Commandments the happier they are with their governance. A Nordic economy today makes it easier to obey God than an American economy. The Nordic economy tomorrow with education, healthcare and employment for all families will make it easier to obey God than the Nordic economy today. It will be expected to be crime free. Every society needs people in all walks of life. In the COVID -19 pandemic it was not the professionals and billionaires but the lowest paid men and women who did the most essential work in society, that died in large numbers in the hospitals. Hockey, football, baseball and basketball players earn more money than their school teachers. If money is the measure of success, they are more successful than their teachers. And what about the sincere Priests and Nuns who took a vow of poverty to serve God and man? They retire and die in poverty. If money is the measure of success, were they successful? How can they and the those who lived in mansions possibly end up in the same place by God's Amazing Grace?

The purpose of life for a lion is to eat other animals and raise offspring who do the same. Should that be the purpose of life for a human being? Economic policy allows men to eat money rather than fresh. That money comes from the pain and misery of others. Those who clean offices in the big cities are invisible. They work at night. Some men may not believe in God. But nobody who believes in humanity would aspire to be the tax -averse billionaire who drives past homeless people to offices cleaned by invisible men and women struggling to make ends meet. Some socialists suggest that nobody should be a billionaire. The billionaires and not the culprits. Regressive taxation made them billionaires.

In 2020, several major corporations paid no taxes to their government. It takes a dead conscience to earn millions of dollars and pay no taxes. That economic policy was not instituted by atheists. Paradoxically, the moral sense of right and wrong is more alive and well among most atheists than in many religious groups. Some men who profess faith in God are more likely to oppose taxation than atheists. Progressive taxation reduces the income gap between the very rich and the very poor, to raise funds for social services for all. It humanizes all citizens high and low. Like atheists, humanists who don't want to bear the baggage of religion support progressive taxation. Apparently, the resistance is from the antisocial cultural conservatives who serve Mammon. If the goal of humankind is to be less like wildlife, and more like a just society, universality of healthcare and education that includes the children of billionaires will be unfair. But it will be fair under progressive taxation.

Jesus told the rich young ruler who kept the law:" If you want to be perfect, go, sell what you have and give to the poor, and you will have treasure in heaven; and come follow Me." (Matthew 19:21 NKJV). He went away sorrowful. He eventually died and left all that wealth behind. It is a lesson about hoarding wealth at the expense of eternal values. To be a Christian has a cost. Everybody came into the world empty-handed and will leave empty-handed. Religion should not be forced on anyone. So, Church and State remain separate. Until the dead phone back to confirm their abode, the Church will be judged by family stability. The State will be judged by the number of parents and grandparents who retire in poverty or die in large numbers in an epidemic because of their living condition. Those who peddle religion and democracy fall short on one or both counts.

By Whose Authority?

The chief priests and Elders of ancient Israel had followed the teaching of Moses for centuries. When Jesus came to heal the sick and teach the Gospel, they exercised a natural human response and asked: "Tell us, by what authority are You doing these things? Or who is he who gave you this authority? (Luke 20:2 NKJV), Through miracles and healing, He showed where His authority came from. As a prefect in a boarding school ran in Eastern Nigeria by missionaries from the UK., I could tell students what to do. They knew that it was by the authority of the principal who could expel an insubordinate student. No student who took an entrance examination to get in would want to be expelled. By whose authority was David king over his parents and Elders? He was appointed by God Almighty. He was a servant king, not their master. "Honor your father and your mother" is one of the Ten Commandments. Man was not created to be a god to fellow mortals but a servant leader. Tyranny gave birth to democracy. But for genuine democracy to endure, the world must know by whose authority a politician rules over his or her parents, grandparents, teachers, professors, classmates and pastors, if any. Anyone in authority is also under authority.

In some nations, the Prime Minister has become the consequential and de facto ruler of the nation. And therefore, rules over the monarch. By whose authority does the Prime Minister rule over the monarch? It should be through the authority of a higher moral power, not in virtue of a ballot box. Being a leader must be by the authority of a higher power. What is the will of the higher power? If they were inspired by the Holy Spirit to serve, they would treat every man, woman and child the same way they want to be treated. Otherwise, they were inspired by a different spirit to serve their party and base supporters. In fact, those who get into politics to use government to do to others what they don't want others to do to them, are not inspired or directed by the Holy Spirit but by the endemic evil spirit in man that panders to human nature.

Over 45,000 people commit suicide in the United States each year. It has created the science of suicidology. If anyone is not happy to be alive, suicide is not the solution. For peace of mind, order and good government, they need a change of administration or a communal settlement like a Canadian Hutterite colony with education, employment and healthcare for all families. In an evil world, it will be called godless socialism or a radical left agenda. Yet, the test of good governance is how many parents and grandparents retire in poverty or die in a pandemic because of their living condition. Thousands of their children commit suicide every year because being dead is better than living in their country.

Who runs what their pastors call an evil world? Is it not human beings, including those who call Jesus "Lord, Lord" and do not what He says? The clergy and laity who lived off the avails of the enslavement of millions of African men, women and children were the supreme power on earth and the administrators of that evil world. That church has not shown repentance and reconciliation with God and man because the cultural conservative members inherit assets, not liabilities. Those men and women of the slave economy were not inspired by the Holy Spirit. Now by whose authority and which spirit inspires the administration under whom thousands of men and women will commit suicide next year? Fifty years from now, there will be another set of politicians in every nation. By whose authority will they rule over their parents, grandparents, classmates,

teachers and professors and those who will commit suicide? To be
the president, prime minister or governor in a nation is not a right. A
dictator or despot has no fear of a higher power and acts accordingly.
He is the State. Christian politicians like President John F. Kennedy,
a Democrat, ran for office to use government to make life better for
their fellow human beings, even beyond their borders. There are
others who, in the name of balanced budget, use government to ruin
the lives of others. Is it not fair to ask who their pastors were, if any?

A conservative politician whose party had been in office for
over a decade got into office to balance a recurrent budget deficit.
He laid off some civil servants, demolished a hospital, sold another
one, and laid off some medical personnel. He balanced the budget
in record time, and distributed oil royalty cheques to the taxpayers,
both rich and poor. His policy ruined some families and increased
the gap between the rich and the poor. Nevertheless, he was hailed
by cultural conservatives for "slaying the dragon." A debt-free and
lean government at all cost, is a conservative ideal. A few years later,
the budget was in deficit again. Was the administration inspired by
the Holy Spirit? Since Adam and Eve walked on this planet, humankind has yet to learn one simple empirical truth - no corpse has yet
left this planet with one penny.

So, to rational minds, a man or woman who has no compassion
should not be in politics. A man or woman who cannot write his or
her own speech should not be in politics. Those who talk big but do
nothing or ignore human suffering but serve the interest of those
who hoard wealth, should not be in politics. Politics is about life or
death. Those who are careless about life should not be in politics.
The future looks bright because future generations will question the
commission of a 40 -year- old president, prime minister, or governor
to control their lives and destiny. Or their divine right to rule over
their own parents, grandparents, teachers, professors and classmates.
Their mandate must be based on the authority that is higher than
government. That authority is the author of the Golden Rule. That

moral authority gives leadership legitimacy. The so-called backsliders hope for a new generation of church leaders who have the vision to abandon victor theology, and raise born again Christians who run an economy that is based on education, employment and healthcare for all families, and let it spread around the world. This 21st century is a critical century in this political denouement: by whose authority do a few control the lives of so many?

The Trump I thought We Knew

When a billionaire is running for public office, one is inclined to believe that he will not need donations because his motive is to help people. That he would be a politician eager to do what is right for God's long neglected common people who are poor. And so, when Donald J. Trump defeated eight Republican party presidential contenders in 2016, including some seasoned politicians, he looked like the anti- establishment man that the common people had been waiting for. He went on to win the presidency. He inherited a response to President Bashar al Assad's war in Syria. When many were killed in a gas attack in April 2017, President Trump told reporters at the White House: "When you kill innocent children, innocent babies, little babies, with chemical gas that is so lethal - people were shocked to hear what gas it was. That cross many, many lines beyond a red line, many, many lines."

I was converted to his vision. Before joining the Biafra Army in the Nigeria- Biafra war (1967 - 70), I Iran a Red Cross feeding center for starving children. In what could be described as a jihad, hundreds of thousands of babies and children were deliberately starved to death for the control of oil. Some were airlifted to Gabon to be fed. My radio message for Obazu Christian mission broadcast on two Radio stations in Eastern Nigeria included this:" In August 1968, a TIME magazine reporter, James Wilde reported that 'There is so little food that one feels guilty every time one eats.' To anti-establishment President Donald Trump, killing babies crosses many, many lines. If he read that report in 1968, would he abide the spiritual callousness it took to let hundreds of thousands of innocent babies and children to be starved to death until 1970? To what end?"

I sent a copy of the message to one of Trumps daughters known to have the ear of the President. She was to tell her father that the key to a successful presidency is to demand compliance to the Golden Rule in the United States and the Middle East. The President I thought we knew went on to thrash African countries and fan the flames of racial hatred in America. In the last year of his presidency, I got a deluge of emails to send money to make America great again. Every month had a fund-raising target. One e-mail reads: Friend, I emailed you. The vice president emailed you. My sons, Don and Eric, both emailed you. Lara emailed you. Newt Gingrich emailed you. Ted Cruz emailed you. Sarah Huckabee Sanders emailed you. The Trump Finance Team e-mailed you. And now I'm emailing you, again. Each day, my team has given me a list of Patriots who stepped up to help us reach our Final End -of- Month Goal, and each day, I've noticed Your Name Is Still Missing."

How can men who mistreat you ask you to send a donation? In the midst of a pandemic, they did not care if you were alive or dead. The e-mail did not stop until I sent this reply: Please do not send any more emails. My father has passed away. It was not a lie. My father passed away in 1970 just after the Nigeria- Biafra war. In fine print at the end of each petition for donation is a disclaimer – "Contributions to the Trump Make America Great Again Committee are not deductible for federal income tax purposes." Those who contributed month after month clearly had vested interest in his re-election. And so, the insurrection of January 6, 2021 should be no surprise. And the lie that they were cheated because he won in a landslide may not assuage those who went to prison in addition to their pecuniary loss. A Canadian cannot donate to an American election. Besides, if the

America that enslaved my fellow Africans was ever ethically great, it was under the administration of President John F. Kennedy when some of my High School teachers were peace corps volunteers, and the United States Agency for International Development lived up to its name.

The Chinese Dimension

Before President Deng Xiaoping, China lived under communism based on State control of the economy. It demanded from each, according to his ability and to each, according to his needs. It seems spiritual but it was unproductive. The needy were growing faster than the able. Under that paradigm, some nations in Africa were ahead of China. But from 1978 when China opened up to the rest of the world, to 2018, about 700 million people were lifted out of poverty. How did such an economic miracle happen? While on a group tour of China in 1989, in city after city the construction cranes poked into the sky. The Chinese leader, Deng Xiaoping had proposed a paradigm shift from communism to "capitalism with Chinese characteristics." Instead of getting rich together under communism, the government became a corporation in competition with foreign corporations.

Foreign corporations established manufacturing plants to take advantage of cheap labor. The government had a development plan with time limits; development zones with leaders expected to meet quotas. Enterprising citizens established businesses in partnership with foreigners. A Steel plants in Wuhan in 1989, for example, retained employees who had nothing left to do. Under modern capitalism they would have been laid off to become homeless. There were no homeless people or beggars on the streets of China. The leaders had a vision and understood that "Where there is no vision, the people perish." The policy lifted millions of people out of poverty in record time, not by giving families gifts of goats, sheep, hens and roosters, but by allowing free enterprise to unleash the power of greed for government, citizens and foreign corporations. Greed is a tonic to economic growth but it must be controlled through progressive taxation.

Nobody can quarrel with success. Whatever serves the common good must be godly. Socialism or inclusive capitalism serves the common good. Marcus Garvey, (1887 - 1940), a Jamaican activist once proposed State capitalism. It was a good idea but from the wrong source. Corporations are tax averse. The State is not subject to taxation and can keep its profit. Cultural conservatives who dictate domestic and foreign policy do not serve the common good. As Christians, will they be willing to use capitalism with Christian characteristics to lift millions of fellow citizens out of poverty? If St. Paul's charge to bear one another's burdens and so fulfill the law of Christ, is a radical left agenda, the answer is no. Capitalism with Christian characteristics is an inclusive capitalism. Inclusive capitalism is the socialism that cultural conservatives who have sold off crown corporations detest. So, it will not happen.

An American entrepreneur raised the price of Daraprim from $3.50 to $750.00. The excuse was that insurance companies will cover the cost. Such capitalism is one of the ways Americans pay more for healthcare, for less outcome than nations with universal healthcare. "American Greed" on MSNBC is a favorite program on television. There are Christians who value human life more than money. There are others who value money more than human life. The same can be said of corporations. In the end, nobody leaves this planet with one penny. "Sleeping With The Devil. How Washington Sold Our Soul For Saudi Crude" by Robert Baer, speaks for itself.

On the corporate side, American corporations produce at low cost in China, to sell high at home. Since every problem has a scapegoat, China is accused in Washington, D.C, politics for stealing technology brought to its doors by capitalist entrepreneurs. Two heads are said to be better than one. No nation has more heads than China. It is not the only reason China will get ahead. It can make a ten- year plan and see it to completion. The U.S. cannot make a plan that will not be reversed by another administration. Democracy honors the free will that allows man to do right or wrong. In nations like China and Cuba, the State controls what serve the common good. The leaders are not in office to enrich themselves or an interest group but to do what they believe to be in the national interest. That is why they can handle a pandemic better than democracies. The democracies can equally do the same if they were obedient to the Gospel. Nevertheless, the U.S. is a microcosm of the world. A nation that is representative of the world has leverage over all nations.

When China Rules the World by Professor Martin Jacques can be frightening. No nation will rule the world. But cultural conservative Christians who look for enemies will do well to begin to practice the Golden Rule. It will lay the foundation for peaceful coexistence rather than confrontation; and ensure the survival of religion in China. In a nation that treats religious extremism as mental illness, compliance to the Golden Rule will also ensure the survival of the children of those who kill innocent men, women and children in pursuit of spiritual imperialism. Spiritual imperialism is no more viable than political imperialism. The world history that has been shaped by monotheists is nothing to be proud of. It has been tragic. Philosopher Confucius of China has this advice: "study the past in order to divine the future." They have studied the imperial past. Atheists do not believe in God or a religion that leads men to do to others what they don't want others to do to them. After slave trade and slavery; and after the historic events of September 11, 2001, monotheists must ensure that the war on terrorism does not become a war on religion that could end with the use of nuclear weapons. In some jurisdictions, people deemed to have the potential to do harm in the name of religion are institutionalized for re-education. It is controversial but extreme action must be avoided or condemned as much as extreme reaction.

Impressionable young men have been led to believe that they are victims, never villains in history; and God rewards good deeds. Killing unbelievers is a good deed. The U.S. Council on Foreign Relations estimated that Boko Haram Jihadists based in Northern Nigeria killed 37,000 Africans between 2011 and 2018. For what? Religion, a Cultural Religion. It cannot happen in China. They don't believe in a God who wants believers to kill or enslave people. Muslims have been killing native Africans in the name of the Arabian religion since the seventh century. Can Atheists study what has happened to Africans and African Americans and believe in God? If one group of victor theologians do not have the moral authority to condemn other victor theologians; if a nation without religion is the only safe nation on earth, there is no hope for humanity.

People can believe whatever they want to believe but must never use what they believe to harm others. The abuse of power by imperial Rome got the world to where it is today. The Almighty God we recognize, has no more Levites. The religious leaders of every religion on earth are volunteers. Practicing the Golden Rule will preempt conflicts between those who don't believe in God and those who do but still do harm to others. It will eliminate the mutual distrust between the East and West and ensure that the past is not prologue to the future. Those who have studied the past know that nothing changes until something changes. The world will not see peace and goodwill to all until the institutions that are producing the bad actors are changed. In the U.S.A and Russia, there are demonstrators for social justice. Each nation's cultural conservatives see their own demonstrators as thugs but the others as legitimate. They do not have a common yardstick for morality. This double standard diminishes genuine Christian faith.

Some nations have done wrong on the right side in the name of capitalism. Others have done wrong on the left in the name of communism. The people of faith do not seem to have a common understanding of right and wrong. As China, a leading nation among the poor nations becomes an economic and military power, what will prevent mutual self-destruction is not the ideology of the left or right but compliance to God's Golden Rule that precludes a cultural perspective. Despite their Christian faith the slave traders and clerics saw the world through a cultural or monocular vision. No matter how religious a man may be, without being born again he has the propensity to do to others what he does not want others to do to him.

An enlightened humanity cannot see the world through the lens of East or west, North or South. As long as two or more people interact, even in the family, without compliance to the Golden Rule they are bound to have problems. How do nations and leaders of all stripes level the playing field? In a video presentation to mark UN 75th anniversary, China's President Xi Jinping noted that "mankind has never been so powerfully capable to overcome the difficulties we face and change the world we live in." He called on the U.N. to stand firm for justice. "Mutual respect and equality among all countries, big or small, represents the progress of our times," he said," and is the foremost principle of the U.N. charter. No country has the right to dominate global affairs, control the destiny of others, or keep advantages in development all to itself." It is imperative, he noted, "that the representation and voice of developing countries be increased so that the UN could be more balanced in reflecting the interests and wishes of the majority of countries in the world."

The great powers should respect international law, and eschew double standards. "Cold war mentality, ideological lines or zero -sum game are no solution to a country's own problem still less an answer to mankind's common challenges," he said in the speech punctuated with "multilateralism. "For those who see from a global perspective, the speech was like a sermon from a church pulpit. Yet, it is fair to say that it was a speech from a nation run by atheists, addressed to Russia and the U.S. in particular that are run by professing Christians. At the end of the Second World War, Japan benefited from multilateralism. Now, no nation has benefited from multilateralism more than China that is also a nuclear power. Should we change the rules? The billionaires of China give it a capitalist credential.

Within all nations there is a concentration of wealth in a few hands. And between nations, technology separates rich nations from poor nations. Is it not true that "mankind has never been so powerfully capable to overcome the difficulties we face and change the world we live in"? Technology can help every nation to be self-reliant but the will to help is not there. Perhaps China can also help spread the technology that capitalism brought to its doors. The Vietnam war was fought to contain the spread of communism. It will be inhuman to contain the spread of technology through war or neglect. Like charity, foreign policy begins from home. Keeping down any group or nation trying to stand up is not a viable policy. Practicing and demanding the Golden Rule at home and abroad is a more viable policy. It levels the playing field for all. With one foot in faith and the other foot outside of faith, an agnostic cannot compete in a laissez-faire economy. Without discipline, rules are worthless. While the capitalist is selling the rope that will be used to hang him, it is imperative to demand from all nations, compliance to the Golden Rule to ensure that the rope is never used. For some men, unfortunately, a life without conflict is boring.

A former Chinese ambassador to the UK, Liu Xiaoming opined that China's goal is a shared future for all humankind. Skeptics may not believe that, but that was the policy of President John F. Kennedy that ended with his assassination. As a rising power, China is filling the void left in Africa by declining powers when goodwill began to recede after the Kennedy administration. The future superpowers will be those that exert influence based on goodwill, not the military capacity to kill and destroy. However, nations like Russia or China are not seen to be an open society. The resources of the World Health Organization (WHO), for example, would have been deployable to contain COVID -19 in Wuhan, China but secrecy cost millions of lives and crippled the global economy for over two years.

Millions of retired people lost their savings; thousands lost their lives as well. It resurrected the demonization of communism and anti-China sentiments. China cannot be as democratic as the United States. About 2,000 people are shot dead each year by their fellow Americans. There are anarchists who would blow up a federal building or carry guns to intimidate politicians. If China with four times the population has that kind of democracy, how many in China will be killed by their fellow Chinese each year? The COVID- 19 casualties in China would have been four times the number in America. However, after COVID -19 toll in human and material resources around the world, the government has a responsibility to the rest of humankind to be an open society where harmless men and women who believe in God are free to worship and speak the truth. In a gated community, outsiders are restricted. To live in a gated community and take advantage of open communities is unfair. Relationships demand reciprocity. It cannot be said enough that within families, within nations and between nations, human beings cannot get along without compliance to the Golden Rule. it makes sense to any human being regardless of culture, ethnicity, gender, religion or political ideology.

The East and West, North and South

Australia is betwixt and between. At the University of Melbourne, Professor Martin Jacques author of "When China Rules the World" removed the filters of culture and offered a candid and unsettling view of China. The look of civilization in China is different from Western civilization. In the western-centric ways of thinking, according to him, modernization is synonymous with westernization. To those who cannot see the world from a different perspective, he opined that China has not been western, has never been and will never be western. It sees itself as a civilization State that is different from Western civilization. China, according to Professor Jacques, had the capacity to conquer most of Asia but didn't. It was constrained by the imperative of civilization. The outside media, Professor Jacques notes, is obsessed over the lack of democracy in China but most of the people are not. The State is not the enemy but the head of the family.

The closest to this mindset, I believe, are the Scandinavian countries where citizens are happy to pay taxes to the government to serve the common good well into old age. His portrait of China is also a contrast to the colonial conquests in the name of the State or religion (vide www.Stephenblanton.com/growth). Slave trade and slavery, among the nations that embraced religion, turned religion into a curse for humanity rather than a blessing. That includes Russia that was once far more advanced than China until Deng Xiaoping came up with the transition to "capitalism with Chinese characteristics." Nevertheless, the Chinese are no saints. Some have done wrong to others who looked different. Everybody in the world cannot be African, Arabian, Chinese, English, French, German, Indian, Japanese, Russian or any other group. It is fair to say that all civilizations have been resistant to Christian civilization because it is counter culture.

The Great Commandment, which is about the love God and neighbor, has been in the Bible since 2,000 BC. Jesus Christ used the Parable of the Good Samaritan to expand the scope of neighbor. But the church in the East and West ignored the Golden Rule, the Great Commandment and the New Commandment. They ignored the Gospel. Pope Pius 1X, the Bishop of Rome and longest serving pope, woke up one morning and introduced the dogma of Papal infallibility. It was all about the use of religion to exercise power. In the U.S., the clergy and laity lived off the avails of the slavery of Africans for nearly 250 years. It was the antipode of Christian civilization. So much for papal infallibility. In the former Soviet Union, the clergy and State hierarchy lived in opulence from the pain of serfs. That is anti-Christian civilization. The Bolshevik revolution of 1917 ended the system and introduced communism. Since that Revolution, some nations have practiced Christianity without Christ. Some have practiced culture embracing Christ. The world was turned topsy -turvy.

Mahatma Gandhi was a Hindu. He read the Gospel and practiced Christianity better than the Christians he confronted in South Africa over apartheid, and in India over colonial rule. In China, Confucius was not the author of the Golden Rule that has been in the Bible for over a thousand years before he was born. But this sage used it to teach moral values, melded with traditional pursuit of integrity, conformity to rituals, self- discipline and the respect for elders that morphed into ancestor worship. China has benefited from technology from Hong Kong, Taiwan and U.S. corporations in search of cheap labor. In a decade, it may overtake the U.S. as the largest economy. Culture is a house. One must get out to see it from the outside. Few historians and journalists are blunt enough to see from a global perspective and call a spade a spade and not a shovel. Whether we believe it or not, the Gospel is at the core of human civilization.

The Greeks and Romans introduced democracy, individualism and rational thinking. But colonialism, slave trade and slavery tarnished the foundational Christian civilization. Men who professed faith in God ignored His Golden Rule for centuries. Consequently, they led friends and Allies from crisis to crisis and the loss of other people's lives. By avoiding colonialism, slave trade and slavery unbelievers became the better standard bearers of civilization. "When China rules the world" is frightening to the people of faith. But when compassion rules the world does not. That's more likely to happen if the Church rediscovers the Golden Rule. And capitalism with Chinese characteristics is matched by capitalism with Christian characteristics. It is not communism or socialism that leads to an empty pew, it is the unfulfilled mandate of the Great Commission that, beginning with slavery, unleashed predatory capitalism, declining trust and declining faith. Those who promote predatory capitalism and the hoarding of wealth; those who make good look evil and evil look good; and the State capitals where right or wrong depends on who is involved, all bear some responsibility when a church goes up for sale.

If world history is to be summarized in one word, it will be "control." Some people do not like to be controlled. While his personal life was questioned, King Henry V111 founded the church of England to avoid the control of the church of Rome. And since no African or Asia has been pope in modern history to demonstrate Catholicism, China has also avoided foreign control through the church. It is an embarrassment that it has gone from a backward nation in 1949 to be the second largest economy in 2021, not because of the influence of religion but by shunning religion. If capitalism is defined by the number of billionaires, there are or will be more billionaires in China than in many capitalist nations. Still, the specter of communism will linger on. Trying to grow billionaires is detrimental to civilization and stability. To deal with the emerging non-Christian nations, monotheists require a superior moral power, not superior weapons. Moral power now trumps military power. Since history does not confer that moral power, monotheists must start anew. It is never too late to start practicing the Gospel.

Slave trade and slavery where the apex of capitalism. The Quakers and the Puritans did not own slaves. They were righteous people. They were persecuted by the Establishment church that owned slaves. So, the righteous people became sinners; the sinners became the righteous and those who suffered or survived slavery became the criminals. That is a counterfeit church whose influence is pervasive in politics and economics.

There are young men in religious or "democratic nations" who have the freedom to carry guns and kill people. Some had no jobs and no food but freedom. A man who has a job but not the freedom to carry guns and do whatever he wants may be happier than a man who has all the freedom but homeless or jobless. Injustice and inhumanity have persisted for centuries because the few who shape domestic and foreign policy see the world through the lens of secular culture. Empires rise and fall. The next empire will endure or fall based on compliance or noncompliance to the Gospel. That is the essence of a stable civilization and the will of God who is above government. Since slave trade and slavery, Christians and non-Christians have run their governments as if there is no God and no Golden Rule. Now, no nation can fix their politics without fixing their religion. If their religion does not teach compliance to the Golden Rule, they cannot fix their politics. In his inaugural address, President Ronald Reagan, a Republican icon proclaimed that "Government is not the solution to our problem, government is the problem." Jesus Christ may like to hear about that. If government is the solution in China and the problem in the United States, by 2040 the world will know who is right.

CHAPTER 11

The Case for Cultural Populism

In any culture, those who have education, wealth or power, have a secure and comfortable family life. If they see beyond culture, they can understand the concept of a common humanity and can afford to be compassionate, as genuine Christians. But the poor and needy cannot. To "love your neighbor as yourself "does not come naturally. It is not part of any culture, particularly when the neighbor is a Samaritan. Every nation cannot be a nation of immigrants. No nation in the Old World, including the nations of Africa, Asia and the Middle East wants the migration or immigration that creates a pluralistic society in conflict with or in opposition to the native culture. People have unlimited right to do as they please in their native land but not in someone else's native land. Without a doubt, no city in the Middle East wants to be like London with people from all corners of the globe who have the freedom to bring their religion and culture. Those who go to Rome are expected to behave like the Romans. The Christian women who go to Muslim nations cover their hair to demonstrate that when you go to Rome you behave like the Romans. Cultural populists expect the same. One must be prepared to walk in their shoes to understand their resentment to the elites and the classroom experts who control their lives and lead them from crisis to crisis.

In the first century, persecution and migration helped the spread of Christianity. In the modern world the cultural conservatives who conserve the past fear that terrorism and bad governance will spread refugees bearing cultural religions that can overcome their culture. Nobody wants any culture to disappear. While the New World is the land of immigrants, premised on a melting pot philosophy, for French Quebec to resist the influx of English-speaking people in order to preserve their language is understandable. The Old World has cultural and ethnic identity to preserve. The European populists do not want theirs to be the land of immigrants as a consequence of colonial guilt. Like the aboriginal peoples of the New World, they do not want to lose cultural identity with every wave of immigrants or migrants.

Every nation in Europe celebrates festivals, carnivals or traditions that distinguish one culture from another, and attracts tourists. Tourists go to other nations to have a different experience. Migrants create economic and cultural anxiety for the jobless and under - employed indigenous population left behind by the elitist policymakers. The English Shires and Midlands do not aspire to be London where Christianity is like one more cultural religion among others. Those who resent the elites wonder in despair, how a nation that controlled one-quarter of the world cannot build a church in the homeland of those who build several worship centers in London. Some cultural populists may not understand the Christianity they profess or even be Christians in the traditional sense. But they are aware that cultural religions can replace the religion of their grandparents in their very own homeland. In Turkey, Hagia Sophia in Istanbul (former Constantinople) was founded as a cathedral in 537 AD. It was turned into a museum and from a museum to a Mosque.

If churches are also disappearing because of poor attendance and are replaced by something different, how long will it be before a man like Adolf Hitler or a cult leader appears as a savior and provoke violence?

The elite only care about their economic interest, not about the poor or disappearing churches. In politics, there are no permanent friends or enemies, only permanent interests, they say. Since the Gospel (not Christianity), is eradicating the culture of "us and them," enlightened Christians have no fear of cultural religions. The Gospel – the Golden Rule, the Great Commandment and the New Commandment- has no equal. Cultural religions were founded by a member or members of the culture. Christianity is not the religion of any culture. It is counterculture. The foundation members were Jews and Gentiles. If Christianity was not corrupted by slave trade, slavery, racism and colonialism, those fleeing from their homeland with all kinds of religions would easily be converted to the global religion that has redeeming value. A Christian can be a missionary without leaving home. The Gospel means the same in every language and in every version of the Bible.

America's populists also fear that what happened to aboriginal peoples in history - being overrun by strangers from nowhere - might happen to them. Such fear by those in economic distress can be exploited by unscrupulous men. Some want immigrants from Europe. But without gun control, safe schools and universal healthcare that Europeans take for granted, America has no appeal to many in Europe. They cannot be comfortable where Christians live in fear and buy assault weapons for Christmas. Besides, immigrants to a new nation inherit the assets as well as the liabilities of the nation. The unpaid liabilities can be a torment to their conscience.

It is said that a rising tide lifts all boats, assuming that everybody has a boat. It is more pertinent in a society whose economy is based on universal employment. The young adults in America who have no college education are used by politicians to stoke hatred. Universal

employment provides the security to end that hatred. With education, healthcare and employment for every family, it is inconceivable
that a young man in a Canadian Hutterite colony or anywhere else,
will get up in the day on nights, to rob a neighbor. And his father
does not need to own a gun "to protect the family from fear and
harm" according to politicians who divide and conquer. The powerless majority in both developed and developing nations suffer the
consequences of political and spiritual elitism. The cultural conservatives who oppose universal healthcare for the poor, or kill African
Americans with impunity, practice the same brand of Christianity as
the slave traders, slave masters and their clergy. It is not Christianity
based on the Gospel - the Golden Rule, the Great Commandment
and the New Commandment. If universal healthcare is "pie in the
sky"; if universal employment is "godless communism" to the cultural conservative policymakers who control society, the church is
not practicing Christianity.

There are small nations in Europe that were victimized by the
powerful nations. They see the refugees and migrants from developing nations as the consequence of colonization that they were not
party to. Their populism is based on keeping those people out to
protect "a Christian culture." But a Christian culture does not yet
exist. The flawed evangelism has the Great Commission bereft of
the crucial component, namely, "teaching them to observe all things
whatsoever I have commanded you." Compliance to all things that
He commanded leads to a Christian civilization. There is none. The
Gospel is counterculture. If culture controls human behavior and the
church; and if the church does not treat others the same way they
want to be treated, the church itself is resistant to Christian civilization. That has been the case since slave trade and slavery. The church
of culture, not the Church of Christ, has been resistant to Christian
civilization. The migrants from Africa, Asia and the Middle East,
thousands of whom drowned in the Mediterranean Sea, are victims
of that flawed evangelism. At the end of colonial rule that should not

have happened, the people would have been better off if the ethnic groups were left the way they were before colonial rule. At the United Nations, every nation is equal regardless of size. The same should have applied to all the ethnic groups at the end of colonial rule. The conflicts and wars could have been prevented if the people of every ethnic group were the masters of their own house under federalism. But many take pleasure in the misery of others.

In the New World, the mass migration from Latin America to the U.S.A., that rears populism, is also the consequence of flawed evangelism. If anyone in the New World should, in good conscience, be resentful of immigrants, it should be the aboriginals on whose land we dwell. But they are few and powerless. There are aboriginals and semi-aboriginal people, "the old stock," who grew up believing that their country is theirs alone just as in the Old World. When a plurality of cultures and sub- cultures are imposed on them by the ruling elite, it can be unsettling.

However, one can forget that the policies that shaped the world were made in the capitals of powerful nations. The strongmen who create conflicts and generate refugees and migrants cannot survive without the support of the big powers who sell the weapons. The major nations of the world are run as if there is no God to whom man is accountable. Christian politicians and capitalists make the policies that shape the world in which technology is reducing employment, concentrating wealth at the top in the absence of progressive taxation. Some activists rail against the "liberal elite" in politics. Some rail against the "conservative elite" in religion. Both are known to be people who are divorced from reality. The Golden Rule, the Great Commandment and the New Commandment- the Gospel - make Christianity an exceptional religion if practiced.

Christianity was tarnished by slave trade and slavery for centuries. Those clerics have passed away. When their successors still avoid preaching the Gospel, and unite in prayer with the clerics of various religions in order to get along, which God or gods are they praying to? It may not matter if we live in a Godforsaken world. But if church leaders resort to syncretism in the name of peace, they no longer stand for the first century Pentecostal church of God, but the church of man and culture. Peace comes through being born again and compliant to the Golden Rule. Treat others the same way you want them to treat you makes sense to anybody who is a human being. Some developed nations that are not having enough babies need immigrants to work and care for the old people. It costs money to raise those immigrants and migrants. It is the policy makers or the elite, who create the environment that now sets one group of neglected people against another.

The victims of populism are also the victims of imperialism, slave trade and slavery. They are victimized left and right. Some young adults have gone from drug addiction to criminality. Some take their lives when the help they need is not coming either from prayer or from the State. When they are tired of reading self-help books; tired of motivational speakers; tired of prosperity preachers; and tired of seeing some immigrants get jobs while they are left behind, they may be receptive to a demagogue who will bring back the good old days. What used to be said behind closed doors is now circulated in the Internet to court likeminded people. If democracy is a government of the people, for the people and by the people, it has not worked for the forgotten people. Unlike a dictatorship, ballot box democracy allows people to choose their own oppressors. Those the electorate elect to serve the national interest, appoint the bureaucrats who run the government and serve corporate interests. It is like electing a Trojan horse. The result is pseudo- democracy. Sadly, the cultural populism that stirs up hatred and violence could have been averted if President Kennedy's vision survived his assassination.

Populists have good reason to be angry when cultural religionists are killing Christians while their kit and kin are running for high public office and demanding equality in the West. For economic reasons, some of their Christian leaders don't care about what cultural religionists do to Christians. In America, there are conservative Christians known as Christian nationalists. They are a subset of the populists and include educated men and women. They are unaware that for 250 to 300 years, the Church lived off the avails of slavery. Was that church conservative or liberal?

Now, some conservatives, mindless of church history, would remind anyone who will listen that their nation was founded on Judeo - Christian values. They want to defend Christianity from liberals and cultural religionists who should have been in their home-land in the first place but for the Doctrine of Discovery and colonial rule. On January 6, 2021, some stormed the US capitol to overthrow American democracy. Some thanked Jesus for allowing them "to get rid of the communists, the globalists and the traitors within our government." They were sincere. Jesus Christ has been misrepresented for the past 2,000 years. That is the problem.

The Decline of Humanity

The 1960s, I believe, were the best of times and the worst of times. Some advocates of social justice were silenced or assassinated. John F. Kennedy grew up in a life of privilege but understood the life of those who were not privileged. To become president, he had to overcome the prejudice of being born a Roman Catholic. His administration was a flash of light in American history. President Kennedy told his fellow Americans that the torch "was passed to a new generation of Americans." He told them to" ask not what your country can do for you -ask what you can do for your country." He planned to confront the common enemies of man: poverty, tyranny, disease and war. He established the Peace Corps Volunteer program for graduates to help in schools, hospitals, and agriculture in developing countries.

He understood that those who were under colonial rule need help while American corporations continued to make money from the natural resources of those countries. The Peace Corps volunteers would see the rest of the world and build bridges between cultures before settling down at home. Helping the people overseas will also keep them in their own homeland. There was the United States Agency for International Development (USAID) in furtherance of diplomacy. There was his Alliance for Progress with Latin America, to create economic stability. As a global citizen he knew that "to live and let live is not enough; to live and help live is not too much." Some developed nations followed America's lead as usual. It was probably the first time that world leaders thought about the collective welfare of the entire human race. Some of my teachers were Peace Corps Volunteers in a boarding school that was run in Southeast Nigeria by missionaries from the UK. They all did what Christians should do, and enabled the missionary face of Christianity to overshadow the colonial face.

But in about 1037 days in office, Present Kennedy would be assassinated. His vision was derailed by Christians who looked inward. Selfish living returned to America. Like a good Samaritan, the spiritual conservative Christians build bridges of goodwill while the cultural conservatives demolished bridges and build walls between "us and them." Furthermore, the foreign aid that they resent is totally senseless because, what is spent on foreign aid is only a fraction of what corporations bring home from overseas. If corporations bring home $100 and the government gives back five dollars as foreign aid, who is giving aid to who? The only meaningful foreign aid is technical assistance in corporate partnership that benefits both sides. That is the real spirit of international development. The Chinese are more likely to do that than Christians. The difference between developed nations and developing nations is technology. The cultural conservatives want to keep it that way. The people must be left to reinvent the wheel.

The resistance to the spread of COVID -19 technology is instructive. The pandemic took over five million lives. The populists will notice that the immigrants and migrants come from their former Colonies. At the end of colonial rule, wisdom suggests that "the Commonwealth "would marry their technology to the natural resources of free nation for the common weal of the Commonwealth. It did not happen. The people confused Commonwealth for commonweal. Instead, at the end of the Second World War, Germany was stripped of its Colonies to join a new alliance of "us and them" who are exploited by remote control. The cultural conservatives who derailed the Kennedy vision did not want foreign aid sent to the colonials to keep them in their homeland. Yet, the policymakers, disposed to arms sales for military solution to every problem on earth, bring the refugees and migrants their rank and file do not want in their country. If the populists look closely with a Christian heart, they will notice that "the enemy is us."

From 2001 to 2021, the United States spent over one trillion dollars on homeland security, over two trillion dollars on the war in Iraq, over two trillion dollars in the war in Afghanistan and thousands of soldiers brought back in body bags. The military - industrial complex has made a lot of money. The men who lament the loss of soldiers and treasures are the belligerent cultural conservative Christians who derailed President John F Kennedy's plan to do good for humanity. President Lyndon Johnson waged war on poverty at home. It was a war that conservative Americans were happy to lose. Then in 2022/23 the United States spent billions of dollars to support Ukraine in a war against Russia. A disgruntled American wrote on social media: "I'm sick of having my paycheck taxed nearly in half, then paying taxes on everything I buy --- only to see it sent to other countries to solve their problems while we inch closer to the cliff." Another one wrote: "Why is there always money for war but we can't afford to feed our school children a decent meal? Why is war our biggest export." Their concerns are understandable.

In Europe, there is the fear that Arab Muslims will replace ethnic Europeans. In America there is the fear that Jews and Latinos will replace the "old stock." President Kennedy had the solution - use the USAID to help the people stay in their homeland. The Peace Corps Volunteer Program and the United States Agency for International Development were to help impoverish nations so that the people culturally conservative Christians do not like, can stay in their homeland and not amass at American borders as refugees. Is it not cheaper to do the will of God than the will of culture? Some Christians raised on victor theology have no regrets over slavery, colonialism and Empire except Hitler's Nazism. Hence the continued resistance to reconcile with God and man.

Populism offers some Christians a tunnel vision that is blind to the cause and effect of slavery and colonialism. The thousands of men, women and children who perished in the Mediterranean Sea and the US - Mexico border, as they fled from manmade nations, would prefer to live and die in their homeland. In April 2022, UK 's Home Secretary traveled to Rwanda to sign a contract for £120 million, to receive asylum seekers from the UK. In his Easter Sunday message, the Archbishop of Canterbury recognized that "sub-contracting out our responsibilities, even to a country that seeks to do well like Rwanda, is the opposite of the nature of God, who himself took responsibility for our failures. "If there are more wars in Europe, will the asylum seekers from Europe be sent to Rwanda?

Since the end of the Kennedy - Johnson administrations, the Cultural Conservatives have no desire to help colonized peoples either in their homeland or to receive them as refugees or asylum seekers fleeing from those man - made nations. Sadly, as a result of doctrines that do not change lives - weekly absolutions and Amazing Grace- the church Establishment has lost influence over its members who run the States. If indeed everyone who calls on the name of the Lord will be saved, as many Christians believe, trying to be a better human being is no longer necessary.

The preachers of the doom and gloom in prophecy now stoke

a new fear. It is the fear of globalization to usher in one - world government and the Antichrist. One theologian would cite another theologian to enhance credibility. In developed nations one - world government frightens the men who feel already left behind by the changing demographics. Yet, to demand an economy that provides employment, education, and healthcare for every family, like the Canadian Hutterites, has not happened in 2,000 years, even under a homogeneous culture. Is the church Establishment dominated by men whose will is for a godly nature or for human nature? Since slave trade and slavery, the Golden Rule, the Great Commandment and the New Commandment - the synopsis of the gospel - are still ignored. So, we live like wildlife while condemning culture for the outcome the church Establishment helped to create through victor theology based on a false premise that "Jesus died to pay for our sins." We live for culture while embracing a counterculture religion.

The greatest antidote to cults and cultural populism is compliance to God's Golden Rule. It should have started 2,000 years ago to preempt the problems of today. The social problems of the world were not created by the victims. They were created by Christians, centuries ago during slave trade, slavery, colonialism and the Scramble for Africa. The populists must be aware that the people they resent are being victimized twice. The world is now reaping the consequences of the imperial brand of Christianity. Nevertheless, continued commitment to the Kennedy policy of the 1960s would have helped people stay in their homeland and avert the mass migration of unwanted people decades later. It would have prevented the recent wave of cultural populism in reaction to the population shift. It would have prevented the wars in the Middle East that summoned willing allies to battle. It might have prevented the terrorist attack of September 11, 2001 that took innocent lives. In addition to the 2977 people who lost their lives that day, the 20 years of war in Afghanistan took another 2461 lives and over two trillion dollars. Could all these have been prevented if the Kennedy vision continued? In these wars, nobody counts the number dead on the other side. Doing the will of God is much cheaper than doing the will of culture.

We do not know who, among the dead, will be in heaven or hell. Therefore, we must judge a good religion or denomination by what we can see. The test of a good religion or denomination must be good interpersonal relations and stable families. And the test of good governance must be the percentage of parents and grandparents who retire in poverty. They are the end product of the economy. No nation should fail on both counts. There is the USAID. If every developed nation, including Japan, has a similar agency and a willing and genuine spirit, the quality of life on earth will improve. But to live selfishly, and sell goods and weapons to the poor and technology deprived, leads to the mass migration to the rich nations and death that nobody wants. Furthermore, nobody attacks the Red Cross because even a sick mind will be condemned for attacking people doing good deeds. The Pope does not need an income. All his needs are provided. The Scandinavians recognize that the more human needs are provided, the less need they have to horde wealth while other people's children starve. In America, to "retire well" is to horde money, and leave some for grandchildren. It raises the bar on cupidity. Yet each year, thousands of people die from suicide and despair in developed and developing nations. What they miss is a just society that grows the Hutterites economy to scale. That is not a priority for those who live by God's Amazing Grace and not by God's Golden Rule.

In the Canadian Hutterite economy, every family has education, healthcare and employment. That is the will of the Holy Spirit that inspires them. How many would commit suicide in Chicago, New York or Los Angeles if the Holy Spirit is allowed to prevails over the evil spirit in man? The church that owned slaves and lived off the avails of unpaid servitude for over 250 years had erased the interface between right and wrong. And since right and wrong are not well defined, every progress is easily reversible. Those who do to others what they don't want others to do to them get a free hand. The neglected in developed and developing nations are set against one another. And there will be opportunists to exploit their discontent.

In the 1970s, the Hippies of San Francisco could not change the American culture. Idealistic youths became adults integrated into the cultural values of human nature. Youthful idealism forbids doing to others what you don't want others to do to you. That sentiment has never had the support of cultural conservatives in church and State. Also, the young and idealistic men and women who graduate and join the media, law enforcement and corporations, for example, are mentored by the adults. They learn the ways of the Establishment and conform for promotion and higher income. It is how culture runs the show and send greedy men to their graves empty-handed. Nevertheless, the influence of the Hippies has made California the most advanced and progressive State in America.

Many immigrants come from non-Christian nations. Is it not abnormal that in politics, with the exception of Nordic nations, second generation immigrants have to plead with the super-rich Christians to pay their fair share of taxes to relieve abject poverty? It is like Mahatma Gandhi teaching Christians how to practice their religion. In Russia, the Bolsheviks will be shocked to see the rich back in power just as many people are shocked to see the Taliban back in power in Afghanistan. In Europe the cultural populists are unhappy with immigrants with different cultures and religions. The immigrants are unhappy to be second- class citizens. They are also unhappy with the geography of their homeland where foreign powers brought together divergent cultures that are killing and turning them into refugees.

It is obvious that those who do to others what they don't want others to do to them are the common enemy of all humankind including the cultural populists. The immigrants and refugees are also the victims of the explorers and colonists who were raised on victor theology. The church Establishment is the ultimate culprit. It did not teach them the Gospel. It did not teach them to observe the Golden Rule, the Great Commandment and the New Commandment. They were Christians on the outside, not Christians in the inside. If the students didn't learn, the teacher didn't teach. The teacher is still not teaching.

Does a nation or government have a goal? A corporation has a goal. It is to be profitable without limit. What is the goal of a nation? While many citizens languish in poverty, new immigrants and migrants have come year after year. Like a leaking bucket that is never full, the human condition remains stagnant - the rich get richer and the poor get poorer, generation after generation. Can a nation close its borders, have nothing to do with other nations of the world and use its resources to lift every citizen out of poverty? That is a goal. But they will have to give up banana, tea, chocolate, coffee, rice or steel from abroad. Boundaries were made by man, not by God Almighty.

The Truth of the Matter

President John F. Kennedy had the wisdom to know that America is not a warrior tribe but a composite of immigrants from all nations of the world. He sent Peace Corps Volunteers to establish good relations with the impoverished global South. The United States Agency for International Development lived up to its name. In 1963, he was assassinated in Dallas Texas. It takes over two generations to forget historic events. By 2023, the USA had a plague of refugees at the Texas border. Kennedy's vision of a shared humanity has been replaced by military bases – over 700 in all. Why? The church that misrepresents Jesus Christ has some denominations that teach their members, not on television but in the sanctum of their church that they will have tribulations. That the world will hate and persecute them. They should accept persecution as a badge of honor. They cite the Scriptures. Where do the hateful world live? The world that was moving forward under President Kennedy began to move backward after his assassination. Indeed, the devil can cite the scriptures for his purpose.

The leaders of the Imperial Church that controlled the entire world passed away several centuries ago. Now, if the church is still following their footsteps with the same false doctrine, it should be no surprise if the church is persecuted by those victimized by the misrepresentation of Jesus Christ. Obviously, the persecution is not because of righteousness. Unless they are dyed in a cultural religion, no human being will oppose those who teach and practice the Golden Rule, the Great Commandment and the New Commandment. That's the Gospel. No tongue rejects honey. President Kennedy had the right vision – use technical assistance to help people stay in their homeland and preempt populism.

CHAPTER 12

War and Peace

The Nobel peace prize was established in 1895. The Carnegie Endowment for International Peace was founded in 1910. There are numerous NGOs purporting to work for peace. They did not prevent the numerals wars since 1895. Many believe that peace is the absence of war. There are streets in the United States where people do not feel safe because of their gender or the color of their skin. There are places in Africa and Asia where people are killed in the name of religion. Yet, the nations are at peace. Humankind has paid a bloody price for the shortcomings of Christian evangelism. It produced Adolf Hitler, Napoleon Bonaparte, Joseph Stalin, Benito Mussolini and Francisco Franco. They were cultural conservative Christians.

It is the cultural conservatives who mobilizes man's brute instinct and lead their nation to war. That was the spirit of colonialism. Adolf Hitler must have died with the realization that the survival of the fittest by natural selection does not apply to humans. What is applicable is the survival of the slickest by cultural selection. The cultures of the world united to subdue him. Some 20 million human beings died in the First World War. Another 50 million died in the Second World War all fighting Nazi supremacy. Now, there are like-minded men who feel free to say and do what the Nazis were condemned for. What lesson then, have we learned from two World Wars? If we have learned nothing, it may be because collectively, we are not much different from the Nazis.

On the 11th day of November, we remember the millions who died in the wars. Those whose German, Italian and Japanese ancestors fought on the wrong side would probably feel uncomfortable. Are we, whose relatives fought on the right side of history better than those whose relatives fought on the wrong side? If we are not, it would be the height of hypocrisy to rejoice over the Nazis. Since slave trade and slavery, Christian nominalism has spread hypocrisy around the world. There is no wrong that pagans are doing that Christians are not doing, if not more. Americans would know how many Christians are born again and live by the Gospel - the Golden Rule, the Great Commandment and the New Commandment. Can the church that owned slaves teach anyone to observe the Golden Rule it did not observe? Yet, the same church today is denouncing culture that is eroding their faith.

Some Americans who went to Europe to fight the Nazis came from segregated churches and had the statues of confederate soldiers looking down on the grandchildren of their enslaved victims. Some Afrikaners who went to Europe to fight the Nazis, came from an apartheid hierarchy based on skin complexion. It speaks to the corrupted Gospel. Over 70 years after the end of the Second World War, Russia's Victory Day is celebrated with a display of modernized weapons of destruction and a matching army. Hitler's Nazis disobeyed God's Golden Rule. Is there a nation whose citizens and governments and not disobeying the Golden Rule even now? It is easier to see the mote in other people's eyes but not the beam in our own eyes. Hatred is a universal currency. We care about what other people do to us but not about what we do to them.

There are people who can be subjugated forever; and there are also people who cannot be subjugated forever. Without the Marshall plan, there would have been World War 111 because all nations are still wrong doers and none has a moral authority over others. The church has changed no nation. Some churches have sung about warfare to cease. Some have sung about laying down sword and spear down by the riverside and study war no more. Is the church creating the environment that makes their wishes to come true? While some soldiers are dying in conflict, their politician prepare for another war rather than for peace. The Christians who imposed pacifism on Japan after World War 11 in 1945, have fought several wars ever since. It is one more "Do as I say, and not as I do." And while some Christians are trading and selling weapons that kill other Christians, those in church instruct God in prayer, to do something. When the church cannot exert a proactive influence for good, that church becomes irrelevant to life and some people leave.

St. Paul wrote: "For we wrestle not against flesh and blood, but against principalities, against powers, against the rulers of the darkness of this world, against spiritual wickedness in high places." (Ephesians 6:12 NKJV). That was true in the first century. If it seems true today, Christianity leaves much to be desired after 2,000 years. The soldiers, Christians and non-Christians who go to kill innocent people follow orders. In the Nuremberg trials, the agents of Adolf Hitler claimed to follow orders. It was not accepted. Apparently, following orders is not a good excuse for the Nazis only. For one nation to invade or conquer another nation is now considered an act of madness. If Christians have to arm and defend themselves against fellow Christians something is wrong. After 2,000 years of the Gospel, why are Christians in a competition for the capacity to kill and destroy? The church must be irrelevant. Military nations with submarines and aircraft carriers can be tempted to leave their borders in search of an enemy an ocean away. A restless cultural militia preaching "peace through strength" on one side of the ocean can overlook their counterparts on the other side of the ocean with the same rights to preach "peace through strength."

They may both wear the cloak of religion, mindless of a show-down. In the days of Napoleon Bonaparte, a nation needed an army to prevent an invasion. Without the prospect of an offence, there is no need for defense. So, in 1948, Costa Rica abolished its military. Costa Rica has not disappeared from the face of the earth. The government would rather spend billions of taxpayers' dollars to improve the human condition and create a just society than on militarism in search of enemies. Is it too much to expect that a nation of people who believe in God should be demilitarized? How can security be an issue between Christians? Yet, can you imagine a military power abolishing its military for Christ's sake? Costa Rica is an example to other nations, particularly the poor nations whose children are dying from starvation. Nations that sell weapons for aggressors to kill people have blood on their hands. So, every nation should produce their own weapons and keep the blood on their own hands. Some nations, even poor and food insecure nations spend billions of dollars on defense. Defense against whom? Many of their putative enemies are fellow Christians.

In the Middle East, conflicts and wars have become part of the culture. Over 3,000 years ago, king David wrote: "Pray for peace of Jerusalem: they shall prosper that love thee" (Psalm 122:6). How many Jews and Gentiles still pray for the peace of Jerusalem? God is not deaf. How can there be peace when the Prince of peace is rejected? How can there be peace when the Golden Rule, the Great Commandment and the New Commandment are ignored? Since there can be no peace without the Prince of peace, many churches no longer pray for peace of Jerusalem. Instead, somewhere in the world there is a Peace Tower, Peace Bridge, Peace Monument and associated structures. Do they bring peace?

In a speech in April 2022, the UN Secretary General, Antonio Guterres, stated that one - quarter of humanity - two billion people - live in conflict areas today and the world faces the highest number of violent conflicts since 1945, when World War Two ended. Was the UN not established to bring an end to the scourge of war? Many nations have normalized the disobedience of God and may fight over an ideology. It is the Gospel - the Golden Rule, the Great Commandment and the New Commandment - that will defeat a wrong ideology, not bullets or the ballot box. The greatest tool any UN Secretary General has to use is God's Golden Rule, to prevent or limit wars. On the basis of the Golden Rule which makes sense to any human being, the Secretary General can convince potential combatants to negotiate. If war breaks out, the UN can call for a ceasefire and immediately deploy troops on both sides or on the side of the willing side and dire the other side to shoot UN troops. They will not if they are human.

A large group of Christians follow Christ without following His Gospel. They follow Christ but do not obey because Jesus has paid for their sins. A very small group of Christians follow Christ and obey His commandments - the Golden Rule, the Great Commandment and the New Commandment – because they are born again. If there will be peace and goodwill on earth the gulf between the two must close. Service in the military or the police may be motivated by the love of country. It is not synonymous with the love of neighbors. it has been used as a steppingstone into politics but people can love their country but not their neighbor.

After the destructive Second World War, there was the Cold War. Since the end of the Cold War, trillions of dollars have been spent in wars in Iraq, Afghanistan and the Middle East. If the experts did not succeed in Vietnam, Afghanistan and the Middle East, it may be time to start listening to God and none experts. In a speech in October 2019, President Donald Trump noted that America had spent eight trillion dollars in the Middle East. "The job of our military," he said, "**is** not to police the world." Other Republican administrations had said the same. But militarism is an addiction for the cultural conservative base they must please.

The war in Afghanistan lasted for 20 years, a duration that

benefited defense contractors. No nation needs aircraft carriers to defend their borders. In fact, the U.S. is doing the work of the United Nations. Future generations will agree that doing the will of God is cheaper than doing the will of cultural conservatives. Statistics show that in 2019, about 20 American veterans a day committed suicide. On an average night in 2021, there were over 10,000 homeless veterans in California. The cost of one F-35 fighter jet can turn 82 homeless veterans into millionaires. War veterans will continue to be homeless and depend on a food bank as long as there are cultural conservatives who send other people's children to wars. Since children are born into a culture and socialized into a tunnel vision, for veterans to be homeless, and dependent on charity or the food bank would seem normal. Every culture has that cultural militia who do to others what they don't want others to do to them. Colonialism is a reflection of that reality. The Church did not teach Christians to observe the Golden Rule.

On Remembrance Day of 2019, Russian and Ukrainian Christians were in another Crimea conflict while remembering their losses in the Second World War. If soldiers are fighting in their homeland while their opponent is fighting away from home, who is the aggressor? Are Soldiers an ocean away from home defending their country? Being the base of the initial aggressor, the war in Afghanistan may be one of the few exceptions in history, where fighting away from home is morally justified. Those who sent out warriors have not learned the lessons of history and the Gospel they profess.

The Gospel is God's guidebook or our maker's instruction Manual. When Jesus Christ came under the Roman Empire, there was peace – Pax Romana or the peace of Rome. It was peace that came through subjugation or the peace of the graveyard. Since colonial wars and World Wars, many nations that have been through war, settled down under Pax Romana. The numerous wars and elusive peace are further evidence of church failure that has frustrated rational men and women who expect a better world. Christianity is a counter culture religion sabotaged by members fighting for culture. In 2,000 years, many churches have not discovered what St. Paul described as "the peace of God that surpasses understanding." It does not come from a ritual handshake in church but from being born again. That's what frees humankind from cultural tunnel vision, wars and the adversarial relationship between the Christians in the East and West. Peace or goodwill is a two- way streets. To demand peace or goodwill from others and not reciprocate is to demand submission.

The Pax Romana and the jingoism that led to the Second World War still exist on a smaller scale to this day in many nations. There are men who find a peaceful world boring. The most affected in these conflicts are women and children. In the Bosnian war, the Muslim women who were raped produced "unwanted" babies and children. The Yazidi community of Syria will not allow their women to rejoin the community with children fathered by their ISIS enemies. Sadly, they make the case for abortion in such circumstances. A United Nations' report in 2019 showed that there were 70.8 million refugees. Since pregnancy is avoidable, why bring children into the world to be victimized by human nature? The greatest conflict zones are the developing nations where the disparate nationalities were forced into an involuntary union (like a forced marriage) by foreign powers. At the end of colonial rule, the wise approach was to leave the people as much as possible the way they were before colonization. Racism has no empathy. Some mistakes are irreversible. A constitution is reversible.

Mali presents a textbook case of war and peace in Africa. In an article in The Walrus (July/August 2019 pgs. 24-33) titled "No Peace to Keep "Richard Poplak wrote: "Twice the size of France, and inhabited by nearly 20 million people, Mali is riven by mind- bending complexities. During the nineteenth century, France split up West Africa in a way that cut through existing tribal relationships. These artificial borders remained when the French left nearly a century later, effectively trapping together ethnic groups that had little history or sympathy for one another and who suddenly had to compete for resources and political power. Land locked, Mali is surrounded by Algeria, Niger, Burkina Faso, Ivory Coast, Guinea, Senegal and Mauritania: States that have suffered at various times their own internal disputes."

In 2018 alone, he noted, "over 120,000 people were displaced by the violence in northern and central Mali. Many risked their lives along the Mediterranean migrant route, the third largest contingent of any nation. Those who did make it -and many didn't - added to a crisis that triggered populist movements across Europe." The U.N. was reported to deploy about 90,000 soldiers and 14,000 civilians in 14 countries. The organization spends about $7 billion (US) a year on "peacekeeping." The temporary stability they create only serves foreign mineral explorations.

The missions can end without resolving the root causes of the people's problems, leaving them worse off than at the beginning. The nations that created the artificial borders enclosing a mosaic of conflicting tribal religionists, left them a standing army to sell them weapons. What does such a standing army with weapons do? Rather than call in the U.N. to share in the loss of lives and waste of treasure, the colonial powers that created these nations can do what was not done by their departing predecessors at the end of colonial rule: Draft a constitution that ensures that the people of every ethnic group are the masters of their own house just as they were before colonial rule. All nations big or small are equal at the United Nations. Such should be the case in the artificial nations.

The Romans were the first to have a standing army. They became very successful at conquests and empire building. The concept spread to other nations that became colonial powers. African nations inherited a standing army that cannot stay and do nothing. The governments continued to buy arms year after year from those who have vested interest in selling arms. So, the government in power has to use the army to suppress the people neglected by the ruling ethnic group. As would be expected, African leaders have neither the vision nor the patriotism to resolve the root causes of their problems because the leaders are the dominant group in power. They are part of the problem, not the solution. Some devious experts would ask: "why would a government kill their own people?" They do not ask how a government can segregate its own people.

There are cynics inclined to believe that the UN has become a self-serving institution some of whose functionaries have vested interest in endless global chaos. And so, they spend billions of tax-payers' dollars annually and call peace enforcement "peace keeping." The taxpayers are totally unaware of the needless expenditures of the United Nations. In 2021, the UN lost 135 peacekeepers. Apart from the U.N., NGOs are also spending money on humanitarian work. Solving a problem is praiseworthy even when the problem is avoidable. The conservative cultural militia and the elites that direct global policy do not mind spending those billions of dollars on "peacekeeping," and humanitarian aid. But in the spirit of schaden-freude, they are opposed to spending a fraction of that budget to mitigate the problems created by past generations, and avoid further bloodshed. History leaves any rational mind frustrated by the counterfeit Christianity that made it possible for cultural conservatives to use a counter-culture religion to rule the world in the name of God.

In Lebanon, Prime minister Rafik Hariri was assassinated in February 2005. In August 2020, the U.N. tribunal came down with a guilty verdict after 15 years of investigation and trial. It cost one billion dollars. That is how they spend taxpayers' money while life on earth goes from bad to worse. How much blood and treasure will it cost if the Church and the U.N. practiced and demanded the Golden Rule as a guiding principle? It would have saved those one billion dollars. Born again Christians are spiritual conservatives who conserve spiritual values and treat others the same way they like to be treated. Evidently, they are rarely in control of any nation. When cultural conservatives are in power, wrongs are never redressed. Sooner or later, as people become more civilized in the light of the Gospel, culture and traditions will change.

Canadians will understand the problems in Mali and other African nations because the colonial structure in Canada has some similarities with the structure in the developing nations. The two founding European cultures had bloody conflicts. In some African countries, there are not two but scores of ethnic groups under one colonial flag. When colonial boundaries were drawn between Canada and the United States, Blackfoot Indians found some of them in Montana USA and the rest in Canada. Mali has seven international borders. In Federal elections, even before polling stations close in British Columbia, the election had already been won in Eastern Canada because of the high population density in Ontario and Quebec. Similarly, when colonial rule ended, ballot- box democracy ceded power to the majority ethnic group or groups. Worse yet, and unlike Canada, the Federal government controls the mineral resources across the nation.

Consequently, post-election bloodshed was preordained. Conflicts between sovereign nations is different from conflicts within nations. The former requires peacekeeping, the latter is peace enforcement because it is about maintaining a forced union between peoples of diverse cultures and religions unequally yoked. Every African nation has an ethnic relations problem. The end of colonial rule should have left all groups in control over their lives. Now, Cameroon is teetering on conflict between the French- speaking North and the English -speaking South. The U.N. may have to provide "peacekeepers" to attempt to stabilize a farrago of unsustainable relationships held together by warlords and arms suppliers. Military missions have supplanted the faith-based missions that failed to teach the world "to observe all things whatsoever I have commanded you "as Jesus said. There are politicians who get into leadership positions with idealism. They always change while in office. They are persuaded that the bad actors in their nation must be allowed to compete with the bad actors in other nations. In that reality, the U.N. and humanitarian nations pay for the mess the bad actors create. That is how since 1945, the U.N. can only buy and send food and medicine to starving mothers and children and abandon the hope of ending the scourge of war. That is good for business.

In 2018, I wrote to young President Emanuel Macron to remind him that the people of France elected him to take a modern approach to politics. The mission in Mali, with the help of the U.N. was not peacekeeping but peace enforcement. We are not responsible for the sins of past generations but to fix them. I noted that the French in Canada have fought to be who they are, and showed the similarities between Canada and Mali. In a federal election, by the time the people in British Columbia go to the polls, the election had already been won because the population is concentrated in the provinces of Ontario and Quebec. If the people in BC were a different ethnic group, as would be the case in Africa, being trapped would be a cause for conflicts or cessation. And to add insult to injury, the Federal government also controls the mineral resources across the nation. And so, every ethnic group must be the masters of their own house. President Macron was gracious enough to acknowledge receipt of my letter but in French. There was no evidence that the government of France tried to solve the problem in Mali by ensuring that the ethnic groups are masters of their own house, as Quebecers are in Canada.

Africa is like a continent planned by Satan. In the Scramble for Africa, scores of ethnic groups were rounded up under one colonial flag. It is like Western Europe under one government. All they have in common is their skin tone. The exception is the Arab Africans whose ancestors came in the seventh century with the mind of spiritual imperialism to Islamize the continent. Some are still doing so through bloodshed. With over 200 ethnic groups in Nigeria, for example, what was Eastern Nigeria (ex-Biafra) is more populous than most nations in Europe. In the Nigeria- Biafra war (1967 – 70), a convergence of ethnic hatred, jihad and oil interest of Christian nations who supplied the weapons, saw hundreds of thousands of babies and children starved to death. Some were airlifted to Gabon to be fed. It was a war crime. Biafra was the most evangelized region on the African continent. In that blood war, Christian leaders in several African countries did not recognize Biafra because the dominant groups control governments. Recognition would embolden the minority groups they control.

A well-funded journalist, not a historian, titled the account of the war as "The Brothers' War" because a "Christian" general used to prosecute the war called it the Brothers' War. When the fog of war clears up, the truth emerges. The fog of the Nigeria-Biafra War has cleared up. Who are the beneficiaries? It is big oil, arms suppliers and collaborators who have or will be going to meet God Almighty with bloody hands. Their children and grandchildren will inherit the blood money. Hundreds of thousands of babies were starved to death. "The outside world viewed the Federal operation as a form of genocide," wrote The Standard Reference Encyclopedia Yearbook (1968, page 342). There are no civil wars in Africa. A war between peoples who have different cultures and languages is not a civil war. This has been the fate of Africans since the Church became a Regent, not the Executor of God's will - the Golden Rule, the Great Commandment and the New Commandment. For 2,000 years and counting, the imperial victor theology deviated from those commandments to create a masquerade of Christianity. Those who fight a war, fight with weapons and their conscience. Sometimes overwhelming force may determine the outcome but a good conscience never loses the war. The truth will always emerge and keep marching on. The pagan gods may be on the side of the big battalions but the Almighty has the last word.

Suffice it to say that if all the ethnic groups in Africa were separate countries, there would be close to one thousand countries in

Africa. It must be where the different languages were born, if the tower of Babel story is true. For peaceful coexistence and to limit the number of countries in Africa, they need wisdom to undo what colonialism has done. Every ethnic group must be the masters of their own house in a confederation. In Ghana, the Akan, Ewe, Ashanti, Fante, and others must be the masters of their own house. In Uganda, the Baganda, Acholi, Lango, Ankole, Gisu and others must be the masters of their own house. In Angola, the Bantu, Kongo, Ovimbundu, Ambundu, Herero, and others must be the masters of their own house. In Ethiopia, the Oromo, Amhara, Afar, Gamo, Beta Israel, and others must be the masters of their own house. In Cameroon, the Bamileke, Bamum, Fang, Duala, Kanuri, Tiv, Njem, and others must be the masters of their own house. In Nigeria, the Igbo, Yoruba, Fulani, Hausa, Efik, Ibibio, Ogoni, Ijaw, Tiv, Kanuri and many others must be the masters of their own house and destiny. In Egypt, Coptic Christians and Pharoah's people need to reclaim their dignity. The Golden Rule – Treat others the same way you want them to treat you, makes sense to any human being. This is the only road to peace in Africa. There is no people group that has suffered more than Africans in the hands of Christians and Muslims. Those who want to sell arms cannot solve Africa's problems.

Peacekeeping is morally defendable to tax payers. The peace enforcement that the UN continues to do cannot. Africa's problems cannot be solved by pretending that every nation is homogeneous in culture and religion. That was the mentality of those who created the problems in the first place. Africa's problems are further compounded by the Islamists bent on the Islamization of Africa. In the war against terrorism, there are allies who are double agents. Their mission of spiritual imperialism began in the seventh century. It is hard to imagine peace where a foreign religion is a weapon of war. And where the only education given to jobless youths is how to pull the trigger. It is the underprivileged people that go to kill or be killed.

Evangelists preach and return to their homeland. Spiritual imperialism uses religion to occupy foreign lands. Those who convert from any cultural religion they were born into, to a global religion, face intense persecution, rejection and discrimination. Christianity is not a cultural religion. It is not a Jewish religion. Judaism is the Jewish religion as Islam is the Arabian religion. Christianity is a global religion and is counter-culture. The foundation members of the first century church were Africans, Arabians, Greeks (Europeans), Jews, Palestinians and Samaritans. There is no other such religion on earth. When a counter- culture religion is controlled by culture, it becomes corrupted by culture and leads to endless problems. That is the fate of Christianity. The peaceful coexistence between Christianity, culture and cultural religions comes from the influence of the Gospel. The Golden Rule is the spiritual power that trumps the inhumanity of human nature. Treat others the same way you want them to treat you makes sense to anyone who is a human being regardless of culture, ethnicity, gender, religion or political philosophy. That is how Mahatma Gandhi practiced one pillar of Christianity and put Christians to shame.

Human society is a concrete jungle. Unlike any leader on the entire African continent, young President Kim Jung Un of North Korea, for example, can rub shoulders with the president of the United States. He has the ultimate weapon of mass destruction, the equalizer. The Gospel of Jesus Christ came to domesticate the human jungle. If the goal of the UN in 1945 was to end the scourge of war, it is fair to say that the UN has failed to do so. The two Africans who have been Secretaries General played the diplomacy card. The Secretary General is well paid to serve humanity not the whims of dominant men. He can relentlessly vocalize the royal law or the Golden Rule to humanize every nation by the end of this decade. Given the history of man in the past 2,000 years, to end war and poverty require the blunt truth not diplomacy. They should not cost taxpayers the billions of dollars the U.N. spends annually on refugees and peace enforcement.

In many nations every jurisdiction is different in the management of human relations. Some follow the example of Pax Romana, to keep the people in peace. It is peace sustained by force or threat of force in order to maintain injustice. Others follow the peace of the Gospel that is based on social justice. Name a social problem that is not rooted in the disobedience of the Golden Rule. There is none. That precept creates the peace that endures. After 2,000 years the Church has to be a disappointment to the Apostles because slave trade and slavery were the opening of the pandora's box. Slave trade and slavery involved buying and selling men, women and children to be put to work without wages until their death. And breed them too. It was the apex of capitalism and the church was a participant. Nothing can be more inhuman. In the American civil war, the men who gave their lives to end the shameful practice did not do so because Africans were their kith and kin. They did so because they were real human beings. God's Golden Rule makes sense to anyone who is a human being.

The Greek philosophers had two categories of war- the just war and the blood war. The American civil war to free African men, women and children that Christians enslaved for life and for centuries, was obviously a just war. In the Nigerian- Biafra war, Christians and Muslims starved hundreds of thousands of babies and children to death because their parents wanted to exit a colonial construct and be who they are. It was clearly a blood war for oil. The Nigerian general used to mask the jihad component of the war was a Christian from Northern Nigeria. He has spent his retirement years in deep regret and prayer. Even his ethnic group would like to secede. All these sad events of history have happened because the imperial church never taught Christians to be born again, as Jesus said, and live by His commandments. It cannot be said enough that to treat others the same way you want them to treat you, makes sense to anyone who is a human being. "Every tree that does not bear good fruit," Jesus said, "is cut down and thrown into the fire" (Matthew 7:19 NKJV). The Hutterite church is one church that bears good fruit. Sociologists who want to know why people suffer and how to mitigate suffering should visit a Canadian Hutterite colony.

In the U.S. A., the cultural conservatives have the gun and the Bible wrapped with the American flag. In Russia they have a cathedral dedicated to the military. It is in human nature to see the mote in the eyes of others but not the beam in our own eyes. They can see the wrongs in other nations but not in their own. When national interest extends beyond national borders; when Christians do not practice the Golden Rule to differentiate themselves from pagans and godless communists; and when both sides have veto power at the U.N. to overrule God and reason, the world may be heading for a nuclear holocaust, when they are under two unstable leaders. General Dwight D. Eisenhower is not a saint to the Congolese people and others who fought against imperialism. But as a Second World War general who saw death and destruction, he recognized that "every gun that is made, every warship launched, every rocket fired signifies, in the final sense, a theft from those who hunger and are not fed, those who are cold and are not clothed." It was a speech made as a Republican president in 1953. Was he a spiritual conservative forced to do the bidding of cultural conservatives?

In the Republican party today, such a speech would be condemned. If Liberals, Socialists and Spiritual conservatives have their way, the nations of NATO and the Russian federation will be demilitarized like Costa Rica to feed and clothe the homeless veterans and support the children of Saint Jude.org and loveshriners.org who are dying from cancer and depend on charity. But the cultural conservatives are the tail wagging the dog. Demilitarization will not happen. The European Union that won a Nobel peace prize for not fighting in over 60 years has been forced to rearm and prepare for war to be fought in their own territory. When the Christians in Moscow and Washington, DC are poised for war; when NATO and the Russian Federation are two Christian groups spending billions of dollars to protect one from the other, something is wrong with their brand of Christianity. The Church of Jesus Christ believes that in God there is no East or West. Does culture believe that? Furthermore, to send weapons to one side in a conflict and "humanitarian aid" to the victims on the other side is good for business but inhuman. Many politicians do not represent the good people of their nation because the political culture controls behavior.

Americans are not one ethnic group but people from all corners of the globe. An aircraft carrier is not needed to defend their borders. It is not the desire of immigrants to America to see their children board an aircraft carrier to fight and die in their old country. They have no desire to see their government spend billions of tax dollars on fighter jets to drop bombs on their own country whether it is in Africa, Asia or Europe. Resolving conflicts through war as a last resort is what they expect from the United Nations. However, the U.S. had a cogent and justified reason to go to war in Afghanistan after losing nearly 3,000 lives in the terrorist attack of 2001. But foreign powers that went to change Afghanistan have left in defeat. If the U.S. spent 20 years in Afghanistan, will nuclear weapons be used the next time to avert defeat? Religion is a powerful tool misused by men who serve as the Regents of God Almighty who has been silent. They have used religion to kill outsiders and abuse insiders. As human beings the Golden Rule, the Great Commandment and the New Commandment - the Gospel - make sense to Priests, Pastors, Mullahs and Rabbis if they believe in the same God. If these volunteers, unappointed by God Almighty do not lead their flock to obey God rather than culture, most people will end up in hell or purgatory if there is such a place. The Almighty God does not need anyone.

In 2012, the European Union won the Nobel peace prize for not fighting for six decades. Since the colonial wars, about 100 million men, women and children have been killed in wars. The perpetual state of belligerence between the Christians, yes Christians, in Moscow and Washington, DC., and within and between many nations is a boon to the arms industry. It also speaks to dysfunctional Christianity. It is as if the Gospel does not exist, and nobody has heard about the Golden Rule. It is what happens when people are raised under victor theology based on control. The harm done by the church that serves as the Regent rather than the Executor of God's will is incalculable. The volunteers who control Christianity, Islam and Judaism show no desire to respond to God's precondition in 2 Chronicles 7:14 for prayers to be answered. They have no desire to notice that as a consequence of disobedience, in all the wars of the past 1,000 years, the Almighty has not, in truth, responded to prayers. The only desire is to lead Bible study that does not see the forest for the trees. And to believe that the prayers that have not been answered in the past will be answered tomorrow without the precondition.

In February 2022, war returned to Europe. Russia invaded Ukraine in order to feel secure from NATO. Given the wrongs nations have done to their own people, is there a nation worth dying for? The church is always on the side of their people, right or wrong. And because culture controls behavior, a military chaplain is able to rationalize war to the soldiers he prays for. Those who fight against their conscience do not fare well. One church hymn calls on "God of Grace and God of Glory; Cure your children of warring madness." It will not happen. The Almighty does not take orders. God's medication for warring madness is to be born again. The church of Amazing Grace is not aware of that. If we don't live by the Golden Rule, it will be hypocrisy to condemn the Nazis. At the end of two World Wars and the Cold War, there was the expectation of a "peace dividend." Warring nations were expected to minimize their expenditure on the instruments of war and spend the money on domestic and international problems that cry out for humanity. It did not happen because cultural conservatives are always looking for enemies to guard against. Besides, a world of peace and goodwill to all is unprofitable to the military industrial complex. Many nations spend more money on the military than on their children. And there is the Institute for the Study of War. Imagine how much better the world would be without the machines of war!

Now, why would people who really believe in God and should follow His commandments, use artificial intelligence to produce autonomous weapons that kill people by remote control, without the intervention of their conscience? The answer is: "If we don't do it, somebody else will do it. If we don't do it to them, they will do it to us." That is how the evil spirit or Satan controls the world. That is how human nature overrules God and reason. A man can see that the land is flat in Africa, America, Asia, Australian and Europe and conclude that the world is flat. An astronaut will disagree. Everyone is entitled to hold on to their belief in things secular or spiritual. But in a Godforsaken world, nobody can dispute what separates men from the beasts; or God's antidote to conflicts – compliance to the Golden Rule, the Great Commandment and the New Commandment. On August 13, 2023, James Nachtway was interviewed on CBS's 60-minute program. He gave up family to document what people do to others in war. One cannot see what people do to others in war and the starvation of babies and children to death and not be ashamed to be a human being.

CHAPTER 13

Christianity for Dummies

At some time in their history, every culture had an organized or unorganized religion through which they reverenced one or many deities. They were cultural religions. There were as many cultural perspectives as there were cultures and cultural religions. If humankind were the product of evolution, cultural religions with different gods will makes sense albeit, a recipe for global chaos because they would serve the interest of the culture. As a genuine religion, Christianity is about good relations between all peoples and between them and God Almighty. It serves the interest of no culture. To believe that all religions are equal is to believe in evolution. But there is the Living God who created the entire universe and the first couple named Adam and Eve. The Almighty was in communication with them until they disobeyed His one and only commandment.

Their descendants spread across Africa, Europe and Asia, lost their moral bearings and became enemies. In the fullness of time, the Almighty revealed Himself to Abraham. Under Judaism, a cultural religion, Abraham's descendants will be groomed through prophets to learn and spread the will of God to all humankind. In a covenant with Abraham, God Almighty will send a spiritual Messiah or Savior through Abraham's son, Isaac the father of Israel. His place of birth was prophesied some 700 years before it happened. He will affirm the will of God the Father, and include the rest of humankind in the plan of salvation. He will be killed in the most brutal way known to man - crucifixion- as the sacrificial Lamb to end all sacrifices. That is the brief message of the Old Testament.

The Almighty God the Father used the virgin Mary to give the Messiah flesh and blood. She was not the mother of God Almighty who used her to give birth to the Messiah. At the fullness of time, Mary and Joseph did go from Nazareth to Bethlehem for the birth of the Messiah, according to prophecy. The priests, rabbis and pharisees were expecting to teach young Jesus about the tribal God of Israel they knew through Prophet Moses. Instead, He taught the people the will of the God of all Creation through a religion that is counterculture. Those who expected a military Messiah to confront and deliver them from the Roman Empire were disappointed. Empires do not endure. Rather, He taught the Golden Rule, the Great Commandment and the New Commandment. He used parables as a prop. The parable of the Good Samaritan was to show that an outsider is a neighbor, not an enemy. He performed miracles to prove His divinity. He was crucified as prophesied, rose from the dead, spent more time with the people before ascending back into heaven. He left them the Great Commission: "Go ye therefore, and teach all nations, baptizing them in the name of the Father, and of the Son, and of the Holy Ghost: teaching them to observe all things whatsoever I have commanded you: and, lo, I am with you alway, even unto the end of the world." (Matthew 28:19 – 20). That is the Gospel of Jesus Christ recorded in Matthew, Mark, Luke and John.

The goal of the Old Covenant was to establish good relations among the Israelites and between them and the Almighty God of Creation so that they can lead the world by example. It was not successful. It was not possible to obey the commandments and be considered righteous. The goal of the New Covenant is to establish good relations between all peoples and between them and the God of Creation. Unlike the Old Covenant, the New Covenant comes with the offer of a Helper, the Holy Spirit, and eliminates animal sacrifices. The Holy Spirit came on the day of Pentecost and marked the birth of the Church. And so, what must we do to be saved? Some monotheists believe that before you die, if your last deeds were noble, you will be saved. Some believe that God weighs your good deeds and your bad deeds. The one that weighs more determines whether you go to paradise or hell. Hence, killing unbelievers would count as a good deed.

Now, do Christians or monotheists know the will of God? If so, what purpose is served by worshiping God without doing His will? "Why call Me 'Lord, Lord,' Jesus said, "and not do what I say?" Did what he said include the Golden Rule, the Great Commandment and the New Commandment? That is the synopsis of the Gospel. Why has there been so much pain and suffering that should not have happened? Still, there is no end in sight. The members of the Church fought numerous wars in Europe, two World Wars, colonial wars, engaged in slave trade, slavery, apartheid, segregation and for about 250 years in the United States and about 300 years in Roman Catholic Brazil, both clergy and laity lived off the avails of unpaid servitude. If over 50 per cent of a company's products are not up to par, that company will not last for 2,000 years.

Christians can believe whatever makes them a denomination. Even after slave trade and slavery, how do Christian scholars explain the state of the world today after 2,000 years of Christianity? Without any doubt, based on the Golden Rule (Luke 6:31), the Great Commandment (Luke10:27), and the New Commandment (John 13:34), Christianity is about good relations between people and between them and the God of Creation. If that is true- and it is - how does the evangelical Christian academia explain the state of the world today after 2,000 years of the Gospel? Christianity is not about Amazing Grace or a revolving door of weekly absolutions. It is beyond dispute that a Christian must be born again (John 3:3).

it does not come naturally or by wishful thinking or through a proclamation. A Christian neophyte must ask for the Holy Spirit, the Helper (Luke 11:13; John 14:16-17; John 15:26) with sincerity, to enable him or her to be born again and progressively live by the Gospel.

Scientists can change their minds because science is self-correcting. But the church Establishment doing the same thing over and over for 2,000 years does not change its mind but demands blind faith. The Pentecostal church of Jesus Christ is spiritually conservative. But for over 300 years of slave trade and slavery, the cultural conservative church convinced educated men and women that from segregated churches and segregated cemeteries they can go home to be with the Lord. That's monumental self-deceit. Is it the Lord who commanded the Golden Rule, the Great Commandment and the New Commandment? But lest our past becomes their future, a new generation of church leaders cannot afford to continue doing the same old things over and over expecting a different result.

The slave traders, slave masters, and auctioneers -the master class- heard the same Sermons that Christians hear today: "Good works cannot save you. Jesus has died and paid for our sins. Your sins have been nailed on the cross and all you have to do is accept the free gifts. You cannot lose your salvation. Once saved, always saved." Some other Christians received weekly absolutions or forgiveness of sins. That is how slavery lasted for about 250 years in America and about 300 years in Roman Catholic Brazil. That is how pain, suffering and neglects persist to this day despite the Hutterite example. That is how babies and children die from hunger and disease while some take trips into space. That is how the Gospel is stuck on the pages of the Bible while Christians try to study the Bible to death. Those who received weekly absolutions in lieu of being born again got an invalid visa to heaven. Surely, nobody can earn salvation. But to live by the Gospel is not too much reciprocity for the crucifixion of the Lamb of God. The eternal life is received by being born again. That's the visa to the Kingdom of God.

The Corruption of the Faith

Men have always done to others what they did not want others to do to them. Social pressure can suppress the endemic evil spirits. For Christians like Adolf Hitler who were dependent on weekly absolutions or amazing grace instead of the transformation that comes by asking for the Holy Spirit, the best that society can do is use social pressure to restrain the evil spirits. The corruption of God's plan for humanity has grave consequences. When St. Paul came to Ephesus, he found some believers and asked: "Did you receive the Holy Spirit when you believed?" (Acts 19 :2). The first church of Jews and Gentiles was Pentecostal. They received the Holy Spirit that enabled them to be born again and live by the Gospel - the Golden Rule, the Great Commandment and the New Commandment.

The Romans who took over the Church changed the Pentecostal Church to a Sacramental church. A Christian no longer needs the Holy Spirit and be born again. Martin Luther and the Reformers did not restore Pentecostalism but introduced the Protestantism that only sanitized Catholicism to address Martin Luther's complaints. If that first century Pentecostal church continued to observe the Golden Rule, after 2,000 years, will the entire world not be better than it is today? And all lives should matter in Christendom regardless of skin tone. But Luther's salvation by faith alone did not change lives either. The same victor theology without the Holy Spirit freed the devil or the evil spirit in man. It led to further corruption of the Gospel and unleashed several wars in Europe, World Wars, colonial wars, slave trade, slavery, colonialism and all that can come out of the Pandora's box. If the world is changing, it is not changing willingly

because of the church Establishment but unwillingly in spite of the
Establishment.

What have we learned in the past 2,000 years? The completion
of catechism is a pass for a nominal Christian; it is not a pass for a
born-again Christian. Being born again is the one and only way a
Christian is able to progressively live by the Gospel and their social
implications. That is the guideline from the God who owns the
world. There is no better guideline and they make sense to anyone
who is a human being. It is what prevents the political, economic and
social morass in the world. It is what prevents conflicts, wars, slave
trade, slavery and the wrongs monotheists had done and continue
to do. Religion can lead people to salvation or to self-deceit. The
Gospel changes lives but victor theology does not. Did it change the
lives of slave traders, slave masters and their clergy? Is it changing the
lives of those who do to others what they don't want others to do to
them? Words spoken or written in Scripture do not change people.
In Christendom the church teaches unity without being united. It
preaches peace and goodwill to all without showing or being the
mechanism to achieve it.

A man can read the Bible from cover-to-cover a thousand times
and not be changed. A woman can read a book of a thousand
Sermons and not be changed. It is the Holy Spirit that changes
people to become a new creation. For centuries the Christian clergy
and laity, high and low, lived off the avails of the unpaid servitude
of African slaves. When Roman Catholic Jesuits were the biggest
slave holders in the world, they totally erased the interface between
right and wrong for more than two centuries - even 300 years in
Roman Catholic Brazil. How many Christians today believe that
they went home to be with the Lord? In what way is the church
today different from the church of the slave traders? If the clergy-
Christians and non-Christians - cannot issue a passport or visa to
heaven or guarantee eternal life, they ought to be held accountable.
After 2,000 years, Christianity demands a review for the good of

succeeding generations. Eternal life is the reward for observing God's commandments; it is not the reward just for believing in Jesus Christ and continue life as usual like the Jesuits. Or continue to do today what Christians and non-Christians don't want others to do to them.

Most Sermons and homilies today are focused on outcome but not on the process to produce the outcome. Absolutions and homilies do not produce a godly woman. Sermons and prayers do not produce a man of integrity. Absolutions, homilies, sermons and ritual prayers have not prevented family violence or the sad events of man's brutal history. And every religion on earth is a cultural religion except one - Christianity. A cultural religion is a blend of culture and religion. It was established by members of a specific culture in their own interest with no outsiders present. Christianity is not the religion of any culture. It is not the Roman or European religion. It is a global religion and it is counterculture (vide Matthew 5: 43 – 44). It serves the interest of no culture. It has universal values rather than cultural values. It is not even a Jewish religion. Judaism is the Jewish religion just as Islam is the Arabian religion despite the efforts of non-Arabs to seize control from the Arabian gatekeepers of Islam.

The foundation members of Christianity were both Jews and Gentiles. Simeon who helped Jesus carry the cross was an African from Cyrene in North Africa. It must have been racism that gave him that high honor of carrying the cross for Jesus Christ. In Acts 13:1 he was identified with the N-word, as one of the teachers and prophets at Antioch, the very first Church. The Acts of the Apostles show that there were probably more Jewish Christians in the first century than in the 21st century Israel. They were converted by the thousands by their Kinsmen. They were in control of Christianity. Then there was a schism and the drift back to the comfort of their cultural religion.

The acquisition and control of the Church by the Romans gave Christianity the semblance of a cultural religion. But Christianity belongs to everybody. The setback that makes Christianity vulnerable is that what belongs to everybody belongs to nobody. Consequently, a community of cultural religionists can be defended by the founding culture. The same cannot be said of Christians. That explains why evangelized Biafra disappeared from the face of the earth. A people that had no organized religion swallowed Christianity hook, line and sinker from the fishers of men. Their story is told by Frederick Forsyth in "The Biafra story "and by John De St. Jorre in: "The Brothers' War." Yes, The Brothers' War. What brotherhood is there in war? What brotherhood is there in the deliberate starvation of thousands of babies and children to death? What brotherhood was there between northern Sudan and southern Sudan which are similar to northern Nigeria and southern Nigeria? There are Christian institutions that, for ulterior motives, would shed more tears for non-Christians than for Christians in similar circumstances. It underscores the need for a Second Reformation to reverse victor theology.

Is the God of the slaves also the God of the slave masters, the slave traders and their clergy? Is the God the Muslims worshipped on Friday the God the Jews worshipped on Saturday? Is He also the God the Christians worshipped on Sunday? If the God of one is the God of all, there must be one standard operating procedure for all. That is what Christianity for Dummies is leading to in a world in disarray. There is nothing in the Gospel of Jesus Christ recorded in Matthew, Mark, Luke and John that needs to be modernized. The Gospel stands the test of time. His coming was prophesied about 700 years before it happened. He was not born to a king or a high priest but to a carpenter. Apparently, the Almighty can use ordinary people. Furthermore, He was born in a manger. Where would the Lamb of God be born if not in a manger for sheep?

He performed miracles, healed the sick by the word of mouth, raised the dead, walked on water, was crucified and buried, rose from the dead, ascending back into heaven, witnessed by a multitude composed of Jews and Gentiles. He was always considered to be a rebel but His disciples defied the Establishment and were willing to die, and they did die for the Gospel. Even the Romans who used Christians to feed Lions embraced the religion we now know as Christianity. There are people who reject Christianity because of what Christians had done wearing the cross. Since they were not born again, they did not obey God's Golden Rule – treat others the same way you want them to treat you. The shepherds and the sheep went astray. There are also people who rejects Christianity because they hate the Jews. And there are people who reject Christianity because they want to avoid people who are different. Given all that is recorded in the Gospel, if Jesus said: "I am the way, the truth, and the life. No one comes to the Father except through Me," does it not make sense to believe Him? One's spiritual destiny cannot be based on sentiment. And given the diversity of views, the diversity of Christian denominations and the multiplicity of religions, clearly," buyer beware" applies to religion.

A co-worker in Canada invited me to their Baptist church. She said: "We are not Southern Baptists." Who were the Southern Baptists? They were Baptists who fought and died in order to sustain slavery in America. Did adult baptism by total emersion change them? Is once saved always saved credible? All the Sermons in the world will not save anybody. Sacraments, Bible study from cradle to grave, baptism, worshipping on Friday, Saturday or Sunday will not save anybody. Rather, unless one is born again, he cannot see the kingdom of God. Nobody can complain about a man or woman who lives by the Golden Rule. The political, economic and social morass of today reflect the unfulfilled mandate of the Great Commission. To those who are doing the work of God but not the will of God, Jesus will say: "Depart from me, ye that work iniquity." Are there such clerics in the world today? He also identified a crowded Broadway that leads to destruction and a scanty narrow and difficult way that leads to life. Are there churches and people who are either on the Broadway or the narrow way today? Your common sense will save you, not an institution.

Nevertheless, cultural conservative Christians have the free will to choose how they live. The spiritual conservative Christians also have the free will to choose how they live because they have read Matthew 25:31 – 46. Members of a club abide by the rules of the club. Christians who are not born again can become impostors who give the church the stigma of hypocrisy. Truth be told, a cultural religion cannot compete with the global religion and vision. Hence the gatekeepers of cultural religions restrict the presence of churches for fear of exposing their people to an open marketplace of ideas and ideals. Still, they offer no guarantees, no passport or visa to life after death. Several men and women have published books in an effort to modernize the religion of their culture. The Gospel of Jesus Christ cannot be modernized because it is from God Almighty.

Although the Gospel has been corrupted and abused for centuries, atheists, cultural religionists and the freedom from religion foundation of America cannot survive in a world without Christian values. Unlike cultural religions anyone forced to be a Christian is not a Christian. It is a religion for the collective accountability to the God of all peoples. It is the only way to peace and goodwill on earth without the smack of the spiritual imperialism of a cultural religion. The Great Commission (Matthew 28 :19 - 20) was to make disciples of all nations. There is no record to show that the God of all nations authorized any group, not even Israel, to kill people and enforce religion in His name. Imagine for a moment that some powerful African men used Voodoo, a cultural religion to seize land and kill unbelievers. All spiritual leaders including Christianity are volunteers. People have the God-given right to believe or not believe them.

As adults, people have the right to change their minds. They have the right to leave the religion or denomination they were born into. They have the right to worship idols or religious statues. And they have the right to practice the religion of their culture. That is

God giving free will. But when any kind of ideology is used to kill innocent men, women and children, it becomes a common enemy to humankind. The website www. Stephenblanton.com/growth is a record of what is tantamount to spiritual imperialism. Nobody of Christian, Muslim or Jewish faith is responsible for the inhumanity done in ignorance by their predecessors. The illiterate and primitive people did wrong in the past. But a more educated generation and beneficiaries of past wrongs are duty bound by conscience to ameliorate the consequences of past wrongs.

In South Africa and Canada, there has been truth and reconciliation commissions aimed to redress the wrongs done to native peoples. For goodness's sake, will there ever be a desire for truth and reconciliation between native Africans and the Arabians who occupied African lands and continue to kill people in the name of a religion alien to Africans? Can they all live in peace on that continent? And will there ever be a desire for truth and reconciliation between African Americans and the Christians whose ancestors fought and died to sustain slavery? The world may not be Christian but the Golden Rule makes sense to anyone who is a human being regardless of culture, religion, ethnicity, gender or political ideology. Yet, the conflict between the will of God and the will of culture will not end soon.

The Hindu religion of India with over one billion adherents may be the World's oldest religion. It was there that Ravi Zacharias (1946 – 2020) was born into an Anglican family. After his education in Canada, he founded Ravi Zacharias International ministry. And a thought- provoking television program," Let My People Think." It makes a difference into what religion or denomination children are born into. That great apologist for Christianity died at the age of 74, two months after being diagnosed with cancer. Why would such a valuable evangelists pass away so quickly? While the Almighty wants thinking men and women to put in a good word for the Gospel, nobody is indispensable to God Almighty.

Some preachers have brought in a celebrity to validate Jesus Christ. God does not need a hero. Whatever will be will be. Children born into a religion, denomination or sect have no choice. It can lead them down the garden path from cradle to grave. As adults if their religion, denomination or sect does not teach them to observe the Golden Rule, the Great Commandment and the New Commandment, they should think twice no matter how magnificent their edifice may be. Treat others the same way you want them to treat you makes sense to any human being. As members of a counter culture religion, born again Christians no longer see the world from a cultural perspective but from a global perspective. They can see the whole elephant, not the parts of the elephant. They are no longer blind. The Gospel has been corrupted and malpracticed since the inception of slave trade. But whether people believe it or not the world can see the difference between nations where Christian influence dominates and nations where cultural religions dominate. Cultural religionists must think for themselves. May God help those who cannot read the Gospel to see the difference between Christianity and their religion regardless of the conduct of some Christians.

There is hardly a social problem on this planet that is not connected to the disobedience of God's Golden Rule. If the Golden Rule (Luke 6:31) is not possible; if the Great Commandment (Luke 10:27) is not possible; and if the New Commandment (John 13:34) is not possible, why would the God who created humankind ask them to do what is not possible? Jesus Christ, the sacrificial Lamb of God came down to teach and proclaim: "I am the vine, ye at the branches. He that abideth in me, and I in him, the same bringeth forth much fruit: for without me ye can do nothing." (John 15:5). Any philosophy or doctrine that asks people to hate or do wrong will be easy to follow because doing wrong comes naturally. In the obverse, to ask people to be good or be happy and practice loving kindness based on their own effort is hard and will lead to frustration. They do not come naturally in an evil world prone to ill will.

To ask for the Holy Spirit (Luke 11:13) is how to be born again and be enabled to keep those commandments. And also have "the peace of God which surpasses all understanding" (Philippians 4:7 NKJV), even when the world is falling apart. Any cleric who has not been teaching parishioners to be born again and observe the commandments has probably sent more people to hell than "home to be with the Lord." If more Christians understand what the Gospel of Jesus Christ is about, and what the church Establishment has done or condoned since slave trade and slavery, they will join the exodus from the church. Ask any protestant Christian youth in Africa what Christianity is all about, the answer will not come from the Gospel but from the Epistles, such as Romans 10:9. A Roman Catholic youth raised on sacraments wouldn't know. Did Jesus Christ come to die on a cross so that Christians can fight wars, colonial wars, World Wars, engaged in slave trade, slavery, colonialism, segregation, apartheid and die and still have eternal life? That is not Christianity but victor theology.

It took a civil war to end slavery in America. Otherwise, it would not have ended to this day because the church was invested in slavery. As a Regency, imperious Roman Catholicism skipped asking for the Holy Spirit, to be born again and observe the Gospel. It offered weekly absolutions. Without "teaching them to observe all things whatsoever I have commanded you," as Jesus said, the Jesuits- the Society of Jesus- became the biggest slave holders in America. They sold 272 of their plantation slaves to save Georgetown university from bankruptcy. So, in 2,000 years, Jesus Christ has one denomination offering forgiveness of sins and the other studying the Bible but not living by the Gospel. Slavery could not have ended without a civil war. Yet there is nothing in the Bible, not even the Amazing Grace that nullified the Golden Rule, the Great Commandment and the New commandment.

The victor theology nullified them to sustained slave trade and slavery for centuries. A nation is as good as their religion. Universally, the Golden Rule makes sense to any human being. No nation can fix their politics without fixing their religion. Conservatism is about conserving the past. Unlike cultural conservatives, spiritual conservatives conserve the good not the ugly past. A nation whose leaders are not compliant to the will of God has citizens who are neither compliant to the will of God nor the will of man. It is a nation in chaos. In the first century the pagans were attracted to Christianity because of the way Christians behaved. Christians were a walking Gospel. Since slave trade and slavery, educated pagans are repulsed by the conduct of Christians, except the poor masses who yearn for relief from poverty and disease. According to one cleric," Medicare is costly. God's care is free." It is that expectation that brings some people to church only to be frustrated by expecting from God what human beings are expected to do.

A previous book titled:" When Culture Overrules God and Reason "was inspired by this epiphany – where would the Lamb of God be born if not in a manger for sheep? Jesus Christ was not only a teacher of good relations between people and between them and the God of Creation, He was also the sacrifice to end all animal sacrifices. The book shows how the Almighty used Caesar Augustus to pass a decree. It forced Mary and Joseph to travel some 150 kilometers from Nazareth to Bethlehem where prophecy said that the Messiah would be born. They must have carried a tent and could have stayed in the tent or in someone's house in Bethlehem if there was no room at the Inn. But they were led to a manger for sheep. Where would the Lamb of God be born if not in a manger for sheep? Surely, "God Moves in a Mysterious Way," wrote William Cowper. Life is not linear. Even so, if God wants people to be saved, He will not make the process complicated. Here now, are what some Pentecostal Christians will acknowledge to be the six steps to heaven or salvation:

1. Acknowledge: Adam and Eve disobeyed God. Sin is the disobedience of God's commandments. "For all have sinned, and come short of the glory of God (Romans 3:23).

2. Repent: "Except ye repent, ye shall all likewise perish. (Luke 13:3)

3. Confess: "If we confess our sins, he is faithful and just to forgive us our sins, and to cleanse us from all unrighteousness, (1 John 1:9)

4. Forsake: "Let the wicked forsake his way, and the unrighteous man his thoughts: and let him return unto the LORD, and he will have mercy upon him; and to our God, for he will abundantly pardon. (Isaiah 55:7).

5. Believe: "For God so loved the world, that he gave his only begotten Son, that whosoever believeth in him should not perish, but have everlasting life. (John 3:16). The intellectuals of a cultural religion who want to discredit Christianity will argue that God does not have a wife and cannot have a son. Prophet Isaiah states: "For my thoughts are not your thoughts, neither are your ways my ways saith the LORD. "(Isaiah 55:8). Jesus Christ is God's begotten son. Christians who are born again are not animals but also the sons and daughters of the Almighty and eternal Father. The Lord's prayer begins with "Our Father which art in heaven"

6. Ask: "If ye then, being evil, know how to give good gifts unto your children: how much more shall your heavenly Father give the Holy Spirit to them that ask him? (Luke 11:13).

This last step is what separates born again Christians from the nominal Christians and superficial spirituality. When a Christian is born again, he or she will live by the Golden Rule because the Holy spirit has replaced the evil spirit. Since few Christians have asked for the Holy Spirit, to become born-again, the past 2,000 years has unleashed an evil world. The state of belligerence between Moscow and Washington, DC this 21st century, and between Russia and Ukraine, demonstrate that the church of the slave traders does not change people. It is a church still led to believe on weekly absolutions for one group and on Amazing Grace for the other group. What will you call doing the same thing over and over for 2,000 years expecting a different outcome? During the Second World War, if all that united a husband and wife in matrimony was shared hatred of Adolf Hitler, the relationship may not last. They will discover that there is a little Adolf Hitler in everyone.

Who You Are

You can recall most of the things that happened in your life. A brain scan cannot recover and print those events on paper. They are in your soul. Your soul is who you are. Only you and God Almighty know the totality of you. A good-looking apple can be rotten at the core. So, when David was beings selected as king of Israel, the Bible states that man looks at the outward appearance but God looks at the heart. The heart is not the organ that pumps blood but refers to the soul. That is the core of the individual. Relationships will not end badly if the individuals looked under the hood rather than on the outward appearance. The body, mind and soul are three in one. Are they the unholy Trinity? When Jesus Christ came into the world, it was under the control of men who did to others what they did not want others to do to them. World history is still a struggle against men who do to others what they don't want others to do to them. The struggle will not end until all men and women are possessed by the Holy Spirit or born again, which is improbable.

Nevertheless, Liberals, socialists and spiritual conservatives outnumber cultural conservatives. A world that lives on peace and goodwill is within their control. There are parents who have not been to church since they were baptized as Christians. Based on history, they know the church to be a place where those who do to others what they don't want others to do to them go to wipe their slate clean. And return to do what they ought not to do and not do what they ought to do. As rational minds, they abstained from the church. Some other disaffected Christians have drifted from meditation to Buddhism in search of peace of mind and peace on earth. In Buddhist Myanmar, the military coup and massacre of civilians in March 2020 changed the minds of some who believed that Buddhism or meditation is the route to peace on earth. Religion cannot transform people and change the world. Meditation offers a temporary relief from stress. It is the Holy Spirit who offers a natural buffer against stress and gives "the peace of God which surpasses all understanding."

Some preachers have told their congregants to be more like Jesus. How can they be more like Jesus without being told to ask for the Holy spirit? We have an endemic evil spirit or the spirit of disobedience; and must sincerely ask God for the Holy Spirit, to replace the evil spirit. The Pharisees were very religions but lost. Without being born again, a Christian can also be very religions but lost. That was the downfall of the clergy and laity of the centuries of slavery. A born-again Christian does not do to others what he does not want others to do to him. That is the litmus test of a born-again Christian. Why did the enslavement of men, women and children not alarm the great Schools of Theology in Europe and America, as anathema to the Gospel? The clergy and theologians were indoctrinated to have a theological and cerebral relationship with God, being conformed to culture and not transformed to a spiritual being. If that is still the case, the church of the slave traders has not changed.

Religion can be forced on people through birth or coercion. A herdsman can force cattle to go in a certain direction not because they want to but because they have to. Anyone forced to be a Christian is not a Christian. The God of Creation gave humankind the free will to choose either the Holy Spirit or the evil spirit - the spirit of disobedience. The evil spirit dwells in a willing host. So does the Holy spirit. In Christianity, a convert has to willingly and sincerely ask for the Holy spirit to replace the evil spirit endemic in man. Jesus said: "If ye then, being evil, known how to give good gifts unto your children: how much more shall your heavenly Father give the Holy Spirit to those that ask Him? The "shall" conveys certainty. "I am the vine, you are the branches," Jesus said, "he who abides in Me, and I in him, bears much fruit; for without Me you can do nothing." (John 15:15 NKJV). Jesus abides in a born-again Christian through the Holy Spirit.

How then can a Christian know when he or she is filled with the Holy spirit? The Spirit-filled Christian is born again and progressively lives by the Golden Rule. While speaking in tongues was the visible sign of a spirit-filled Christian in the pioneer church, compliance to the Golden Rule is the visible evidence of a spirit -filled Christian in the modern era. There is hardly a social problem in the world that is not linked to the disobedience of God's Golden Rule. Sooner or later thinking men and women of the world will consider the very long list of social conflicts in the past 2,000 years. They will conclude that the conflicts could have been prevented by compliance to the Golden Rule. Their fingers will point to the church Establishment that did not teach Christians to observe the Golden Rule. It would have prevented all the sad events of human history. Instead, because the leaders were not born again, they became participants in malfeasance. They elevated cultural conservatives dyed in human nature.

To tell is different from to teach and observe. How many Christians go to a church that teaches them to observe (or obey) all things whatsoever that Jesus Christ commanded. Suppose pioneer Christians - Jews and Gentiles- and their successors were taught all that Jesus Christ commanded including the Golden Rule. Will there be slave trade, slavery, two World Wars, the Holocaust, segregation, apartheid, terrorism, scams, family violence and the growing epidemic of divorce and singleness. The failure of the church fathers to teach Christians to observe all things whatsoever that Jesus Christ commanded has created an endless list of problems for humankind. Every Christian is a nominal Christian until he or she is born again. The clergy and laity of the slave economy were nominal Christians.

After 2,000 years of Christianity how do you explain why a Minneapolis, Minnesota policeman would arrest a man named George Floyd whose ancestors survived over 200 years of slavery in the hands of Christians, handcuff him behind his back, place his face down, kneel on his neck for nine minutes and kill him? Does it not show that the victor theology of the imperious church of the slave traders has not changed? It raises the question: what makes a person human? Racism and hatred cannot be stopped by legislation. The ideology of the Islamic states and terrorism cannot be stopped by legislation. The resulting Islamophobia cannot be stopped by legislation. Legislation cannot change human nature. It is by being born again to live by the Golden Rule can man be humanized to stop inhumanity. There is no other way. Weekly confession and absolution create a revolving door for malfeasance. It offers mass admission to heaven and does not require being born again, as Jesus said. Mass admission to heaven is not consistent with "narrow is the gate and difficult is the way which leads to life, and there are few who find it" (Matthew 7:14 NKJV).

There are educated people called scholars, who have not read the Jewish Torah, the Christian Gospel or the Arabian Koran to see the difference. Why? Because people want to believe what they are born into. The most famous Indian was born a Hindu. Mahatma Gandhi read the Gospel of Jesus Christ and embarrassed Christians by practicing Christianity better than they did. He would not be persuaded to be a Christian; not because of the Scripture but because of the conduct of the Christians he encountered in apartheid South Africa and colonized India. Slavery and imperialism disgraced the Christian faith. Gandhi practiced Christianity, not Hinduism, and put Christians to shame. If there is purgatory to give good people a second chance to accept Jesus Christ, it will be for such people as Gandhi, Confucius and other non-Christians of similar moral character. Gandhi chose to die as a Hindu rather than as a Christian or monotheist. That should be a concern to evangelical Christians in the Dixie culture.

In America, Christianity sits at the table with all other religions including Voodoo as equals. Why? Because the religion that subserved slave traders, slave masters and their clergy lost moral authority. It is like losing the Ark of the covenant in ancient Israel. It is equally lamentable and should keep genuine Christians awake at night. The use of Law and order as a tool for police brutality against the survivors of centuries of slavery; the use of a Bible for photo opportunity to win support, are further abuse of the Gospel of Jesus Christ. Hindsight shows that the clergy and laity that lived off the avails of unpaid servitude for over 200 years, did not live according to the will of God. In doctrine and liturgy, there is nothing that suggests that the church has changed. What has changed are the preachers. "No servant can serve two masters," Jesus said. If church and state do not live by the will of God, by whose will do they live? The will of God is the Golden Rule, the Great Commandment, the New Commandment and their social implications. There is no other way but to trust and obey. In any homogeneous ethnic group, caring for one another is beyond dispute. It becomes disputable in a multi-cultural society that the Gospel represents.

If the Ten commandments were not to be obeyed, the Almighty God would not have given them through Moses. If the Golden Rule, the Great Commandment and the New Commandment were not to be obeyed, the Almighty would not have given them through Jesus Christ. Those three precepts are about good relations between the peoples of the world and between them and their Creator. Unlike Moses, Jesus Christ had to come from heaven for the whole world. To continue to do wrong to others and rely on weekly absolutions or

Amazing Grace is nothing but amazing self - deceit. By emulating the weekly confession and absolution, some politicians have gone from one wrong deed to another and all they have to do is apologize. One's life must be based on the Gospel. Only then is it "well with my soul." Choosing to be a godly couple with integrity under the auspices of the Holy Spirit is what prevents divorce and churches from being sold. If belief in Jesus Christ is the only difference between a Christian and a pagan or godless communists, the pastor or priest needs malpractice insurance. Unfortunately, the pastorate is one profession that does not require malpractice insurance. Therefore, buyer beware applies to religion. If God wants people to be saved, why would He make the process complicated. A car owner must follow the instructions in the manual, for the car to perform according to specifications. To perform according to God's specifications, a Christian must be born again and show it by compliance to the Golden Rule, not by speaking in tongues nobody can interpret or understands.

Since Adam and Eve walked on this planet, countless millions of people have died. In about 120 years, everyone alive today will also be dead. Some of those past generations accumulated and left untold wealth while some died from starvation. Some, like King David chose the way of truth (Psalm 119:30) while others chose the way of culture. Everyone left the world as empty handed as they came into the world. Nobody has come to tell the story about life on the other side except one - Jesus Christ. It is wise to pay attention to what he said. If church history during slavery is instructive, at the hour of death <u>Christianity for Dummies</u> will make sense. For some it may be too late.

If The Dead Could Speak!

Consider the numerous wars and sad events the church has been involved in since the Apostles and their Pentecostal church passed away. Include the enslavement of Africans for about 300 years. Satan has cherry picked the Gospel to keep the Broadway to destruction over-crowded. For example, "Jesus loves you "does not change lives. "Your sins are nailed on the cross" does not change lives. "Jesus died for your past, present and future sins "does not change lives. Such people will continue to do to others what they don't want others to do to them.

Luke 11:13 changes lives. The Almighty offers to download the Holy Spirit and replace man's evil spirit to enable him become born again. And live by the Golden Rule, the Great Commandment and the New Commandment. That is the Gospel. But Satan has kept that verse hidden for 2000 years. It is not taught. "Because narrow is the gate," Jesus said, "and difficult is the way which leads to life, and there are few who find it (Matthew 7:14). Yes, there are few who find it. So, if the dead could speak; if Adolf Hitler, slave traders, slave masters and their clergy could speak, this would be their message to the world: "A Christian must ask for the Holy Spirit to replace the evil spirit, and be born again. A born-again Christian lives by the Golden Rule, the Great Commandment and the New Commandment. That is genuine Christianity otherwise, it has no redeeming value regardless of the magnificence of their cathedral. Genuine Christianity would have prevented what we did. Any business or institution that is not genuine will eventually collapse. Buyer beware!"

America's PBS television runs a program titled "Finding Your Roots," by Harvard Professor Henry Louis Gates Jr. The men and women profiled get to know their ancestors as far back as possible. In the view of those ancestors of centuries past, if relatives are forgotten after a century or two, what is life all about? What advice would they offer the men and women on Wall Street, the young politicians who rule over their parents, grandparents, teachers, professors and classmates, and the volunteers who now control the church? They might repeat those words of wise King Solomon: "Let us hear the conclusion of the whole matter: Fear God, and keep his command-ments: for this is the whole duty of man." (Ecclesiastes 12:13). That is the bottom line.

CHAPTER 14

The Party of God or Sabotage

The world did not create itself. Atheists would believe in the tenets of the Golden Rule, the Great Commandment and the New Commandment as long as God Almighty is excluded. Some who profess faith in God would also believe in the Golden Rule, the Great Commandment and the New Commandment as long as Jesus Christ is excluded. But whether we believe or understand it or not, God the Father, the Son and the Holy Spirit are one mind. And so, those three precepts are about good relations between peoples and between them and the God of Creation. They spell Christian civilization. That is what a good religion should be about – good relations between humanity and between them and their Creator. All civilizations are resistant to Christian civilization. Paradoxically, even the church is resistant to Christian civilization. The church whose clergy and laity lived off the avails of slave trade and slavery; the church that owned and sold 272 slaves to save Georgetown university from bankruptcy; the church involved in colonialism, segregation and apartheid that are anathema to Christian values, was resistant to Christian civilization.

Jesus Christ told a crowd of people: "Many will say to me in that day, 'Lord, Lord, have we not prophesied in Your name, and cast out demons in Your name, and done many wonders in Your name?' And then I will declare to them, 'I never knew you: depart from Me, you who practice lawlessness!" (Matthew 7:22-23 NKJV). The "we" are not atheists or pagans. They are Christians -nominal Christians apparently doing wonderful things. It is easier to destroy an institution as an insider than as an outsider. The greatest threat to Christianity is not from atheists and pagans. It is from Christians. For slave traders, slave masters, the auctioneers and clergy, for example, going to church made them religious. But they were practicing lawlessness or disobedience. They ignored the Golden Rule because it did not serve their interest. The abolitionists were called radicals.

Christianity is about good relations between people and between them and the God of Creation. That, cannot be said enough. We know that from the Golden Rule, the Great Commandment and the New Commandment. It has not been taught by the church that does not believe in the Golden Rule. The cultural conservatives have no interest in Truth and reconciliation with God over modern man's original sin - slavery. They are opposed to universal healthcare or any program that will benefit the people they hate. To "bear one another's burdens and so fulfill the law of Christ "is a "radical socialist agenda." Some preachers avoid the Gospel of Jesus Christ and the practical Christianity of St. James, but use the Old Testament and Revelation to peddle prophecy. African children dying from starvation, for example, are shown as a fulfillment of Bible prophecy. So, they do nothing to help. That the devil can cite the scriptures for his purpose is more pertinent now than in the days of William Shakespeare.

The disaffected young men who commit acts of hatred and mayhem are indoctrinated and radicalized by men who sit in safe air-conditioned offices. Some publicly express support for Israel. But some of their members gun down Jews in Synagogues. Others have T-Shirts that read 6MNE (Six million not enough) and Camp Auschwitz. For some ulterior motives, some care about Jerusalem but not about Bethlehem, the birthplace of Jesus Christ they follow. Jesus Christ, the Messiah and Lamb of God was not born in the home of a king or chief priests. He was born in a manger for sheep through the home of a carpenter. His disciples were not the educated elites of society but lowly fisherman. St. Paul wrote: "But God hath chosen the foolish things of the world to confound the wise; and God hath chosen the weak things of the world to confound the things which are mighty; and base things of the world, and things which are despised, hath God chosen, yea, and things which are not, to bring to nought things that are: That no flesh should glory in His presence." (1 Corinthians 1:27–29).

First, a proviso. No modern bishop is responsible for leading the church astray but for returning it to the straight and narrow way. The Romans who took over the pioneer church of Jews and Gentiles were not foolish, weak, base or despised. They were the most powerful empire known to man. Hence, Christianity became the spiritual arm of imperial power. A counterculture religion became the religion of culture. The Kings of Europe were at the mercy of the pope. The church Establishment used slavery to enforce celibacy, condoned the enslavement of the nearest pagans at the bottom of the totem pole, and laid the foundation of the master class and racism that has bedeviled the New World since slave trade began. The Protestant Reformation did not address slavery and racism but only the sins of Rome.

So, for nearly 250 years in the U.S. A., and for over 350 years in Roman Catholic Brazil, all clergy and laity lived off the avails of slavery. The president who ended slavery was assassinated. Abraham Lincoln was succeeded by vice President Andrew Johnson, a democrat, a southerner and slave owner known to be a racist at the core.

As the Democrats began to purge the party from hate mongers and segregationists, Lincoln's spiritually conservative Republican party morphed into the party of cultural conservatives, to resist the Golden Rule and conserve feudal cultural values. President Lincoln's transformed party, in partnership with the Dixie church, became the voice of southern gospel, even "the moral majority." The Democratic party became the voice of women seeking suffrage and the voice of African Americans demanding civil rights. From whom? It is from Christians, cultural conservatives, fellow mortals.

Now, imagine for a moment how world history could have been different if Jewish Christians, as trustees, continued the Golden Rule, the Great Commandment and the New Commandment, and did not abandoned Christianity to Rome. Africans might not have been enslaved. The Tuskegee syphilis experiment (1932 to 1972) might not have happened. There would have been no Jim crow laws and lynching of emancipated African Americans. The Holocaust against the Jews might not have happened. The Tuskegee experiment may have inspired the Nazi experiment on Jews under Dr. Joseph Mengele. What Christians did to Africans in Dixie inspired the Nazis for the Nuremberg Laws and the Holocaust. They might not have happened. The three people groups most abused by the corruption of the Gospel are Africans, Jews and the Irish, in that order. A world that stifles the uncomfortable Truth will never get better. The Golden Rule is the rule in any family- a unit of the family of God. In a homogeneous society like the Nordic nations, it is easier to live by the Golden Rule. In a heterogeneous society like the U.S.A., a microcosm of the world, it is much more difficult to live by the Golden Rule. There are people who look different, speak different languages and come with all kinds of religions. To treat them like family is almost an impossible mission. That is where the sabotage of Christianity is most evident.

The Golden Rule came under increased stress test when the door of immigration was opened after the end of slavery and colonial rule. In the most heterogeneous nation on earth, the "patriots and nationalists" want to close the door and build a wall between the United States and Mexico. Those patriots who wrap the gun and the Bible with the flag of patriotism forget the Aboriginals of America. No nation, including Mexico, needs an open border to immigrants. And no nation needs an open door but a window to immigration to reflect the kingdom of God in their nation. Immigration is the consequence of colonialism. Since the colonial history cannot be reversed, President John F. Kennedy offered a solution. He sent peace corps volunteers to impoverished nations to build bridges between the United States and other cultures. As the name implies, the United States Agency for International Development (USAID) was born with great expectations. He also proposed an "Alliance for Progress" with Latin America to stabilize their economy. It would have helped the people that Christianity has not helped since Christopher Columbus landed.

Other advanced nations followed the American lead. Like President Abraham Lincoln, President Kennedy was assassinated. Those policies that would have kept people in their homeland were derailed. Those who conserve culture and human nature would neither help those who survived slavery nor those who survived colonialism. People may not hear what was said behind closed doors but they can see the outcome. The United States consulate in Eastern Nigeria which is more populous than many nations in Europe was closed. A Pfizer plant there was closed. It would have helped in a pandemic. If China fills the void left in neglected Africa, it will be criticized. Who is coming to America and how much doing good will cost are two factors that set the cultural- conservative agenda. A cultural conservative minority dominates the majority view. They forestall peace and goodwill on earth. In the endless clash of cultures between the East and West, Africans, African Americans, Asian Americans, Aboriginals and Pacific Islanders are not sure if they belong to the East or West. They would like to see Christianity practiced to end their own misery because in God there is no East or West. One cannot think of any social problem that does not emanate from the failure of the Regent church Establishment to fulfill the mandate of the Great Commission.

The Pastoral Racism in Ministry

Why would a man read the Gospel of Jesus Christ with the Golden Rule, the Great Commandment and the New Commandment and decide to be the pastor of a segregated church? It is incomprehensible that a cleric who preached about our common origin from Adam and Eve, could pastor a segregated church. To use the counterculture religion to serve culture is antichrist. There are well educated, mostly men, who have acted in ways that suggest that they have lost their minds. They did not lose their minds. They lost their conscience. Education alone does not change a man. It is the Holy Spirit that changes a man. The conscience dies before the soul dies. If that conscience can be revived, the soul can be saved. That is the task for those who want to save the soul of their nation. An influential few who have lost their conscience can corrupt millions of impressionable men and women. That has been the history of Christianity particularly in Dixie. The Dixie church was not there to "preach good tidings unto the meek; bind up the broken hearted; proclaim liberty to the captives; open the prison to those who are bound; proclaim the acceptable year of the LORD and the day of vengeance of our God; and comfort all who mourn. "Instead, the Dixie church was there to bless the cage of slavery. If world history can be summarized in one word, it would be - control. No man has the right to control the life of another.

The leaders of the American Revolution (1765 – 83) recognized that war was necessary to free themselves from British control. Yet, they did not want the same freedom for the men, women and children they held in slavery for centuries. That is the nature of the culture of entitlements. Like Rev. Dietrich Bonhoeffer who opposed Adolf Hitler in Germany, one of America's great icons of faith was John Brown (1800s - 1859). Like the revolutionists, he recognized that war was necessary to strike a death blow to slavery in America. The church could not end slavery. Left to the church, there might still be slave trade and slavery to this day. The church establishment was not even part of the problem or part of the solution. It was the problem. They never saw anything wrong with slave trade and slavery. It is unfortunate that social evolution is so slow that those who do not have abundant patience resort to revolution.

John Brown raided the Federal armory at Harpers Ferry, Virginia, to arm the slaves for insurrection. The fear of such insurrection might have been one reason for the right to bear arms and the gun culture not seen in any other nation. John Brown was convicted for treason. He sat on his coffin on the way to his execution for the sin of the nation. It was like Jesus Christ carrying the cross to be crucified as the Lamb of God. The first person executed for treason in American history stood for and died for the Golden Rule that the church ignored. Treat others the same way you want them to treat you, makes sense to anyone who is a human being regardless of culture, ethnicity, gender, religion or political ideology. It is one of the pillars of the Gospel of Jesus Christ. John Brown died for the Truth and like Jesus Christ, "his truth is still marching on."

Those who conserve the feudal past and resist change called John Brown a terrorist. Similarly, those who stand for humanity and compassion today are called "the radical left." Every generation has the same cultural conservatives. And since that slave liberation movement, there has been several movements either to free or to counter the freedom of the human conscience. Before the subsequent civil war, there were times when northerners and journalists were run out of Dixie. They were the enemy of the people. John Brown, President Abraham Lincoln and those who fought to end the sin of slave trade and slavery understood the Gospel better than the church Establishment. The church used slavery to enforce celibacy; condoned slave trade and slavery; erased the interface between right and wrong; and for nearly 250 years in the U.S.A., and over 350 years in Roman Catholic Brazil, clergy and laity lived off the avails of the unpaid servitude of African men, women and children. Nobody alive today is responsible for those events but that is the legacy of the church that left roadblocks on the way to civilization.

The church run by man is not infallible. That church has not changed. It cannot change without reconciliation with God under a Second Reformation. Some denominations still offer weekly absolutions or forgiveness of sins. Other denominations still count on God's Amazing Grace, while piling on new transgressions. Did Jesus Christ die for our past, present and future sins; and free us from the Golden Rule, the Great Commandment and the New Commandment or did He die for our past sins before repentance, so that we can go and sin no more with the help of the Holy Spirit? Few recognize that a Christian must be born again through the Holy Spirit and live by the Golden Rule. If a bus driver is heading towards an abyss, should the passengers keep quiet out of respect for the driver? That is the question that faces Christendom. Since we are all born into a religion or a denomination, caveat emptor is applicable to religion.

If most Christians do not learn to be born again and live by the Gospel, future generations of mindful students cannot read about the Trans -Atlantic slave trade, slavery, colonialism and even the divorce rate among Christians, and not wonder if the church serves any useful purpose to either the living or the dead. In politics, the same dogmatic and cultural -conservative mindset still influences both domestic and foreign policy. Those who wish to use government to do good are asked where the money will come from. But there is always money for weapons and war. American mothers and sisters fought for suffrage until 1920. African Americans still fight for civil rights. Against whom? It is against the Christian cultural -conservatives who demand submission to man, not mutual submission to God Almighty. And certainly not mutual compliance to the Gospel - the Golden Rule, the Great Commandment and the New Commandment. The pandemic of 2020 exposed a world that is economically and socially in disarray. If Christianity is about good relations between people and between them and the God of Creation; if the Golden Rule - Treat others the same way you want them to treat you makes sense to any human being, how effective has the Gospel been in 2,000 years? Other religions must also question if they offer any benefits to the rest of the world. No nation can fix their politics without fixing their religion. If the religion does not instill the Golden Rule into the functionaries of Church and State, they cannot fix their politics. That is what makes a nation more livable than others.

Not knowing what Muslims have done to Africans since the Arabian invasion of the Seventh Century, some African Americans converted to Islam in their reaction to what Christians had done to them in spite of the Gospel. They formed the Nation of Islam in 1930, and abandoned the Lamb of God in resentment of the perverted Gospel. There are Christians, past and present, who have done some good to mitigate the pains of history. I attended a boarding school in Southeast Nigeria ran by missionaries from the UK., went to the hospital ran by their medical missionaries who were my role models, and listened to sermons by peripatetic preachers. The thousands of Africans with that exposure in the 1960s can separate the spiritual conservatives from the cultural conservatives. By contrast, for African Americans who survived slavery, attended segregated churches, survived Jim crow laws and the Ku Klux Klan, and faced racial oppression in every facet of life - watched by a silent majority - it is difficult to separate the cultural conservatives or what one politician described as the "deplorables" from spiritual conservatives. Those deplorables will continue to sabotage Christian civilization generation after generation. They are not liberals. They are not socialists. They are not spiritual conservatives who conserve spiritual biblical values like the Quakers and Puritans. They are cultural conservatives who conserve feudal cultural values that keep down women and those who look different.

By professing Christianity that is counterculture, cultural conservatives corrupted the Christian faith. The progression of history will show that the Gospel of Jesus Christ is the embodiment of civilization. However, there are men and women whose purpose in life is to slow down civilization. The nearly 250 years of slavery in the U.S., and over 350 years of slavery in Roman Catholic Brazil slowed down civilization. Because of Adolf Hitler, millions of fathers and mothers went to their graves with hatred for all German people. If they looked into their history, they would have discovered that their nations did wrong to Africans. The Nazis did not represent the German people. The church that lived off the avails of slavery for centuries did not represent Christians. The workers of iniquity do not represent Americans or the West. The cultural conservatives who do to others what they don't want others to do to them, do not represent the majority. But the silent majority who sit on their conscience can make it difficult to believe in God. The followers of the cultural conservatives who blende Christian values with cultural values are laying their treasures on earth. Nobody has left this planet with one penny. It includes the slave traders and slave holders. It will include the richest men and women on earth today. In fact, 120 years from today, everyone will pass away. Those who conserve culture and human nature and impede Christian civilization have enticing talking points:

"We have fought to lower taxes."

Conservatives are divided politically because they are divided spiritually. The dogmas of centuries past do not appeal to all conservatives today. Many cannot defend a belief in small government or lower and lower taxes at the expense of social services, a belief inherited from grandparents. Still, the tax cuts keep coming up during and between elections, particularly in a multi-cultural society. Regressive taxation has been a limiting factor to good governance. It is the tool used for centuries to keep the rich richer and the poor poorer. Aversion to taxation is a defining characteristic of the antisocial taker, unwilling to give to pay for civilization. A jungle can be run tax free. But if it is to be civilized, it cannot be run tax free. Yet, during elections and between elections those who live selfishly wrangle over tax cuts. A conservative is not conservative without preaching tax cuts. It is the mantra of cultural conservatism. Those tired of the tirade wish that taxes could be eliminated completely to see if cultural conservatives can run a government without taxes. Or see rational minds come up with a progressive tax code written in stone, to let politicians focus on governance. That would be a tax code that does not create billionaires and paupers in "a nation under God." Also conscious of the fact that everyone leaves this planet as empty handed as they came in.

Yet, for generations the gap between the very rich and the very poor continues to grow. And every year someone wins the Nobel prize in Economics. It seems like disdain for the poor. Economists are fallible human beings. They are not prophets. Economics is everyone's responsibility because it affects everyone. Without progressive taxation, plantation capitalism creates billionaires and paupers. The regressive taxation that allows the hoarding of wealth at the expense of starving children is an impediment to civilization. It is unfathomable that anyone can take home millions of dollars a year with a good conscience. Consider the parable of the rich man and Lazarus, the beggar. With progressive taxation, the rich man will be less rich, Lazarus will be less poor, and both will be in Abraham's bosom. Is it not the better option? That is the Scandinavian approach to life.

Parents want to elect a caring government not the better deceivers who would later be voted out of office. They are deceived by a few men and women who are liberal to their children but conservative to other people's children. They are deceived by a few rich men who assemble in a comfortable place to talk about improvements but do nothing. American Christianity is on trial because nobody can serve God and mammon. The master and the slave do not share the same Christian values. The billionaire and the homeless pauper do not share the same Christian values. The Christianity many profess forbids laying treasures on earth. Sadly, before other non-native religions came to America, Christians laid a corrupt foundation through slavery. Hence, Christianity is on trial in America more than anywhere else on earth. Those who do wrong to the people they hate will eventually do wrong to the people they love. Family violence is an example. Still, some are willing to oppose progressive change as long as the people they hate are suffering more than themselves.

The animosity that exists at the bottom of society involving youths deprived of good education, economic prospects and moral upbringing is exacerbated by the concentration of wealth at the top. It has been enabled by the opposition to progressive taxation, universal basic healthcare and social justice. With tax cuts and reduced social services, more women are in prison than ever before. Some desperate youths do commit suicide. Others would commit petty crimes like drug offenses and shoplifting to be in prison for shelter, food and medical care. Spending more on education, vocational training, housing, universal basic healthcare and employment cost less than running a prison industry. If benign neglect at home and conflicts abroad cost more than doing good, why not do good? The recidivism rate can be reduced through a chaplaincy that teaches the Golden Rule. And an offer of an early release to the penitent. But how can the Establishment teach the Golden Rule that it had not practiced?

Crime is the result of a dysfunctional religion. No good religion condones an economy that creates multibillionaires and
destitute people prone to crime. Those Christians, Muslims and
people of Jewish faith who truly believe in God will be remiss not
to proclaim that an economy that is more Scandinavian than plantation capitalism, is more in line with the will of God Almighty.
Most nations are developing nations. A few nations are advanced
nations. How many are both advanced and civilized? Based on
the Gospel of Jesus Christ, a civilized nation would have universal education, healthcare and employment for all families like a
Canadian Hutterite colony. There is no such nation. Civilization
has a limit but development has no limit. As a nation under God,
for example, ancient Israel was more civilized than it is today. A
nation can be more civilized than a nation that is more developed.
Such an economy may be difficult to contemplate in a pluralistic
society. Yet, all the Sermons in the world are meaningless without
that objective.

Social evolution has been a very slow process. By the time
America has an economy based on universal access to education,
healthcare and employment, the present generation shall have passed
away. Like the slave holders, all will leave this life without a penny.
"For we brought nothing into this world," wrote St. Paul, "and it
is certain we can carry nothing out." (1 Timothy 6:7 NKJV). So,
why do mortals who go to their graves empty handed support an
economic pyramid that creates conflict for those at the bottom?
Why do some people oppose social democracy or inclusive capitalism
that uses progressive taxation to turn the pyramid to a plateau and
improve social services for all? Socialism has not destroyed Nordic
nations. Since no man has yet left this planet with his wealth, they
are content to pay taxes for a welfare States. The happiest people on
earth and there, not in the nations will multibillionaires. In fact, a
socialist government is the genuine democracy because it serves the
common good. It reflects a government of the people, by the people

and for the people. A nation that lives by the Golden Rule and its social implications is bound to be a happy nation. Genuine faith cares for both the spiritual and the temporal needs of the people.

Presidents Joe Biden's administration was the most inclusive and democratic in American history. But as a pluralistic society, plantation capitalism will still prevail. Does anyone need a billion dollars while children languish in poverty? And while Shriners Hospital and Saint Jude's Hospital go on television to raise money to support children with cancer. There are men and women who have the billionaire status thrust on them as a result of regressive taxation. Some have pledged to give away most of their wealth to worthy causes. Some are pleading to pay more taxes. Some have taken up philanthropy to redeem their conscience. The Bill and Melinda Gates foundation in partnership with Warren Buffett, for example, have humanity on their minds. So does Mackenzie Scott, the ex-wife of Jeff Bezos. In the Covid-19 pandemic, she reportedly gave $4.2 billion to charity to help vulnerable people. With a net worth of $185 billion in 2020, Jeff Bezos was at the top of the list of the richest people on earth. A few multimillionaires have formed "Millionaires for Humanity." Their goal is to persuade the super rich to pay more taxes, particularly as essential workers who provided them food and sanitation services bore the brunt of COVID- 19 pandemic deaths. Their humanity is commendable. It shows how regressive taxation has imposed untold wealth on compassionate people who have no interest in laying treasures on earth. During the slave economy, cultural- conservative Christians sold men, women and children for labor. Those considered to be liberal or spiritual conservative put up with the leadership of the cultural- conservative Christians and clergy. For about 250 years, they did not derail the gravy train to save their conscience and soul. Today, that is the case with Christians who tolerate the tax cutters that create the billionaires while paupers and children languish in poverty for lack of social services.

"We are Pro-life. We protect the Unborn."

To be pro-life cannot be a Liberal or Conservative issue. All human beings, Christians and non-Christians are Pro-life. Abortion
has been a divisive issue exploited by politicians who want to be
on the side of righteousness during an election. Christians and
non-Christians are opposed to abortion as a birth control measure.
However, Christian values are devalued when practiced with hypocrisy. Being antiabortion is pitched as pro-life. But pro-life does not
include the babies and children born to languish in ghetto zip codes.
When people wear the cross on their chest and express concern for
the baby in the womb but not for those born to languish in ghetto
zip codes; when the life of a baby in the womb is prioritized over
the life of the mother, it is not Christianity but politically motivated
hypocrisy. To terminate a conscious life without a good reason is
murder. President Bill Clinton said it best: "Abortion should be legal,
safe and rare." That's the way it is in a Hutterite colony that bears
one another's burdens, leaving nobody prayer dependent.

Women are condemned for abortion. When the men involved in
the pregnancy are part of the brouhaha, abortion may cease to be an
election issue. The words of Jesus Christ are instructive: "He that is
without sin among you, let him first cast a stone at her" (John 8:7).
Is it not better to remove the beam in our eyes before worrying about
the mote in other people's eyes? As long as the woman, not the taxpayer, pays for the procedure, she and her doctor are not accountable
to any man but to God. One sinner is not accountable to another.
Politics, religion and racism thrive on ignorance. It may be easy to
fool the electorate. It may not be easy to fool God Almighty who sees
the soul. Since Christianity is about good relations between people
and between them and the God of all creation, it is abundantly clear
that those who live by the Gospel are on God's side.

Selective morality was used to lead slave traders and slave masters to believe that God was on their side. And so, both clergy and

laity lived off the avails of slavery for centuries and were prepared to die in a war for their belief. Abraham Lincoln, who seemed to know more about the will of God than the clergy reportedly said: "Sir, my concern is not whether God is on my side; my greatest concern is to be on God's side, for God is always right." The cultural conservative faction of his party has made the journey to God's social justice very slow. In that slow journey, there are men, women and children suffering and dying along the way. After 2,000 years of Christianity, some issues of right and wrong remain unresolved for lack of pastoral guidance. Such has been the case with abortion. The church identifies with conservatism. But there are cultural conservatives who conserve cultural values of self-interest; and there are spiritual conservatives who conserve inclusive spiritual values and are pro-life and pro-choice because it is the soul that sins that shall die, not the community. The spiritual conservatives of Lincoln's party care about babies in the womb as well as the children in ghettos. They are proponents of the Leave no Child behind Act and care about environmental stewardship.

There are protestants who use pro-life to drum up the Roman catholic vote. But it took until 1960 to elect the first Roman catholic president and 60 more years to elect another through the effort of African Americans. Several centuries ago, some job advertisements included "No Irish need apply." Legislation and social pressure can erase overt prejudice. It is only the Holy Spirit that can erase covert and insidious hatred and prejudice by transforming anyone dyed in culture into a spiritual being who does not do to others, what he does not want others to do to him. The cultural conservatives are at the root of the social injustice in America. The spiritual conservatives have to stand up and be counted. In the 2020 U.S. election, the world expected a repudiation of racism, hatred, police brutality and division. Instead, many misguided Christians cared more about abortion and voted accordingly.

Pollsters are more wrong in the United States than anywhere

else. Many American voters tell pollsters what many want to hear or pretend not to have made up their mind. But in the privacy of the voting booth, they yield to the basic instinct of American culture." The heart is deceitful above all things," wrote Prophet Jeremiah," and desperately wicked: who can know it?" (Jeremiah 17:9). However, the parents who decide to bring a baby with genetic abnormality into the world deserve commendation. The Almighty did not design the genetic code to be perfect. Like the man in Scripture who was born blind, they are here to teach a lesson (John 9:2). They do not blame God for their condition. In fact, they are happier and more content than the billionaires. They humanize society, including those who, for political reasons care about them in the womb but not about those languishing in poverty. One of the foundation members of the Lincoln project was a former Republican strategist. He told MSNBC in December 2020, that the Republican party is an organized conspiracy for the purposes of maintaining power for the donor class. Evidently the preservation of worldly treasure takes priority over the life of lesser mortals.

Consider this: If Jesus Christ returned when the world population was one billion, millions of souls would have perished. If He returns when the world population is 10 billion or more, billions of souls, the majority, will feed the fire of Hell. If only a few find the narrow way that leads to life, (Matthew 7:13-14) does it not make sense to have fewer children?

"Our deregulation has released the entrepreneurial Spirit and created millions of Jobs."

Liberals regulate while Conservatives deregulate. The so-called free market allows greed and avarice to run amok. When it reaches a peak the bubble bursts into a recession. All too often a liberal government would inherit and manage the recession, enact legislation to control greed and provide economic homeostasis. If the economy is not growing fast enough to absorb job seekers in the absence of universal employment, a conservative leader will offer to get the unemployed all employed. If voted into office, the regulations are lifted, the greed and avarice return, and the boom and burst cycle is repeated. If one government regulates and the other deregulates, how can they compete with China where all hands are on deck? Texas is America's Energy Capital and the most underregulated State. In the February 2021 winter storm, some families received power bills of over $16,000. That will be forgotten within a year or two. The economic and social push and pull have become an American tradition. Deregulation of greed invites economic lawlessness. It is a hypocritical policy for a political party strident on social law and order. A small government is also a conservative ideal. The cultural conservative philosophy that the government that governs the least governs the best, is a wild -west philosophy and an invitation to jungle politics. If the goal of a government of the people is to provide jobs for all families; if the goal of the church is to "bear one another's burdens and so fulfill the law of Christ," why would Christians be opposed to a big government as a tool for full employment when technology is reducing labor? Why would they oppose universal employment? Many Christians believe in small government because their grandparents believed it in the hate-filled past.

When he is not in power, the cultural conservative is enthusiastic about creating and protecting jobs. Now, suggest an economy based on universal employment, the enthusiasm disappears. A television preacher noted that in running a race in ancient Greece, the athletes stripped all encumbrances to the point of nudity. In running God's race, he argued, a Christian must strip all encumbrances too. If so, why do many Christians resist running an economy based on universal education, healthcare and employment to make the race easier and end prayer fatigue or prayer dependency? Why do the poor who blame Marmon for their problems not demand such a caring government that lives up to the ideals of the faith they profess? The cultural conservatives who want a government that is run like a plantation, can oppose universal healthcare. Their allies can include some comfortable minority leaders who claim that their country will be turned into "a socialist utopia." It is reminiscent of Quisling and Uncle Tom. There are those who care more about money than about human lives. Under plantation capitalism, if the slave masters were doing well, the economy was doing well. The rest of the people were the tools of production. Today, if the stock market is doing well, the economy is doing well regardless of the number or people who are homeless, jobless or dying in a pandemic. The market is a cheerleader of deregulation and also a divided Congress because some elected politicians who rely on corporate donors may never vote to raise taxes. It is an indirect plutocracy.

The markets can become the new trading post of plantation capitalism. As in plantation capitalism of centuries past, capital rules and without progressive taxation, it creates a chasm between the billionaire and the pauper. Hence, some men live by bread alone because enough is never enough. The super rich men in history like King Solomon and the pharaohs are reminders that nobody has left this planet with a penny. The neglected Americans who have been disillusioned by the two- party system with no viable third party, often express their longstanding resentment or discontent against the urban elites by boycotting the polls. Sooner or later, it will be obvious that with an economy based on universal education, healthcare and employment for every family, a nation performs at its highest potential. It begins by identifying the captor and the captive.

"We have secured our borders."

Those who have read the Bible know about the wall of Jericho. The great wall of China is a tourist attraction. During the Cold War there was the Berlin wall. Walls between people groups have been rare. They were built to keep invaders out. In modern times, wars and brutal regimes have caused men, women and children to abandon their homeland and flee for safety or for a better life elsewhere. In 2015, the number of such displaced people reached 65 million. In the target destinations, border walls became a political issue for those running for office, just as cutting taxes was a winning strategy in the past. In the United States, terrorism and the 9/11 attack raised concern for security. Walls are expensive and would be for about 2,100 km U.S - Mexico border. While running for president, Donald Trump promised to build "a beautiful wall" and Mexico would pay for it. It helped him defeat a field of Republican opponents. But since 1990, the U.S. has discovered about 150 elaborate tunnels between Mexico and the U.S. In the hot Arizona desert, migrants have died in increasing numbers. In 2015 alone, a record 3771 migrants- men, women and children like you and me-died on their way to Europe. They were fleeing ungodly rulers. Since 1960, more walls have been erected than in all of history. The purpose is to keep migrants out. And since 1960 to 2020, the world population has doubled and so has inhumanity and empty church pews.

In every social problem, be it the murder that will happen next week or the family violence and cybercrime of tomorrow, one thing should always come to mind. Did the church Establishment obey Christ's command and teach converts "to observe all things whatsoever that I have commanded you"? One of those things commanded is the Golden Rule – Treat others the same way that you want them to treat you. It makes sense to any human being and deters all social problems. On the issue of migration and walls, 1960 comes to mind because it was the year one of Africa's favorite presidents was elected. The Kennedy administration was a flash of light in American history. President John F. Kennedy told his fellow Americans that the torch was "passed to a new generation of Americans." He told them to "ask not what your country can do for you- ask what you can do for your country." He planned to confront the common enemies of man: poverty, tyranny, disease and war. He established the Peace Corps volunteer program for graduates to help in schools, hospitals and agriculture in developing countries. There was his "Alliance for Progress" with Latin America, to create economic stability. And there was the United States Agency for International Development (USAID) that lived up to its name. He was the first Roman catholic president in American history and a global citizen.

I listened to his speeches through my transistor radio tuned to The Voice of America and the British Broadcasting Corporation. Some of my secondary school teachers were Peace Corps volunteers in a boarding school that was run in Eastern Nigeria by missionaries from the UK. They all did what genuine Christians do and enabled the missionary face of Christianity to overshadow the colonial face. The U.S. was playing a leading role in human civilization. Many advanced nations followed their lead because it was the kind of Exceptionalism the world applauds. That spirit of humanity began to fade away after his assassination in 1963. The cultural conservative hawks saw the developing nations of the world as the enemy that deserves nothing but exploitation. They began to reduce humanitarian aid mindless of the wealth American corporations bring home from foreign lands. That self-absorption was the beginning that culminated in Donald Trump's "America First" agenda. Since the 1960s, the U.S. has spent trillions of dollars and lost thousands of lives in wars that could have been avoided through the Kennedy vision. Since the 1960s, the Kennedy vision -Peace Corps volunteers, the United States Agency for International Development, Alliance for Progress - would have kept hundreds of thousands of migrants and refugees in their homeland in Latin America. President Kennedy understood pain in the land of his ancestors.

Since the First Century, world history could have been different through compliance to God's Golden Rule. It is important to notice the negative role those cultural conservatives unleashed on this planet through antisocial movements. You may not know what people discuss behind closed doors but you can see the result. The migrants, immigrants and refugees to the United States bring their potential, not their wealth. It is in the best interest of the world as an entity to take fewer migrants, immigrants and refugees and help the rest stay in their homeland and maximize their potential. Technology is what separates advanced nations from developing nations. That technology could have saved countless lives if all nations could produce their own vaccines in a pandemic. Those who flee from their homeland flee from the men (usually men), who do to others what they don't want others to do to them.

Colonialism created artificial nations that became a death trap for many. Now, every nation has a responsibility to identify the captors and the captives. In the past 2,000 years, the church has failed to teach the captors to observe the Golden Rule. The Kennedy administration did the will of God for humanity. The Peace Corps Volunteer program and aid to developing nations through USAID cost less than sending soldier abroad in aircraft carriers to kill or be killed in developing countries. Nations do not defend their homeland by fighting outside their borders. That is the responsibility of the United Nations. The evil world has been programed for confrontation, not for cooperation. The party of culture is conservative. After Abraham Lincoln was Assassinated, his Republican party became the party of culture with standard campaign lines.

"We believe in Religious Freedom"

Freedom of religion is considered to be a fundamental human right. The first amendment to the U.S. constitution guarantees freedom of religion. So, why do cultural conservatives still reiterate their belief in religious freedom? There are nations that prohibit a foreign religion or any religion. They have no freedom of religion. Also, when people are persecuted, terrorized or killed to convert to a religion, there is no freedom of religion in that nation either. While African Americans struggle for social justice, Africans are murdered on their own continent in the name of religion. Organizations like "The Voice of Martyrs" request monthly prayers for Christian pastors and laity persecuted or murdered in Africa and Asia. Some immigrants to America fled from such countries. But for economic reasons, no political party has made any serious effort to confront the religious intolerance of their trading partners.

In America, Roman catholic institutions can pray all day in school. Protestant institutions can also pray all day. But school boards discourage prayer in public schools with students who come from several faith traditions. That is what irritates the cultural conservatives who may not even pray at home. And so, when conservative evangelicals reiterate their believe in freedom of religion, it is to show that liberal democrats are mindless of the persecution of Christians. And also, to protest the absence of prayer in public schools and stir up their base. It is cheap politics. All relationship problems must be seen as the consequences of the church that went astray. The church Establishment failed to teach Christian converts to observe all things whatsoever that Jesus Christ commanded, in order to avert man's inhumanity to man. If they followed the mandate of the Great Commission, after 2,000 years there might not be many cultural religions in the world today.

"Our neglected Military is the greatest in the World"

As fifty nations in one, the United States should have the greatest military force. But as the home of the peoples of all nations, who is the enemy? Cultural conservatives want a powerful military force. That is understandable under imperialism. Europe's colonial powers understood it and now refrain from excessive and needless military spending. Today, how does militarism conform to the peace and goodwill of the Gospel if the church is serving God? The Gospel and militarism are incompatible. Yet, after 2,000 years of Christian civilization, nations go to war despite God's Golden Rule. Even the aggressors claim that God is on their side. Adolf Hitler believed that too. Religious people must bear in mind that if godliness is increasing, militarism should be decreasing. Wearing religious symbols while modernizing weapons of destruction is a display of hypocrisy.

The Romans ruled the known world as if there is no God to whom man is accountable. Since the ancient Romans, both Christians and non-Christian governments still govern as if there is no God to whom man is accountable. No ethnic group has been or will ever be righteous. Even so, those who do to others what they don't want others to do to them are not the Liberals, Socialists or Spiritual conservatives. They are the cultural conservatives in every culture. They tend to be closed minded. They are the cultural militia who mobilize to do wrong on behalf of the culture. So, just like non-Christians, Christians have gone to war for the same reasons including starving children to death because the people wanted to be left alone. If the Golden Rule – Treat others the same way you want them to treat you - is the will of God, the aggressors were not inspired by the Holy Spirit. What spirit inspired them? Does a secular society care?

There was a time when a man like Napoleon Bonaparte would wake up one morning and decide to invade another nation. Those nations are not delighted to hear his name. Similarly, the British, French and the Jews are not delighted to hear the name of Adolf Hitler. The Irish are not delighted to hear the name of Sir Walter Raleigh. The Spaniards are not delighted to hear the name of Sir Francis Drake. African Americans are not delighted to hear the name of slave traders, slave masters, Confederate soldiers and Klansmen. The aboriginals in Canada are not delighted to hear the name of Sir John Macdonald. The aboriginals of Mexico are not delighted to hear the name of Spain's Hernando Cortez. The aboriginals of Australia had similar experiences in those Empire days. Portugal that was occupied and ruled by Muslims for 800 years would be the first to start and the last to stop slave trade and slavery in Brazil. One would expect that those who have suffered pain and injustice would become the founding fathers and mothers of a just and better world. Sadly, abused people also abuse other people. Such has been the history of man. If that history were to be summarized in one word, the word will be - control.

In North America, the Chinese, Irish, Japanese, Jewish and Ukrainian immigrants have sad stories that are untold. People have done to others what they did not want others to do to them. The Boston tea party was not a tea party but a rebellion against British taxation on tea without the taxpayers being represented in parliament. The American War of Independence was fought to free the colonies completely from British control. Men and women want to be free from the control of other men and women. Now consider the centuries of slavery and the fate of African Americans to this day. How does the British control of the colonists compare to the centuries of enslavement of lesser mortals by the same colonists? It is always important to keep in mind how different world history would have been, if the Church Establishment taught converts to observe all things that Jesus Christ commanded, including the Golden Rule.

During the Cold War to check the spread of "godless communism," free military assistance was provided to those fighting against socialism, in support of unfettered capitalism that creates multi-billionaires and paupers through trickle -down economics. Even the secret service was used to overthrow or assassinate some leaders while useful dictators and totalitarian governments were tolerated. Insecurity also drives the military budget. The insecurity in Russia evokes corresponding insecurity in America. That Costa Rica can live without a military force is instructive. God's people want to lay down sword and spear down by the riverside and study

war no more. But they are not the policy makers who want to spend or invest billions of dollars each year on weapons of destruction.

Investments in militarism rises when a conservative president and legislators are elected. Is it not unseemly for a Christian to invest in warfare? How do the followers of Jesus Christ justify such investments on instruments of death while St. Jude and Shriners hospitals are on television pleading for donations to support children with cancer? Some Christians will rationalize defense spending on the need to protect themselves. If Christians in America and Russia want to protect themselves from one another, are aircraft carriers needed to defend their shores? Those who have not lived in more than one country, have a tunnel vision that sees only through the eyes of culture. There is the cultural truth; and there is the global truth. Now imagine a world that lives by the Golden Rule. Imagine a world where people treated others as they would like others to treat them. There might not be a need for a police force and the military. That is God's world. Those institutions exist because people do to others what they don't want others to do to them despite the Gospel, now 2,000 years old. Most cultures cannot yet imagine such a world. Will it not be a better world if nations spent less on a military in search of enemies, and more on Peace Corps programs and Agencies for International Development, to make friends and spread their humanity?

"We Support Our Great Law Enforcement, to Maintain Law and Order."

Colonial Law and Order, not seen in Europe, became the party refrain. African Americans are not the enemy, but the victims of secular and church history. Black history began from Genesis. It is the history of humankind, a history that went wrong. In 2020, the world watched American sociology unfold on global television. The daylight asphyxiation of an African American named George Floyd, was caught on camera and shown around the world. A policeman handcuffed him on a street in Minneapolis, Minnesota, knelt on his neck laid on a pavement, and in about nine minutes he was dead. African men, women and children were enslaved by Christians for over 200 years and abandoned in poverty. They survived segregation and lynching. Over 400 years later, they still have no respite. When David was being chosen out of seven sons, to be the king of Israel, the Bible states that "the LORD does not see as man sees, for man looks at the outward appearance, but the LORD looks at the heart." So, what makes a person a human being? When people do things that are inhuman, one should feel ashamed to be a human being because morphologically, everyone is a human being. After 2,000 years of the Gospel, we still have not discovered what makes a person a better human being.

There are cultural conservatives who see only what they want to see and hear only what they want to hear. They saw and heard about that inhumanity in Minneapolis. That epitome of centuries of Law-and-Order awakened men and women who have a social conscience. But like Pharoah, many hearts remained hardened. Man's capacity for evil is unlimited. Satan or the spirit of disobedience, is like a virus that needs a host. That host is a willing person. A lion or bear that kills a human being is doing what animals do. Without the Holy Spirit to replace the evil spirit, there is little difference between a human being and the human animal. That's why a Christian must be born again and "observe" or live by the Golden Rule. That is the sermon that has yet to be preached.

For centuries, judges were too willing to give the police who kill unarmed African Americans, the benefit of doubt. In recent years, some police incidents have been caught on camera as evidence. Still, not much changed until the murder of George Floyd. The men and women who stormed the U.S. capitol on January 6, 2021 represented almost all professions including the police and the military.

It shows how the more things change, the more they stay the same. The enemy is within. A Klansman can wear a police uniform for the opportunity to kill with impunity, under Law and Order and go Scot free. Since anyone who is not trigger happy is gun shy, no police man or woman wants to be seen to be gun shy. For African Americans under a militarized police force, a traffic stop can end in death. In the Denver suburb of aurora, Colorado, four police constables used choke-hold on Elijah McClain, an African American youth who later died in August 2019. The constables returned to the site to take a reenactment photo as a memento. The trigger-happy policemen and women who have killed African Americans in the home front would have won the wars in Vietnam and Afghanistan, had they been deployed.

Until the civil rights movement of the 1960s, those who lived under subjugation lived a life of learned helplessness. They sang spirituals to let faith in God make the unbearable bearable. Yet, it was a time when most Christians behaved themselves because God is watching from a distance. Now, the fear of God is completely gone in a secular society and a man or woman in uniform can kill people with impunity. For centuries, the root cause of social problems has not been addressed in America. Instead, the police force is militarized to deal with the growing consequences of centuries of abuse in a community that is undermined and overpoliced. The learned helplessness and injustices of life can trigger depression or mental illness in some. When relatives call the police to deal with a mental case, the victim can be shot dead. Problem solved. A call to reduce police budget or "defund the police" to fund some social services, is sacrilege to those who sustain injustice through fear or cannot walk in the shoes of others.

In a secular -minded family court, many children's lives have been ruined. Some lawyers allow a decision that they will not allow for the children of their own relatives. A judge can grant sole custody of children to an intransigent parent and arguing that when they grow up, they will look for the other parent. By then the damage has already been done to children who should never grow up without both parents. It is the highest limit of child abuse. That dysfunctional family life is propagated to form a stereotype. Those who have no power in society, have no justice in the Justice Department. Even at its best, the Department of Justice cannot offer justice. A decade of imprisonment for murder is not justice. According to the Scriptures, "the soul that sinneth, it shall die." It has to otherwise God's commandments are meaningless. Those who forgive murder do not forgive but let go in order to move on with their lives. To forgive murder is to seem more righteous than God Almighty. It cannot be said enough that there is no social problem anywhere on earth that is not the result of the failure of the imperial church to teach them to "observe all things whatsoever I have commanded you." One of those things is the Golden Rule. That was 2,000 years ago.

The crime statistics for African Americans and aboriginal peoples all over the new world is similar. They are overrepresented in the prisons and blamed for their circumstances. While some citizens are innocent until proven guilty others are guilty until proven innocent. With five percent of the world's population, the United States holds about 25 percent of the world's prisoners, even more than China with four times the population. Is it not true that every society has the criminals they deserve? They also have the politicians they deserve. Social injustice produces criminals to feed the prison institution, particularly where prisons are privatized for profit. The cost of doing the will of culture is more than the cost of doing the will of God. The cost of hatred is more than the cost of love. By the end of 2019, according to statistics, 1.4 million Americans were prisoners. The cost of policing and incarceration is more than the cost of social justice and will cost more as declining spirituality leads to rising crime.

Since the days of Charles Dicken's Oliver Twist, when nations were homogeneous, it is the deprived, not the rich, that commit what the rulers consider to be crime. Among African American young men who inherited poverty from enslaved ancestors, some would sell drugs to support the family. Some will end up in the infamous Angola prison in Louisiana, and be incarcerated for decades. It's a longer sentence than for murderers. There are others who would be there for crimes they did not commit. Or for possession of cannabis the Federal government found embarrassing to follow some State governments to legalize, after so many have been killed or incarcerated." Emptying the books" is the practice of sending a "likely suspect" to prison to close a cold case. It is said that "the police always get their man." The general impression is that the police are trained to be always right and professional. The reality is that every profession is a sample of society because nobody can be trained to be righteous. That sample includes Klansmen who wear the uniform as a license to kill.

A Hutterite colony is a just society. They read the same Bible. Policing an unjust society with all the gadgets needed is expensive. Besides, no amount of training will make every police constable compliant to the Golden Rule. The evil spirit in man can only be exorcised by the Holy Spirit. In Norway, the prison serves to humanize criminals. It is mostly a homogeneous nation where people are like the family of God. In Japan, no citizen is suppressed by structured injustice. The government is guided by the Rule of Law, not by Law-and-Order. They are not even Christians. But in the United States, a very heterogeneous and most evangelized nation, the prison institution dehumanizes and hardens inmates. It is inconceivable that human beings can be ruined because of the tone of their skin. Farm animals don't even care about skin tone. Those prison inmates have at some time recited the Pledge of Allegiance to "the flag of the United States of America and to the Republic for which it stands, one nation under God, indivisible, with liberty and justice for all." Outsiders are embarrassed by the hypocrisy but not those inside.

Most of the young men in conflict with the police, regardless of ethnicity, lack a college education or a steady job. They hardly go to the polls to vote for change. But the women whose brothers and fathers were brutalized in the Civil Rights movement of the 1960s, have become the leaders of change and are dubbed the backbone of the Democratic party. While apologists may blame "a few bad apples" for institutional, structural or systemic racism; and for sexism, discrimination, conscious and unconscious bias, the core of America's problems is spiritual. The social problems of today result from the church that went astray centuries ago. On the issue of human relations, the invisible elephant that is out of sight and out of mind, is the church Establishment itself. For instance, in Brazil that was the first to start and the last to stop slavery; a nation whose church saw slave trade and slavery as God-ordained, the survivors of slavery are abused and neglected more than anywhere on earth. Yet in Rio, there is the statue of "Christ the Redeemer" with arms stretched to both ends of the world, to demonstrate the global limit of our hypocrisy. Slave trade and slavery, and the transition from slavery to Law and Order demonstrate what people who are powerful do to those who are powerless when the Church of Jesus Christ is corrupted. So, that imperial temple that stood for might is right has to be demolished, rebuilt and returned to the Church of Jesus Christ that stands for the Golden Rule. The cultural conservatives who do to others what they don't want others to do to them count on God's Amazing Grace. But the victims of history imprisoned under Law and Order cannot count on man's amazing grace.

Being in compliance to the Golden Rule separates human life from wildlife. In the wildlife, some animals eat others without a second thought. Through economics rather than cannibalism, human life can mimic wildlife. When humans live in communities like a zoo, social services are different and political campaigns are driven by the fear of others. The Almighty who created and knows man inside out, gave the Golden Rule -Treat others the same way you want them to treat you. Hence, the Rule of Law, a principle under which all persons and institutions are accountable to laws that are publicly promulgated and equally enforced, is a godly system that is no respecter of persons. But Law and Order is what would be expected in wildlife where injustice is the law. Injustice is the law because justice will destabilize the food chain. So, all lives do not matter. If injustice has no consequences, it never ends. That has been the experience of African Americans since emancipation. Under Law and order, a revolt against injustice is the problem, not the injustice. By contrast, the Rule of Law is a pillar of democracy compliant to the Golden Rule. Law and order are used in a dictatorship for control. In developing countries, dictators and despots use law and order for suppression. Truth be told, African Americans have lived under a dictatorship within a democracy. The same applies to Brazil.

If you inherited poverty from centuries of slavery and abandoned in ghettos without restitution, do you have any reason to protest, revolt or commit survival- motivated crime? Don't you deserve more than Sermons and prayers from the church Establishment that sentenced your ancestors to slavery? When asking has not worked; when demanding has not worked; after 400 years, any people group may be forced to take matters into their own hands. Some may even fly planes into buildings. What religious people did in the past shows that a man who is not born again is not different from a pagan. However, left to African Americans alone slavery could not have ended. Left to South Africans alone apartheid could not have ended. Left to colonized people alone colonialism could not have ended. Left to women alone, their enfranchisement could not have happened sooner. Those who are oppressed cannot liberate themselves. It takes a critical mass of humanity to do what is right. The freewill allows everyone to choose humanity or inhumanity. Humanity comes through the Holy Spirit by being born again. A born-again Christian, not the counterfeit one, does not do to others what he does not want others to do to him.

At home and in Diaspora, Africans are the greatest consumers of religion as well as the greatest victims. In the first century, the Romans threw Christians to Lions in the coliseum for entertainment. It did not discourage believers or the conversion of new ones. Since life is controlled by those who have power, the Romans took control of Christianity and shaped it as a useful tool to exercise power and control. In Brazil, they enslaved Africans for over 350 years because they controlled the narrative of Christianity. Their Christianity was not about compliance to the Golden Rule, the Great Commandment and the New Commandment that would include lesser mortals, but about sacraments, weekly confessions and absolutions. In Dixie, the protestant master class - clergy and laity - enslaved Africans for about 250 years and thanked God for His amazing grace and their prosperity. Some of those slaves were Muslims. Back in the seventh century, Arabians invaded Africa, seized some land and forced their religion down the throat of those who could not resist. Christians brought them and other Africans to the New world as slaves. Praise houses became a center of life and mutual support for all. The things that happened in the distant past are open to conjecture. One can argue that those African Americans paid their attention to the Gospel, not the Epistles. Their faith in God and spiritual songs made the unbearable bearable for emancipated people who had no money. Their victimization was premised on disregard for the Gospel of Jesus Christ.

Now, through victor theology, African and African American preachers have become part of their own victimization. Some are either pulpit entertainers, preachers of prophecy, preachers of illusory prosperity, the endurance of persecution or anything but the Gospel. The poor are rich in faith, and can be exploited. Does anyone need to read a pastor's 10 books to understand the will of God? Missing in action are preachers of the Gospel who are "teaching them to observe all things whatsoever that I have commanded you" as Jesus said in the Great Commission mandates. That's preachers whose congregants are genuine born-again Christians who observe the Golden

Rule, the Great Commandment and the New Commandment. Compliance to the Golden Rule is the visible evidence of a born-again Christian. That is what stabilizes families and reduces crime. Couples who are genuine born -again Christians have a lifelong relationship. Religion is the linchpin that supports society. When it is corrupted, there will be victims just as in wildlife. The COVID -19 pandemic of 2020 exposed the dysfunction in Christianity since slave trade and slavery. The number of single men, single women and single mothers is an embarrassment to 2,000 years of the Gospel. There is little difference between the divorce rate of Christians and pagans. Why? The non-Pentecostal church did not teach that a Christian must be born again. Additionally, that "man looks at the outward appearance, but the LORD looks at the heart" is instructive in choosing a spouse. A good-looking apple can be rotten at the core.

Africans who went to boarding schools, hospitals and churches that were run by missionaries are embarrassed and uncomfortable on issues of racism in the homeland of the missionaries. So are the missionaries and genuine Christians too. The role of the imperial church Establishment bears repeating at every juncture. It used slavery to enforce celibacy; condoned slave trade and slavery; erased the interface between right and wrong and between Truth and fallacy; created the master culture that wrapped the Bible and the gun with the American flag; lived off the avails of unpaid servitude of Africans for about 250 years; and created the social pathology that bedevils the world. The statues of history's wrongdoers are finally coming down because few want to be associated with inhumanity. Retired professionals who did not have minorities or women in their class, understand how the craft of systemic prejudice and discrimination were practiced covertly and surreptitiously. Now, governments no longer allow institutional racism and sexism despite continued resistance by cultural conservatives. Corporations that used to employ only people who are "socially compatible," are becoming more humane and inclusive. That's after 2,000 years of the Gospel.

The Dreaded Socialism

When unbelievers become addicted to money, socialism becomes a frightening proposition. A plutocracy - a government of the rich, by the rich and for the rich, dreads socialism. To try to redistribute wealth as a policy, feels like extortion. The slave economy was plantation capitalism. Some slave masters owned over 100 slaves to make them richer while the slaves were kept in penury. As long as the masters were prosperous, the nation was prosperous. The slaves were the tools of production. The church Establishment did its best to cover up the Gospel Truth. "Thy will be done on earth as it is in heaven" was lip service. Since politics and religion thrive on ignorance, the Establishment used the Gospel to subserve culture.

In a world where might is right, the slave traders and slave masters were the good people. Their slaves were the bad people, perceived as criminals. The Establishment erased the interface between right and wrong. So, both clergy and laity began what will be over 200 years of living off the avails of slavery. It was a mockery of God Almighty who remained and will remain silent until the end of history. Revisionist Christianity is evident in economics where the plantation capitalism that creates billionaires and paupers is glorified while demonizing socialism. Can one of those street beggars be a theophany of Jesus Christ who would someday say: "I was jobless and homeless and you did not help me"? The spirit of revisionism was modernized in the 1980s when conservatives who became icons proclaimed that government is the problem even when they are the government. A government can do what an individual, even a multibillionaire philanthropist cannot do. The government is not the problem but the solution to serve and protect the common good.

The American civil war brought extreme capitalism to an end. The Bolshevik revolution of 1917 brought an end to another group of clergy and laity who lived luxuriously at the expense of peasants and indentured servants. They introduced communism and excluded

God. It could not survive. The cold war was about containing the spread of communism. But the abject poverty of the masses was abated through the industrial revolution. So, communism was no longer appealing. The anti-communism of the 1950s turned into antisocialism. The anti- socialism can equally turn into antichrist. The economic ideological struggle is now in the USA between the advocates and lobbyists for the billionaires and the advocates for the paupers. It is a sad commentary on the Christian faith when cultural religionists have to plead for compassion. The Good Shepherd who left 99 sheep to go for the one that was lost is a hint on socialism. It leaves no one behind. In the story of Ananias and Saphira, the pioneer Christians shared their resources. That was a lesson on socialism. "Bear ye one another's burdens ---" is a lesson on socialism. If the Apostles of Jesus Christ were to run a government, will the economy be one that creates multibillionaires and homeless people or more like the Nordic welfare State? Those who have read the Gospel know the answer. An antisocialist should not pretend to be a Christian.

Some preachers marketing illusion and a false faith have turned the Gospel and the world upside down. Is it possible for Satan to join the church and call good evil and evil good? Prophet Isaiah (Isaiah 5:20) proclaimed "woe unto them that call evil good, and good evil." Some Christians who condemned socialism wear the cross that is counterculture. Some are liberal to their children but conservative to other people's children. A few generations ago, to be liberal in America was pejorative; to be a socialist was a sin; and under McCarthyism, to be a communist was a crime. In some States like Florida, there are many homeless people and senior citizens dependent on the food bank. They don't want anything to do with socialism. According to the Scriptures, St. Peter denied Jesus Christ to save his own life. To win votes in Florida, Christian politicians would deny Jesus Christ by denouncing socialism. Surely, religion and politics thrive on ignorance. But there are occasions when socialism is acceptable to cultural conservatives. In 2008 government intervention saved American Banks. In 2020, government intervention saved the airlines. Socialism is good when corporate profits are privatized and the losses are socialized. It is also good when a select few of suffering people are helped in order to use them for propaganda at national conventions. Any attempt to help everyone is "godless socialism" or "big government socialism" to those who are antisocial. Some speakers at those political conventions are known to promote or condone benign hatred, benign neglect and plantation capitalism, and still end a speech with "God bless America." Is it not a mockery of God Almighty?

In Canada, Rev. Tommy Douglas, a Baptist- preacher -turned politician introduced universal basic healthcare in his home province of Saskatchewan in 1947. Despite the opposition to his Socialist party, it spread across the nation. No government -liberal of conservative - has dared to dismantle it without peril. Nobody should die because they cannot afford healthcare, Rev. Douglas argued. Rev. Tommy Douglas was an Executor of God's will. Elsewhere, his counterparts serve as the Regents of God Almighty. Christians outside America have long expected the Democrats to do the same in healthcare and dare the cultural conservatives to dismantle it. The best that the Democrats could do was the Affordable Care Act, a half measure that tried to steer clear from being called socialists, in order to win the next election. They didn't. Donald Trump was elected president by a minority of voters frustrated by the two-party Establishments. The leading edge of change and the pursuit of social justice is not from the church but from the streets. The activists range from Christians to atheists. When non-Christian immigrants come to America to demand practical Christianity, it is a sad commentary on theoretical Christianity. They can see practical Christianity in December but not the other months of the year. Paradoxically, the practical Christianity they demand does not exist in the homeland they fled. Even infidels expect Christians to lead the way.

A View of the American Constitution

Every people group in the world, including Russia, has citizens who are Americans. Therefore, a dysfunctional America is not in the best interest of any nation. During a presidential election, if the heads of diplomatic missions at the United Nations held a secret ballot, to choose an American president, the choice will be the best president for the United States and the world. The U.S. constitution was drafted with the mind of slave masters. Can it be flawless? To likeminded Americans, it is written in stone and even more so than the Gospel if one is an atheist, an agnostic or belongs to the Freedom from Religion Foundation. The original intent of the Constitution has been used to sustained prejudice and injustice as in centuries past. When the Supreme Court ruled that separate but equal was constitutional, it was no surprise. After over 200 years of slavery, Chief Justice Roger Taney declared that the survivors of slavery could not be citizens. He became a cultural icon. Cultural conservatives acted like gods over lesser mortals. Every institution in the land were participants or defenders of slavery, segregation, racism, discrimination and privilege against the conscience of Liberals, Socialists and Spiritual conservatives who had a conscience.

The American constitution has undergone several amendments since it was drafted in the 18th century by men who did not practice the Christianity they professed. Now, some of those amendments need amendment in the light of civilization. It is like fixing different parts of a very old car that should be discarded. If the constitution has not led to a perfect union in 200 years, it is because it was not structured for a perfect union but for an incremental progression to a more perfect union. The masters did not expect a woman or an African American to be president. They devised a now obsolete electoral college that has become a quad-annual nightmare. As a result, a presidential candidates can win three million more votes than the opponent and still lose the election. That minority rule by the masters cannot continue without redefining and restructuring democracy. No nation can preach on democracy abroad without democracy at home. Rational minds in America will agree that their democracy is not the gold standard of democracy beyond the peaceful transfer of power.

Several centuries ago, democracy was conceived to serve the common good. If it has not done so, it is pseudo – democracy. For genuine democracy to endure, the world must know by whose authority a politician rules over his or her parents, grandparents, teachers, professors, classmates and pastors, if any. It is inconceivable that the men who drafted the American constitution in the 18th century are more brilliant than the men and women of the 21st century. Social evolution is a very slow process in the transition from the medieval mind with no compassion, to the modern mind with knowledge and compassion. Yet, the founding fathers are exalted for the social construct that impedes social evolution and Christian civilization. Also, every nation needs more than two political parties to avoid polarization and a bipartisan gridlock.

In party politics, one of the parties of a nation will be on the right or conservative, to protect wealth, privilege and cultural values. The Republican Party has won the Law and order as a badge of honor. Wise leaders recognize that they are mortal and will not be in office forever. Therefore, it is better to do what is in the best interest of future generations, and not what is in their own best interest for the moment. Within the Department of Justice, there is the Rule of Law for the majority and Law and Order for the minority that has to be kept in their place. The Supreme Court, for example, is apolitical. But the U.S. supreme court is gradually being transformed into the legal arm of Congress rather than the apex of justice under an independent judiciary. Cultural conservatives want a Supreme Court packed with constitutional originalists to interpret cases based on the mindset of the founding fathers (there were no founding mothers), most of whom were slave masters and racists.

Common sense has no classroom. It does not require a legal mind to postulate that every generation deserves a constitution that keeps them accountable to their own conscience, and not use the Supreme Court to determine the constitutionality of a case, based on the mindset of a distant generation. Furthermore, if the separation of powers is genuine; if the judiciary is a co- equal branch of government, the functionaries and Justices of the Supreme Court should be appointed by the National Bar Association and not by politicians who expect loyalty. Until then, judicial appointments will always divide Americans. Human beings desire freedom and good governance. And on moral issues, to be accountable to God and not to the government. Now, some nations have freedom but not good governance. Some have good governance but no freedom. If the American Senate, like the Roman Senate of Julius Caesar was designed to resist progress and change, how many want to be in the shoes of those waiting for change?

American politics is convoluted. The party of conscience became the party of culture and the party of culture became the party of conscience. Abraham Lincoln's Republican party was the anti-slavery party that went to war to free men, women and children from slavery. It was a spiritual- conservative party that conserved spiritual values. When he was assassinated in 1865, he was succeeded by his vice president, Andrew Johnson. He was a Democrat and a cultural conservative who conserved cultural values. He was a slave owner known to be a racist. He opposed the 14th amendment that granted citizenship to the survivors of slavery. He rescinded the plan to resettle emancipated families with 40 acres of land and a mule. They were men, women and children who inherited poverty from centuries of slavery by Christians who exercised the power of life and death on earth. He did his best to honor Confederate soldiers and reverse everything Abraham Lincoln and spiritual conservatives stood for.

A president can change the tenor of his party. For his misdeeds, the president was impeached in the House of Representatives but escaped conviction in the Senate that tends to preserve cultural values. Andrew is a Bible name. Those Christians saw the Church as a social event. Party politics is also personality politics. Every four years, presidential candidates tell Americans what he or she will do for them. A nation should not rely on one brain. "I will fight for you" they say. Fight against who? To address police brutality against the underclass, a presidential candidate will propose to train the police to be sensitive to the culture of the ethnic groups they police. Why is the Golden Rule missing from the church? To treat others the same way you want them to treat you is the solution to all social problems regardless of ethnicity.

In 2020, President Donald Trump claimed to have done more for African Americans than previous presidents except Abraham Lincoln. True or false, if the fate of a segment of the population depends on the goodwill of one person- the president-something needs to change. The young men fighting and killing each other on the streets of America are not the brightest in the nation. They have a common problem. They need education and gainful employment. An empty stomach obeys no laws. Those who are needy don't even care about the injustice inflicted on others who inherited poverty from centuries of slavery. Ideally, an executive branch should execute the collegial will of his elected colleagues and pursue human rights at home and abroad without hypocrisy. To allow a president to use executive order to bypass elected officials and execute his own will, creates a personality icon. Perhaps in deference to the eponymous George Washington, the founding fathers made the president an imperial president without a crown, but on a long leash. Hence, Americans can wake up each day, wondering what the president will do. And surely, through executive order, he can dismantle the labor union, withdraw from international agreements and organizations, invade a weak nation, erase the legacy of the predecessor, establish his own legacy or doctrine, pardon criminals who have connections, and may even pardon himself for his malfeasance on his way out.

No president has escaped criticism for what he has done or failed to do with that executive power. What is right or wrong depends on who is involved.

Now, imagine this: Some "primitive" cultures had an ancient wisdom of governance that can be described as village democracy. They had no King or Emperor. Instead, a consultative assembly of respected Elders decided on what the leader or executive should do. He was a servant leader. They did not depend on one head but on many. That's how they survived for millennia against all odds, without the ballot box and party politics. It is like a municipal government whose politicians are elected without a party platform. The mayor executes collegial decisions. No corrupt politician can count on the protection of the party establishment or be subservient to the leader or dismiss an allegation of wrongdoing as politically motivated. Those primitive people had order without a written law. In Washington, DC politicians who walk across the aisle to find partners to solve a problem are lauded. That's the collegiality of the ancient cultures. Colonial rule introduced party politics, the ballot box and major rule for the ethnic majority, with the attendant ethnic and religious mayhem. Corrupted Christianity corrupts majority rule because it does not have the moral authority to infuse the Golden Rule into the fabric of culture. Now, when elections are won with less than 60 percent of the popular vote, genuine democracy cannot be achieved without the Golden Rule to accommodate the 40 percent on the outside.

American Democracy

The United States is the oldest and longest lasting attempt at constitutional democracy. That is true. It was deemed to be a democracy when it was no longer ruled by the King of England, but by the people. It was said to be a government of the people, by the people and for the people. But truth be told, it was a pseudo- democracy. The master makes the rules and determines what is right and what is wrong. Their mothers and sisters were not enfranchised until 1920. African Americans and aboriginals were once considered to be two-thirds of a person in that democracy. Literacy test and property ownership where tools used to keep minorities and the poor away from the ballot box. When they were enfranchised, gerrymandering and voter suppression were used to keep them out. Christians, not godless communists, introduced the filibuster to obstruct progressive policies. That is not the hallmark of democracy. The animal jungle cannot be changed by the majority at the bottom of the food chain because they are animals. Among humans, suffrage is the tool to change their own jungle barring voter suppression.

A genuine democracy is an aspiration that no nation has attained. If democracy is a government of the people, by the people, and for the people; a government where the people are treated equally under the rule of law, the Golden Rule must be embedded into the fabric of culture to make it possible. It has not happened. In World War 11 and the Vietnam War, African Americans went overseas to fight and die for democracy without the full benefit of democracy at home. A democracy is more than the peaceful transfer of power. It is about serving the common good. When about 90 people at the top own as much wealth as the bottom 50 percent of the population, democracy is not serving the common good. A government of the people is like running a nation as a family unit. What the world has seen is indirect plutocracy, funded by corporations and masquerading as democracy. The hand of capitalism should serve the common good. The progressive taxation that should tax excess wealth to care for children and reduce poverty has been sabotaged through regressive taxation. The party of regressive taxation solicits election funds like a debt owed to them to stay in office. For the billionaires who are their benefactors, it is a debt owed to the party to stay in office. But not to Spiritual conservatives who care about people more than money. If since Adam and Eve walked on earth no corpse has left this planet with one penny, it makes no sense to horde and lay treasures on earth.

A democracy does not leave some children behind, and parents jobless or homeless. Democracy is glorified because it offers the freedom to be who you are and recognizes the humanity of all citizens. Even so, some people groups have survived for millennia without the ballot box. If democracy is melded with hypocrisy and not the Golden Rule; if one man's dream is another man's nightmare, it is a pseudo- democracy. It is fragile and cannot endure. Rhodesia had the Rule of Law for the privileged, Law and Order for the underclass. They called it a democracy. It was a cultural truth that did not endure. Apartheid South Africa was the same. They also called it a democracy. It was a cultural truth, not the universal Truth. It did not endure. The Democratic Republic of the Congo bought the patent of democracy. It has been a bloody patent.

For over 200 years, those who survived centuries of slavery in America have been suppressed without restitution, and their voices have been muted. Since the master makes the rules and determines what is right or wrong, many see their nation as a shining city on a hill or the cradle, the temple, the champion, the beacon of democracy. If these are mere slogans of a cultural truth, sooner or later a lie will destroy itself. It came close on January 6, 2021. A joint session of Congress assembled to ratify the electoral college votes of the November 2020 presidential election. The men and women invited to Washington, DC to riot and storm the capitol represented the millions of impressionable Americans amenable to the deceit that corrupted the Christian faith. Some policemen guarding the capitol reportedly, took selfies with the rioters.

One of the rioters, a female Air Force veteran from California was shot and killed. Apparently, every profession, including those in uniform and robes, has men and women with the mindset of the cultural conservatives who ruin the lives of those who look different. Every profession is a sample of society. African Americans, for example, have Mayors and police chiefs who could not improve respectful policing. They were token gestures. While all people groups want to see themselves represented in governance and in all walks of life, it is more important to see public figures, whoever they may be, practice the Golden Rule or act like Jesus Christ they claim to follow, and obey God in whom they trust. That is civilization.

The American culture was established by the church of the slave masters who corrupted the Gospel. They created the dissonance between the Socialist and the plantation Capitalist who justified slavery for centuries. A good thing can be corrupted. So has the Gospel and democracy which make them difficult to promote in many parts of the world. Democracy or good governance must be assessed and rated by those at the bottom, not those are the top of society. A democracy will not be a government of the people, by the people and for the people unless "one of the least of these My brethren" says so. Until then, it is a pseudo- democracy. However, a pseudo -democracy is better than an autocracy because a pseudo -democracy will eventually lead to a genuine democracy. It takes centuries to get there.

Social evolution is snail slow. The thousands of people who commit suicide want to get out. They have no love for America. Those who love America do so, not because of what it is but because of what it can become- the shining city on a hill for other nations to emulate, according to the Puritans. Every nationality on earth is represented in America. It is the microcosm of the world. While some groups do not feel free in the free world, the U.S. A is the leading nation in both the "free" and the not -so -free world because no nation is more representative of the world than the United States of America. Therefore, a dysfunctional America is not in the national interest of any nation. Finally, there are people who want the kind of democracy that allows people to do whatever they want. There are others who do not want that kind of democracy. The handling or mishandling of the COVID -19 pandemic that killed six million people shows that every nation needs discipline, either from the will of God or from the will of men. That discipline is better to come from the obedience of the will of God Almighty.

By Whose Authority?

Some citizens have written to express their concerns to professional politicians without any response. Still, the self-centered or dogmatic politician would send mail, asking them for donations because the next election is the most important in the nation's history. About 30 percent would send donations again and again, even when their circumstances did not improve under that government. In an election in which over 40 percent of the electorate did not vote for the winners, by whose authority do they rule over the entire nation? There are school yard bullies who will be politician, with no motivation to serve but to legally do to others what they don't want others to do to them. And get more attention than their more academic classmates. "Treat others the same way you want them to treat you" is a guideline for governance because it is biblical. "Bear one another's burdens and so fulfill the law of Christ" is a guideline for governance and accountability to a higher power. The authority of Jesus Christ was questioned: "Now it happened on one of those days, as He taught the people in the temple and preached the gospel, that the chief priests and the Scribes, together with the elders, confronted Him. And spoke to Him, saying, 'Tell us, by what authority are You doing these things? Or who is he who gave you this authority?' "(Luke 20: 1-2 NKJV). Since the Israelites had been guided by Moses, Joshua, the prophets and Kings for 2,000 years, it was human nature to question where His authority came from. Jesus Christ cited the prophets, performed miracles, raised the dead, walked on water – things no human being could do - to show that he was the prophesied Messiah whose authority came from Jehovah.

As a prefect in a boarding school that was run in Eastern Nigeria by missionaries from the UK., I could tell fellow students what to do. They knew where the authority came from. Since the end of colonial rule, Africans have seen a few despots and dictators. Teachers have watched a student with little Intellect exercise political power like demigods. Can a blind man lead people who have sight and vision? Yet men (always men) with little education like Uganda's Idi Amin, led a nation with university professors. Their authority to rule came from the gun. If a ruler does not rule by the Golden Rule ethics, the authority was not inspired by the Holy Spirit but by a different spirit. So, by whose authority does a politician or a dictator rule over his parents, grandparents, teachers and classmates? By whose authority does a supreme leader lead men and women twice his age?

Someone's grandparents do not want to be ruled by the whim of someone else's grandson. By whose authority does a young President, Prime minister, Governor or Mayor rule over his parents, grand-parents, professors and classmates? To whom are they accountable? The church in America owned slaves. At the end of slavery and the assassination of President Abraham Lincoln, his successor, President Andrew Johnson rescinded the 40 acres of land and a mule to resettle families that survived over 200 years of slavery. Women- their own wives, mothers and sisters -were not allowed to vote. By whose authority did those cultural conservative men control the lives of other mortals? By whose authority do terrorists kill innocent men, women and children in the name of a religion? The God of the Bible who created the slaves, the slave masters and terrorists commanded the Golden Rule, the Great Commandment and the New commandment. Any administration or religion that is not based on what we know to be the will of God, is not inspired by the Holy Spirit but by a different spirit. Governance must be based on biblical authority.

The COVID -19 pandemic showed how the sloppy leadership of one man can cost thousands of people their lives.

As in the past, so it is today. A little boy running around in the school yard will grow up to be a general or politician who rules over his parents, grandparents, teachers and classmates, and toy with the lives of lesser mortals. That cannot be allowed to continue. The U.S. exercises influence on all nations. The card- carrying members of the Republican or Democratic party are less than 40 percent of the American population. The men and women who control power-the White House and Congress- are less than 10 percent of the American population. The same applies to many nations. Now, by whose authority do 10 percent of the population control the fate of 90 percent of the population? By whose authority in America, do 10 percent of the population suppress the vote and aspirations of millions of men and women who inherited poverty from over 200 years of slavery in the hands of Christians?

If the politicians are Christians, and the authority is not from the Holy Spirit or from the God who commands the Golden Rule, the Great Commandment and the New Commandment; if men and women who wear the cross and hug the Bible hate people, obviously, "Church for Sale" is long overdue. Some nations can be governed by the values of their culture. One culture has its way, while another culture has its own different way. A multi -cultural society can only be governed by the global values of the God of all peoples and cultures. The clergy ministered to segregated churches. Based on the Gospel of Jesus Christ, slave trade, slavery, racism and segregation were not inspired by the Holy Spirit. What spirit inspired that church? There is yet nothing to show that the Church has changed, from the values of slave traders to universal values. "Do unto others as you would like them to do unto you" or "Treat others the same way you want them to treat you "is the modus operandi that binds a civilized or multi-cultural nation. A church and State that is based on that Golden Rule ethics can claim to be directed by the Holy Spirit, otherwise it is directed by a different spirit.

As men and women of different religions and different denominations, Republicans do not all agree on any given issue. Similarly, the Democrats do not all agree on any given issue. But they are all expected to agree on the Golden Rule because it makes sense to any human being regardless of culture, ethnicity, gender, religion or political ideology. That is why ethnic minority individuals can join a Conservative party. There are African Americans in the Conservative party. There are also antisemites and Ku Klux Klansmen in the party. Do they all share the same values? Do African Americans oppose gun control, affirmative action and restitution to right the wrongs of centuries of slavery? Do they support all the manifestations of racism or a Supreme Court that upholds the originalism of the slave masters' Constitution? They do not share racist values either as small-c or large-c Conservatives. The African Americans are spiritual conservatives. The cultural conservatives do to others what they don't want others to do to them. It's the antipode of God's Golden Rule. They conserve the cultural values of human nature that have impeded Christian civilization for over 2,000 years. If they are purged from the Liberal and Socialist parties, they are left with the Spiritual conservatives. Hence, the conservative party is more divided than any other party in every nation because it has both the Spiritual and Cultural conservatives.

A nation cannot fix their politics without fixing their religion. If their religion does not teach them to observe the Golden Rule, they cannot fix their politics. The U.S. supreme court can have nine conservative Justices. The president and vice president can be conservatives. The House of Representatives and the Senate can be controlled by conservatives. Like Abraham Lincoln, despite his flaws, if they are all spiritual conservatives who observe God's Golden Rule, that would be a good government. But to care about babies in the womb but not about babies and children born to languish in ghetto zip codes; to discriminate against men and women who inherited poverty from centuries of slavery without restitution because their lives do not matter; that is a mockery of God Almighty and a disgrace to Christianity. Without laws and regulations equally enforced, human life and wildlife are similar. That is why the Almighty God of all Creation sent Jesus Christ to teach the Gospel. The synopsis is the Golden Rule, the Great Commandment and the New commandment. That's all that is required of man – good relations between peoples and between them and the God of Creation. Life has no other purpose. So, if the ruler of a nation is not a servant leader doing the expressed will of the Creator of life; if there is no church, "teaching them to observe all things whatsoever I have commanded you" as Jesus said, obviously, the people have the cultural and dogmatic politicians and clerics they deserve.

In this 21st century, the Truth is under attack both inside and outside the community of faith. While God's Golden Rule makes sense to any human being, it cannot be achieved through legislation because it takes the Holy Spirit to replace the evil spirit in a willing host who wishes to change. How many, even among those who wear the cross and hug the Bible, want to change? "Choose you this day whom ye will serve," frustrated Joshua told the Israelites. The Klan cannot change until their church changes.

How an American Votes

The United States is a nation with many grievances. When African American women join a demonstration for women's rights and wage parity, they share a common cause with some racists. When Hispanic Roman Catholics join a demonstration for pro-life, they share a common cause with some hate mongers. In Florida, the sunshine State, some of their retired seniors who are dependent on the food bank, don't want anything to do with socialism. A homeless

Latino in Florida can be persuaded to see universal healthcare as a death trap and reject any hint of socialism that could get him off the street. Similarly, a homeless African American in the Bible belt can be persuaded to ignore centuries of benign neglect and the character of a candidate and vote for "the party of Abraham Lincoln who freed the slaves." He is told that he is not voting for the candidate, but for the party. Since they will not vote for a confederate flag-waving party, they are reminded that it is the party of Abraham Lincoln, a party that has long morphed into a cultural conservative party. It shows the power and effectiveness of propaganda in sustaining ignorance. And surely, politics, religion and racism thrive on ignorance.

Abortion is a lightning rod for Roman Catholics as prayer in school is for protestants, even those who don't pray at home. Protestants have used abortion to rally the support and votes of Irish Catholics for centuries. Yet it took until 1960, to suspend their prejudice and elect the first Irish American president. And 60 more years to elect the next one with the help of African Americans. When it lived by the antipode of the Golden Rule during centuries of slavery, the church erased the interface between right and wrong. Consequently, social justice has never ranked high on the hierarchy of concerns. There are cultural conservatives who hug the Bible and want Muslims sent back to the Middle East because "we don't want Sharia law in America." That sentiment determines what party they vote for. Those men and women did not study the past. African Americans formed the Nation of Islam and became Muslims. They resented how they have been treated from 1619 to the 1960s by the church that ignored the Gospel - the Golden Rule, the Great Commandment and the New Commandment – the core of their faith. If the church establishment that has escaped scrutiny preached and practiced the Gospel when they took over the first century church, there might not be new religions and much of the sad events of human history. Those who have suffered historical injustice are duty bound to exercise a civilizing influence on the world because

God's Golden Rule- "Treat others the same way you want them to treat you" – makes sense to any human being. That is difficult to do when stigmatized by crime.

And so, giving a smorgasbord of grievances and issues, Americans cast their votes based on a hierarchy of concerns. Some issues are higher than others on the hierarchy of grievances or worries. They cast a single vote or switch parties where the likes outweigh the dislikes. The fear of emancipated slaves and the bravery of Haiti might have created the gun culture in America. For some, the second amendment and support for the National Rifle Association (NRA) are high on the hierarchy of their worries. Both Democrats and Republicans are repulsed by the persecution and killing of Christians overseas. But economic interest has restrained action when any party was in power. To the evangelicals, it is the Democrats that turned the blind eye to freedom of religion and welcome to America those who persecute and kill the Christians they pray for. It is an issue high on the hierarchy of concerns for the evangelicals but not so much for the African Americans of the Nation of Islam. Their organization was founded in the 1930s because of the corruption of the Gospel. The evangelicals want a government and culture that cares for their values. So, the anti-Muslim faction is different from the anti- immigrant faction. The independent minds vote for either the Democrats or the Republicans based on the prospect of good governance rather than on political dogma. As a nation with many grievances, splinter groups, some of whom hate each other can be united to a common cause. It takes an enigmatic politician to play all sides and exploit the human condition. In these circumstances, election pollsters in America have rarely been accurate. The voters tell pollsters what the world wants to hear.

Notice that if the imperial church had stood for Christian values from the beginning, those who come to America with all kinds of religions would see the difference between a cultural religion and Christianity, and be converted. The Nation of Islam would not have been founded in Detroit. And since Lincoln's spiritually conservative party became a cultural -conservative party, lobbyists have been used to ensure that politicians do not serve the common good. Then gerrymandering and voter- suppression by every means possible, has become the extra leverage to subvert democracy in what is said to be the greatest democracy on earth. A Christian observer will notice that one party governs like the masters, while the other governs like servant leaders. The master- spirit is not open to humility for a nation said to be under God, and not above God.

It bears repeating- no nation can fix their politics without fixing their religion. The God of boundless compassion, mercy and amazing grace, is also a God of accountability. Afghanistan is one of those places, where a religious few controls the masses. In the secular world, a few can also control the masses. In 2020, for example, the population of California was 40 million people. The population of Wyoming was 582,328 people. Both States are represented by two senators. In addition to voter suppression and gerrymandering, a minority can control the majority in America and by extension, the world. Despite the American history of centuries of slave trade, slavery, segregation, Black church burning and endless social injustice without restitution or repentance, the cultural conservatives claim to be the moral majority. In this scheme designed by victor theology, the future generations will determine if their America is truly a nation under God or a nation above God.

A stressful society can cause depression and mental illness. A phone call to the police has left some with mental illness shot dead. A proposal to "defund the police" and transfer the funds to social services would make sense anywhere with limited funds. In 2020, the Democrats lost seats for that slogan because "Law and Order," not social justice, is higher on the hierarchy of worries. Clearly, there is a correlation between a dysfunctional church and the politics of its members. No nation can fix their politics without fixing their religion. What the world saw in that 2020 election was the consequences of an imperial church that has been dysfunctional since slave trade and slavery.

The universal healthcare that many advanced nations take for granted, a livable minimum wage, accessible education for all, an accountable police force, and addressing climate change were portrayed as a "radical left agenda." The youths of today are more educated and progressive than their grandparents. The church Establishment supported cultural conservatives and plantation capitalism without regret, repentance or reconciliation with God Almighty for centuries. It has not opposed a taxation policy that encourages Christians to lay treasures on earth at the expense of starving children, even when nobody has ever left this planet with their wealth. It has ignored the core of the Gospel of Jesus Christ including the Golden Rule. After 2,000 years of the Gospel, if Black lives still do not matter, the problem or solution is not in politics; it is in the church. That church needs another Reformation to accommodate genuine Christians who have the mind of Christ. Otherwise, "Church for Sale" will be as normal as "House for Sale."

Latinos in the U.S. come from different nations, different cultures with different interests. Many are on the conservative side of the border control issue, to limit the influx of migrants because they threaten their own status and job security. The conversion of millions of Latinos from Catholicism to evangelicalism creates a divergence of views in politics and economics. President Fidel Castro still comes up long after his death. History shows that he created the greatest caring economy in Latin America. And helped free some African countries from colonialism. His goal was godly but the means may be ungodly. His greatest critics are politicians whose goal and means are both ungodly. The political right stands for control, privilege and entitlement. The political left stands for the common good. It is an aberration to have a dictator on the left brutalizing some dissenting citizens. It is a personality issue, not based on the collective ideology. It is similar to church history. What

some Christians have done has nothing to do with the Gospel of
Jesus Christ and the Golden Rule.

On the other hand, a right-wing dictatorship, even when benign,
is in conformity with ideology. For over 200 years, the U.S. has been
moving at a snail's pace towards "a more perfect union." That slow
pace has a physical toll on the victims and a spiritual toll on the
villains. When Senators act like Caesar's Senators resisting change,
the United States will be no more united than the United Nations.
Creatures of culture cannot recognize that a problem exists until
they are personally affected. Nothing will change in America until
the imperial church Establishment that laid the foundation of all
that ails the nation changes. That elephant has evaded attention and
scrutiny. A reformed Church that is not in denial but repentant for
America's original sin; a Church that teaches Christians to observe
all things whatsoever that Jesus Christ commanded, including the
Golden Rule, will make it possible in the privacy of the voting booth,
for grandparents to vote for humanity and not for the fear of those
under endless repression. No longer will there be a cabal resistant to
Christian civilization and the will of God.

Amazing Grace or Amazing self-deceit!

Is this a God- forsaken world? It is written: "If my people, which
are called by my name, shall humble themselves, and pray, and
seek my face, and turn from their wicked ways; then will I hear
from heaven, and will forgive their sin, and will heal their land."
(2 Chronicles 7:14). The people did not listen. So, the world was
forsaken until Jesus Christ came. If He is the same God that we
worship in the last 4,000 year, it should be no surprise that we are
back to a God- forsaken world. Jesus Christ the Messiah, came to
teach the way to salvation, die as the Lamb of God, the sacrifice to
end all sacrifices, rose from the dead and returned to heaven. In the

First Century, His Church- Jews and Gentiles- was inspired by the Holy Spirit on the day of Pentecost. The Church was Pentecostal. It was a new beginning since 2 Chr.7:14 was ignored. The church that took over from the pioneer Christians was based on imperial power and control. Was it inspired by the Holy Spirit? Between then and now, Christians- clergy and laity- lived off the avails of slave trade and slavery of African men, women and children for nearly 250 years in the United States, and for over 350 years in Roman Catholic Brazil. Was the church inspired by the Holy Spirit? The church Establishment never fulfilled the mandate of the Great Commission – "teaching them to observe all things whatsoever that I have commanded you." All things would include the Golden Rule. As a result, Arabians invaded and occupied North Africa, and killed some in the name of a brand-new religion, Islam. And Africans became the greatest consumers as well as the greatest victims of religions that have lost redemptive value in a God-forsaken world. Can prayers be answered in a God-forsaken world?

In the First World War, about 15 million people perished. The Almighty God did not intervene. In the Second world war, about 40 million people perished. The Almighty did not intervene. About six million Jews faced a holocaust death. The expected Messiah did not come to intervene. In the Biafra war, the world watched hundreds of thousands of babies and children starved to death in the oil war. The Almighty did not intervene. In 2020, the pandemic killed over six million people. The praying crowd deserted St. Peter's Square, knowing that the Almighty will not intervene. On some days in 2021, over 4,000 people died in Brazil in a single day. The Almighty did not intervene. Did the church expect the Almighty to intervene in the Russia - Ukraine war of 2022?

How can God intervene in an unrepentant world that cannot be humble, pray, seek His face, and turn from their wicked ways? Many of us have left religion because we have lost faith in the institution, but not in God. How do you change an institution that cannot be changed through the ballot box? The United States is said to be the most religious nation on earth. It is the most evangelized nation. Polls show that about 10 percent are atheists and agnostics. Given what those who believed in God have done in human history, one can sympathize with the atheists and agnostics in America and in communist nations. If terrorism is associated with religious people; if slave trade, slavery, wars, colonialism, segregation and apartheid are associated with religious people, one can sympathize with those who don't believe in God. How do you change an institution that cannot be changed through the ballot box? It is by leaving with the hope that an exodus will force a Second Reformation. The Klan will not change until their religion changes.

There are good Christians, and there are bad Christians. African men, women and children were enslaved by a bad church and State, subjected to segregation, lynching and endless abuse. Those who were abused in Europe by the big powers, would emigrate to join the abuse of weaker people, usually African Americans and Aboriginals. Abused people usually abuse other people. With victor theology, the Christian cultural conservatives turned the Gospel of Jesus Christ upside down. President John F. Kennedy came into office in 1960, to revive the conscience and save the soul of America. He was assassinated. The many good deeds presidents John F. Kennedy and Lyndon Johnson did in the 1960s began to collapse under cultural conservatives.

President Richard Nixon won the presidency on the theme of Law and Order. President Ronald Reagan won on the theme of "the welfare queen." Reciting the pledge of allegiance in school has been a training in hypocrisy. And so, with total disregard of God Almighty and the Golden Rule; without regret, apology or repentance for centuries of historical wrongs, succeeding generations of cultural -conservative Americans close every political convention speech, commanding God Almighty to bless America. The world would watch their audacity and bravado in disbelief. With the childhood training in hypocrisy, the people are conditioned to lie to themselves that a nation above God is a nation under God. That blatant defiance of God and common sense is an insult to all humanity. Prophet Jeremiah recognized that there are men who call good evil and evil good. Such men have dehumanized humankind. When a policeman handcuffs an African American whose ancestors survived centuries of slavery and abuse, kneels on his neck for nine minutes to kill him, even a godless communist would feel ashamed to be a human being. What makes a person a human being? The world is in a struggle between good and evil. The United States will determine if God or evil wins that struggle.

It is said that history was written by the victors. Similarly, it is clear that the narrative of the Gospel of Jesus Christ was schemed and controlled by powerful men. It was to their spiritual detriment and would be to ours too, if we continue to follow their footsteps. The church of the slave traders, slave masters -clergy and laity-lived off the avails of slavery for centuries. They were not born again as required. If the Gospel and the crucifixion of Jesus Christ, mean anything, the church of the slave masters and clergy have no hope for salvation. The world should not be the way it is today if they followed the Gospel. Man must submit to God, not the reverse.

The cultural -conservative Christians see their gain from the pain of others, as God's blessing bestowed on them. So, despite the Golden Rule; despite the Great Commandment; and despite the New Commandment, some clergy and laity see imperialism and centuries of slave trade and slavery as a blessing from God, who is unlikely to be the God of the Bible. Therefore, since the first slaves were brought to Virginia in 1619 to this 21st century, there has been no regrets, no remorse, no apology and no repentance and recon-ciliation with God. Based on those commandments, was slavery inspired by the Holy Spirit or some other spirit? Now, should the church grant itself absolution for living off the avails of slavery for centuries? The response of those whose ancestors owned slaves is:

"I didn't do it." The modern church can also claim the same alibi. Even immigrants may feel the same, particularly those who are not Christians. But people who inherit assets also inherit the liabilities.

Wherever people immigrate to, they inherit both the assets and the liabilities of that nation. Immigrants cannot go to a new nation to attend the best schools and inherit the assets, but not the historical liabilities. Should they come to America to think like the slave masters or like the activists for redress? Should they join the church that says the Lord's prayer but do nothing to ensure that God's will is done on earth as it is in heaven? Those who resist Affirmative Action to ameliorate the past sins of their new nation, add another layer of inhumanity. Before the saints go marching in, they start marching here on earth. They start doing the will of God on earth as it is in heaven. Immigrants to the United States do well because they are not inhibited by the learned helplessness that keeps some African Americans in perpetual poverty in ghetto zip codes.

What is the equivalent of 40 acres of land and a mule today? Whatever it is, a conservative government and Senate cannot afford it. They cannot walk in the shoes of others. However, a scholarship program for the downtrodden and an economy based on universal education, healthcare and employment that lifts up all those at the bottom of society regardless of ethnicity can be a significant contribution to the restitution and reconciliation with God and man. With progressive taxation, a rising tide will lift up all boats because everyone has a boat. Even that may be unacceptable to those conservatives who are paranoid about bible-based socialism. Nobody can be chastised for the sins of their father but for following his footsteps. Nobody can be chastised for the wrongs of history but for being indifferent to the consequences. Millions of Christians have purportedly "gone home to be with the Lord" without doing the expressed will of the Lord. Going home to be with the Lord without doing the will of the Lord is not Amazing Grace; it is amazing self-deceit. Christianity is not one of those religions that lets people forget past malfeasance and move on. Christianity calls for repentance. Where there is no repentance, there is no humility to God Almighty, no common ground and reconciliation among men because the Gospel has been corrupted.

South Africa and Canada have made an effort at Truth and Reconciliation with the victims of history. But not the United States and Brazil where the clergy and laity did more wrong than anywhere else in the world. So, it is unsettling to see evangelist whose nations have not reconciled with God and man come to Canada to preach. The church Establishment has been a disinterested observer of social justice. And through silence, it is still on the side of the selective morality that served the slave masters. That silence is responsible for the spiritual decay that allowed a policeman to handcuff an African American named George Floyd, kneel on his neck in broad-daylight in Minneapolis, Minnesota. When he died, the constable called the "police hearse, "an ambulance to take the body to the hospital.

Most Christians do not measure up to the faith they profess. In 400 years, the American church Establishment has not apologized for its participation in slavery or seen the need for reconciliation with God Almighty. Absolution is perhaps the greatest obstacle to reconciliation and restitution. When sins are forgiven every week in a place called church, there is no inclination to apologize and be a better human being but a spiritual robot, going through the motions of religion. That explains why, after 2,000 years of Christianity, and despite the church and the United Nations founded to end the scourge of war, in March 2022, Russia invaded Ukraine, a different linguistic group and sovereign nation. The Apostles of Jesus Christ performed miracles. They did not forgive sins. That would be playing of God here on earth. One can hypothesize that the Roman magisterium assumed the role of forgiving sins, to intimidate the Kings of Europe into submission. Confession and the offer of absolution and remission of sins promote endless malfeasance and misfeasance. It has conditioned those who know right from wrong, particularly politician's, to choose to do wrong and apologize.

In the Vietnam War, the politician's sent their soldiers to fight and die in that distant land, to prevent the spread of communism. "In the Presence of Mine Enemies, "by Howard E. Rutledge was about his experience in Vietnam. On Christmas Eve, he heard "Silent Night, Holy Night" played while in captivity. It was, perhaps, to underscore the gulf between those who profess Christianity and the practice thereof. Non-Christians in America get a better understanding of Christianity in the month of Silent Night. December is the month to show peace and goodwill to all. December is the month they will see choirs of men and women, boys and girls of every ethnic group in the world, sing O Holy Night: "Truly He taught us to love one another; His law is love and His Gospel is Peace. Chains shall He break, for the slave is our brother. And in His name, all oppression shall cease---" The Russia-Ukraine War of 2022 shows that it is all a sham. December is also the month for the rule of law. But after December, non-Christians will see the return of Law and Order, to suppress the descendant of those brought in chains for over 200 years of slavery because the church was a scheme designed by victor theologians. It was not established to teach converts to "observe all things whatsoever I have commanded you" as Jesus said.

In some genuine Christian families where parents have different skin tones, there are, scientifically, three or more skin tones. And around the world there are scores of skin tones. Rabbits change their coat for summer and winter. Yet, after 2,000 years of the Gospel, "Black lives Matter" is still contentious in Christendom because going to church was a social and cultural event. There is not a "biracial" man or woman who is not on the side of the oppressed minority. It is God's side. To the atheists, religion is also about good and evil competing for dominance. When one month of the year is focused on giving, and 11 months are focused on taking; when one month is dedicated to God, and 11 months are dedicated to culture, it does not look like God is winning. And so, they will see babies come into the world and be received with open arms from coast to coast. Some will grow up homeless in the richest nations on earth because of policies made by man.

To add to the confusion about Christianity, atheists will also learn that December is the month, according to history, when on the eve of Christmas 1914, a group of German, British and French troops laid down their arms. Enemies became temporary friends. They sang Christmas carols, drank beer on the "No man's land," and even played soccer on Christmas Day. The Christmas truce ended after Christmas. They returned to the trenches in a war that took about 38 million lives. They made Christianity look like a joke. Unlike other religions, anyone forced to be a Christian, even by birth, is not a Christian. Being a Christian is a choice based on conviction. For over 300 years, clergy and laity of the slave economy, professed the Christian faith but did not live by the Gospel. They were said to have "gone home to be with the Lord." It is not Amazing Grace; it is amazing self-deceit.

"If my people, which are called by my name, shall humble themselves, and pray, and seek my face, and turn from their wicked ways; then will I hear from heaven, and will forgive their sin, and will heal their land." (2 Chronicles 7:14). With that in mind, one would expect that the Almighty and Holy God must have forsaken the church and the world since the clergy, even the Jesuits, lived off the avails of slavery for nearly 250 years in the United States, and over 350 years in Roman Catholic Brazil. And once again, the world paid no heed to (2 Chronicles 7:14). If we pretend to believe in God; and pretend to obey the Golden Rule, the Great Commandment and the New Commandment, God will pretend to answer our prayers. Whatever has been resolved in Dixie with prayer, has been resolved in a pagan community without prayer. Those who assume that the Almighty God will answer their next prayer will be disappointed. But those who assume that we live in a world God-forsaken for

defiance of God will not be disappointed. A stubborn and wayward child cannot expect pocket money from parents. Without a
Second Reformation, repentance and reconciliation, the church is
that stubborn and wayward child who will pray and get no response.
Christian soldiers cannot win a war between good and evil with
many saboteurs, in a God forsaken world.

CHAPTER 15

When Pastors Retire

When I was a resident in "Small town Alberta" in 1991, I paid occasional visits to Rev. Father McCrae for conversation. He lived in an annex to his church. As human beings, priests need a break from isolation. That was before I took the Right of Christian Initiation of Adults (RCIA) in 1992 and sang in a choir with Filipino parishioners in a Calgary Catholic Church. As a result of his family experience, Fr. McCrae did not drink alcohol. The physical combat in hockey upset him. One day, he told me that he will retire. I said to him: "Father McCrae, you can't retire. The Apostles didn't retire." He repeated himself and added, "you can have my job." He was beginning to get angry, he said. He had repeatedly told congregants not to leave the church before Mass was over. Still, some continued to leave in order to get out of the small parking lot as fast as possible. That's why he was getting angry. It was to him unpriestly to be angry. When I moved away and had a family problem, I invited him over for advice. He told me where to go for help. It did not solve my problem. Apparently, without the wisdom of Solomon, being brought up a Protestant and being brought up a Roman Catholic can be a problem for a couple.

By the time I inquired about the good and faithful servant, it had been nine years since he passed away. It is an extraordinary life-long commitment to be a Pastor, Priest or a Nun. Being in the service of the Almighty should be the most important profession but not in a secular world. For the 10th anniversary of father McCrae's death, I dropped off money at the church to order flowers in memoriam. I learned that it was an unusual request.

A thousand years ago, there were no millionaires. Only the king lived in comfort. Even then, he did not own a car, air conditioner or refrigerator. In the materialistic world today, corporate executives, sports professionals and television personalities take home millions of dollars a year and live in mansions. Those who are required to take a vow of poverty and celibacy to serve them will be remiss not to condemn, not only abortion but also the hoarding of wealth and trashing of socialism by tax dodgers and Christians laying treasures on earth. How many Roman Catholic congregations today are worth the sacrifice of taking a vow of poverty and celibacy to serve? For priests and nuns to give up family, take a vow of poverty, and celibacy, serve God and humanity, die and be forgotten, is a shame. They all deserve beatification. Many priests and nuns like Mother Teresa made personal sacrifices and lived by the Gospel - the Golden Rule, the Great commandment and the New Commandment, by happenstance. By following tradition, Christians are all spiritual hostages in an Establishment whose theology and liturgy were designed by imperial medieval minds. Decisions and choices have consequences. It took almost 2,000 years to see the consequences of forced celibacy by an Establishment that became a Regency and not the Executor of God's will. Clerics can be trapped in an Establishment.

Is there a retired pastor who has no regrets? When the end is near, every pastor would want to depart with those words of St. Paul: "I have fought the good fight, I have finished the race, I have kept the faith." (2 Timothy 4:6). However, many will have regrets because their society was safer and more moral at the beginning of their ministry than at the end. That has been the case for more than a thousand years. Some may feel that they should have tried harder. If they tried harder or prayed more, would it have made any difference? Some pastors will lament the growing materialism and unrelenting decline in Christian values. But no enlightened and born-again pastor can retire without a conscience that feels guilty of the institutional neglect in "teaching them to observe all things whatsoever that I have commanded you," as Jesus said. No enlightened pastor can retire without noticing that "The peace of God that surpasses all understanding "does not come from a handshake in the church or through meditation. Yet, as a loyal employee of a denomination, no pastor can change society. In a divided multi- denominational Church, no pastor can influence change on a city.

Companies do surveys to know how they can serve their customers better. Even when many members have left; even when Christians go to war after 2,000 years of sermons, the Church Establishment does not do surveys. The people are seen as the problem, not the Church. Some clergy who had seen empty pews Sunday after Sunday take comfort in the words of St. Paul: "Now the spirit expressly says that in latter times some will depart from the faith, giving heed to deceiving spirits and doctrines of demons." (1 Timothy 4:1 NKJV). It can be argued that the Church itself departed from the Pentecostal faith in the Fourth Century, after the Apostles passed away. That departure made slave trade and slavery guilt-free for centuries. The spiritual conservatives practiced the Golden Rule while the cultural conservatives did the opposite. This gave the church a split personality.

When I was younger and foolish, I heard about a peripatetic Baptist preacher named Rev. Billy Graham. I thought that he would change the world. Did he? He did his best. He began his ministry in the 1950s and converted millions of people around the world to Christianity. How many of those millions of Christians became born again Christians is unknown. A Christian who does not live by the Gospel, lives by paganized Christianity, like the slave masters. Rev. Dr. Graham's home State in Dixie is just like any other State. In fact, even in Dixie, America was more moral at the beginning of Dr. Graham's ministry than at the end. That will be the case for all popes, bishops, pastors and priests. The truth is that no pastor, priest, evangelist or prosperity preacher can bring theoretical Christianity to an end without activism and reformation. After 2,000 years, the question now is: "Shall we continue in sin that grace may abound?" Should we change course or stay the course?

All the Sermons that a pastor preached in his career cannot change a town. The inhabitants of any town today are more educated than their predecessors. Yet, their doctrine and liturgy are based on the mindsets of medieval men who believed that the world was flat, and persecuted those who were right. The incongruity between the ancient and the modern is a factor in empty pews. As people become more enlightened, they are bound to challenge ancient believes and assumptions. How do you convince an educated, rational and analytical mind, that the Almighty God will solve their problems when it has not happened in 2,000 years; and the semantics of Mary as "the mother of God"? Many pastors who are addressed as Reverend, do not always feel reverend. One would assume that anyone addressed as holy father, does not always feel holy like God Almighty, who is the Holy Father.

Jesus Christ complained about the Pharisees, and their hypocrisy. If people do not complain about governance, it will not change. And if they don't complain about the church, it will not change. To refill the empty church pews, the fishers of men need practical Christianity as the bait, not more prayers. And certainly not more threats of fire and brimstone. On any given Sunday, there are more worshippers in Anglican churches in Southern Nigeria than there are worshippers in all of the United Kingdom. But they are not the gatekeepers of the denomination. More than anyone else, if they were called, the gatekeepers in the denominational headquarters can change the liturgy and instruct Christian politicians, the corporate executives and laity who profess the faith, to be born again and observe the Golden Rule for the good of their souls. That is the un-fulfilled mandate of the Great Commission that will reverse the tra-jectory of the church. That is the route to the practical Christianity that will save the church from collapse. So, it is imperative for church leaders to focus on changing the dynamics of the urban jungle before changing the victims suffering from prayer fatigue. A Christian must be born again and live by the Gospel. If the Christian slave traders did not know that, it shows that the evangelists were not spreading the Gospel but hypocrisy around the world.

"Bear ye one another's burdens, and so fulfill the law of Christ" is not godless communism in the Church. Like the Hutterites, it should have happened more than a thousand years ago, long before the Bolshevik Revolution toppled the religious elites in church and State who enjoyed privilege based on injustice. When the Establishment changes, the society or nation will change. Americans, for example, know that it takes a Richard Nixon, not a liberal, to go to commu-nist China. When cultural conservatives change in their social and economic relations to the rest of society, the nation changes. Clerics who have a genuine desire to serve and save the world will discover that doing the same things over and over expecting a different result, cannot save the world if those same things are wrong. While church attendance is declining, any pastor doing the same things over and over expecting a different result is preaching in a cemetery.

Can a retired pastor, then criticize an institution that pays his pension? They served an Establishment created in the era of imperi-alism to serve not one but two masters- God and culture; the sacred and the secular. Nowhere on earth, were men free from ethnocen-trism. The church fathers laid the foundation for a dysfunctional world. The American culture in particular was created by the church to be a master culture. The theologians knew that their slaves were the same descendants of Adam and Eve, tanned by the sun. Like

Adam and Eve, they were scantily clad because they lived under the hot sun and not in Siberia.

The Jesuits (the society of Jesus) sold 272 of their inventories of slaves to save Georgetown university from bankruptcy. Evangelism co-existed with the buying and selling of men, women and children for slavery despite the Golden Rule – Treat others the same way you want them to treat you. Good relations between people and between them and God constitute Christian civilization. Paradoxically, the church was resistant to Christian civilization. Still there has been no repentance, no restitution, and no reconciliation with God or man since the end of slavery. During and after slavery, how could the clergy retire for centuries, and were able to say like St. Paul: "I have fought a good fight, I have finished my course, I have kept the faith"?

Without learning from Rabbits that change their hue in winter and spring, it is inconceivable that after 2,000 years of Christianity, skin color is an issue in Christendom. Some American demonstrators in June 2020, held placards that read:" Silence is complicity." From the emancipation of slaves, to the Civil Rights Movement, to the enfranchisement of women and the quest for social justice, no institution has been more silent than the church. The leading edge of change has come from the streets, not from the church. American women used petitions, protests, parades and pickets for decades, to demand the right to vote. The right from who? From their cultural conservative sons in a master culture created by the church. In 1917, Alice Paul, one of the ring leaders of the right to vote was sentenced to seven months in prison for picketing the White House. They won the right to vote in 1920.

The Civil Rights Movement of the 1960s was also peaceful. Sadly, change is snail slow. Human beings have to beg other human beings for their rights because some men exercise power like the gods. And wherever they made progress towards freedom from the strictures of life, they encounter a backlash and regression. The church that was complicit in slavery and erased the interface between right and wrong has yet to become the solution to social problems. In the U.S. A about 4,000 churches close down each year. It may be counterintuitive to wish them all closed down. And hope that out of the decadence and demise of the church that stood for might is right, will emerge the Church of Jesus Christ that stands for the Golden Rule. Institutional pastors and freelance pastors still serve an Establishments that is difficult to change.

How did the issue of absolution, come about? Jesus Christ said to Peter:" And I also say to you that you are Peter, and on this rock, I will build My Church, and the gates of Hades shall not prevail against it. And I will give you the keys of the kingdom of heaven, and whatever you bind on earth will be bound in heaven, and whatever you loose on earth will be loosed in heaven." (Matthew 16: 18 – 19 NKJV). The Romans assumed that apostolic authority. As the most powerful empire on earth, they established the papacy, "the seat of St. Peter" on that premise. The apostolic prerogative granted to Peter is not transferable to anyone who is not Simon Peter. But the priests became sub-contractors offering absolution or forgiveness of sins after confession. Apparently, everyone can go to heaven on the coattails of St. Peter.

Now, how many retired pastors or priests believe that they were qualified to offer absolutions or forgiveness of sins to their brothers, sisters, mothers and fathers? How many believe that the continued enforcement of celibacy can be justified, given the sex abuse scandals and the millions of dollars paid out in compensation? How many believe that the Great Commission, including "teaching them to observe all things whatsoever that I have commanded you" is a mission being accomplished in 2,000 years? No pastor or priest could have changed the policies made in their denomination's headquarters.

The history of the U.S. A does not make Christians proud. President John F. Kennedy, Rev. Dr. Martin Luther King and Senator Robert F. Kennedy strived to make America and the world better but were all assassinated in the 1960s. There may or may not be a correlation but out of despair, the exodus from the church began in the 1960s, according to research. In all mainline churches - churches whose members had owned slaves - that exodus is now more evident. The empty pews show that something is wrong. The focus on the sins of the flesh had overlooked major social and structural problems. In the 1960s, the focus of displeasure on the pulpits was rock and roll. If they studied the past, they would have noticed that the clergy and laity who lived off the avails of slavery for centuries, opened the pandora's box for the ills the church continues to condemn to this day. Those disaffected Christians leaving pews empty want freedom, not control; practical Christianity not endless prayers and Bible study; and an end to hypocrisy. When the good that is voiced from the mind is not in the soul, it is hypocrisy. That is not the case with born again Pentecostal Christians taught to observe all things that Jesus commanded.

It is manifestly obvious from history, that preceding generations of Christians that we follow did not understand or practice Christianity as a church. It is difficult to believe that in his childhood, Adolf Hitler was a Christian. His mother was known to be a devout catholic. If Adolf Hitler, Francisco Franco, Benito Mussolini and Joseph Stalin were taught that a Christian must be born again; that the identifiers or characteristics of a born-again Christian are compliance to the Gospel - the Golden Rule, the Great Commandment and the New Commandment – obviously, world history would have been very different. The theology and liturgy that served those men have not changed. The pastorate has continued to do the same things over and over expecting a different result even when the pews are half empty.

The first century Christians attracted new members because of their character and behavior. They cared for everybody. Some Christian politicians have been doing the opposites for centuries. There is a correlation between how people are governed and church attendance. Yet since the 1960s, as every crop of retired pastors and nuns knows, it is more acceptable to criticize culture or the "backsliders" than the institutional headquarters where the policy that misguides humanity are made. In all professions, retired people can use the media to expose the flaws of the institution they served, in order to improve it. The consequences of forced celibacy continue to plague the Roman Catholic church. And even after centuries of slave trade and slavery, nothing has changed in both the Roman Catholic and Protestant denominations to show improvement or lessons learned. In the 1970s, pastors in some denominations retired leaving a few empty pews. In the 1980s pastors retired leaving more empty pews. The trend has continued. A regression analyses will show that as fewer and fewer members bear the cost of running the church, sooner or later the doors will be permanently closed and the building deconsecrated and sold for commercial use.

Jesus Christ chose His disciples; they did not choose Him. Thereafter, clerical duty is supposed to be a calling. The Levites were no longer needed. Those who teach good relations between people and between them and God are the ones who are called because that's what religion should be about. The gatekeepers of all religions are volunteers. Little children volunteer to help their parents. The spirit and efforts are warmly appreciated. But the work has to be re-done. Evangelism has to be redone by "teaching them to observe all things whatsoever that I have commanded you, "as Jesus said. How the Almighty will raise the clerics to redo evangelism is unknown. Many churches will close down for good when the COVID -19 pandemic ends. The only groups not economically affected were politicians and Canadian Hutterites. In such an epidemic or pandemic, one should either be in politics or in a Hutterite colony with education healthcare and employment for all families.

In the 16th century, the Vatican began to sell access to heaven in the name of Indulgence. A dissident priest, Martin Luther, helped change the course of church history by leading a reformation of the church. From hindsight, it is now obvious that the Roman Catholic and Protestant clergy and laity who lived off the avails of unpaid servitude for centuries also went astray - again. How could they go home to be with the Lord without doing the will of the Lord spelled out in the Gospel? The church has not changed since slavery. What has changed are the preachers. Now, how can there be a change without dissident clerics like Martin Luther? The church that stood for might is right; the church that was seen as the face of colonialism all over the world, has yet to be seen as the church of Jesus Christ that stands for the Golden Rule.

There is no transgression worse than the misrepresentation of God and Jesus Christ. In fact, no religion including Islam and Judaism, should wait for the day when the God of Creation will hold spiritual leaders accountable. It will be too late for the millions who have died with a false faith and a false hope; and the millions who will die in the centuries ahead with a false hope. That includes the suicide bombers led to believe that they are heading straight to paradise for killing people. Leaving the church, one by one, is not a substitute for an urgent second reformation of all the denominations. Every nation, every jurisdiction and every pastor is accountable to God Almighty, and not to a religious headquarters an ocean away. God's temple is everywhere.

There are hundreds of Christ- like pastors helping thousands of families in need at the expense of their own families. The millions and billions of people in need require an institutional response. A Hutterite colony has that institutional response and their pastor can live a normal life. There is a lesson here for denominational church leaders. The church must either demand good governance and risk losing tax -exempt status or remain silent and be one more "church for sale." There is no group of people who go to church more than African Americans. Yet, over 50 percent of the children are raised by single mothers. Any Christian couple who does not live by the Gospel is not born again. That is the key to family and social stability. That is the secret of stable marriages. Are the pastors preaching that Gospel or are they doing marketing and running a theater church? Before his conversion, St. Paul persecuted Christians and believed whole-heartedly that he was serving God Almighty. Every Christan denomination has clergy who whole-heartedly believe that they are serving God Almighty. Yet, they do not teach the flock to ask for the Holy Spirit, become born again and be enabled to live by the Golden Rule, the Great Commandment and the New Commandment. That is how Russia and Ukraine fought a savage and barbaric war after 2,000 years of Christianity that did not follow Christ. How can their clergy retire with no regrets?

Therefore, it will be wise to unite and restore the church to the original Pentecostal Church of the first century. The Church led by St. Peter and the Apostles could never have been involved in wars, slave trade, slavery, colonialism, segregation, apartheid, racism, misogyny and more. And be in a war in Europe in 2022. The change or reformation can be led by those most abused by religion. They include the people of Northern Ireland torn between Roman Catholicism and Protestantism. The reformers can also include Chinese Christians who must defend their faith against those who wonder if religion has done the Russians and Ukrainians any good. The imperial church did not practice the Gospel of Jesus Christ. To know Jesus Christ as Lord and Savior – is it all there is to Christianity? In "A Tale of two Faith Traditions," is it a pastor's fault that one church preaches while the other practices?

Finally, it must be said that a preacher's wife is hardly celebrated. But she is also a preacher, not with words but by conduct. She is a missionary of the Gospel who lives by the Golden Rule, the Great Commandment and the New Commandment. Conduct is as important or even more important than sermons. At some point in life, people should retire and make room for others. But human beings were not created to sit and do nothing. When employment to make a living ends, volunteering to help others defines a human being. AfricanGuestHouse, org is a concept being actualized for that purpose.

CHAPTER 16

To the News Media

The News media covers events in all walks of life. Therefore, journalism must be the most learned profession grounded in the Truth. The News media has come a long way. From the slave economy to the 20th Century, the media served the interest of the Establishment that owned the institutions. Some still do. Many civic leaders had the mind of the Roman Empire and feudal lords. They enforced imperial laws and ignored social justice. The reporters employed as journalists were high school graduates who understood the rules of grammar coupled with a good typing speed. They were the products of culture, not the products of higher education. Just as a lottery winner is portrayed as the norm rather than the exception; and just as an "answered prayer" is presented as the rule rather than the exception, a criminal was presented as a representative of the group and the victim was presented as one of more future victims. Up to the 1950s, an African American seen on the pages of a newspaper was likely to be a man wanted by the FBI.

Then came the tabloid media that has been selling fake news for generations. There was a market for the insatiable appetites for gossip to fill the minds of idlers; a market for those inclined to conserve the ignorance of the past, and for the human nature that sees evil only in others. Because the Golden Rule makes sense to anyone who is a human being, it controls the tongue even when granted the freedom of speech. So, tabloid journalism degrades the profession and has no place in a civilized nation. An enlightened media is futuristic, lenient on those whose sins do no physical or economic harm to others, but biased against those who conserve the feudal past that did harm to others. The men and women who have lived in more than one culture have a more balanced sociological perspective than those whose way is the only way they know. Hence, tabloid journalism can be deployed to create the distrust of those dedicated to the pursuit of the Truth. In the United States, fortunately, over 90 percent of journalists have college education. They can overcome the few driven by greed and ignorance. They chase multiple sources to distill the Truth rather than pursue the cultural truth.

What is Truth?

In the Scriptures, Pontius Pilate asked Jesus: "What is Truth? "Jesus Christ created a division among the people of the first century because the Truth divides people (John 7:43; 9:16; Luke 12:51). The Truth landed Jesus Christ on the cross. There is the cultural truth and there is the global or Gospel Truth. A cultural truth will make sense to a culture or bloc, but the global or Gospel Truth will make sense worldwide. Culture can raise their children in conditioned ignorance that constitutes their truth. In slave trade and slavery, for example, men fought and died in the defense of conditioned ignorance. It made sense to those who died. Yet the Bible upholds the universal Truth that makes sense globally. Nazism, also, was a cultural truth. So were slavery, segregation, apartheid, imperialism, racism, and terrorism. By contrast, the Golden Rule is the global or Gospel Truth. The cultural truth is unstable but His Truth endures and matches on forever. Any statement in the Scriptures that requires modernization is not from God Almighty. The Truth cannot be updated. Since the Father and Son are one, nobody should expect anything that Jesus said to require modernization.

He said: "For everyone practicing evil hates the light, and does not come to the light, lest his deeds should be exposed," (Jn 3:20 NKJV). Should it be a surprise that as cockroaches shun the light, wrongdoers hate the limelight of the Truth media but not the culture media? Should it be a surprise that dictators hate a free press? No individual or institution can go wrong being on the right side of history. In many world capitals, right or wrong depends on the party of the person involved. Educators have used children to shame and educate such adults who have lost their way. When schoolchildren in North America became "tree huggers," their parents relented in their opposition to the cause of acid rain. The News media can be part of the educators because so much is wrong in the world. An aversion to the Truth or war on the Truth is a disservice to future generations who will suffer the consequences or bear the shame of the deeds of their grandparents. There is no greater truth than observing the Gospel - the Golden Rule, the Great Commandment and the New Commandment. Those who do, will always be on the right side of history.

What cultural religionists do is a reflection of their Scripture. Similarly, those who have not read the Gospel of Jesus Christ believe that what Christians do reflects the Gospel. Slave trade, slavery, colonial wars, colonialism, segregation, apartheid and racism have nothing to do with the Gospel. The Israelites went into captivity. They were punished and forsaken for noncompliance to 2 Chr 7:14. Since the Apostles passed away, Christians and Muslims have done worse, particularly to Africans, than the Israelites who were forsaken. If the Almighty God is still the same, this must be a God forsaken world. Life makes sense to those who believe in a God forsaken world.

When a pastor is changed, his congregation will be changed. When the News media understands the Gospel Truth, the world will be changed. Roman Catholicism is based on sacraments, weekly confession and forgiveness of sins (absolutions). For Protestantism, it is salvation by faith alone. That means that Jesus died for our sins; our sins are nailed to the cross, believe on the Lord Jesus Christ and carry on. And they did carry on with wars, slave trade, colonialism, social hierarchy and all that can emerge from the Pandora's box. That's the Amazing Grace. If the Epistles were not discovered, will the world be better or worse than it is today? In the First Century, a believer received the Holy Spirit and lived by the Gospel and the ethics of the Golden Rule. Ever since that Pentecostal Church became Roman Catholic and split into two, both denominations have acted like institutions with a split personality. Part of the Church is doing good through the Holy Spirit while the other is not through the evil spirit of disobedience. That is still the case to this day. As, perhaps the most learned or informed profession, the News media may be a better medium than the pulpit to communicate the Gospel of Jesus Christ.

The cultural truth has been at war with the Gospel Truth that victor theology disabled. Nevertheless, the Truth will catch up with us either in life or in death. Agnostics who want to be on both sides of the fence mix the cultural truth with a sliver of the Gospel Truth. Since social evolution is very slow, agnostics are in all walks of life. Good journalism is shaped, not by the truth of culture, but by the Truth that rises above culture. The media's pursuit of the universal Truth serves the cause of democracy regardless of who is in power. Because they are human, some journalists report with pain in their voice, the blatant social injustice or the senseless murder of a person because of the tone of his skin - in their own country. It may not end without the boycott of the church, to force reformation. Someday, those journalists will be comfortable reporting human rights abuses in other nations without looking like hypocrites.

Time constraint or the rush to meet deadlines can be an excuse to report the news and leave out the historical background. With the passage of time, the victims become the villains; the aggrieved become the rebels. It has been a disservice to humanity. Some journalists see every day as a new day. But trained journalists recognize that while every day is a new day, there are events that are the consequences of what happened in the past. The Middle East is a prime example. The past explains the present. But the media cannot go back to the 16th century to explain 21st century events. They cannot cover every day, the root cause of every problem. However, once a week, a panel must remind the people the root cause of a problem to ensure that they see the whole elephant and do not pile on injustice on injustice.

Some comedians have used satire to laugh at American politicians. Some artists like Tom T. Hall sang about politics and small-town hypocrisy. They are not usually seen as contributors to human civilization. An enlightened media is the last best hope, not the church. The journalism profession has also faced criticism for blurring the line between news and opinion. Those who give their opinion must first study the Gospel of Jesus Christ. To treat others the same way you want them to treat you is the future. The Golden Rule has no exception. Every adult human being has an opinion. Talk show hosts are paid to give their opinion. It is not journalism. Radio talk show hosts syndicated across the United States, disseminate their prejudicial and divisive views. They are the bane of genuine journalism. If the goal of civilization is to present material facts based on the Truth, the majority of Americans will do what is right.

Conflicts in such places as Afghanistan, Yemen, Ethiopia, Somalia, Palestine, etc. did not attract celebrity journalists as the Russia - Ukraine War. The western media was accused of double standard and racism. Racism has been and will always be part of life. How can there be equal coverage in conflicts when people are not treated equally in America? The response to the COVID-19 pandemic shows that in many developed countries, most people would rather vaccinate their dogs before Africans, if it came to that. That's the outcome of victor theology. For preachers to go to Africa to teach them the same victor theology that sustained slave trade and slavery for over 200 years is an insult to the human intellect.

What is it that indicates that a Christian is born again? What is the test of a born-again Christian? Is it belief in Jesus Christ and nothing more? That was the doctrine of the slave economy. A Christian who does not live by the Golden Rule, the Great Commandment and the New Commandment is not born again. That is the litmus test. Every problem goes back to the corruption of the Gospel. It is said that what goes around comes around. A few centuries ago, the only people in distress in North America were African slaves and the aboriginal peoples. Today, a lot more people are in distress because the disobedience of God comes around. Do journalists who report other people's problems have problems of their own? They do because they are human. Rather than cover up their problems, they can be part of the solution. Sadly, when journalists critical of politicians use their name recognition to get into politics, they behave like the same politicians they criticized. It exposes the hypocrisy in both professions.

The first women to run for public office faced a hostile media. Any national media that is focused on opinions will lose credibility particularly when the opinions are not based on the Gospel Truth. A journalist said to President Donald Trump: "Putin is a killer!" His response was: "Do you think our country is so innocent?" It is human nature to see from a cultural or regional perspective rather than from a global perspective. Sometimes people see and speak the global Truth. But most of the time, they see and speak the cultural truth. The Gospel Truth is the global Truth. It is different from the cultural truth. If journalism is about the Truth, there is no better ally than the Gospel. Blurring the interface between right and wrong can lead the East and West into a nuclear war. No nation can fix their politics without fixing their religion.

In December 2020, the Kansas City Star joined a list of

American Newspapers and magazines to apologize for racially biased coverage since its inception. Mike Fannin, president and Chief Editor apologized for past decades of racially biased coverage that helped keep Kansas City segregated. The newspaper noted that a detailed examination of its past coverage documented how they wrote about African Americans only as criminals or people living in the crime- plagued neighborhoods and ignored segregation in Kansas City, Missouri, and its public schools. Fannin wrote that The Star had reinforced segregation, disenfranchised, ignored and scorned generations of Black residents and for decades, robbed an entire community, dignity, justice and recognition. Before the video showing the murder of George Floyd surfaced, one newspaper headline was: "Man dies after medical incident with police interaction." Christian civilization has suffered from such diabolical opposition to the Truth for over 2,000 years.

Let us be honest to God and to ourselves. With the exception of a few Christians who followed their conscience, it is difficult for an African to have a good word to say about the church and clergy who ignored the Gospel of Jesus Christ, from slave trade and slavery to this day, and raised Christians who were comfortable with injustice. Why were Roman Catholics forbidden, for centuries, to read the Bible and see the Scripture for themselves? As a consequence of being born into a religion, there are educated men and women who have not read the Bible or the Scripture of the religion they profess. In any language or translation of the Bible, the Golden Rule, the Great Commandment and the New Commandment are the same. In any language or translation of the Bible, the Great Commission – "Go ye therefore, and teach all nations, baptizing them in the name of the Father, and of the Son, and of the Holy Ghost: Teaching them to observe all things whatsoever I have commanded you;" is the same. How can the men of the cloth or anyone read the Gospel of Jesus Christ and not understand it? Any man who attended a Seminary and did not understand the Gospel and the full mandate of the Great Commission, must have been brainwashed. Were they afraid to disagree for fear of being expelled? The victor theology that tolerated racism, turned the Church into a good- looking apple rotten at the core.

So, the learned profession must recognize that the problem in many nations is not politics. It is corrupted religion. No nation can fix their politics without fixing their religion. If politicians use the title "Honorable," it should not be to deceive people. They must be seen to be honest and honorable. In the UK, the BBC is doing more than the church to keep their politicians honest. In the U.S. A, it is CNN, not the church that is keeping politicians honest. It raises the question -if the church is not teaching their members who run the nation how to treat others the same way they want to be treated; and to care about other people's children the same way they care about their own children, is the church part of the problem or part of the solution?

Some clerics will argue that their role is to preach the Gospel. But victor theology is not the Gospel of Jesus Christ. The Gospel of Jesus Christ cannot produce the outcome we have in the world after 2,000 years. The mandate is not only to preach the word, but also to teach them "to observe all things whatsoever I have commanded you---." By teaching them to observe the Golden Rule, the Great Commandment and the New Commandment, believe it or not, there would have been no slave trade, slavery, colonialism, world wars, the holocaust, new religions, terrorism, segregation, apartheid, divorce and the social chaos in the world today. Now, by teaching them to observe the Golden Rule alone, the Christians in the East and West would stop spending billions of dollars on arms for war annually, while the children of those who were colonized and en- slaved die from hunger, disease and neglect.

In 2,000 years, the world has not changed as expected because if the students didn't learn, the teacher didn't teach. The News media has a significant role to play in human civilization. Based on the Truth of enlightened journalism, the News media can save more lives and souls than the clergy whose victor theology has not changed. The Pharisees misrepresented God Almighty. If the Church Establishment misrepresented Jesus Christ, that should be no surprise. But people are suffering from the consequences ever since the Apostles passed away.

When the COVID - 19 pandemic is over, the News media may want to revisit their constitution that left so much life and death in the hands of one man or woman. Should a new constitution be drafted every 10 or 20 years to reflect a more educated society? In pre -colonial Africa, some ethnic groups had no political parties or monarch. A consultative assembly of Elders told a leader what to do as the executive of the common weal. Their time-honored wisdom made it possible to survive for millennia without the ballot box. Now, in the modern world, hundreds of thousands of people can die in a pandemic because a president or prime minister can do as he or she pleased, with limited constraints. He can also reverse the policy of his predecessor. By whose authority or values does he rule over his classmates, schoolteachers, professors, parents and pastors, if any?

If Congress, the executive branch, and the judiciary are indeed equal branches of government, does it make sense for politicians to appoint and confirm judges? A conservative president will choose conservative judges and a liberal president will choose liberal judges neither of whose judicial philosophy is guided by the values of un-corrupted faith. Justice is neither conservative nor liberal. Politicians always claim that the charges laid against them was politically mo-tivated. Therefore, the Law Society or Bar Association should run the Department of Justice and appoint judges who believe in the Golden Rule regardless of their faith. Oversight institutions must be independent of the government of the day. Under a police com-missioner, a police force is the enforcement arm of the Department of Justice. Governments come and go. Consequently, the police will be less robotic in their response to those, including friends and relatives, demanding human rights or social justice for all. The demonstrators would be more civil to the police because they are seen to be serving public interest, and not agents of partisan politics or an autocrat. Politicians cannot claim that an indictment was politically motivated.

On the American economy, it is the view of the laymen that the economy collapses when greed gets out of control. A president who inherits a recession will institute regulations to control greed. The stock market slows down and the real economy begins to recover slowly, perhaps too slow for avarice. Then, another president comes into office to deregulate what was regulated. The stock market takes off, and the boom-and-bust cycle is repeated. This is a layman's observation of the push and pull at the center of capitalism under a presidency the founding fathers allowed to be a dictator on a leash. When Jesus Christ returns to reign for a thousand years, as evangelical Christians teach from the Book of Revelation, what kind of government will it be? Will there be homeless and jobless people? If not, why don't Christians have such a government? Why are the Hutterites the exception?

"I have come that they may have life," Jesus said, "and that they may have it more abundantly." If Jesus is coming soon; if this is the end time, where is the abundant life He offered 2,000 years ago? Has He not been misrepresented since the Apostles passed away? The Canadian Hutterites have employment for every family, education for their children, universal healthcare for all, and life after death. That is the abundant life.

The imperial church built the top- down world order that has caused so much pain to the lesser mortals at the bottom. The institutions owned by the corporate Establishments have resisted change. But the Nordic nations appear to have control over the tug between greed and stability. Theirs is not an economy where a billionaire can pay no taxes while children languish in poverty and perpetuate the Rich man and Lazarus Culture. They have a better understanding of what life is about. By contrast, America's slave masters left all their wealth from slavery behind. It should be a lesson for the billionaires; and the victor theologians who want thinking people to believe that the Holy Spirit is in every believer. That would include the Christian slave traders, slave masters, and their clergy purported to be saved by grace, just for believing in Jesus Christ and nothing more. Did they go home to be with the Lord? Spiritually, ethnocentricity is destructive. It is unfair that theologians do not need malpractice insurance.

Confucius of China was not a Christian. As a moral leader, he was better than many, if not most Christians today. Mahatma Gandhi of India was not a Christian. But he practiced Christianity and put Christians to shame. Schadenfreude paints Africa as a continent where Satan is on the loose, keeping them poor and dancing for tourists. But when Moses was here on earth, the greatest nation on this planet was in Africa. In a book titled "Things Fall Apart," Chinua Achebe showed that the men of his culture who worked hard to become affluent, took a title. In the Igbo heartland, they took the title of Duru. They had a code of conduct called "Iwu Nze." It allowed polygamy, if desired, in order to shun the temptation next to the love of money. It was like the Ten Commandments but without God Almighty. They were irreligious but believed in the unknown God, just like the ancient Greeks. They had a fetish called "Ofor." It sealed them to the oath of Iwu Nze, as they upheld the moral compass that guided their pre-colonial culture. They did not form a political party to protect their wealth and keep others down. Their survival as a people depended on everyone. It was a meritocracy that anyone who worked hard could join. So, they did what is right because it is right, not because of a reward or punishment after death. And without an organized religion, it was also a culture that did not fight and kill in order to force religion on anyone.

Kings tend to go to war. If few of their people ended up as slaves, it was because they had no kings. As children, we helped lead my father's sheep and goats into the bush. We tied them to shrubs and left them to feed all day. We returned in the evening to lead them home. Nobody can do that today and return in the evening to find all of the sheep and goats. Christianity should have made a moral culture better, not worse. In Africa and the New World, the conquerors destroyed anything that was different because what is different is abnormal. The ethics that replaced the native one was not based on the Golden Rule, the Great commandment and the New Commandment because conquest, in the first place, was anathema to the Gospel. Compliance to the Gospel of Jesus Christ should make a pagan but moral culture godly, and transform the world in 2,000 years.

Instead, victor theology peddled sacraments and weekly absolutions for Roman Catholics and Amazing Grace for protestants. The victor theology discarded the Golden Rule and enabled clergy and laity to trade in human cargo and live off the avails of slavery for centuries. The victor theology and The Doctrine of Discovery unleashed the Scramble for Africa which brought together disparate and discordant ethnic groups within national borders created by foreigners. At the end of colonial rule, they were left with an army to buy weapons to kill one another for economic and religious reasons. One such deadly consequence of colonialism was the Nigerian - Biafra war in which thousands of babies and children were deliberately starved to death.

Regardless of Culture or ethnicity, the Golden Rule is the Truth. The Great Commandment is the Truth. The New Commandment is the Truth. They stand the test of time. Yet, generation after generation, the cultural militia who defend culture, like the Pharisees, have waged war on the Truth and resisted redressing historical wrongs. If Jesus Christ appears as a politician running on a platform based on the Golden Rule, how many Christians would vote to Him? The Church He founded preaches what is popular. "Go and sin no more "is not popular. What is popular is Amazing Grace. An anecdote of a God who is soft on sin gets an applause. Like politics, secular religion is not about doing what is godly but about doing what is popular.

If you speak the Truth, those who don't want to change will be offended. It is true that going to a Bible College or Seminary is not the same as going to heaven to know everything about God beyond what is revealed in the Bible, to become an expert. It is true that Israel was established to be the missionaries of the world. In 2,000 years, it has not happened and may never happen. None had gone to Africa to tell them about the will of God. Judaism is about good relations between Jewish people and between them and Jehovah God Almighty. But Christianity is about good relations between the Jews and all Gentiles, and between them and God Almighty. When some people reject Jesus Christ and others turn the Gospel upside down, the consequences are hatred, wars, the Holocaust, colonialism, slave trade, slavery, crime, family conflicts and family breakups. As a result of the disobedience of God, no people group has suffered more than Africans. They were colonized, auctioned like animals and enslaved for centuries. They have a responsibility to portray the will of God.

If truth be told, the News media has a major role to play in human civilization. Reuters has a long-established gold standard in journalism. In June 2023, it published online, research on the genealogies of Americans in high office, who were direct descendants of ancestors who enslaved Africans. Some who inherited the assets but want nothing to do with the liabilities of slavery, even the liabilities to their conscience, argued that someone today should not be responsible for what someone else did 150 years ago. It resonates with cultural religionists and nominal Christians who do not understand the Gospel. In the slave economy, many Christians saw what they had as a blessing from God. That should be no surprise since they were raised on the false doctrine that Jesus died for their past, present and future sins.

However, there are also good people who see "a moral imperative to confront the legacy and impact of our nation's original sin." And one who "rejects the efforts of those who would sugar-coat our history." The Imperial Church turned the Gospel of Jesus Christ upside down. The world has been reaping the consequences of what they sowed - wars, colonialism, slave trade, slavery, segregation, apartheid, social chaos, family dissociation and relentless social injustice. American historians should not teach their students that they are the descendants of bad people, but the practitioners of the corrupted Gospel they should fix and move on.

The descendants of the slave traders, slave masters and clergy, are a very small fraction of the American population. But they offer the greatest resistance to restitution and social justice because a false doctrine is not amenable to repentance. Since the spiritual destiny of a congregation is in the hands of their clergy, whether they are born again or not; call Jesus 'Lord, Lord' and do what He says or not; go to heaven or not, all depend on their clergy. And so, what Reuters or the News media has to do next is a similar report on the church Establishment that misled Christians, owned, bought and sold slaves. The Epistles have been a distraction. The Acts of the Apostles and the Gospel recorded by St. Luke should provide the global News media the template to reason from first principles, what Christianity is about and what the world has lost by the misrepresentation of Jesus Christ. The faulty doctrine dehumanized not only the slaves but everyone in America.

The evangelical media has continued to perpetuate that false doctrine that misrepresents Jesus Christ. Stories are covered only if they have a faith angle. A person who got out of a cultural religion and embraced Christianity by faith; a person whose prayer or faith restored their marriage; ended an addiction or got healed from cancer will be covered in newsletters. It is to show that belief or faith in Jesus Christ is all that Christians need. Before it is too late, the question everyone must ask is:" How do I know if I am born again?"

Finally, the Scramble for Africa was a hurricane that swept across Africa. African Americans will eventually recover from learned helplessness. But Africans will never recover from the Scramble for Africa. There is no thinking student who would study history, and not wonder if the church served any useful purpose. That era shows that for Christians who did not live the faith and the pagans who lived in huts, the Gospel did not do them any good. They were not born again. Even now, the social problems that the News media will report tomorrow can be prevented today by compliance to the Golden Rule. Yet, the victor theology is still the norm to this day. The victims of history want to see Truth and Reconciliation with God and man, and let bygone be bygone. But if culture controls behavior and the cultural conservatives who do to others what they don't want others to do to them are periodically in control of government, change will be difficult. When the weak, the poor and spiritual conservatives can lead the cultural conservatives to the God who established the Gospel and demands repentance, and humility from His people; it is then, and only then can we all sing "It Is Well With My Soul."

"There is nothing noble in being superior to your fellow man; true nobility is being superior to your former self." – Ernest Hemingway.

CHAPTER 17

Notes

1. Life's Little Instruction Book. Vol 11, Jackson Brown Jr. Rutledge Hill Press, Nashville, Tennessee 1993 page 691.
2. Leaving Christianity. Changing Allegiances in Canada Since 1945. Brian Clarke and Stuart Macdonald. McGill- Queen's University Press 2017.
3. The Philadelphia Trumpet. Edmond, OK, USA. November – December 2017 page 16.
4. Why You Can Disagree and Remain a Faithful Catholic. Philip S. Kaufman. The Crossroad Publishing Company, New York, NY 10017 page 46 – 49 (2002).
5. My Answer, My Answer, My Answer by Billy Graham. Pocket Books, Simon and Schuster, New York, N.Y 1967 Page 155.

Printed in the United States
by Baker & Taylor Publisher Services